SOVIET RUSSIAN NATIONALISM

SOVIET RUSSIAN NATIONALISM

FREDERICK C. BARGHOORN

NEW YORK   OXFORD UNIVERSITY PRESS   1956

PRINTED IN THE UNITED STATES OF AMERICA

IN MEMORY OF *Laurence Bradford Packard*

PREFACE

ABOUT THIRTY YEARS AGO one of the most solid works yet produced in Soviet Russia in the field of social and political science contemptuously defined patriotism and nationalism as ideological weapons of the reactionary *bourgeoisie*. National patriotism was castigated because it elevated fatherland and state to the level of absolute values.* Today, although Soviet propaganda appeals to 'proletarian internationalism,' a unique and exceptionally intense form of nationalism is perhaps the central element of Soviet ideology. This new Soviet nationalism is an often bewildering combination of traditional Great Russian nationalism, elements of Western universalist Marxism, and, most important of all, a system of rationalizations of the political order which has taken shape in the Soviet Union since 1917.

We have attempted in this study a historical, descriptive, and analytical treatment of Soviet Russian nationalism. It is hoped that this book, besides adding to our knowledge of Soviet ideology and policy, may contribute usefully to the growing literature on modern nationalism. Perhaps, among other things, it may shed light on the relationship between political symbols and social forces in Soviet Russia and thus in some degree assist those whose task it is to translate their interpretation of Soviet reality into policy recommendations.

The influence, inspiration, assistance, and counsel of many persons have helped to shape my thinking on the subject of this

* *Encyclopedia of State and Law*, Moscow, 1925-7, 3 vols., iii, pp. 252-4. The Russian title of this work is given in subsequent references.

study since I first began to contemplate writing it during World War II years in Moscow. I hope that I have not reflected all this light too badly. Naturally I alone am responsible for all the omissions, errors, and misinterpretations from which this study suffers. I cherish memories of conversations with Russians which helped me to understand the complexity and the value of communication across the ideological and organizational barriers that separate their lives from ours. I am similarly grateful to the Soviet refugees in contact with whom, in postwar government service, I deepened my acquaintance with Soviet thought. Whatever value this book possesses must be attributed in large part to knowledge and insight gained through association with teachers at Amherst and Harvard, particularly the late Laurence B. Packard and Michael Karpovich, and with other friends and colleagues at these institutions, in the Russian Institute of Columbia University, and, of course, at Yale University. I should also like to express here my appreciation of the great privilege of serving in Moscow and in Germany with many able and devoted Russian specialists of the Department of State.

Special mention should be made of the generous support made available to me through the Provost of Yale University and others concerned with the administration of the Stimson Fund and other financial resources of the University. Without this aid it is difficult to imagine how this work could have been performed. Among many other things, financial support from Yale made it possible for me to have the part-time assistance of Mr. Paul W. Friedrich. I benefited enormously from many stimulating conversations with Paul Friedrich. Whatever scientific qualities this study possesses, it owes in considerable measure to our association. Useful assistance was also rendered by Mr. Sol Polansky, Mr. Sidney Heitman, Mr. Patrick McGrady, and Mr. George Chranewycz. I deeply appreciate the patience and devotion to detail of Mrs. Elizabeth Martin and Mrs. Eunice Jones, who typed the manuscript, and the great and generous helpfulness of Miss Veronica E. O'Neill, secretary of the Department of Political Science of Yale University.

It is impossible to name all the colleagues and fellow workers in the Soviet field who helped me with advice or information during the researching and writing of this book. My participation in conferences, programs, and seminars at Notre Dame University, the Russian Institute of Columbia University, and the Russian Research Center of Harvard University helped me to clarify my thinking on the subject of this study. For these opportunities I am indebted to many persons associated with the foregoing institutions, particularly to the late Professor Waldemar Gurian, to Clyde Kluckhohn, and to Philip E. Mosely. Other persons who were kind enough to help me in various ways are mentioned in footnotes but I should like to record here my special appreciation to Raymond A. Bauer and Alex Inkeles of the Harvard Russian Research Center, and, with respect to Ukrainian questions, to John S. Reshetar, Jr., and Mr. Timothy Sosnovy. I am grateful to Mr. Mose Harvey for a helpful critical reading of the manuscript.

F. C. B.

New Haven, Connecticut
March, 1956

CONTENTS

SOVIET RUSSIAN NATIONALISM

Soviet Patriotism

In political analysis, and in 'practical' politics also, it is difficult to agree on, or sometimes even to know, the meanings of words. Perhaps this is one reason why men have often killed in the name of ideas which they did not understand. Scholars assume that such waste of effort might be reduced if people perceived more clearly the relationships between words and their referents.

Is the concept of 'nationalism' relevant to the study of Soviet ideology? We think that it is, and therefore begin with a survey of pertinent definitions. One recent formulation characterizes nationalism as 'the justifying ideology of a nation-state or of a nation aspiring to become a state.'[1] Many scholars agree that the modern nation and national consciousness are to a very significant degree concomitants, or even creations, of the state, and that the characteristics of a particular nationalism depend in large measure upon the political authority with which a given body of nationalistic sentiments is associated. In this view, governments and ruling classes shape the political concepts of peoples.[2]

But each society, though politically controlled by a state, has its own 'way of life,' and its traditional body of images and symbols by which those who belong to it identify themselves and differentiate themselves from other peoples. Students of nationalism must deal not only with political but also with cultural problems. Some scholars, in particular Catholics appalled by the divisive effects of nationalism upon what once was, or seems to have been, the spiritual unity of Western Christendom, condemn modern nationalism as a revival of 'tribalism.'[3]

Karl W. Deutsch defines a people as 'a community of complementary habits of communication.' [4] Another writer, emphasizing the manipulative elements of nationalism, defines the nation as 'the social system created deliberately in order to permit the identification of people and state.' [5] Many writers attempt to distinguish between 'nationalism' and 'patriotism.' Patriotism is described as a 'healthy' feeling of love of one's native country, which in modern times has gradually grown out of an earlier attachment to a small local community, and nationalism as 'the over-estimation of one's own nation and thus the detraction of others.' [6] This differentiation between patriotism and nationalism occurs in a distinctive form in Soviet sources, which assert that patriotism attains its highest development in Soviet 'socialist' society but that nationalism is a pernicious product of the 'capitalist' system.

Political scientists such as Robert M. MacIver have warned of the dangers inherent in the attempts of governments to control culture. As MacIver points out, 'There is grave peril when government usurps control over the myths of the community.' [7]

The foregoing calls attention to some of the problems with which we are concerned in this study of nationalist sentiments in Soviet thought. We consider that despite the 'internationalism' attributed by communist propaganda to Soviet thought and behavior, the Soviet Union is in fact the most highly integrated and centralized nation-state that has yet existed in the world. Like all extreme forms of nationalism, that of the Soviet Union is imperialistic. It is expansionist and its horizon of ambition is bounded only by the realities of geography and counterbalancing power.

This new kind of integral nationalism is the 'justifying ideology' of a new type of politico-economic structure, that of Soviet 'state monopoly capitalism.' In this system, a disciplined, centrally controlled, and exceptionally monolithic elite, uniformly indoctrinated and hierarchically ranked and graded, administers and co-ordinates all social activity. Status is a function of loyalty and efficiency as evaluated by the supreme decision-makers at the center of the mechanism. Soviet Russian nationalism, described in Soviet sources as 'Soviet patriotism,' is the unifying symbol pattern of this political system.

This type of nationalism is appropriate to an order in which the ruling class is the collective owner of the means of production and the collective exploiter of the 'masses.' The Soviet ruling class functions somewhat like an army, under the command of the Kremlin. Not only separation of political powers, but separation of political, economic, military, and cultural spheres of life are minimized in such a society.[8]

Soviet sources emphasize that public administration is effected by the 'unified activity of the state.' [9] Textbooks used in training state officials point out that unity of policy is assured by Party direction, and rests upon a 'single plan of national economy.' [10] According to one text, 'in the USSR, where the economy is in the hands of the state, state administration assures the unity of economic and political leadership on the basis of a unified state plan of development for the national economy.' [11] Authoritative administrative handbooks emphasize that 'Soviet state organs inculcate in the citizens of the USSR the sentiment of duty to the motherland.' [12]

Credence is lent to the view that Soviet nationalism is the ideology of 'state monopoly capitalism' by the fact that Stalin, who developed the conception of the Soviet nation, based it upon a 'bourgeois' model. A 'capitalist' institution was renamed; the 'socialist' institution bears significant resemblances to the pattern which it replaced. It is, however, a more oppressive form of an institution traditionally regarded by Marxists as peculiar to capitalism.

The official conception of the 'Soviet nation' must be pieced together by non-Soviet scholars from scattered materials. The predominance of the implicit over the explicit reflects the situation of a regime which cannot allow its doctrines to face the scrutiny of critical analysis, as well as the astuteness of politicians who realize the advantages of ambiguity, and are concerned with the manipulation rather than with the definition of symbols.

A careful reading of major official statements on the problems of state and nation reveals that although Stalin never admitted that the Soviet Union was a nation, he and his collaborators attempted to mold a Soviet national consciousness.

Before defining this form of national consciousness we should say a few words about the ethnic structure of Soviet Russia, which is analyzed in detail in other contexts subsequently. Soviet nationalism is very largely the creation of the Soviet regime. But even the most powerful 'social engineers' must establish identities between their state power and the society which they govern. It is a mistake to consider that Moscow is indifferent to 'public opinion.' On the contrary, the Kremlin is deeply concerned with the manipulation of opinion. This requires ability to communicate with 'masses,' and 'elites,' in terms which will elicit desired responses.

The Bolsheviks gained control first of central Russia and then of the Ukraine and other non-Russian areas by a combination of propaganda, playing upon social tensions and national sentiments, and force. They have sought to win the loyalty of both Russians and non-Russians by claiming to represent the national interests and traditions of these various peoples, although at the same time they have attempted by indoctrination and agitation to make 'Soviet men' out of the people under their control. As one scholar has written, 'the Russian Communists are well aware that they must rely on the national loyalty, not merely on the class solidarity, of the 110 million Russian people, both in defense against foreign aggression (as during the German invasion) and in aggressive expansion.' The same methods are used in developing and maintaining the national solidarity of Soviet Russians as have been used in other 'national culture societies.' [13]

The Great Russians remain, as they were in imperial days, the dominant nation of the Soviet Union. Soviet communism bolshevizes Russians but it both bolshevizes and Russifies non-Russians. We need not accept at full value the Kremlin's claim that all Russians identify with the Soviet system. We are reminded that not all Russians regard themselves as 'Soviet men' by such statements as that of the Soviet refugee who said: 'I left the Soviet Union so that I could be a Russian.' [14]

The Soviet system of political control is characterized by great flexibility. As internal and external situations change, the Kremlin alters its pattern of slogans and symbols. But the objective of maximum integration at home and maximum disintegration in the non-Soviet world persists, and probably will as long as the internal Soviet power structure remains substantially unchanged.

Lenin and Stalin were aware of the disintegrating forces which are at work in large political systems. Stalin indicated such awareness, for example, in a major statement in 1950 when he referred to the empires of Cyrus and Alexander the Great, Caesar and Charlemagne as 'conglomerates' of tribes and peoples, lacking economic unity and 'a language understood by all members of the empire.' [15]

Occasional candid statements in the Soviet press reveal an astutely instrumental attitude toward nationalism and other group sentiments. For example, the Army newspaper *Krasnaya Zvezda* [16] for 1 January 1940 stated: 'History knows many instances when large nations and splendid armies fell to pieces, only because they were not supported by national unity, the unity of the country.' [17]

A study of Soviet nationalism cannot be fully meaningful without awareness of its relationship to international communism, which is one of the most potent foreign policy instruments of the Soviet state. Communists abroad, whether they know it or not, are Kremlin instruments. Perhaps this may become less true, or even cease to be true at all, after foreign communist parties achieve state power. Soviet propaganda may persuade the relatively uninformed rank and file members of foreign parties that they are patriotic Frenchmen, Indians, or Brazilians but of course the members of the Party apparatus derive cynical amusement from their success in disseminating such an illusion, which is one of the reasons why Soviet national socialism is so well equipped to exert influence throughout the world.

The concept of a 'socialist camp' carries a step further that of the 'anti-imperialist and anti-fascist camp' propounded by Andrei A. Zhdanov in his address at the founding of the Cominform in 1947. An important contribution to the doctrine symbolized by this term was made in Stalin's article 'Economic Problems of Socialism in the USSR' published on the eve of the 1952 Party Congress. In 1954 the new Soviet textbook on political

economy devoted a chapter to 'economic co-operation of the
countries of the socialist camp.' [18]

In an article in *Pravda* for 5 March 1955 the outstanding theoretician F. V. Konstantinov, in a long article entitled 'J. V.
Stalin and Problems of Communist Construction,' attributed to
Stalin 'the important proposition concerning the formation of a
unified and powerful socialist camp, opposed to the camp of
capitalism.' He asserted that this bloc defended 'peace and civilization,' and engaged in peaceful competition with the opposing
camp. Numerous articles of this kind refer to the 'enormous,
compactly located territory,' to its 900 million people, and to the
friendship and harmony which allegedly reign in the socialist
sphere.

The consolidation of this 'camp' is accompanied by extension
of Soviet culture to formerly independent national culture areas,
and by the debasement of symbols once associated with free cultural life. In Soviet propaganda all this takes place under such
slogans as development of the 'world democratic market' and 'embodiment of the principles of proletarian internationalism.'

From the non-Soviet point of view this process may be characterized as the development of an 'arrested culture,' remarkably
isolated both in time and space, 'based much more on the organizational, "external" (on the physical force in the long run) than
on the inner individualized values.' The national cultures are
inundated by 'the great influx of symbols from the sphere of the
Soviet Russian area.' [19]

The formation at Warsaw in May 1955 of a United Command
for the armed forces of the Soviet Union and its captive states,
and the accompanying treaty envisaging 'further development
and strengthening of economic and cultural relations' in the 'socialist camp' was soon overshadowed by the Khrushchev-Bulganin
'apology' to Tito and other events indicating to some optimistic
observers that perhaps the Kremlin was prepared to 'abandon the
hallowed principle of the infallibility of Communist leadership.' [20]

Increased emphasis upon the concept of the 'socialist camp'
was accompanied by a continued effort to safeguard the doctrinal supremacy of Russia. In striving toward integration of a

vastly enlarged sphere of influence, the Kremlin was at pains to achieve a flexible synthesis of Soviet Marxism and Russian nationalism.[21]

We have identified, in sufficient detail for this stage of our analysis, major elements which we shall examine. Let us turn to Soviet sources for official definitions of patriotism, nationalism and related concepts. These ideas are expressed by four terms, 'Soviet patriotism,' 'proletarian internationalism,' 'bourgeois nationalism,' and 'cosmopolitanism,' reflecting the polarism of official Soviet thought. The first two are considered good, even sacred, while the other two are unqualifiedly evil and are always used in a pejorative and condemnatory sense.

'Soviet patriotism' is the master symbol of Soviet Russian nationalism. It is the most abstract, general, and frequently repeated slogan of a system of demands for loyalty to the leadership of the Communist Party of the Soviet Union. It symbolizes the priority of these demands, and the values and identifications associated with them, over all other social and political relations. In this system the Party leaders define the attitudes and values of the Soviet peoples, and, by extension, of all mankind.

A leading Soviet theoretician defines Soviet patriotism as follows: 'Soviet patriotism constitutes the fusion of the progressive national traditions of the peoples with the common vital interests of all the toilers of the USSR. This marvelous fusion was created by the Party of Bolsheviks. The Party of Lenin and Stalin is the inspirer and teacher of Soviet patriotism, the founder of the new patriotic traditions of the working people of the USSR.'[22] Another definition of Soviet patriotism reads as follows: 'Boundless love of the Soviet people for the Socialist motherland, the unity of all the fraternal peoples around the Party of Lenin and Stalin and the Soviet government.'[23]

Soviet sources almost invariably discuss internationalism together with patriotism, and they make it perfectly clear that the two concepts are integrally and logically connected. The Soviet theoretician quoted above writes that 'The unity of patriotism and internationalism of the Soviet people is manifested in the support, moral, political and material, which the workers of the USSR have rendered and continue to render to the international proletariat in its struggle for democracy and socialism,' [24] and the Soviet dictionary of foreign words defines 'internationalism,' as 'The international class unity and solidarity of the proletarians and working people of all countries in the struggle for overthrow of the domination of the *bourgeoisie,* the destruction of imperialism and the construction of communism in the whole world.'

A corollary of this doctrine is the obligation of foreign communists to support the Soviet Union, sometimes stated in terms of support for 'Russia.' Thus a scholar writes, 'What Lenin said about the national pride of the Russian proletariat also applies of course to the proletariat of every other nation, because the class interests of the workers of Russia coincide with, or are identical with, the interests of the workers of other countries.' [25] Soviet patriotism requires not merely love for the socialist motherland but also 'hatred for the enemies of the Soviet State.' [26] The statutes of the Communist Party of the Soviet Union, adopted at the Nineteenth Party Congress in October 1952 prescribe for members the obligation to 'contribute in every way to the active defense of the Soviet motherland against the aggressive activities of its enemies.' [27]

We should now familiarize ourselves with the official definitions of 'bourgeois nationalism' and 'cosmopolitanism.' A typical Soviet definition of nationalism is as follows: 'the ideology and policy of the *bourgeoisie,* defending its class, exploiting interests at the expense of other nations, interests which it presents as those of the whole nation.' [28] The same work defines cosmopolitanism as 'the other side, the mask, for aggressive bourgeois nationalism,' and asserts that cosmopolitanism is, under present conditions, 'the reactionary ideology of American imperialism, seeking under the flag of cosmopolitanism to establish its world domination in the interests of monopoly capital.' [29]

The Soviet argument is that Soviet patriotism and proletarian internationalism—internationalism and nationalism are used sometimes with, sometimes without their qualifying adjectives— are progressive, revolutionary, and universal. In contrast, nationalism and cosmopolitanism are retrogressive, reactionary, and narrowly limited. True national pride, and the efflorescence of the 'best' and most 'progressive' cultural traditions are possible only on the basis of Soviet patriotism and proletarian internationalism. According to one important Soviet source 'Soviet patriotism by its very essence is incompatible with nationalism, which seeks to set the peoples of the USSR apart from one another, to separate the peoples of non-Russian nationalities from the Russian people and its culture, from the highest achievement of Russian and world culture, Leninism.' The same source goes on to say that 'Soviet patriotism is equally incompatible with national nihilism, renouncing national traditions and traits or with the rapid elimination of all national differences. Such national nihilism is only superficially opposed to nationalism, but in reality it always has been, and remains, its other side, containing nationalist, colonizing and chauvinist tendencies.'[30]

These official definitions may sound somewhat tedious but they provide a necessary foundation for subsequent discussion. They make it clear that, at least on the explicit level of official documents, Soviet patriotism differs from non-Soviet concepts of patriotism or nationalism. It is based upon Marxist-Leninist doctrine, it is universal in its pretensions, it refers to a supranational entity, the USSR, and it takes priority over, and asserts the right to transform, national cultural traditions. But it is also clear that it does not disregard local cultural factors. We may view Soviet patriotism as a complex of the highest values and loyalties of Soviet citizens, with loyalty to the particular culture of one's own nation in the second order of priority and loyalty to international communism on the third level. National pride, often mushrooming into chauvinism and messianism, which, as we shall see, is virtually synonymous with pride in Russian achievements and Russian culture, is a vital 'irrational' element in this pattern.

The categories which we have adduced reflect an unstable equilibrium among various elements of Soviet ideology. It has always been the avowed intention of the Party to minimize the role of traditional values. But in times of crisis, particularly during World War II, substantial concessions have had to be made to national traditions, particularly those of the Great Russian people. When the Party feels strong, it tends, other things being equal, to reduce concessions to popular traditions and attitudes. It tends to broaden its symbolic and attitudinal base when it feels threatened. As the regime recovered from the effects of World War II, the use of traditional symbols, particularly in the daily press, gradually diminished. Quantitative samples which are referred to later in this work, indicate the overwhelming predominance of the Marxist, or, more precisely, 'Soviet' symbols.

This does not necessarily mean that traditional symbols of Russian nationalism, and attitudes associated with them, are as unimportant as quantitative measurement seems to indicate. Russian national symbols are 'censored' out because of formal allegiance to Marxism, and because of the Kremlin's desire not to lose influence over those to whom it broadcasts its message of 'internationalism.' To a considerable degree, the 'Soviet' themes and symbols in Soviet ideology mask 'covert' or 'latent' Russian attitudes.[31]

Let us turn now to a brief historical sketch of the development of Soviet patriotism. For at least fifteen years following the Bolshevik revolution the term 'patriotism' was scorned by communists. Samuel Harper observed in 1931 that the Bolsheviks could move ahead 'not handicapped by patriotism.' Such concepts as patriotism and religion were, he noted, 'sentimental idealisms to the materialistic Bolsheviks.' In their view, people acted as members of classes, and social classes were guided by 'concrete, material interests.' [32] Such attitudes, at least with respect to patriotism, belonged to the period when what was soon to be denounced as a 'vulgar materialist' and a 'mechanistic' interpretation of Marxism was dominant. Problems posed by tension between Russians and non-Russians by industrialization and by national defense led later to somewhat paradoxical developments. For, since the early 1930's, and with increasing emphasis, Soviet thought has stressed both the value of previously rejected traditional attitudes and at the same time the necessity of a strictly 'goal-oriented,' [33] 'conscious' approach to action.[34]

The attitude which prevailed prior to the early 'thirties could not be better illustrated than by the article on patriotism in the excellent *Encyclopedia of State and Law*, edited by the gifted and erudite legal scholar P. Stuchka, who later fell victim to the great purges. According to this work, 'in our times patriotism plays the role of the most reactionary ideology, whose function

is to justify imperialist bestiality and to deaden the class consciousness of the proletariat, by setting impassable boundaries to
its struggle for liberation.' The *Encyclopedia* added that the
proletariat by the defense of its 'class state' fulfilled its internationalist mission, and that it defended the Soviet 'socialist
fatherland,' but not the 'national unity' which it contained.[35]
It emphasized that the *bourgeoisie* of the Soviet 'fatherland' was
not expected to display Soviet patriotism. Hence, service in the
Red Army was forbidden to 'non-toiling' elements.

The stress in the above statement is upon allegiance to a revolutionary social class rather than a nation or a state, but the
latter identities are also implied. The use of the term 'socialist
fatherland'[36] is interesting, particularly in view of the fact that
Marx had proclaimed that the workers had no 'fatherland.' Yet
if the view is accepted that in Marxism the attitude toward nationalism was determined by the question of the stake that a
class had in its country, the idea of Soviet Russia as the 'socialist
fatherland' was not necessarily inconsistent with Marxism.[37]
The expression 'Fatherland War,'[38] revived by Stalin in 1941,
had been used by Russian conservatives and nationalists in the
nineteenth century to describe the war against Napoleon. And
yet Lenin himself proclaimed that the Bolsheviks became 'defensists' after the Revolution.[39] As early as 21 March 1918 the
front page of *Pravda* was dominated by a flaming call for the
'organization of the defense of the socialist fatherland.'

This slogan became deeply embedded in the consciousness of
Soviet communists. Foreign intervention, and particularly the
war of 1920 against Poland, did much to give it more than a
purely 'proletarian' meaning. It always had latent Russian nationalist connotations. The Party leaders strove to subordinate
this nationalist element to their Marxist program, however. A
front-page *Pravda* editorial of 1 August 1920, for example, declared that the proletariat had nothing to lose but its chains and
that the task of the working class was to conquer the world. Its
most powerful weapon was the 'great proletarian power.'[40] After
universal victory, this 'power,' like the state, would not be
needed. An overtone of Russian nationalist resentment against
the capitalist West was suggested by the editorial's statement

that the 'capitalists' could no longer treat 'us' like a 'semi-colony.'

The victory of the Bolsheviks throughout most of the former Russian empire, combined with the failure of the Bolshevik Revolution to spread to other countries, left the Soviet regime facing three main sets of problems in the area of the theory and practice of nationality and statehood. The first was that of the relations between the Russian and non-Russian peoples of the new state. The second was that of the relationship between the 'socialist fatherland' and the non-Soviet world. The third was the question of the nature and continued existence of state and nation within the area under communist administrative control. The broad lines of solution to the second of these sets of problems were laid down by Stalin in 1924 and 1925 in his doctrine of 'socialism in one country.' In turn, the policies and doctrines based upon 'socialism in one country' led to the development of the ideas of Soviet and socialist 'democracy,' nation, and state which were embodied in the 'Stalin Constitution' of 1936 and in other major documents.

In May 1925 Stalin, in a speech to the leaders of the Moscow Party organization, made a famous statement 'On the results of the work of the fourteenth conference of the Russian Communist Party.' [41] Although many works on the Soviet Union have dealt with 'socialism in one country' it will be useful for our purposes to quote briefly from Stalin's crucial statement. Stalin asked, 'In general, is it possible to build socialism by our own efforts in our country,[42] technically and economically backward, if capitalism persists in other countries for a more or less considerable period?' He replied, 'Leninism answers this question in the affirmative.' It would be possible to construct a 'fully socialist society,' under the leadership of the working class and on the basis of an alliance of workers and peasants. But the 'final victory of socialism,' its complete assurance against attempts at intervention and the restoration of capitalism, presupposed 'the final victory of socialism' on a 'world scale.' [43] Stalin indicated in a general way that the chief means of achieving socialism in one country was industrialization. He quoted with approval a statement by Feliks Dzerzhinski that the country must become 'metallic.' [44]

The carrying out of Stalin's program required efforts, achievements, and sufferings which far surpassed in scale, intensity, and significance those of the original Bolshevik revolution of 1917–21. First of all, realization of this program led to the 'liquidation' of ideas inconsistent with it, and in many cases to the imprisonment, exile, or physical elimination of persons associated with doctrines formerly approved but later regarded as useless or harmful. Second, there was a semantic revolution in the course of which the Soviet regime claimed, and appropriated for its own use, symbols which had formerly been anthematized as Tsarist, bourgeois, or democratic. The new reality created by the 'revolution from above' received formal, codified expression in the Stalin constitution of 1936 and in the changes in the statutes of the Communist Party adopted at the Eighteenth Party Congress in March 1939. After the interruption of World War II, the finishing touches were put upon this system of rationalizations, particularly in the spheres of nationality and culture in Stalin's pronouncements of 1950.

Before examining this threefold operation, we should stress that while it broadened the base of the regime's power at home, and in important ways changed its character, it never led to renunciation of the Kremlin's claim to leadership of the world 'proletariat.' The most important element of continuity in Bolshevik thought since 1917, and, in some ways, since Lenin formulated his basic concepts in *What Is To Be Done*,[45] is the idea of irreconcilable and ceaseless struggle between the principles of 'socialism' and 'capitalism.' A concept of 'internationalism' which insists upon the necessity for centralized monolithic unity of the Party vanguard but makes expediential concessions to what are regarded as historically 'relative' facts of culture, such as national sentiments, has shaped the attitude of Bolsheviks toward non-Bolsheviks.

The combination of transcendent loyalty to the Party with the Party's internal organizational principle of absolute centralism, determines the character of Soviet thought and action. Traditional and spontaneous forces struggle to break out of this totalitarian structure and those who control it have been forced to reckon with them, but to a surprising degree the rulers have succeeded in utilizing for their own purposes these traditional and spontaneous forces without themselves succumbing to their appeal. It was not until 1950 that Stalin, in his official rulings on language and culture, explicitly recognized and legitimized the role of traditional, culturally determined elements in Soviet society and thought.

It is a fascinating experience to study the emergence of Russian nationalist symbols in the Soviet newspapers of 1933–4. The stage was set by administrative measures which increased Moscow's power at the expense of the already limited powers of the provinces. Thus *Pravda* for 24 April 1933 published a decree which abolished the right of the constituent republics to grant orders of distinction. The Russian Association of Proletarian Writers and its affiliated but partly autonomous non-Russian associations were abolished by a decree of April 1932, and in 1934 all Soviet writers were put under control of a single, Moscow-directed Union of Soviet Writers. Henceforth, education, scholarship, and the arts, as well as the mass communications media, were to inculcate pride not only in the Soviet present but also in the officially interpreted Russian revolutionary heritage of the past. Symptomatic of these developments was an article in *Izvestiya* for 15 April 1934 which called upon Soviet writers to intensify their efforts to 'create the new Soviet man.'

Much patriotic propaganda in those days revolved around the building of the 'giants' of 'socialist construction' and around heroic feats of small groups of Soviet citizens or of individuals. During the first six months of 1934 hardly a day passed without one or more banner headlines in the newspapers about the 'Chelyuskintsi,' a group of Arctic explorers and scientists headed by Professor Otto Schmidt, who had drifted for many months on ice floes after leaving their ships, the *Chelyuskin* and the *Krasin*. In connection with this expedition the appealing but previously taboo term *rodina* [46] was revived, in a famous *Pravda* editorial of 9 July 1934 entitled 'For the Motherland!' The editorial extolled 'creative and self-sacrificing patriotism' and demanded the destruction of all who betrayed the motherland.

The propaganda of heroic feats of industrial construction and military training reflected pride of achievement of Party and Komsomol [47] activists and the increasing authority and self-confidence of the new, tough Soviet 'technical intelligentsia.' But concessions were made in these years also to other elements in the population upon whom the success of economic development and war preparations depended. Stalin had already called for a halt to the baiting of non-Party engineers and scientists who were working faithfully for the regime. His program for making Soviet Russia a great power may have appealed to many of these men. P. Bardin, an outstanding Soviet engineer and a member of the Academy of Sciences, perhaps reflected this feeling in an article in *Izvestiya* for 1 May 1934 in which he emphasized that, in contrast to the new regime, engineers had not had an opportunity in pre-Soviet Russia to use and develop their ability to the full. The thesis that scientists, engineers, artists, and soldiers received real opportunity for self-development and useful service to the community only after the Bolshevik revolution has, ever since the early 1930's, been a prominent and probably effective feature of Soviet ideology.

The rehabilitation of traditional values and in particular of the Russian past, which began in those years, reflected genuine pride and enthusiasm, but it also reflected a growing tendency to relapse into the worst features of pre-revolutionary chauvinism. This tendency was intensified during the industrialization drive and developed eventually into a pattern far more dogmatic and authoritarian than even the official nationalism of pre-Soviet Russia. Many brilliant articles which helped to smooth the way to the new outlook were written, ironically enough, by Nikolai Bukharin, one of the chief victims of the great purges. Despite these articles, Bukharin was to be denounced, not many months before his arrest, for allegedly 'despising' the Russian people. It would be an oversimplification to attribute Bukharin's fall to his rejection of nationalism and chauvinism, but it is significant that among Great Russian communist leaders he was the sharpest critic of a chauvinistic attitude toward non-Russians. Bukharin's attitude was reflected in his warning at the Twelfth Party Congress, in 1923, that if the 'trampling upon of national minorities' continued, the existence of the Soviet Republic would be at stake.[48]

Bukharin's approach to the new 'proletarian humanism' which

he, together with the most respected of Soviet writers, Maxim Gorki, defined and popularized, was summed up in his statement in *Izvestiya* for 30 March 1934, that 'we are the heirs of everything progressive.' In the same paper, for 6 July, Bukharin argued that words like 'patriotism,' 'fatherland,' and 'motherland' which had sounded hateful and disgusting when associated with Tsarism, had now taken on thoroughly positive connotations. Interestingly, he criticized the Menshevik *émigré* publication *The Socialist Courier* for viewing the growth of Soviet patriotism as a reactionary development.

Another powerful and sinister theme must be mentioned here, namely, the propaganda which justified the savage crushing of 'nationalist deviations' in the Ukraine and elsewhere. 'Bourgeois nationalists' were denounced as allies of foreign 'interventionists,' who allegedly desired the restoration of capitalism. Already in 1926 Stalin had written to Lazar Kaganovich, his lieutenant in the Ukraine, that an incorrect policy of extreme 'Ukrainization' might assume the character of a fight 'against "Moscow" in general, against the Russians in general, against Russian culture and its supreme achievement, Leninism.' [49] In 1930 he wrote an angry letter accusing the popular 'proletarian poet,' Demyan Bedny, of 'slandering' the Russian proletariat by depicting Russians as lazy and backward, when in fact the revolutionary workers of all countries hailed the Russian working class, as 'the advance guard of the Soviet workers.' [50]

Let us examine the main concepts of Soviet patriotism as set forth in the 'thirties and subsequently. This doctrine is based on the claim that 'socialism' has been achieved in the Soviet Union, and that Soviet society is moving toward 'communism.' It was established dogmatically and it is interpreted dogmatically. Neither the process of identification of Kremlin policy with Marxist doctrine by which it was established, nor its application in policy, is subject to the discussion, analysis, comparison, or other methods by which the legitimacy of doctrines can be tested in a democratic society.

In 1913 Stalin, in his well-known essay, 'Marxism and the National Problem,' defined the nation as 'a historically developed, stable community of people, arising on the basis of community of language, territory, economic life and psychological pattern, manifested in a community of culture.' [51]

He also stated that 'the nation is not only an historical category, but an historical category of a definite epoch, the epoch of developing capitalism.' [52] But in 1929, in his essay, 'The National Problem and Leninism,' first published in 1949, Stalin introduced the concept of 'socialist nations,' which 'have developed on the basis of old, bourgeois nations as the result of the liquidation of capitalism.' These nations, of course, differ radically from 'bourgeois' nations. The overthrow of capitalism in Russia, and of 'national oppression,' led to the efflorescence of national culture, and to the 'consolidation of friendly international relations among the peoples of our country.' [53] Stalin's 1929 essay, and his much more famous letters on linguistics published in the daily press in 1950, are basic documents of the Stalinist totalitarian evolution. Taken together with Stalin's formulation of the increasing role of the state under socialism, and even under communism, set forth in his 'report' to the Eighteenth Party Congress in March 1939, they indicate the determination of the leaders of the new Soviet ruling classes to make maximum use of traditional concepts of political power. This return to old methods and values, however, was accompanied by increasing emphasis upon the differences between the Soviet and non-Soviet 'worlds.'

It is obvious that a stable community of sorts exists in the Soviet Union and that it is based upon a unified national economy. In 1925, Stalin made an important speech, 'On the political tasks of the University of the peoples of the East,' in which he declared that 'the universal human culture toward which socialism is moving' was to be 'proletarian in content, national in form.' Subsequent Soviet doctrine has maintained that the USSR has a 'proletarian,' or a 'socialist,' culture.[54] Stalin made it clear that adoption of national cultural forms was regarded as a more or less temporary concession facilitating extension of Soviet control over oriental populations of peasants, pastoralists, and hunters. He even predicted that some nationalities would have to be 'assimilated' in the process of building a 'universal proletarian culture.' [55] Stalin's slogan of 'universal human culture' concealed the extension to non-Russian peoples of Soviet Russian

culture. Before this process could reach its modern form, however, major social and economic developments had to occur.

Stalin interpreted some of these changes in his report 'On the
draft constitution of the USSR' on 25 November 1936.[56] He
hailed the 'complete victory of the socialist system in all spheres
of the national economy' and stated that Soviet society consisted
of two friendly classes, the working class and the peasant classes,
plus the new 'working intelligentsia,' which was a 'stratum' and
never could be a class.[57] Although Stalin did not say so, and
Soviet sources have subsequently carefully refrained from admit-
ting the fact, it is perfectly clear that the intelligentsia is the elite
of Soviet society. This reality has, however, been obliquely suggested in some of the Party's directives, such as the resolution of
the Central Committee of 14 November 1938 urging that special
forms of intensive propaganda should be devoted to 'the com-
manding cadres of our Soviet Party and non-Party intelligentsia,
consisting of yesterday's workers and peasants.' [58]

In his report on the draft constitution, Stalin established the
practice of distinguishing between the 'class structure' of the
USSR and the 'sphere of national relationships.' The country was
homogeneous with respect to class structure, but with respect to
national structure it was 'a fully formed multi-national socialist
state, which has stood all tests and whose capabilities might well
be envied by any national state.' [59] But even within the sphere
of national relationships, Stalin implied that homogeneity was
increasing, when he referred to the period of 1924, after the first
constitution of the USSR had been adopted, as a period when
'survivals of distrust toward the Great Russians had not yet disappeared.' [60] Stalin's distinction between class structure, which
was obviously regarded as fundamental, and the secondary sphere
of national relationships, was consistent with his earlier distinction between content and form in the field of culture. On the
basis of this distinction the Party authorities can so interpret national forms as to rob them of any real meaning.

The 1936 Constitution, particularly in Article 14, conferring a
long list of crucial powers upon the central government, was
federal in form but unitary in content. Its adoption was followed
by centralizing measures such as the abolition of national mil

ary formations. Voroshilov stated in his speech at the Eighteenth Party Congress in 1939 that, 'the workers' and peasants' Red Army was the sole army of the Soviet State.' The existence of national military formations was in contradiction to fundamental principles of the constitution.[61]

Even before World War II, which intensified nationalist trends, the Soviet Union met to an increasing extent Stalin's 1913 criteria and also those of Pillsbury, according to which 'the nation is in a sense a mental aggregate, and ability to be developed and controlled by common ideals and to carry out acts in common is the prime criterion of the existence of a nation.' [62]

We have left to the last the first of Stalin's criteria for a nation, a common language. Even with respect to this criterion, the Soviet Union was, before the war, already moving toward the status of a national state. A decisive step was taken in 1938 when the study of the Russian language was made a compulsory subject, beginning with the third grade, in the schools of the non-Russian units of the Union. By 1952 a Soviet author could write that 'the Russian language is the means of communication among the peoples of the Soviet Union and for the peoples of other countries it is the synonym of a new world and a new culture, the culture of socialism.' [63]

It is apparent from the foregoing that, at least in terms of Stalin's definition, the Soviet Union is a nation. Although there is no subject on which there is more confusion in Western social science than on the nation, it is safe to say that Stalin's 1913 definition does not differ radically from generally accepted Western definitions of a modern nation. Nevertheless, neither Stalin nor any other Soviet authority has ever openly admitted that the Soviet Union was a nation or a nation-state. Soviet sources do, however, often imply that this is the case. Let us first discuss the implied recognition that the USSR is the Soviet, 'socialist' nation and then explain Soviet failure to go beyond mere implication.

The expression 'Soviet national pride' has become very common in recent years. A text used in all Soviet pedagogical institutes states that the building of a communist society requires people 'with a highly developed feeling of Soviet patriotism and national pride.' [64] M. I. Matyushkin, whose *Soviet Patriotism* has

been cited several times wrote in 1952 that as a result of World
War II the 'Soviet national pride' of the working people of the
USSR had risen to new heights.[65] Such expressions as 'Soviet
man,' 'Soviet culture,' 'Soviet music,' and 'Soviet science' are
constantly used. Perhaps more significant, in view of the claim
that the USSR is a multi-national state, is the extremely common
use of the expression 'Soviet people.' [66] The term 'Soviet people'
was not used by Stalin in his report on the draft constitution, nor
is it contained in the constitution itself. It seems to have come
into common use by about 1939. Volume 8 of the *Small Soviet
Encyclopedia* published in that year boasted that in the event of
attack the 'Soviet people' would crush the enemy on his own
territory.' [67] Volume 9 of the same work, published in 1941,
stated that the Lenin-Stalin nationality policy had 'created a
single great Soviet People.' [68] Currently this expression is used at
least several times in every *Pravda* editorial. Confusingly, however, the expression 'peoples of the Soviet Union' continues to
be used. It is also important to note that the period of the late
'thirties and early 'forties which saw the introduction of the
concept of the 'single Soviet people' witnessed the glorification
of the Great Russians as the 'first among equals' of the 'family'
of Soviet peoples. It became a commonplace to say that 'the
Great Russian people leads the struggle of all of the peoples of
the Soviet land for the happiness of humanity, for communism.' [69]
We may assume that 'Soviet people' became more and more
synonymous with 'Russian people.'

The development treated in the last few pages would seem to
have two main implications. The first is that the Kremlin did,
increasingly after 1936, regard the Soviet Union as a super-nation.
The second is that the Great Russian people, and their traditions
and language, exercised an increasingly predominant influence
within the Soviet nation. It is interesting that during the fifteen
years or more since these ideas became prominent in Soviet
thought, the first has never been more than implied, and the
connection between the two has never been precisely or fully
stated.

There are compelling, and understandable, reasons why the
implications of the combination of Soviet patriotism and Russian

nationalism are not spelled out. In the first place, the Kremlin did not want to diminish its appeal to various elements outside the Soviet Union who might be attracted by Soviet 'internationalism.' There is another consideration of a similar practical character, related to Soviet domestic affairs. Kremlin control not only over non-Russians, but over the Great Russians also, would tend to be impaired if the more traditional and familiar symbols of nationalism were entirely given up in favor of the newer and more synthetic concepts of Soviet patriotism. The implicit idea of the USSR as the Soviet nation probably represents the goal of the Kremlin in so far as it regards the nation as a value at all.

That it does is indicated by many vital statements of top Soviet leaders. *Pravda* for 28 December 1954 contained an interesting example of Soviet nationalism. N. S. Khrushchev reportedly told a conference of Soviet leaders in the construction industry that 'Nowadays the whole world recognizes the might of the Soviet Union as a great world power and the imperialists are forced to reckon with this fact.' He added that this achievement was the result of support by the Soviet people of the Party of Marx, Engels, Lenin, and Stalin.

The Kremlin's ultimate ambitions and interests of course exceed those of any 'capitalist' nation-state. In 1951 an authoritative Soviet philosopher wrote that Soviet patriotism 'combines the genuinely national interests of the socialist state with the international interests of the working people of the whole world.' [70] In his farewell address at the Nineteenth Party Congress Stalin declared that the communist parties must lift up the banner of national independence and national sovereignty if they wished to become 'the leading force of the nation.' Post-Stalin Soviet policy has combined the lines of policy suggested in Konstantinov's and Stalin's formulas.

Soviet propaganda attacks efforts toward political or cultural co-operation in the non-Soviet world as 'war mongering' and 'cosmopolitanism.' At home, Soviet citizens suspected of interest in or sympathy for ideas not explicitly endorsed by the Party are accused of being 'cosmopolitans.' If they are non-Russians, they are more likely to be attacked as 'bourgeois nationalists.' It is very dangerous to fall into either one of these categories, for since the great purges they have been tantamount to treason.

The dissemination of 'Soviet patriotism' is one of the main functions of Soviet communications media. In this respect, as in so many others, the Soviet system has vastly intensified, by virtue of modern techniques and superior organization, major features of the Tsarist regime. It has added an element which Professor Karpovich calls 'ideocracy,' consisting in an attempt to put into practice an official philosophy.[71] As in Tsarist Russia, official patriotism is disseminated in the schools. The Party replaces the Orthodox Church as a major organ of ideological control.

Tsarist Russia had its patriotic school textbooks, under such titles as *Native Language*, and *Native Country*. An excellent example of the much more ambitious Soviet equivalent of Tsarist patriotic handbooks is the work entitled *Our Great Motherland*, the most recent edition of which was published a few months after the death of Stalin.[72] Attractively bound, illustrated by patriotic photographs, and provided with an excellent political map, this is a work well calculated to intensify national pride, as well as aversion toward the ideologically 'alien.' The handbook asserts that 'Soviet citizens hate the capitalist system with all of its vile characteristics and they are prepared to defend the Soviet socialist fatherland to the last breath.'[73]

Its central theme is the partnership of the Soviet people and the Communist Party in the building of a communist society.[74] The work assumes complete harmony of opinions and aspirations in Soviet society. It states, for example, that the 'unity of interests, aspirations, aims and outlook,' among the population constitutes the chief superiority of Soviet society to capitalist society.[75] A reader who does not share the professed values of this manual can scarcely fail to be shocked by its self-righteous tone, as in the assertion that 'it is not surprising that the Soviet Union is the most advanced country in the cultural sphere.'[76] The title of this book might well have been 'Russland ueber alles.' And yet it claims insistently that 'proletarian internationalism' is the dominant concept of Soviet ideology.

The concept of Soviet patriotism discussed in this chapter is a pattern of rationalizations for Kremlin imperialism. It has many sources of strength, including traditional Russian patriotism and messianism, the appeal of purposefulness and social dynamism in Marxism, and the success of the Soviet leadership in power politics. Its weaknesses include its 'synthetic' character as a doctrine imposed from above, as well as the internal contradictions of Soviet society, which it helps to conceal.

The Doctrine of Russian Leadership

All nations possess a sense of mission, and this is likely to become especially strong during the rise of a nation to world eminence. National pride, messianism, and chauvinism are aspects of 'ethnocentrism,' one of the useful concepts formulated by William Graham Sumner.[1]

As Robert Michels pointed out, each nation develops a complex and distinctive myth of its origins and destiny.[2] Surveying the American scene a few years ago, Merle Curti asked 'May perhaps a future historian conclude that the dominant faith of our time is the religion of nationalism—the American way?'[3]

We should not be surprised that despite 'proletarian internationalism' Soviet propaganda portrays the Great Russians as the bravest, wisest, and most virtuous of men.[4] The official nationalism, chauvinism, and messianism of the elite strata of Soviet Great Russians, however, as manifested in Soviet sources, are more intense and more disturbing than similar phenomena in the case of other great modern nations.

The official Soviet image of the Great Russian people is that of the leading nation of the supranational Soviet Union. Eventual world leadership by the Russian nation is suggested in the fact that the Soviet Union, by virtue of its structure, and in terms of authoritative interpretation, is viewed as the nucleus of a future world federation of Soviet nations. The role of the Great Russians is attributed to the priority and preponderance of their contribution to the Bolshevik Revolution and to the building of Party and state. On the cultural and ethical level the official image is that of a nation which deserves respect because it best exemplifies conformity to 'socialist' norms.[5] This image corresponds to Soviet reality. The Great Russians set the norms to which the non-Russian peoples are urged and compelled to conform.

Stalin defined the leadership role of the Great Russians at a Kremlin reception in honor of Red Army commanders on 24 May 1945. Addressing this group, consisting primarily of Great Russians, Stalin said,

> I would like to propose a toast to our Soviet people, and in particular to the health of the Russian people.
>
> I drink first of all to the health of the Russian people because it is the leading nation of all the nations belonging to the Soviet Union.
>
> I propose a toast to the health of the Russian people because it earned in this war general recognition as the guiding force of the Soviet Union among all the peoples of our country.
>
> I propose a toast to the health of the Russian people not only because it is the leading people, but also because it has a clear mind, a firm character and patience.[6]

Stalin's standard, foreshadowed before the war, has been adhered to since. After the war, there was a retreat from Russian nationalist symbols. Although often disguised by use of the word 'Soviet,' however, the concept of the leading role of the Great Russians has remained relatively constant. The death of Stalin caused no substantial alteration of this image, as is suggested by a typical statement in *The Teacher's Newspaper* more than a year after the supreme leader's death. In its editorial for 7 April 1954, *The Teacher's Newspaper* asserted that the most important task of the 'national' schools was to improve the teaching of the Russian language.[7] According to the editorial:

> Ukrainians and Belorussians, Latvians and Estonians, Kazakhs and Uzbeks, Georgians and Armenians, Tatars and Udmurts, Yakuts and Evenks, in fact all the great and small peoples of the USSR study with love the language of their

elder brother, the Great Russian people, which marches in the vanguard of contemporary mankind. By mastery of this language, they obtain access to the treasury of the most advanced culture and science of our age.

The Russian language has also achieved universal recognition beyond the borders of our motherland. It is studied with deep interest by our friends in the Chinese People's Republic, and in the countries of peoples democracy, who thus adhere to our culture.[8]

The quotation above, which could be duplicated many times, reflects the surge of Russian nationalism unleashed by Stalin. This unabashed Great Russian nationalism contrasts with the modesty of most of Lenin's utterances on the historical role of the Russians. Even after the successful Bolshevik revolution of 1917, Lenin made many such statements as the following: 'We know that not our merits, but our backwardness, brought victory to the Russian detachment of the proletariat.' [9] Pride in the revolutionary role of the Russian working class, but at the same time restraint, is suggested by Lenin's belief that the fate of socialism not only in Russia, but, perhaps, in other countries also, depended on the success of the Russian workers in solving their problems.[10]

Stalin's applications of Leninism were as significant in the nationality field as in many others. It will be interesting to survey the evolution of Stalin's views on the relationship between Russians and non-Russians, and between Russian and non-Russian cultures, since they underly the Soviet policy as we now know it. Despite, and partly because, he was not born into but had had to assimilate to the dominant culture, Stalin was in some ways closer to the traditional Russian nationalist pattern than Lenin. It is significant that one of his first important published works demanded unity of action of 'proletarians of all nationalities of Russia' and attacked Georgian and Armenian 'Socialist-federalists.' [11]

Some writers have attributed decisive significance to Stalin's desire to play a role on the all-Russian stage.[12] Stalin's appreciation of opportunities afforded to an ambitious leader by a vast empire was, in some ways, similar to that of Napoleon or Hitler. Personal factors played a part in making him, like his Austrian and Corsican counterparts, a superimperialist. Other factors, however, were much more important.

Political realities forced Stalin to exploit Russian nationalism. Even Lenin had been compelled to employ the slogan of the 'socialist fatherland,' which for many Russians was a disguised form of traditional Russian patriotism. Expediency for the sake of survival was sanctioned by Lenin, and demagogy in the service of power was elevated by Stalin to the level of a science.

To understand the process by which Stalin discarded Leninist inhibitions concerning Great Russian chauvinism it is necessary to realize how strong this sentiment was within the ranks of the victorious Bolsheviks. Characteristically, a delegate to the Tenth Congress of the Party, in 1921, declared that 'the transformation of Russia from a colony of Europe into the center of a world movement has filled with pride and with a special kind of Russian patriotism the hearts of all those who are connected with the revolution.' [13]

The stenographic reports of this congress and of the Twelfth Congress, in 1923, are indispensable sources for understanding of Party attitudes toward nationalism and operational principles developed to deal with it. It is clear from the reports of these Congresses that Russian nationalism and chauvinism were powerful forces in the Party. Some leading communists, such as Bukharin and Rakovski, and outstanding men like the Ukrainian Skrypnik and the Georgians Mdivani and Makharadze, who may be regarded as 'national' communists, were deeply concerned about Russian chauvinism. Stalin was already moving toward his formula of a balance between the extremes of local nationalism on the one hand and Great Russian chauvinism on the other. In form, Stalin's position was a compromise but in its practical effect it always emphasized centralism, which favored the Great Russians and their culture. Stalin was wise enough, however, to cloak this policy in Leninist phraseology and to present it with sufficient regard for the susceptibilities of the non-Russians to avoid needlessly antagonizing them.

A word count based on debates on Russian-non-Russian relations at the Tenth Party Congress reveals that 'Russia' and variations thereof, such as Russian, all-Russian, and so on, occurred 183 times. The Ukraine was mentioned only 12 times, and other nations less often. As delegate Safarov pointed out, opposition to Russian autocracy persisted in the guise of opposition to the Communist Party, which consisted largely of Russians, especially in the borderlands. So long as there were no factory workers among the Kirghiz and Uzbeks, the proletarian dictatorship became a Russian privilege. Many speakers at this Congress, including Lenin, emphasized the importance of a struggle against the heritage of Russian imperialism and of Russian colonization among the non-Russian peoples. Although Lenin expressed satisfaction that some of the borderlands of the former Russian empire had been recovered by Soviet Russia after a temporary loss, he also pointed out that it was not possible 'to submit the Ukraine, Russia and Siberia to the same stereotype.' [14]

A long article would be required to summarize the wealth of material on Russian chauvinism contained in the report of the crucial Twelfth Congress. The results of its deliberations were summed up in its seventh resolution, according to which the most important obstacle to the carrying out of the Bolshevik nationality policy was 'survivals of great power chauvinism,' reflecting the pre-revolutionary privileged position of the Great Russians. These survivals lived on in the attitudes of members of the bureaucracy, both central and local.

They were expressed in a 'contemptuous and soulless' attitude on the part of Russian officials toward the needs and requirements of the national republics. The situation was complicated by the fact that in a number of national units, such as the Ukraine, Belorussia, Azerbaidzhan, and in Turkestan, a large part of the working class, which was the main support of the Soviet authority, was of Great Russian nationality. Under such conditions, talk of the inevitability of victory of the 'higher' Russian culture over the more 'backward' cultures was only an attempt to strengthen the domination of the Great Russian nationality. The resolution stated that a decisive struggle against Great Russian chauvinism was the most urgent task of the Party.

The resolution urged that economic inequality between the

center and the borderlands be overcome by economic assistance to be given by the Russian proletariat to the 'backward' peoples. It noted that among the non-Russian peoples there were powerful chauvinistic attitudes directed against other non-Russians. Georgian chauvinism was directed against the Armenians, the Osetins, and the Adzharians. There was also Azerbaidzhanian chauvinism against the Armenians, and Uzbek chauvinism against the Turkmen and Kirghiz.[15]

Scattered in the often sharp debates on the nationality problem at this Congress, are numerous statements, still helpful for understanding Soviet nationality problems and policies. Skrypnik referred to 'great power prejudices, imbibed with our mothers' milk,' which, he said, were 'instinctive' with many comrades. Mdivani argued that the Russian proletariat think not in terms of mere formal equality of nations but give special consideration to the proletariat of the formerly oppressed nationalities. National equality, he argued, was not merely a question of language and culture. The non-Russian nationalities must be given an economic basis on which to develop.[16] Bukharin agreed that economic concessions must be made to the non-Russians, to 'put a firm foundation under our authority.'[17] Yakovlev declared that the Soviet bureaucracy consisted overwhelmingly of 'Russians and Russified Jews.'

Many of these 'Russifiers' refused to learn the language of the peoples among whom they worked.[18] Makharadze raised the crucial issue of the relationship between the non-Russian nationalities and the powers of the Party Central Committee. He complained that the central authorities made all the important decisions, including appointments to Party and Government posts in the most remote localities. Makharadze and other Georgians were indignant because the Georgian railroads had been co-ordinated with the general Soviet railroad system without consulting the Georgians. Also, the Georgians had been denied the right to establish customs frontiers and had, together with the Azerbaidzhanians and the Armenians, been forced into the Transcaucasian Federation instead of being allowed to belong directly to the Soviet Union, formed in 1922.[19] In 1936, perhaps because by that time this 'federation' represented a potential danger to

Moscow's policies, it was dissolved. Similarly, in the late 'twenties and early 'thirties separate Central Asian 'nations' were set up.

The principal opponents of the foregoing speakers were Stalin and his fellow Georgian, Ordzhonikidze. Stalin gave the main speech, an indication of his already well-established authority as an expert on nationality problems. He took the line that only he and his supporters were true continuators of Lenin's policy. Stalin accused Bukharin of wishing to put the Great Russian proletariat in a position of inferiority to the formerly oppressed nationalities. What to Lenin was a 'figure of speech,' said Stalin, Bukharin had turned into a political slogan. He opposed Bukharin's and Rakovski's demand that a statement referring to the harmfulness of local chauvinism be removed from the resolutions of the Congress. Stalin turned the tables on his opponents, particularly Bukharin, by pointing out that they had formerly been opposed to Lenin's insistence on the right of nations to self-determination.

At least three main positions on the nationality problem were advocated at the Twelfth Congress. One position, represented by Makharadze and other non-Russians, emphasized the necessity of giving a wide range of economic, political, and cultural autonomy to the non-Russian peoples. In this view, the revolution would not achieve its purpose, and would indeed become a mockery, if a firm base of local power was not placed under the formal rights granted by the Soviet constitution of 1922 to the national units of the Soviet 'federation.' Although formal concessions were made to this position, it was not to prove victorious in the long run.

After the relatively liberal interlude of 1923–9 many of those who had advocated it at the Twelfth Congress were liquidated as 'bourgeois nationalists.' This position might be characterized as one of 'national' communism, and that of Bukharin as one of 'cosmopolitan' internationalism. At this time Bukharin still belonged to the 'left' wing of the Party. To Party leaders like Bukharin, solution of the national problem was a means of enhancing the international revolutionary appeal of the Soviet Union, particularly in Western Europe.

It is interesting that Trotski, subsequently to be branded by the Stalinist leadership as the ringleader of the 'Trotskyite-Buk-harinite' gang of 'wreckers' and 'capitulators,' did not even participate in the nationality debates at the Twelfth Congress. He was one of the numerous Russified Jews to whom the strong local patriotism of a Skrypnik was alien. On the other hand, because they were internationalists, men like Bukharin and Trotski could be more tolerant, in practice, of the aspirations of the non-Russian peoples than could the centralist Stalin.

Stalin's position, which had been embodied in propaganda from early 1918, was set forth systematically as early as the Tenth Party Congress in 1921. It was simple in conception but complex in application. Its core was 'socialism in one country.' The Soviet power base was to be the major instrument for the extension of communism.[20]

Within this framework Stalin was willing to make minor concessions to non-Russian communist nationalists. In his victorious concluding speech at the Congress he stressed that the fight against local nationalism must, to the greatest possible extent, be carried on by Tatars, Georgians, Bashkirs, and other non-Russians. If this were not done it would seem as though Great Russian chauvinism were being strengthened. Unlike Rakovski, who favored giving the Ukraine representation in the second chamber of the supreme legislative body of the Soviet Union proportionate to its relatively large population, Stalin argued in favor of a relatively larger representation for the smaller Eastern peoples of the Soviet Union.[21] The Western-minded Rakovski was concerned with the impact of Soviet constitution-making on Germany but, suggested Stalin, 'the Eastern peoples, organically linked with India and China,' were more important. In Stalin's words,

if we make a small mistake in the Ukraine this will not be felt in the West but if we make a small mistake in Adzharistan, with its one hundred and twenty thousand people, this will be reflected in Turkey, and in the whole East, for Turkey is most closely connected with the East. If we make a small mistake with respect to the small region of the

Kalmyks who are linked with Tibet and China, this will affect us much more than a mistake in the Ukraine.[22]

Consequently, argued Stalin, each people belonging to the Soviet
Union should have equal representation in the upper house of
the Second Chamber. In retrospect Stalin's concern about the
Kalmyks is ironic. He deported them for 'collaboration' with the
Germans in World War II.

The discussion regarding nationality representation in 1923
illustrates an extremely important aspect of Soviet tactics. The
Soviets are alert to the importance of creating politically useful
impressions on non-Soviet public opinion. In the making of the
First Soviet constitution, which was discussed at the Twelfth
Party Congress, and was in force from January 1924 until December 1936, the propaganda value of the constitution was taken into
consideration. Similarly, Stalin in his 25 November 1936 speech
on the draft constitution of the USSR stated pointedly that 'the
international significance of the new constitution of the USSR
can hardly be exaggerated.' [23] There is no doubt that important
features of the 1936 constitution, such as the right of the constituent republics to 'secede,' and retention of a bicameral 'leg-
islature,' were determined largely by foreign propaganda
considerations.

The problems posed at the Twelfth Party Congress by intense
Great Russian chauvinism, even within the Party, were recognized as extremely serious. The position taken by Stalin would
ultimately favor attitudes of Great Russian chauvinism and
policies of Russification. But these negative features were for
many, especially outside of the Soviet Union, disguised or overshadowed by secondary concessions to the non-Russians. The
importance of these concessions and the difficulties involved in
implementing them should not be underestimated. One fact that
helps us to understand that Stalin's policy, at least at this time,
was not mere demagogy but required courage is the fact that, as
Skrypnik pointed out, many Party members were shocked when
the Soviet Union, on Stalin's initiative, received the name, not of
Russian Union of Soviet Socialist Republics, but of Union of
Soviet Socialist Republics.[24]

The subsequent history of Soviet nationality policy can be summed up as a gradual whittling away of restraints imposed by the conditions of the 1920's upon a weak regime. This process is reflected in many of Stalin's most significant statements. Let us compare Stalin's reports on the work of the Central Committee to the Sixteenth, Seventeenth, and Eighteenth Party Congresses of 1930, 1934, and 1939, respectively. Stalin devoted almost three pages to the 'national problem' in his 1930 Report.

In form at least, Stalin's position was an attack on Great Russian chauvinism, which he characterized as 'the chief danger within the sphere of the nationality problem.' The 'deviationists' in the direction of Great Russian chauvinism, according to Stalin, considered that with the victory of the proletariat, individual nations should begin to disappear in the USSR and there should begin to develop 'a single common language within the borders of a single state.' This deviation toward Great Russian chauvinism reflected the desire of dying classes of the formerly dominant nation to regain their lost privileges.

By identifying the deviation toward Great Russian chauvinism with the remnants of the Great Russian *bourgeoisie* who were in many cases undergoing persecution for alleged sabotage against the first Five Year Plan, Stalin drew a subtle distinction between the practices associated in the minds of both Russian and non-Russian communists with the old regime, and the new stress on centralization necessitated by rapid communist industrialization. Bolshevik leaders, including Stalin himself, had warned members of the *smenovekhovtsi* [25] group, headed by the returnee Ustryalov, formerly an anti-Soviet *émigré,* who had returned to Soviet Russia after he became convinced that Lenin was leading the country to a new rebirth, that they would be tolerated only as long as they did work useful to the new regime and refrained from interfering in political questions.

The case of the smenovekhovtsi—Ustryalov himself disappeared—illustrates how very precarious the situation of the Soviet intelligentsia still was at the time. And it underlines the fact that throughout the history of the regime, Soviet Russian policy has never been a simple continuation of prerevolutionary policy.[26]

As early as 1930, Stalin seems to have been setting up a straw

man in his attack on Great Russian chauvinism. He conjured up
a vision of a non-existent coalition of Great Russian chauvinists
and Utopian internationalists disguising their fight to restore
Great Russian privileges by false interpretations of Marx. More
significant than his disingenuous defense of 'proletarian internationalism' was Stalin's pointed attack on 'local nationalism.'
He defined the 'deviation' toward local nationalism as 'the desire
to separate oneself and shut oneself up within the framework of
one's narrow national shell.'

In the effort to defend themselves against Great Russian chauvinism, the adherents of this deviation shut their eyes to factors
which were bringing the toiling masses of the nationalities closer
together. This deviation, said Stalin, reflected discontent among
the dying classes of the formerly oppressed nations with the dictatorship of the proletariat, and their desire to 'separate themselves into their own national state and establish there their
own class domination.' Stalin significantly warned that this deviation was dangerous because it 'cultivates bourgeois nationalism,
weakens the unity of the toiling peoples of the USSR and plays
into the hands of the interventionists.' [27]

In his 1934 report, Stalin devoted less than a page to the national question. This speech was delivered after the sensational
suicide of Skrypnik, who killed himself, following denunciation of
his policy, in July 1933; many other tragic events had already occurred incidental to the suppression of leaders and tendencies opposed to centralization and Russification. Stalin now began his
discussion of the national question with the statement, still often
quoted in Soviet political journals, that 'survivals of capitalism in
men's consciousness are much more tenacious in the sphere of the
national problem than in any other sphere.' He dwelt on the
case of Skrypnik and he added that such cases were not exceptional, there being many such in other national republics. Stalin
defined the deviation toward nationalism, whether toward Great
Russian or local nationalism, as 'the subordination of the internationalist policy of the working class to the nationalist policy
of the *bourgeoisie.*'

In contrast to his 1930 position, he declared that it was 'empty'
to ask which of the two forms of nationalism represented the

greater danger. The chief danger, at any given time, was the deviation against which the Party had stopped fighting and which had consequently become a threat to the state. Stalin made it clear, however, that he regarded local nationalism as the greater danger. In the Ukraine, until recently, the deviation toward Ukrainian nationalism had not represented the chief danger, but when the struggle against it ceased, it joined forces with the interventionalists and became the main threat.[28] The grim doctrine on 'national deviations' summarized in this speech became a permanent part of the Soviet political arsenal. Thereafter any kind of actual or suspected deviation, whether Great Russian or local, was to be regarded as collaboration with the 'capitalist' enemy.

It is not our task to trace the developments which led to this situation. In essence, they amounted to the undermining of the federalism of the 1924–9 period and many of its cultural concomitants. The events in the Ukraine illustrate a process common to all of the non-Russian national units. Beginning in the late 'twenties, Moscow instituted repressive measures against many of the old Ukrainian Communist Party (Borotbists) who, after their party's merger with the Bolsheviks in 1920, obtained leadership in Ukrainian political and cultural life.

Writers such as Khvylovi, who proclaimed an 'Asiatic Renaissance,' in which a Western-oriented Ukraine, not Moscow, was to be the leader of socialism, statesmen such as education Commissar Shumski, economists like Volobuev, who in 1928 denounced Moscow's 'colonialism,' leaders like Petrovski, who as early as 1926 attacked the habitual use of the Russian language at Ukrainian Party meetings, were imprisoned or shot, committed suicide, or simply disappeared. Petrovski alone came back from Siberia in 1953 and was even awarded a decoration. In 1932–4, and again in 1937–8, thousands of Ukrainian and other non-Russian intellectuals and professionals were exiled or shot. The victims of these genocidal policies included not only 'bourgeois' intellectuals and almost all of the original 'nationalist' communists but even men like Postyshev, Stalin's lieutenant in purging the Ukraine in 1933. Thus Muscovite centralism triumphed over Ukrainian national communism, which had failed to provide it-

self with a local military force and the other weapons of power
which alone might have assured some possibility of real autonomy, cultural or otherwise. As Iwan Majstrenko has emphasized
in his recent study, *Borotbism*, this lack of a local national power
base was a major difference between Ukrainian communism and
Titoism of today.

By 1939 the doctrine of Soviet patriotism was in full vigor.
Stalin in his report to the Eighteenth Party Congress stated that
'on the basis of this community there have developed such moving forces as the moral-political unity of Soviet society, the friendship of the peoples of the USSR and Soviet patriotism.' One of
the five major tasks of the Party in internal politics listed by Stalin in this speech was the strengthening of the unity of Soviet
society and the 'friendship of the peoples,' together with other
aspects of the 'democratization of the political life of the country.' [29] Stalin's complete silence after 1934 regarding the danger
of Great Russian chauvinism is a fine example of Soviet totalitarian logic, in which state policy defines social reality. The
implicit assumption was that in the by now fully developed Soviet socialist society large-scale national deviations had vanished
forever. The new formula, consistent with suppression of incon-
venient aspects of reality, was to be accompanied, during and
after World War II by unacknowledged and unexplained acts of
genocide, which reflected the continued existence of acute national tensions.

In the Soviet communications system an important theme
often makes its debut relatively inconspicuously before it is included in a policy statement at the top level. There are many
reasons for this, including the desirability of allowing a reasonable interval between statements that might otherwise be revealed to be conspicuously inconsistent. The top leadership
speaks to many audiences, both domestic and foreign, communist and non-communist. To understand this pattern it is often
necessary to study not only major policy statements but also
premonitory signals, as well as later glosses upon doctrinal pronouncements.

As early as May 1938 a Party propagandist wrote in the Central
Committee's chief political organ that the Russian people 'lead

the struggle of all of the peoples of the Soviet land for the happiness of mankind.' [30] On 2 July 1940, *Pravda* published an item which anticipated subsequent rewriting of the history of the pre-revolutionary relationships between Russians and non-Russians. Reviewing the second volume of the very substantial university level history textbook which had recently appeared under the editorship of M. V. Nechkina, I. Mints, a leading Party theoretician, criticized the work for failing to demonstrate the enthusiastic participation of 'national units' in the Russian army during the war of 1812. Mints's criticism was within the framework of one of the major demands made in the Party's decrees on the study and writing of history in 1934 and 1936. These decrees demanded that increased attention be paid to the history of the non-Russian peoples of the Soviet Union but that the negative view of pre-revolutionary Russia as a 'prison of peoples' and of Tsarist policy toward non-Russians as one of plunder and exploitation of the non-Russians be modified.[31]

The article on 'Russians' in the second edition of the *Small Soviet Encyclopedia* repeats again and again that the Russians stand 'at the head' of the peoples of the Soviet Union. It asserts that 'the culture of the peoples of the USSR is historically linked with the culture of the Russian people. It has always experienced and continues to experience the beneficent influence of the advanced Russian culture.' [32]

The 'leading role' of the Great Russians was enhanced during the Soviet-German War. Stalin's first war speech, delivered on 3 July 1941 set a tone of patriotism and defense of 'national culture and national statehood' of the Russians, Ukrainians, and other peoples of the Soviet Union against Germanization and enslavement. But within this framework, especially after his speech of 6 November 1941, Stalin emphasized the uniqueness of the Russian role. Assailing the German Fascists, Stalin declared,' and these people, without conscience or honor, people with the morality of animals, have the impudence to demand the destruction of the Great Russian nation, the nation of Plekhanov and Lenin, of Belinski and Chernyshevski, of Pushkin and Tolstoi, of Glinka and Chaikovski, of Gorki and Chekhov, of Sechenov and Pavlov, of Repin and Surikov, of Suvorov and Kutuzov.' [33] Stalin's list of names was reproduced thousands of times in subsequent Soviet press and magazine articles. All of the persons named by Stalin were Great Russians, many of them figures revered by patriotic, conservative Russians of the pre-revolutionary period.

The state anthem adopted by decree of 20 December 1943 is an interesting synthesis of Russian and Soviet elements. The first stanza reads as follows: 'Great Rus has joined together for all time the unbreakable union of free republics. Long live the united and mighty Soviet Union, created by the will of the peoples.' [34] Commenting on the adoption of the new anthem the Soviet youth newspaper *Komsomolskaya Pravda* for 28 December 1943 emphasized both the leadership of the Great Russians and the friendship of the peoples of the Soviet Union.

The Great Russian people under the leadership of the Bolshevik Party had united all the peoples of the country. First among equals, it had gathered the peoples into a 'single family.' The article emphasized that not only Russians but also Uzbeks, Kazakhs, and members of many other peoples had been awarded medals for gallantry at the Front. Thus, while the new anthem hailed the exemplary role and status of the Russians it did so within the framework of a formal cultural pluralism. It should also be remembered that in February 1944 an amendment to the Soviet Constitution was adopted which gave the national republics the right to establish diplomatic relations with foreign states. This gesture was to be followed in 1945 by the inclusion, at Soviet insistence, of the Belorussian and Ukrainian Soviet republics in the United Nations.

In addition to appealing to the national sentiments of the Great Russians, and, to a lesser degree, the non-Russian peoples of the Soviet Union, Soviet war propaganda also made use both of the more abstract symbol of the 'Soviet people,' and of more tangible local associations and sentiments. An example of continued emphasis on the abstract, 'Soviet,' symbology is furnished by a lecture delivered by the prominent writer and Party leader, Alexander Fadeev, in 1943. Fadeev's lecture, entitled 'On Soviet Patriotism and the National Pride of the Peoples of the USSR,' emphasized that the basis of Soviet morale was 'the Soviet character of our patriotism,' which distinguished it from any other

kind of patriotism.[35] Such statements reflected the determination
of the Party leadership to keep a firm grip on the weapon of
patriotism.

At the same time, basic human attachments to native places
and familiar ways were associated, in the propaganda, with national survival. An interesting example of this appeal to 'local
patriotism' is a statement contained in *The Teacher's Newspaper*

> It is necessary from the earliest years to teach children in
> the school to love everything native: the pine groves and the
> birch trees, and the banks of the native rivers . . . and the
> native villages, and their collective farms; towns and fac-
> tories, the native language, history, national literature, the
> native regions and our glorious customs and traditions. We
> must teach the love of these dearest and closest things, as
> a patriot teacher said, in order that the thought of the
> motherland may evoke tears of joy, while the thought of los-
> ing her may make our blood run cold.[36]

Thus both the general propaganda of Soviet patriotism, and
local lore, or *kraevedenie*, as the Soviets call it, continued to
figure significantly, along with traditional nationalism, in the
Kremlin's propaganda.

Some well-informed Westerners saw in the cult of Tsarist generals such as Suvorov and Kutuzov, in the new anthem, and in
related developments clear proof that 'the new patriotic Russia'
was free of the 'hangover' of Soviet internationalism.[37] In the
long run the forces of national sentiment and tradition reflected
in these developments may in fact prove so strong as to vindicate
this judgment, incorrect as it seems to have been proved so far.
The Soviet press, however, even at the height of the nationalist revival in 1942–3, contained many warnings that the new 'line' in
no way repudiated Marxist internationalism. And although the
patriotic hymn to the fatherland became the state anthem, the
Internationale has remained the anthem of the Communist
Party.[38]

Glorification of the Great Russians as the dominant nation
of the Soviet Union has remained a conspicuous ingredient of

the post-1945 symbol pattern. It has not, however, been a stable, precisely defined element, nor should we expect this. The Soviet communications mechanism is regulated by central controls. But Soviet propaganda symbols must be selected with many audiences in mind. As a rule, subject to careful checks against relevant contexts, moods of confidence in the Kremlin, whatever their causes may be, are reflected in increased emphasis upon 'internationalism' in Soviet domestic propaganda, while a sense of urgency tends to be reflected in increased use of traditional 'nationalist' symbols. These include not only positive symbols such as 'motherland,' but negative ones such as 'imperialist cannibals.' Choice of symbols is intimately related to policy. As one student suggests, Stalin's toast to the Russian people 'supplied the key for the understanding of the purges carried out after 1945 among the non-Russian peoples of the Soviet Union.' [39] Similarly, an intricate pattern of variation in use of Great Russian and internationalist symbols since the death of Stalin has reflected shifts in tactics of Russification.

Politburo members continued to quote or paraphrase Stalin's toast to the Great Russians after 1945. In December 1949 G. M. Malenkov said 'the Soviet people all remember the moving words uttered by our great leader on 24 May 1945 . . . when Comrade Stalin proposed the health of our Soviet people and expressed warm thanks to the Russian people . . .' [40] L. P. Beria spoke similar words in his speech at the Nineteenth Party Congress in October 1952. Such top-level statements were backed up by a spate of scholarly and popular articles. [41]

The ideological reconversion after the war was accompanied by a shift of emphasis from the Russian people to the Communist Party. A number of spectacular cultural developments occurred in connection with this shift of emphasis, among which a prominent one was the rewriting by Alexander Fadeev of his novel *The Young Guard* because it did not sufficiently glorify the role of the Party. [42] But despite the Kremlin's fear of idealization of the pre-Soviet past, and other 'incorrect' kinds of Russian patriotism, there has been no repudiation or serious diminution of the emphasis upon the leading role of the Great Russians.

Komsomolskaya Pravda for 15 November 1952 published a

poem entitled 'To the Great Russian People' by an Uzbek, Hafur Gulyam, which had been translated from Uzbek into Russian. Hailing his 'Russian Brother,' the author wrote:

> You showed me Communism's paths; on you I can rely.
> Hail brother!—from the Uzbek land your younger brother I!
> You are the one who gave the world the mighty aeroplane.
> Rise higher, and the endless heights will then be your domain.

These lines from a long poem indicate the demands for fealty imposed upon the non-Russian peoples of the Soviet Union. At the Uzbek writers' congress in August-September 1954, the same Gulyam devoted his speech to proving the 'traditional love of the Uzbek for the Russian.' [43]

There is considerable agreement among students of quite varied points of view that the trend toward Russification was partially reversed during the three months between Stalin's death on 5 March 1953 and the arrest of Lavrenti Beria on 27 June.[44] There is less agreement with regard to the course of Russification since the fall of Beria, but on the basis of careful study of the opinions of other scholars and of a wide range of Soviet publications I am inclined to the following view. The pace of Russification was again accelerated after the elimination of Beria but the means employed were considerably less rigorous than in Stalin's last years.

The Kremlin decided after Beria's fall to attempt to enlist the services of the Ukrainians and the Belorussians on the side of the Great Russians in a policy which tends to favor the Slavic as against the non-Slavic peoples of the Soviet Union. This revival of a wartime policy has also included conspicuous gestures to the Poles and Yugoslavs and may ultimately be motivated as much by foreign policy considerations connected with the German question, as it is by internal factors.

Without attempting to set up rigid and inflexible categories where we know so little, it is safe to say that a totalitarian regime tends to make concessions or change its policies only in response to strong pressures or enticing opportunities. It is against this background of totalitarian behavior that we may view post-Stalin nationality policy and propaganda. As in other areas of choice, the new leadership apparently felt under pressure to at least create the impression in the nationality field of a relaxation of Stalinist controls. In international affairs, it led off with the slogan of 'relaxation of international tension.' The May Day 'calls' [45] of 1953 asserted that there was no disputed question which could not be resolved by negotiation. A year later this statement disappeared from the slogans, indicating confirmation of the basic hardening of Soviet policies which set in after the fall of Beria. The slogans for May Day and for 6 November 1953, as well as the May Day slogans for 1954 and 1955 gave first place to the call 'raise still higher the banner of proletarian internationalism!' The slogan of 'proletarian internationalism' is one of the most ambiguous in Soviet propaganda. It can serve both 'offensive' and 'defensive' purposes. It would seem that in the post-Stalin situation it was used domestically to suggest something of a return to the policies of Lenin while in foreign policy it was intended to appeal to the anti-imperialist mood of the 'colonial' peoples.

A number of impressive gestures were made to the non-Russian peoples of the Soviet Union during the three months following Stalin's death. 'Internationalist' language featuring the expression 'friendship of peoples' was employed more frequently. Beria's funeral oration, one of the three delivered at the ceremonies for Stalin, laid particular stress on the theme of the unity and the friendship of the Soviet peoples. After Beria resumed operational control of the political police, which he had relinquished, at least formally, in 1946, measures were taken against those responsible for the notorious anti-Semitic 'doctors' plot.' Party and police officials were removed in the non-Russian republics, particularly in the Ukraine and Georgia, under charge of having brought false accusations of 'bourgeois nationalism' against innocent persons.

Probably the most significant item of this kind in the early post-Stalin years was the publication in *Pravda* for 13 June 1953 of an announcement by the Central Committee of the Communist Party of the Ukraine of the dismissal of L. G. Melnikov as first secretary of the Party in that republic. The plenary session

stated that Melnikov 'permitted a distortion of the Leninist-Stalinist nationality policy of our Party, expressed in the defective
practice of advancing to leading Party and Soviet work in the
Western provinces of the Ukraine personnel drawn primarily
from other oblasts of the Ukraine and also in the conversion of
instruction in the Western Ukrainian higher educational institutions to the Russian language.' The limited importance of the
demotion of Melnikov is indicated by the fact that he was soon
appointed ambassador to Rumania. In April 1955 he received a
new and important post in Moscow, indicating that Khrushchev
was placing members of his old entourage, built up in his years
in Kiev, in key posts.

Melnikov was replaced in the Ukraine by A. I. Kirichenko,
the first Ukrainian in the history of the Soviet Union to hold the
post of First Secretary of the Party in that vitally important republic. In July 1955 Kirichenko became a member of the Party
Presidium.

Indications of a return to a semblance of 'proletarian internationalism' were manifested in some of the other non-Russian
republics. On 27 June 1953 the Latvian Party leader, Kalnber-
zins, stated that not enough 'Latvian national cadres' had been
promoted in the Latvian Party and Soviet organs.[46] The new line
was summed up in an article in *Kommunist* released by the censors on 18 June.[47] This article indicated that the new course
involved no fundamental changes. It emphasized the leading role
of the Russian people in Russian and Soviet history. Peoples of
the borderlands, wrote Fedoseev, had long ago linked their destinies with that of the Russian people. The best Russians had
been sincere friends of 'all the peoples of Russia.'[48] As is so
often the case, however, in Soviet political articles, which must
be read with an eye for subtle nuances, Fedoseev's article contained statements indicating that a somewhat new line had been
adopted in the nationality field.

The Party, wrote Fedoseev, educates Soviet people in the spirit
of respect for the national traditions of other peoples and mili-
tantly struggles against infringements on the rights of citizens of
any nationality. Fedoseev wrote

... in this respect the struggle against attempts of certain historians to glorify the reactionary policy of Tsarism, and also against manifestations of national exclusiveness, against nationalist distortions in certain books on the history of peoples of the USSR and in certain works of literature and art, has great significance.

Fedoseev added that the Party was concerned with the further development of the economy, national culture, and statehood [49] of all of the Soviet republics.[50]

The emphasis of Fedoseev's article was on the international significance of Soviet nationality policy. He emphasized the ideological unity of the peoples of the Soviet Union with those of China and of Eastern Europe. He asserted that

... socialist patriotism, love and devotion to the socialist motherland, have great international significance. The successes of the Soviet Union inspire not only Soviet peoples but also the toilers of the Chinese People's Republic and the European countries of people's democracy, and also the advanced people of the whole world. In the same way, the achievements of the Great Chinese People ... are ... dear to all Soviet people and to all of progressive humanity.[51]

It should be noted, incidentally, that in applying the word 'great' to the Chinese people Fedoseev was following the practice established since Communist China assumed its position of leadership among communist countries. Careful reading of many tens of thousands of words in Soviet sources reveals that the Chinese and the Russian peoples are the only two peoples to which the word 'great' is consistently applied. This adjective, however, has been used increasingly since Stalin's death, with respect to India.

Perhaps even more significant than the article by Fedoseev was another, in the same issue of *Kommunist* by S. Yakubovskaya entitled 'The Formation and Flourishing of Socialist Nations in the USSR.' [52] Yakubovskaya divided the 'Socialist nations' into three groups. One group, including Russians, Ukrainians, Georgians, Armenians, and others had already been consolidated into 'bourgeois nations' before the Bolshevik revolution. The second group, consisting of the peoples of Central Asia and Kazakhstan had already, before 1917, entered on the path of capitalist development, but feudal-patriarchal relations had still been predominant at the time of the revolution. The third group consisted of nationalities [53] which had been in the stage of 'disintegration of the clan order' [54] before the revolution. 'The nation which was most highly developed, economically, politically and culturally among the nations of Russia was the Russian nation.' [55]

On the basis of the development of the 'Russian socialist nation' all of the other nations of the Soviet Union had also grown into flourishing socialist nations. The author took pains to demonstrate that the Uzbeks, for example, were definitely a separate nation at the time of the revolution. She applied similar arguments to other non-Russian nations. This is in line with a basic tenet of Soviet nationality policy which seeks to confer the attributes of 'nations' or of 'nationalities' [56] on as many groups as possible but at the same time to tie each one of these groups to the guiding Party center and to the leading Russian nation. Each of these socialist nations, as a result of the aid given to it by the 'Great Russian people,' had developed an advanced economy, technology, and literary and artistic culture.[57]

The summary of Yakubovskaya's article given so far would seem to indicate that it represented little change from the Stalinist emphasis upon the leading role of the Great Russians. But, as in the case of Fedoseev's article, the article by Yakubovskaya contained several important paragraphs warning against the excesses of the previous policy. Yakubovskaya emphasized the value of the 'mutual enrichment' of cultures in the Soviet Union.[58] The major works of 'the national literatures of all the peoples of the Soviet Union,' she stressed, were translated into Russian and of course the works of Russian Soviet writers were translated into the languages of all of the Soviet socialist nations.

Exhibitions of national art held in Moscow had great significance. Further development of the 'spiritual individuality and national character' of all of the socialist nations would take place under conditions of gradual transition to communism.

Yakubovskaya criticized 'distortions of the nationality policy of
the Party' in the Ukraine, Lithuania, and elsewhere. The heart
of her exhortations was contained in the following significant
paragraph:

> the struggle against any sort of distortion of the nationality
> policy of the Party is the most important requirement for
> the development of nations on the path toward Communism.
> For the future, the task consists in carefully developing and
> promoting local cadres who know the language, customs,
> ways of life and norms of the people, and in developing the
> local school and theater, in improving the work of all So-
> viet institutions, and in raising the material and cultural
> level of the broad masses of toilers of all the national re-
> publics and oblasts.[59]

In view of subsequent developments, perhaps the most interesting point in Yakubovskaya's article was the fact that the
only Party leader whom she quoted was L. P. Beria. She referred
at considerable length to the speech delivered by Beria at the
Nineteenth Party Conference in 1952. The main theme of Beria's
speech on that occasion was the achievements of the Soviet nationality policy. Tsarist policy, Beria had argued, denied all
rights to the non-Russian peoples. They lacked 'statehood,' and
they were governed by officials who spoke only the Russian language, which was not understood by the local nationalities. But
in the Soviet system all the peoples of the country had acquired
and developed their statehood and their own high culture. Public business was conducted in the native language and account
was taken of local customs and 'the psychology of the local population.' The inequality of peoples, a heritage of the Tsarist past,
had been liquidated.

Beria compared the non-Russian peoples of the Soviet Union,
in respect to industrial, cultural, and educational developments,
with Near-Eastern countries such as Turkey, and with Western
European countries such as France and Italy, to the great disad-
vantage of the latter. With the aid of a battery of seductive
statistics he set forth the Soviet nationality policy as a model for

non-Soviet countries. Also, he made one statement which in retrospect takes on considerable significance. Noting that the friendship of peoples was being enhanced in the gradual transition to communism, Beria asserted that 'the high level of economy and culture achieved by the Soviet republics has opened up developments for active participation in the solution of the most important all-union tasks.' This implied that they had not hitherto played a sufficient role, and may have reflected Kremlin awareness of their discontent.[60]

The *Pravda* editorial of 10 July 1953 discussing the expulsion of Beria from the Party and his indictment for 'criminal activities' laid considerable emphasis on the nationality question. The editorial stated that 'by various sly strategems Beria attempted to undermine the friendship of peoples of the USSR, the foundation of foundations of the multi-national socialist state and the chief condition for all the achievements of the fraternal republics, to sow discord among the peoples of the USSR, and to activate bourgeois-nationalist elements in the union republics.' It seems probable that Beria sought to utilize and strengthen his connections among non-Russians, particularly in the political police, to strengthen his own machine in the struggle for supreme power against his rivals in the Presidium of the Party.[61]

Beria owed his career to the favor of his fellow Georgian, Stalin. A major landmark on his path to power was his publication of a book eulogizing Stalin's role in the history of the Communist Party in Transcaucasia which originated in a very long 'report' given by Beria in 1935. After Beria replaced the paranoiac Ezhov as head of the political police in 1938, he brought with him from Georgia a number of fellow countrymen who played a role in the Soviet police organs far out of proportion to the size of the Georgian nation. There is no doubt in my mind, on the basis of conversations with Soviet acquaintances during my four years in Moscow from 1943–7 and interviews with Soviet refugees, that there was considerable resentment among Russians against Stalin, Beria, and other Georgians in high places.[62]

The animosity of Great Russians toward these Georgian rulers may well have been shared by many non-Russians, particularly by Armenians, among whom there is still considerable anti-Georgian sentiment. But we should not exaggerate the significance of the national factor in the Beria case. While I have been very much impressed over the years by the role played by Georgians in Stalin's secret police, and while confirmatory evidence of the possible significance of this factor is furnished by the fact that several of Beria's 'accomplices,' whose executions, along with that of their leader, were announced in December 1953 and again in December 1954, were also Georgians, it is extremely difficult to separate the national from the other factors in such a complicated situation.[63]

It is not surprising that the summer and fall of 1953 were marked by a partial return to emphasis upon the dominant role of the Great Russians in the Soviet 'family of peoples.' An article by one of the editors of *Kommunist* released for publication at the end of July 1953 indicated a reversal in the vitally important area of selection of nationality cadres. A. Kravchenko inveighed against the selection of cadres in the national republics on the basis of an 'amateurish' approach. Among other things, Kravchenko noted that the problem of personnel was directly connected with the nationality question and that enemies of the people had resorted to various disguises, among them being the pretext of a struggle against violations of the nationality policy of the Party.[64] Beria's fall was followed by one more in the series of purges which had rocked the Communist Party in Georgia between 1951 and 1953. This largest in the series involved top Party and government leadership and affected more than 3000 Georgians.

As far as is known, however, the top local leadership remained in Georgian hands, although the Russian General Antonov, apparently of Jewish origin, was appointed Commander of the Transcaucasian military district. General Antonov took the May Day parade in Tbilisi in 1954, an honor which had previously been reserved for the Chairman of the Council of Ministers of the Georgian Republic. Antonov, like the new Secretary of the Georgian Communist Party, Mzhavanadze, in his speech at the Sixteenth Congress of the Georgian Communist Party in February 1954, stressed the 'altruistic assistance of the Russian people' to the Georgians.

In Azerbaidzhan, M. D. Bagirov, despite the fact that he had, at least since 1951, energetically pushed the Russian supremacy line, was removed as First Secretary of the Party organization. It is of course, possible that he was removed for reasons not connected with the nationality question, such as his long and close association with Beria. After a few months of promises of greater intellectual and cultural freedom, Central Asia and Kazakhstan were again subjected to renewed intensity of propaganda regarding the debt owed by their peoples to the Great Russians.[65]

That the Baltic area continued to be subjected to intense cultural pressure was indicated by numerous items, among which the article by the Latvian Communist D. Latsis entitled 'The Great Force of the Friendship of the Peoples' in one of the November 1953 issues of *Kommunist* is a good example.[66] Discussing the entire Baltic region, Latsis extended Baltic-Russian friendship back into the fifth century. He attributed the political and cultural achievements of the 'free' Baltic peoples exclusively to Russian influence. Latsis did not confine his tribute only to services allegedly rendered to the Baltic peoples. Among other things he wrote that the Belorussian people had established their own 'national State' only under the Soviet authority. And he stated 'under the direct influence of the most advanced Russian literature, the peoples of our country have produced talented prose writers, poets, and dramatists under the Soviet power.'[67]

As is always true in the case of any major Soviet propaganda line, examples could be multiplied virtually *ad nauseam*. The intensity and wide dissemination of this theme has been indicated. It might, however, be well to point out that as far as the smallest peoples of the Soviet Union, such as the Yakuts, were concerned, there is abundant evidence in Soviet sources that even during the 'Beria interlude' they were not relieved of the obligation to express gratitude to the Great Russians.

A Soviet work published in 1953 contained much material exemplifying the official post-Stalin attitude toward the internal Soviet nationality problem. This attitude is somewhat self-contradictory. The work in question denies that there is a 'ruling nation' in the Soviet state and argues that the Soviet peoples adhered voluntarily to the union. In contrast, the United States was built up by the conquest and extermination of 'unarmed Indian tribes.'

Asserting that the Soviet Russian nation has precisely the same rights as, for example, the Estonian, this work at the same time characterizes the Russian Soviet republic as the 'mother republic,' and expatiates in the Stalinist manner upon the leading role of the Russian people.[68]

Let us now turn to the rather special case of the application of the Russian supremacy theme to the Ukraine since the fall of Beria. On the organizational side, it should be pointed out that as far as is known no significant purge took place in the Ukraine after the fall of Beria. The Ukrainian Kirichenko remained First Secretary of the Party. The inclusion of Kirichenko in the inner circle of top Party leaders may well be a 'sop' to Ukrainian pride. According to one expert the fact that there was no Ukrainian in the Politburo after 1938 was a significant source of resentment.[69]

A full treatment of post-war or even post-Stalin Russian-Ukrainian relations might well require a book. What follows deals primarily with the celebration on an all-Union scale, mainly from January to June 1954, of the 300th anniversary of the 'reunion' of the Ukraine with Russia. The celebration began officially on 12 January 1954 when all Soviet daily newspapers, in a special section, published four 'theses' on the anniversary, proclaimed by the Central Committee of the Communist Party of the Soviet Union. For a week following the publication of the 'theses,' Russian-Ukrainian relations were the chief topic in the Soviet newspapers, and they again became the main topic in the last week of May, when special Jubilee sessions were held of the Supreme Soviets of the Russian and Ukrainian Soviet Republics.

The celebration of the 'reunion' was one of the greatest propaganda campaigns of all time, and certainly the most spectacular in the history of Soviet nationality policy. Besides official decrees, editorials, and thousands of news items, it included the special Supreme Soviet meetings, already referred to, the visit of an official Polish delegation, exchanges of greetings between the heads of the Soviet and Ukrainian 'governments,' and also a wide range of literary and artistic events. The nation-wide celebration included such curious events as a celebration in Tbilisi, in which factory workers observed the 'reunion' anniversary by expressing gratitude to the Russian people.[70]

As is usual on such occasions, it was widely reported that workers and farmers were redoubling their productive efforts under the stimulus of enthusiastic responses to the celebration. Part of the preparation for the event on the higher intellectual levels, was publication of three large and handsome volumes, each containing more than 500 pages of 'documents and materials,' by the Academy of Sciences of the USSR, jointly with the Academy of Sciences of the Ukrainian Republic.[71]

This propaganda exercise illustrates strikingly the importance of the interpretation of history in nationalist ideology. As Karl Deutsch and other students of nationalism have emphasized, national cohesion requires a group memory.[72] A totalitarian regime can, to a greater extent than is possible in other types of society, deliberately utilize instruments of communication and of recording, including historical archives and the historical profession, to create what one might call a synthetic community memory. This is the sort of operation in which the Kremlin was engaged in celebrating the reunion of the Ukraine with Russia. Of course this particular operation, vast though it was, only illustrates the effort constantly in progress in the Soviet Union, to shape and tailor the consciousness of the population to the Kremlin's specifications.

Since this particular operation revolved around an historical symbol, namely the alleged 'reunion,' which occurred in January 1654 at the Ukrainian Rada[73] of Pereyaslav, between representatives of Tsar Aleksei Mikhailovich and the Ukrainian Hetman, Bogdan Khmelnitski,[74] a word must be said about the 'facts.' The significance of the Pereyaslav treaty of 1654 has long been disputed by Russian and Ukrainian historians. The extreme Russian view was that the Ukrainians agreed to annexation by Moscow. On the other hand, Ukrainian historians such as Michael Hrushevsky considered that the Ukraine had been recognized as an independent state, bound, however, to Muscovy in the person of the Tsar.[75]

From the Ukrainian point of view, the oppression of the Ukrainians in the Russian Empire was based upon the 'Pereyaslav legend'; originally the Russian interpretation was that the 'Little Russian'[76] people had voluntarily joined the Muscovite state since they were of the same religion as the Muscovites. At the end of the nineteenth century the idea of 'one nationality' replaced the idea of one faith. The 'Pereyaslav legend' was the basis of the Russian imperial theory of a 'reunion of Rus.'[77]

A rough approximation of the historical truth would seem to be that the Russians, particularly at the time of the Ukrainian revolt against Peter the Great in the early eighteenth century and again and still more flagrantly in connection with Katherine II's abolition of Ukrainian rights and privileges, distorted and misinterpreted the 'Pereyaslav legend,' but that Ukrainian historians, in their turn, indulged in a great deal of historical anachronism in the nineteenth and twentieth centuries in tending to attribute to the Ukraine of 1654 too many of the attributes of a modern sovereign national state. Similar interpretations were made by the Tsarist regime of agreements with the Georgians and other non-Russian peoples, whose rights were subsequently whittled down by the imperial government.

It is ironic that Soviet interpretation of the Pereyaslav treaties has reverted to an extreme Russian imperialist position, which is forced upon the Ukrainian people in the name of the 'friendship of peoples.' The official 'theses' published in *Izvestiya* for 12 January 1954 stated that the 'reunion' was 'the completion of a prolonged struggle of the freedom-loving Ukrainian people against foreign enslavers and for reunion with the Russian people in a united Russian State.' This statement is in contradiction with numerous previously accepted historical facts. The Soviet interpretation now is that Khmelnitski was a great Ukrainian national hero who liberated his people from Polish and Turkish threats by 'reuniting' them with the Russian people.

This view contrasts sharply with that presented by the first edition of the *Small Soviet Encyclopedia* in 1931.[78] This earlier, and more accurate, Soviet account stated that 'the great power-chauvinist historians' viewed the so-called 'accession of the Ukraine to Russia' in 1654 as a 'reunion' of two parts of a single Russian nationality and 'denied the independence of the historical process of Ukrainian development.' [79] According to Soviet historiography before the glorification of Great Russian chauvinism became obligatory, Khmelnitski was a 'traitor' who betrayed the Ukrainians to the serf-holding Muscovite autocracy.

As early as 1938, however, the essential features of the post-war line on this question had been worked out. The important film produced by Sergei Eisenstein in 1938 depicts Alexander Nevski as the leader of the united 'Russian' people. This people included 'Kievan Rus,' the ancient state centering in Kiev, which is claimed as their ancestral homeland by both Russians and Ukrainians. Volume ten of the second edition of the *Small Soviet Encyclopedia* published in 1940 stated that the acquisition of the Ukraine by Russia, brought about by Khmelnitski and the Muscovite Tsar, 'corresponded to the desires of the greater part of the peasantry, the Cossacks and the leadership, who wished union with the brother Russian people.' [80] Soviet manipulation of the Khmelnitski symbol takes on peculiar overtones in view of the fact that Khmelnitski's cossacks were notorious for their slaughter of Jews.[81]

The view that the Russians and the Ukrainians had always been 'brother' peoples with common interests and common enemies was temporarily modified beginning about 1947. The 1946 edition of the standard Soviet medieval history textbook, used in all the schools of the country, stated that the 'heroic struggle of the Russian and Ukrainian peoples had saved Europe from enslavement by the Mongols.' [82] But the 1950 edition of the same text stated, 'in their cultural level the Mongols stood much lower than the Russians. Their power was maintained by force alone. The Russian people deeply hated the fierce conquerors and gradually gathered strength in order to throw off the terrible yoke. At the cost of tremendous suffering and constant struggle with the merciless conquerors, the Russian people shielded Western Europe from the horrors of the Mongol yoke.' [83]

The last quotation would suggest that Soviet historiography had returned to the most extreme version of the Tsarist interpretation according to which the Ukrainian people did not exist as a separate nationality. Actually there has been a good deal of contradiction in the Soviet position. On the one hand, lip service has always been paid to the idea of the 'Soviet Ukrainian nation,' while on the other hand there is a tendency, noted by Walter Kolarz, to regard the Ukrainians, Russians, and Belorussians as members of a 'Russian super-nation' comprising almost four-fifths of the population of the USSR.[84] A Soviet patriotic hand-book published a few months after Stalin's death contained a description of Kiev as 'the mother of Russian towns.'[85] This interpretation of course conforms to Tsarist and Soviet centralist traditions.

The novel and significant feature of the celebration of the Russian-Ukrainian 'reunion' was that it officially elevated the Ukrainians to the rank of 'junior elder brothers.' Not only was more attention devoted to the Ukrainians than had ever been devoted to any other single non-Russian people, but some acknowledgment was even made of the 'debt' which the Russians owed to the Ukrainians. A symbolic expression of mutuality of interest and obligation was afforded by the 'gift' of the Crimean oblast to the Ukrainian republic in February 1954. In an election speech on 9 March 1954 Kirichenko hailed the transfer of the Crimean oblast as an expression of the 'boundless love and confidence of the Russian people in the Ukrainian people.'[86]

It has been suggested that the Kremlin's purpose in transferring the Crimean oblast to the Ukrainian republic was to set the Moslem peoples of the Soviet Union against the Ukrainians, in continuation of Moscow's traditional 'divide and rule' policy. Once the seat of a mighty Tatar empire, the Crimea had, as late as 1944, been known as the 'Crimean Autonomous Oblast' so-called because a considerable but ever diminishing minority of the population consisted of Crimean Tatars. The Crimean Tatars, in distinction from the Tatars of Kazan, were exiled for alleged collaboration with the Germans. Hence, the argument runs, the Kremlin is making the Ukrainians imperialists by giving them an area which by right belongs to the Tatars.

It was also suggested that in view of the considerable animosity displayed toward Turkey in the propaganda for the 'reunion' the handing over of the Crimea might figure in plans to make demands on Turkey in the name of the Ukraine.[87] Another price which the Ukrainians have had to pay for this 'gift' is contribution of a large share of the manpower required to colonizing virgin soil in East Siberia and North Kazakhstan. It appears that this colonization is being carried out to a considerable extent by Ukrainians. Kirichenko in his 9 March 1954 speech, referred to above, stated that 40,000 'young patriots' had already 'requested' that they be sent to Kazakhstan and that 15,000 tractor drivers from the Ukraine were going to be 'given' for the Kazakhstan region alone. Subsequent press reports confirmed the impression of a considerable influx of Ukrainians, and also members of other ethnic groups, into Kazakhstan.

For example, the lead article in *Molodoi Kommunist* [88] for February 1955 reported that about 25,000 boys and girls had already been sent out to Kazakhstan and Siberia by the Ukrainian Komsomol organization, and more than 25,000 by the Moscow organization of the Komsomol. The article reported that more than 150,000 'young patriots' had left various parts of the country for the virgin lands. It also made it clear that the resettlement process would reach much larger proportions before its final goals were achieved. It seems likely that this drive is a major factor making for further Russification and 'Slavization' of areas into which, especially since 1941, an influx of Slavic settlers has already poured. One is tempted to speculate as to whether it may not, in the long run, have anti-Chinese implications. Such speculation also is encouraged by Khrushchev's statement early in 1955 that the Soviet Union needed to increase its population by an additional 100 million or more persons.

It seems probable that the post-Stalin emphasis upon the 'partnership' between Russians and Ukrainians was connected not only with Khrushchev's career as a Great Russian who built a personal political machine in the Ukraine, but also with the major role played by Russians and Ukrainians jointly in the resettlement drive.

Following the June 1954 celebration of the Russian-Ukrainian 'reunion,' the theme of Ukrainian-Russian relations remained a minor but persistent one. M. Z. Saburov devoted a paragraph to it in his address on the thirty-seventh anniversary of the revolution, on 6 November 1954. In December 1954 a handbook for teachers was published on this topic.[89] In March 1955 both the Russian and the Ukrainian republics were granted the Order of Lenin in commemoration of the 'reunion.' [90]

The celebration of the 'reunion' involved concessions to Ukrainian national consciousness which might in the future pose problems for the Kremlin.

It is important to realize, however, that the major theme of propaganda on nationality relations, although presented in a somewhat more subdued vein than previously, has continued to be the supremacy of the Great Russians among the Soviet peoples. The value to the Ukrainians of membership in the Russian-dominated Soviet state also continued to be emphasized. In speeches by Kirichenko and other Ukrainian leaders the old characterization of the Russians as the 'elder brother' and the reservation to the Russians of the adjective 'great' continued to be a conspicuous feature. Occasionally, however, the 'reunion' propaganda applied this adjective also to the Ukrainians. The preface to the three volumes of documents referred to earlier made it clear that emphasis upon the value of centralization continued to dominate the Soviet view of relations between the Russian and the non-Russian peoples. It stated that 'the great friendship of the peoples of the USSR, and Soviet patriotism, has deep historical roots and rests on the glorious traditions of the liberation and struggle of all the peoples of Russia headed by the Great Russian people, against social and national oppression.' [91] The preface asserted that all of the Soviet republics were developing together 'as a single socialist economy,' and were moving as a 'single family' to the 'starry heights of communism,' thus showing the way to a happy future for mankind. Without friendship with the Great Russian people these achievements of the Ukrainian and other Soviet peoples would have been impossible.[92]

The doctrine of the services of the Russians to non-Russians and the debt of the latter to the 'elder brother' is complex and deep-rooted. Perhaps we should pull together the various strands into a clear pattern, which can then be evaluated. In the first place, Russian nationalism is formally subordinated to Soviet patriotism.

The Great Russians have earned their leading position in Soviet society by virtue of leadership in the revolution, in the building of Socialism, and in the defense of the motherland against foreign enemies. Testing the logic of this assertion, it might be asked why no special honor is accorded to Soviet Jews, who, at least in the early period of the revolutionary regime, played such a conspicuous role. At this point we shall confine ourselves to pointing out first that according to Soviet doctrine Jews are not considered a nation, but only a 'nationality.' [93] They do not meet the criteria set up by Stalin in 1913. Among many other reasons, a high degree of assimilation of Russian culture by Soviet Jews and the existence of a great deal of anti-Semitism in the Soviet population as a whole should also be mentioned. I have already noted that the Chinese people share with the Russians the honor of being called 'great' in Soviet propaganda. This practice fits into the framework of attempting to rationalize the relative value of a people by its officially defined attitude toward Communism.

Since 1945, use of the terms 'Russia,' 'Russian,' and cognates has for the most part been restricted to historical and cultural items. A careful counting of words in the editorials in *Pravda* for February 1953 yielded 191 uses of the word 'Stalin,' 37 of 'Party,' 94 of 'Soviet Union,' 10 each of 'motherland' [94] and 'country,' [95] 17 of 'American imperialist,' but not a single use of the word 'Russia.' Another count, this time of the entire content of *Pravda* for the first eleven days of May 1953, yielded 140 uses of 'Soviet Union,' 132 of 'Soviet people,' 90 of 'motherland,' 56 of 'country,' and 31 of 'Russian,' 10 of 'Russian people,' and 5 of 'Russia.' In addition, the term 'old Russia' was used 3 times, in each case in a derogatory sense.

In another word count based on every fifth editorial in *Pravda* from 2 September to 27 September, inclusive, the terms Communist Party, followed by 'Party organization,' and Communist, respectively, held the first three places among symbols of Soviet patriotism. Then came Soviet Union, Soviet organ, Party enlightenment, Soviet people, and Soviet persons. In this count, no derivatives of 'Russia' were found. Finally, the same type of count for the January 1954 *Pravda* yielded a number of uses of Russia, Russian people, Russian Communist, and 'the Russian proletariat, the most revolutionary in the world.' These symbols, however, were overwhelmingly outnumbered by the more general symbols of Soviet patriotism and of proletarian internationalism.

In view of the data examined in this chapter we can say that the Russian supremacy theme is used to support Kremlin policies which do not necessarily have the enthusiastic support of the Great Russian element within the Soviet Union. It is important to make this point strongly because it might be easy to conclude from some of the evidence examined here that Soviet Russification is a mere continuation of pre-revolutionary Tsarist policy, or at least that it is a Russian nationalist policy. There is of course an element of continuity with the Tsarist regime, and there is also at least some reflection of Russian popular sentiment in the policy of the regime.

The Soviet regime utilizes traditions and other elements of national culture if it is forced to by circumstances, or if it is advantageous for it to cloak its policies in traditional or national guise. I believe that it would be naive to argue, as some anti-Soviet Russian refugees seem to, that everything 'Russian' is good and everything 'Soviet' is bad.

The Russian, Soviet, and other elements in the pattern of the USSR are all very complicated. The regime exploits some of the worst elements in the Russian tradition, but it also tolerates some of the good ones. At the same time, it struggles against some of the negative features of the Russian heritage, such as inefficiency and lack of discipline. Until the years immediately before World War II, the regime endeavored to suppress the extremes of Great Russian chauvinism and messianism.

Since the war it has attempted to make use of these aspects of the Russian cultural heritage in so far as they could be harnessed to Communist power and its promise of 'peace, democracy and Socialism' for the whole world. If 'spontaneous' Russian nationalism were allowed free reign within the Soviet Union, or, to speculate for a moment, after the disappearance of Soviet power, its excesses might in some ways be as difficult to deal with as those of the Bolshevik regime.[96]

The foregoing remarks are intended to warn readers against drawing the conclusion that the author is unaware of at least some of the dangers and complexities involved either in identifying completely, or refusing to identify at all, the Great Russians and the Soviet regime. Perhaps even more difficult is the question of the impact of Russification, and its ideological justification, on the non-Russians.

It is difficult to doubt that the 'elder brother' role of the Great Russians is resented. It should be emphasized, however, that as a rule statements regarding the leading role of the Russian people are made by non-Russians. Since Stalin himself was not a Russian, this statement can be applied even to his famous toast. Malenkov and Khrushchev, apparently Great Russians, refrained from using language which might be considered to reflect overt Russian chauvinism.[97]

The history and cultural development of the non-Russian peoples has been interpreted in the light of a retroactive Great Russian messianism. According to this doctrine, the contacts and intercourse between non-Russians and the Great Russian workers, peasants, and 'progressive intellectuals' in the past, as distinguished from those with representatives of the Tsarist government, were invariably beneficial to the non-Russians. Although the Tsarist government is denounced as reactionary, its incorporation of non-Russian peoples into the Russian empire is considered a positive achievement. The intensity of Soviet propaganda on this problem indicates the Kremlin's fear that even a moderate degree of cultural autonomy for non-Russian peoples fosters development of dangerous attitudes.

By late 1943 the Kremlin was convinced that it could withdraw concessions made to national sentiments, particularly of the non-Russians, to which it had been compelled to appeal to beat back the Nazi onslaught. A history of the Kazakh people, for example, warmly praised in *Pravda* for 10 July 1943, had been by 1945, after numerous individual criticisms, included in a systematic denunciation of histories of Tataria, Yakutia, Bashkiria, and other non-Russian areas. Georgi Aleksandrov, at that time the Chief of the Administration of Propaganda and Agitation of the Party Central Committee, criticized non-Russian historians for allegedly emphasizing experiences that had divided the 'peoples of Russia,' when in fact the history of these peoples had been a record of the overcoming of mutual antagonisms and of consolidation around the Russian people.[98]

Aleksandrov also made a contribution to a campaign, which in the post-war years took on vast dimensions, which was designed to change the images held by non-Russian peoples of their traditional national heroes. He castigated Tatar writers for glorifying the legendary hero Idegei who, in 1408 had 'headed a bandit raid of Tatar-Mongol hordes against Moscow.' The Central Committee as early as 1944 began to issue very specific decrees to eliminate 'incorrect' nationalist views from history, literature, and the arts. The campaign to eliminate anti-Russian sentiments from the historical memory of the non-Russians was intensified in the fall of 1946.

The purge inaugurated by Zhdanov in Leningrad was almost immediately extended to the non-Russian intellectuals. Provincial newspapers published in October 1946 carried a mass of material along these lines. Several newspapers for 16 October, for example, attacked a number of Soviet Uzbek poets for producing works 'permeated with a nationalistic spirit,' and for presenting the past of the Uzbek people in an overly attractive light. *Soviet Kirghizia* for 22 October 1946 complained that 'lack of ideological educational work has led to a situation in which some of our writers are prisoners of survivals of capitalism, of Shamanism.' The nostalgia for the heroic 'feudal' past attacked by Soviet central and provincial press probably reflected discontent and disillusionment with many features of the Soviet system.

By 1951, a series of anti-national decrees had been implemented by the Party organizations, Academies of Sciences, and other control bodies of the non-Russian units. The attack centered largely on criticism of the theory of a 'single current' [99] in the development of national cultures. The 'single current' theory it was alleged, minimized the significance of the class struggle and of the progressive influence of Russian culture.[100]

This campaign has deprived the Turkic peoples of the Soviet Caucasus of their nineteenth-century hero, Shamil, who until March 1950 was considered sufficiently respectable for the Stalin

Prize to be awarded to Gaidar Guseinov for a historical work glorifying Shamil's struggle against Tsarist oppression. The Stalin Prize was withdrawn and Shamil denounced as an agent of British capitalism and the Turkish Sultan. Strange as it may seem, 'withdrawal' of Stalin Prizes and even of academic degrees is a rather common Soviet practice.[101]

In Kazakhstan, the historical figure who must be eliminated from the people's consciousness is the nineteenth-century leader of a 'feudal-monarchical' movement, Kenesary Kasymov. The historian E. Bekmakhanov was a prime target of this attack. Prior to 26 December 1950, Bekmakhanov and his colleagues were in the good graces of Moscow. But then *Pravda* delivered a crushing blow in an article entitled 'For a Marxist-Leninist treatment of problems of the history of Kazakhstan.' Subsequently, the Central Committee of the Communist Party of Kazakhstan carried out a purge against the offending historians and their publishers. This campaign included special meetings of the Academy of Sciences of Kazakhstan and resulted in an order that by 1952 a presentation of Kazakh history, particularly Kazakh-Russian relations, 'free of bourgeois-nationalist and cosmopolitan distortions' should be well under way. Kenesary, like Shamil, was henceforth to be regarded as an agent of the English 'colonizers.'

From February to May 1952, there occurred a 'grim and thoroughgoing purge of scores of local and national museums all the way from Lithuania to Kazakhstan.' [102] In Latvia, the campaign against the people's memory involved suppression of traditions, holidays, and folklore, and obliteration of historical monuments. In the summer of 1952 a traditional Latvian folk holiday, which for centuries had been the high point of Latvian national life, was no longer celebrated.

Here as elsewhere, the campaign to eliminate anti-Russian sentiment is an attempt to remake the future by altering the past. The non-Russians are deprived of the spiritual refuge of history.[103] If highly developed peoples, such as the Latvians, could be treated in this fashion, we should expect more extreme measures in the case of smaller and less advanced peoples. It is not surprising that the legendary Mongolian hero, Geser, was discovered in 1948 to be, in reality, Genghis Khan in disguise and a symbol of 'feudalism, pan-Mongolism and religious prejudice,' and that he has been replaced in Sovietized Mongolian folklore by the figure of Peter the Great.[104]

In the Ukraine, even such a favored and politically powerful writer as Alexander Korneichuk, was subjected to sharp criticism for allegedly yielding to a local nationalist tendency, although Korneichuk, together with other favored Ukrainian intellectuals, regained some of his prestige after the death of Stalin. Particularly strange was the attack on Volodymir Sosyura for his poem 'Love the Ukraine,' written in 1944 and highly praised for years, but attacked in 1951 as an example of Ukrainian 'bourgeois nationalism.'

The attack on the theory of the 'single current' survived the death of Stalin. M. Matyushkin, perhaps the leading theoretician of official Soviet patriotism, wrote in April 1954 that this 'theory' inevitably led to the 'glossing over' of the class struggle. Matyushkin also returned to the attack on alleged idealization of the 'feudal and patriarchal-clan way of life' by 'bourgeois nationalist and cosmopolitan' intellectuals in Kazakhstan and elsewhere. Like other post-Stalin pronouncements on the nationality question, Matyushkin's article partially balanced the emphasis on Russia by criticism of 'great power chauvinism' but the main stress was on the necessity of struggle against 'nationalist survivals,' which, to Matyushkin, were weapons of international imperialism against the USSR.[105]

One feature of Soviet thinking on the nationality problem which we have not yet discussed would seem to indicate that the ideological measures just surveyed may be partially motivated by fear of 'separatist' movements or at least of such moods, among the non-Russian peoples. This is the Soviet criticism of the 'false and harmful theory' according to which a nation is not really a nation unless it has its own 'separate national state.' [106]

According to Soviet scholars, 'the despised traitors of the motherland, hirelings of foreign intelligence services, bourgeois nationalists, maintained that the Soviet nations ceased to be nations after they were united as national republics with the USSR,' but this, of course, is not true.[107] In the light of this argument, a statement made by Presidium member Pervukhin in Tbilisi during the 1954 campaign for elections to the USSR Supreme Soviet takes on considerable significance. Pervukhin quoted a statement made by Stalin in 1921 to the effect that neither Georgia nor any other Soviet country could exist in isolation in view of the hostility of the capitalist states toward the Soviet countries. Bourgeois nationalists, he said, had attempted to separate Georgia from the Soviet Union but they would never succeed. He called for a decisive struggle against any manifestations of bourgeois nationalism, which sought to sow discord among the people of Transcaucasia.

Another significant feature of Pervukhin's speech was its implication that Beria had opposed the plan of the majority in the Kremlin to increase production in Georgia of certain crops, such as tobacco, tea, and so on for distribution throughout the Soviet Union as a whole.[108]

Some three years have passed since the death of Stalin and evidence continues to mount that the concept of Russian cultural leadership in Soviet society and of the superior status of Russians has become a stable feature of Soviet doctrine. This doctrine has been formulated, however, in a somewhat less aggressive fashion since Stalin's departure. There is a tendency to place greater emphasis upon a postulated common desire of all the peoples of the Soviet Union to participate in building a modern, technologically advanced society. Typical is the statement that 'During the course of socialist construction, with the fraternal aid of the Russian people, the real inequality of peoples, a heritage of the old order, was eliminated.' The article containing this statement also asserted that the growth of 'socialist nations' in the USSR had proved that the capabilities of development of all peoples depended mainly on the social system under which they lived.[109]

It is interesting that the adjective 'great' (*veliki*) was omitted from the above quotation. Its omission before the word 'Russian' has tended to become the norm since the death of Stalin. Even in the reports in *Pravda* on the March 1955 meeting of the Supreme Soviet of the RSFSR, the expression 'great Russian people' occurred relatively infrequently and the term 'Russian' was vastly outnumbered by the term 'Soviet.' [110]

Probably the formula to which expression was given at the March 1955 meeting of the RSFSR Supreme Soviet represents a fairly stable position. In this post-Stalin formula the conception of Russian leadership, although essentially unchanged, was expressed in a less irritating manner. At the same time, the doctrine of Russian supremacy was tactfully subordinated, in statements about the outside world, to the Leninist conception of 'proletarian internationalism.'

Similarly, the non-Russian intelligentsias of the Soviet republics are brought into more active participation in Soviet cultural life. A variety of projects such as the 'preparation of surveys of the literature of the peoples of Central Asia and Kazakhstan,' reported in *Pravda Vostoka* for 9 June 1955, or the unusually well-publicized 'festival of Bashkir culture' in May-June 1955, indicate a desire to reward loyal non-Russian intellectuals in prestige and cash. But the Bashkirs were reminded by Party Secretary S. D. Ignatiev on 27 May that Bashkiria 'linked its fate with Moscow' in the sixteenth century. And Nikolai Tikhonov in *Pravda* for 17 July 1954 reiterated the twenty-year-old claim of the 'unity' of Soviet 'multi-national literature.'

Underlying Factors in Soviet Russification

We have already indicated that 'Russification' has not been abandoned as a result of the Bolshevik revolution. Soviet Russification, however, presents a pattern of demands and values which differs considerably from its Tsarist counterpart. The Soviet doctrine conveys a more urgent sense of mission and has far broader horizons than the imperial Russian creed of orthodoxy, autocracy, and nationalism. By subscribing to revolutionary Soviet Russian ideology one participates, however humbly, in the Kremlin program for transforming the world. In contrast, the official ideology of old Russia was parochial 'despite occasional traces of messianic doctrine.' [1]

Another difference between Soviet totalitarian and Tsarist traditional Russification is that the Soviet variety does not require a non-Russian people to renounce its language and perhaps some other cultural traits. Tsarist policy required that non-Russian peoples give up their language if they were to participate on anything like even terms in the imperial Russian pattern. Instruction in state and church schools was exclusively in Russian. It was officially decreed that the Ukrainian language, for example, did not exist. The Soviet formula is 'bi-lingual,' and to a limited and probably temporary degree, 'co-cultural.' [2] Although Soviet policy violates the integrity of non-Russian languages, it permits their teaching and use for educational and local administrative purposes. A serious effort is made to use the mother tongues of non-Russian peoples for the most effective communication to them of Soviet ideology. In return for a measure of linguistic freedom and other officially selected elements of national culture the non-Russians are expected to acquire a knowledge of the Russian language, and other prescribed features of Russian culture. To a limited degree, the Great Russians are expected to be familiar with the contributions of non-Russian peoples to general Soviet culture.

We may define Soviet totalitarian Russification, or 'Sovietization,' as the process by which non-Russians acquire the Russian language and other required elements of Great Russian culture. It may be useful to distinguish between 'objective' and 'subjective' Russification. Complete 'objective' Russification would mean acquiring the necessary elements of Russian culture without necessarily 'inwardly' accepting Russian values and beliefs. Complete 'subjective' Russification means, for all practical purposes, becoming a Russian, including not merely the acquisition of behavorial traits necessary to 'pass' as a Russian, but emotional identification with the Russians.

To understand what follows, we must define 'culture.' Throughout the remainder of this study, this term is normally used in the sense employed in modern, particularly American, anthropology. In this 'scientific' usage, culture 'means the total life way of a people, the social legacy the individual acquires from his group.'[3] Soviet scholars seldom use the term in this way. Although Soviet sources refer very frequently to 'Soviet' or to 'Russian' culture,[4] this is usually more or less equivalent to our term 'civilization.' 'Kultura' means technological achievement; it also means 'refinement,' and 'spiritual values.' Contemporary Soviet doctrine maintains that only in the 'socialist' Soviet system can material as well as spiritual values develop and flourish.[5]

The Soviet Russian attitude toward the world role of Russian culture is somewhat paradoxical. It is in part an 'imitative-defensive' attitude, as indicated by the ludicrous boastfulness of Soviet propaganda regarding Russian contributions to culture and civilization.[6] The Soviet Russians have attempted to 'nationalize' their borrowings from the 'West.' Particularly unsure of the loyalty of the non-Russians, the Soviet regime displays a nervous insistence that they appreciate the blessings of 'Russian culture.' Ironically enough, among non-Russians, especially those whose cultural development has differed radically from that of the Great Russians, hostility engendered by the harsh pressure of Westernization has often been directed against its agents, the Great Russian communists.

The Soviet combination of industrialization and Russian control did not sufficiently take into account the values and beliefs of non-Russians, in some cases pre-industrial peoples. Kalinin, the nominal chief of the Soviet State from 1920 to 1946, said in 1929 that it was the aim of Soviet policy 'to teach the people of the Kirghiz steppe, the small Uzbek cotton grower, and the Turkmenian gardener to accept the ideals of the Leningrad worker.' [7] 'None of the various national groups have been allowed to continue their native culture, using the word "culture" in the broad sense of a stage and characteristics of a civilization.' [8] One scholar observes that 'the bed of Procrustes pales as a metaphor before the practice of the Soviet nationality policy.' [9]

Not Russification alone, but its employment by a totalitarian regime is a threat to cultural freedom. It would be absurd for an American to condemn the Soviet regime merely because it pursues a policy of cultural assimilation. The United States is the prime example of a successful policy of assimilation. The important considerations are the content of what is assimilated and the means by which assimilation is effected. Assimilation in the United States is voluntary, and 'spontaneous.' Immigrants have accepted assimilation to American norms as part of a process which began when they chose to exchange one set of allegiances for another. In Tsarist Russia and especially in the Soviet Union, whole nations, regardless of cultural background, have been forced to accept norms arbitrarily prescribed by a despotic political authority.

Granted the existence of a 'multi-national' Russian, or Soviet, state, some degree of Russification is inevitable for linguistic, demographic, economic, and administrative reasons. These have been reinforced by Marxist-Leninist theory.

The centralizing and assimilatory policies of the Soviet regime were not necessarily the only ones available. More cultural 'autonomy' and a greater measure of 'federalism' might have been granted to the non-Russians. Soviet policy might have been more 'pluralistic.' Let us discuss briefly the alternatives of political and cultural policy available in a society composed of several distinct national elements.

It is probably impossible to completely separate the political and legal from the economic, social, and cultural questions involved.[10] Historical evidence, at least that of the last century or two, indicates that political and economic factors tend to 'determine' the nature of a culture. In a society in which political and economic power is relatively widely distributed, freedom and diversity of all kinds, including 'cultural freedom,' can develop. But where political and economic power are concentrated and centralized, and where the central government is not subject to controls of constitution and custom, the tendency is toward compulsive homogeneity. The experience of our times has made it clear that totalitarianism means the 'politicalization' of as much of the life of a country as the totalitarian rulers can control without threatening their power. In the words of Peter Meyer, 'Democratic society tolerates a diversity of beliefs, traditions, emotional attachments, and group ties and solidarities. Totalitarian society cannot.'[11]

There is of course no complete correspondence between political forms and the treatment of ethnic groups. However, at least in modern industrialized society, cultural pluralism is to a significant degree dependent upon the existence of constitutional government. It is also dependent upon the feeling of security or lack of security of governments in relation to foreign governments.

Soviet totalitarianism has been impelled, both by domestic pressures and by fear of external enemies, to resort not only to an oppressive policy of assimilation but to a wide range of other 'reactionary' policies. Although the basic policy with regard to national and ethnic groups is one of willingness to bring the members of these groups into the dominant cultural pattern, extreme 'discrimination' and even persecution, flowing into genocide, have been employed against recalcitrant groups.

To understand the Soviet approach to problems of autonomy, assimilation, discrimination, and persecution we must among other things survey the facts regarding numbers, distribution, and characteristics of the national components in the Soviet population. The outstanding demographic factor is the predominance of the Great Russians. In addition to being by far the largest national entity, they possess important geographical advantages. The area from which, beginning in the sixteenth century, they extended their power by settlement and conquest, first to the north and east and then to the south and west, is the strategic center of the Soviet Union, and, in the opinion of some geographers, of the Euro-Asiatic 'heartland.' [12] Substantial minorities of Great Russians, established over centuries, but especially in the period after 1905, existed in almost all of the non-Russian political units of the Soviet Union even in 1926, when the first and by far the most detailed Soviet census data were published.[13]

Industrialization, which brought Russians and non-Russians together in new factories and enterprises, intermarriage, which is relatively limited in Central Asia, and the tendency of some non-Russians to identify with the dominant national group, are among factors which subsequently fostered assimilation to the Great Russian pattern, especially since the first Five Year Plan.[14] Transfers of population connected with World War II and postwar Soviet economic and security policies still further intensified the trend toward intrusion of Great Russians into the non-Russian groups. The effects of colonization, especially in Central Asia, were somewhat limited, however, by the fact that colonists and natives lived in separate villages. The impact of 'automatic' processes has been enhanced by a deliberate policy of scattering and intermingling of peoples. In the long run, this consciously organized process of 'fusion of nations' may perhaps aid in the formation of the 'new Soviet man' and of the 'Soviet nation.' [15] In the short run, it exacerbates national tensions, but it strengthens the power of the authorities against hostile groups.

In addition to numbers and location, the Great Russians enjoy other advantages. Traditionally they have been the ruling nation and they long ago acquired the techniques of power and the self-confidence common to dominant nationalities. Over a period of several centuries the Great Russians have gradually acquired perhaps unsurpassed skill in the arts of 'divide and rule.' Russian experience with Asiatic peoples has been rich and intimate, and the Russians are unusually free from attitudes of 'racial' snobbery, although some condescension toward technically less advanced peoples has developed in recent decades.[16]

Among 'great' peoples, the Russians have a perhaps unique tradition of adapting for their own use borrowings from other cultures. The Great Russians enjoy in the Soviet Union, as they did in the Russian Empire, the advantage of being relatively 'advanced' in the arts of civilization. With respect to such objective indexes as urbanization, literacy, and formal education, the Great Russians have throughout the history of the Empire and the Soviet Union ranked above most of the non-Russian peoples, although some of these peoples, particularly the Baltic nations, the Georgians, the Armenians, and the Jews are in some ways more advanced.

With a literacy rate of 45 per cent in 1926, the Great Russians were ahead of most of the other peoples. They were far more urbanized than the Ukrainians.[17] About 50 per cent of the population of the Soviet Union are or consider themselves to be Great Russians. It is necessary to be cautious about percentages, a fact which points to one of the abnormalities of Soviet life. No ethnic data has been published since 1939. The national composition of the population is treated as a secret. According to the special USSR volume of the *Large Soviet Encyclopedia*, the 99,019,000 Great Russians constituted 58.41 per cent of the Soviet population in 1939.[18] At that time, the total population was 170,467,186 persons.

After acquisition in the fall of 1939 of parts of Poland inhabited mostly by Jews, Ukrainians, and Belorussians, and of Northern Bukovina and the Baltic states in June and July 1940,[19] the Soviet population increased to 193 million. In 1945, additional non-Russians were taken into the Soviet Union when it incorporated the Polish Lwow area, and was presented with the Trans-Carpathian Ukraine by Czechoslovakia. The 'People's Republic' of Tannu-Tuva was added during the war as an 'autonomous oblast' to the Russian Soviet Republic, although this fact was not disclosed by the Soviet press until 16 August 1946. If it is assumed that the nearly 100 million Great Russians, as of 1939, had increased by 1955 to about 110 million and that the more than 90 million non-Russians as of 1940 had grown to about 105 million, an almost even division between Russians and non-Russians is found.[20]

The obtainable data demonstrate the existence of large minority groups and yet emphasize the numerical preponderance of the Great Russians. There seem to be somewhat over 40 million Ukrainians in the Soviet Union.[21] Since the 1939 census recorded a figure of only 28,070,000 Ukrainians, it is clear that more than ten million Ukrainians were added by conquest between 1939 and the post-war period.

There would seem to have been a loss of some three million Ukrainians. If one allows for natural increase, this loss amounts to much more than three million. Lorimer calculates the average rate of increase of the Soviet population as a whole for the period 1926–39 as 15.9 per cent, that of the Russians having been 27 per cent. If the rate of growth of the Ukrainians had been even only 16 per cent during those years, there should have been 36 million Ukrainians in 1939 instead of 28,070,000.[22]

The main reason for the deficit of Ukrainians seems to be the famine of 1932–3. Estimates of deaths of Ukrainians as a result of the famine range from three to ten million.[23] Part of the deficit may have resulted from migration to other areas in search of a better food situation. Many Ukrainians were exiled as 'kulaks.' Others moved voluntarily to the predominantly Russian Donbas industrial region. In some cases, Ukrainians moving to regions of Russian culture prudently 'passed' as Great Russians.[24]

Some authorities are of the opinion that the loss of life in the Ukraine, Kazakhstan, and the other non-Russian areas was the result of the employment of starvation 'as an instrument of national policy.' [25]

The 'Western Ukrainians' differ considerably in culture from their Eastern compatriots. Several millions were, until 1946, members of the Roman Catholic Church of the Eastern Rite, usually referred to in English as the 'Uniate' church, which was founded in 1596 under Polish auspices. Centuries of Hapsburg and two decades of hated Polish rule, as well as Polish, Austrian-Hungarian and Catholic cultural influences, shaped and sharpened the national consciousness of the Galician, Trans-Carpathian,

and other Western Ukrainians, especially of the Catholic majority. Heightened national consciousness was stirred among the
Eastern, Orthodox Ukrainians, also as a result of the revolutions
and wars of 1917–21, and in 1921 an 'Autocephalous' Orthodox
Church was established, although it was from the beginning an
object of antipathy to the official Russian Orthodox Church and
of suspicion to the Kremlin. It was suppressed in 1930 and its
leaders induced to confess that for ten years they had been conducting covert anti-Soviet Ukrainian nationalist activity. This
branch of Orthodoxy experienced a partial revival under German
protection during World War II, but found it impossible to co-
operate with the Ukrainian Catholics and was denounced by the
Russian and Ukrainian clergy under leadership of Metropolitan
Sergii, who loyally supported Stalin.

Prior to 1939 neither Western Ukrainians nor Western Belorussians had lived under Soviet rule. Like the Great Russians,
the Ukrainians even before 1917, but to an increasing degree
since, have colonized the North Caucasus, Central Asia, and
Siberia. Apparently many remote enclaves of Ukrainians have
kept alive elements of national consciousness. According to 1933
Soviet data, 13.2 per cent of the population of the Kazakh republic were Ukrainians. At that time 7.8 per cent of the population of the Russian Republic were Ukrainians. Six and
eight-tenths per cent of the population of the Northern Osetin
Autonomous Republic were Ukrainians.[26] According to another
Soviet source, 'compact masses' of Ukrainians are to be found in
the Voronezh and Kursk oblasts and in the North Caucasus, as
well as in Western Siberia, in Kazakhstan, and in the Far East.[27]

So far as the eponymous populations of Central Asia and
Eastern Siberia are concerned, the Ukrainians are apparently regarded as 'Russians,' and it also seems that the Ukrainians living
among the non-Slavic populations of these areas tend to identify
themselves with the Russians. Some 10 million of the 40 million
odd Ukrainians of the Soviet Union live outside of the Ukrainian
Soviet republic. In some Ukrainian farm settlements in Eastern
Siberia, for example, Ukrainian continues to be the basic language.

More than three million persons of Ukrainian origin live in

the United States, Canada, Brazil, and other countries of the Americas or Western Europe, a fact which has considerable political significance, underlined in the case of Soviet refugees among them by the post-Stalin pressure for 'repatriation.'

The next most numerous people of the USSR are the Belorussians, or White Russians. With the addition of Belorussians in territory acquired in the Nazi-Soviet partition of Poland in 1939, and allowing for subsequent increase, there are probably some nine million Belorussians. According to the USSR volume of the *Large Soviet Encyclopedia*, the three Eastern Slavic peoples constituted, in 1939, 78 per cent of the Soviet population. Kolarz states that 'this Russian super-nation makes up almost four-fifths of the population of the USSR and is thus largely identical with the Soviet Union.' [28] In contrast to the Ukraine, with its fertile black soil and its vast coal, iron, and other mineral resources, Belorussia is largely a country of marshy land, scrub forest, and relatively slight industrial development.[29] The Belorussians have displayed less national self-assertiveness than the Ukrainians. Their national consciousness awoke later than that of the Ukrainians; Belorussian literature—and literacy—are largely Soviet developments.

Numerically next in magnitude among the peoples under Kremlin rule, but vastly different in culture, are the Turkic peoples of the Volga-Ural region, sometimes referred to as Idel-Ural, and those of Central Asia and the Caucasus. In Soviet usage, Central Asia consists of Uzbekistan, Tadzhikistan, Kirghizia, Turkmenistan. Kazakhstan is regarded as a separate area. Until the Samarkand Conference of Central Asian historians in 1935, this whole area was usually described as 'Turkestan.' At that conference a new line was laid down which demanded of historians that 'they repudiate the view of Central Asian history as embracing the political and cultural developments of the individual Turkestan tribes and peoples.' Since then the concept of an area or culture of 'Turkestan' has been taboo.[30] Cultural division, however, is accompanied by administrative consolidation in some important respects. The basic principle appears to be one in which every means is employed to strengthen Moscow control over the area. For example the Turkestan Military District, with its headquarters in Tashkent, in Uzbekistan, embraces a territory considerably larger than that of Uzbekistan.[31] Except for 1,400,000 Chuvash who are, or were, Christians, the Turkic peoples of the Soviet Union had a Moslem cultural-religious background. Since the Turkic and Moslem groups overlap so much, it will be convenient to list here the various Moslem peoples of the Soviet Union.

Six of the sixteen constituent republics of the USSR have a predominantly Moslem heritage: The Azerbaidzhan, Kazakh, Kirghiz, Tadzhik, Turkmen, and Uzbek republics. The same is true of the following autonomous republics: Bashkiria, Dagestan, Northern Osetia, Tataria, and Kabardinia, all in the RSFSR, as well as Abkhazia and Adzharia and Southern Osetia in the Georgian Republic, Nakhichevan in Azerbaidzhan, Kara-Kalpakia in the Uzbek Republic, and the Gorno-Badakhshan territory in the Tadzhik Republic. Some 23 million Soviet Moslems belong to the Sunni rite while over 3 million of the remainder are Shiites. Of the approximately 26 million Soviet citizens of Moslem background, constituting about 13 per cent of the total Soviet population, more than 22,000,000 are of Turkic stock, about 2,500,000 are of Iranian extraction, mostly in Tadzhikistan, 400,000 are Finno-Ugrians inhabiting the Volga region. The Soviet policy of dividing the Turkic peoples into as many 'separate nations' as possible has a kind of parallel in the field of religion. Four separate 'administrations' were set up during the war to deal, respectively, with the affairs of the Moslems of the RSFSR, those of Central Asia, those of Transcaucasia, and those of the North Caucasus.[32]

According to the latest available Soviet statistics, the population figures for the major Turkic peoples of the USSR were as follows: Uzbeks, 4,844,000; Tatars, 4,300,000; Kazakhs, 3,098,000; Azerbaidzhanians, 2,274,000; Chuvash, 1,367,000; Kirghiz, 884,-000; Bashkirs, 842,000; Turkmen, 811,000.[33] The 1939 census, incidentally, listed 21,000 Arabs.

According to the 1926 census there were 2,968,289 Kazakhs, almost a million more than in 1939.[34] Like the Ukrainians the Kazakhs suffered frightfully during collectivization. In addition, they were subjected to the rigors of enforced transition from a nomadic to an agricultural economy. The impact of Soviet industrialization was complicated in Central Asia by the fact that the Bolsheviks instituted a drastic and brutal reform in the complex and ancient water supply system of the area.[35] Olaf Caroe in his account of the effects of collectivization in Central Asia, writes 'the whole conception was indeed two-headed—to collectivize and mechanize agriculture and use the displaced peasants and nomads as unskilled labor for the new industries which were being set up.' [36]

There is a considerable Finnic ethnic group in the USSR. As of 1926 there were almost 600,000 persons of Finnic extraction in the Baltic region, and 2,658,700 in the Volga-Ural region. The largest Baltic-Finnic group are the Karelians. In 1940 after the Soviet Union by conquest during the Russo-Finnish war had acquired Vipurii [37] and much Finnish territory, the Karelo-Finnish Autonomous Republic was redesignated as a Soviet Socialist Republic. Since the Karelians were a minority of the population in this very backward unit, this was obviously a political move directed against Finland. Among the more important peoples of the Volga-Ural region are the Mordvins, with a population of 1,340,415 in 1926, the Mari, or Cheremis, with 428,192, and the Votyak, now usually called Udmurts, who in 1926 numbered 504,187. In addition, there are the Komi, divided into the Zyryans and the Permyaks, both undergoing assimilation which turns Finnic reindeer breeders into Russian-speaking coal miners.[38]

Among the peoples of the Caucasus and Transcaucasia, the Turkic Azerbaidzhanians have already been mentioned. The most advanced, and politically most important, peoples of this area are the Georgians and Armenians. According to the 1939 census there were 2,248,600 Georgians and 2,151,900 Armenians.[39] Both peoples had a very ancient Christian culture, with a rich literary tradition centuries older than that of the Great Russians. The dozens of smaller nationalities in this ethnographic museum include the mosaic of peoples in Dagestan. One tiny people, the Svanetians, a picturesque group of mountaineers, is apparently the latest Soviet people to lose its political identity. They gave their name in 1950 to two of the administrative districts of the Georgian Republic but it did not appear in connection with the 1954 election.[40]

According to the 1939 census the Jewish population of the USSR was 3,020,141. Despite the existence of the Jewish Autonomous Oblast, a sparsely settled political unit near the Manchurian frontier, in which Jews are and always have been a minority, Soviet Jews have long been the most Russified of the Soviet non-Russian peoples, but their 'cosmopolitan' heritage and international links were to create difficulties for them after World War II. Zionism has always been suspect and Hebrew a forbidden language. We do not have space for further population figures on individual peoples.[41]

It will be illuminating to examine some figures on the distribution of Great Russians in predominantly non-Russian areas. The USSR volume of the *Large Soviet Encyclopedia* contained figures on the Russian population of the non-Russian republics and autonomous republics, mostly as of 1933. In the Tatar Republic in 1933 the population was 50.4 per cent Tatars and 41.8 per cent Russians; in the Mordvin Republic 37.4 per cent Mordvins and 57.3 per cent Russians; in the Mari Republic 51.4 per cent Mari and 43.6 per cent Russians; in the Chuvash Republic 80 per cent Chuvash, 15.8 per cent Russians; in the Bashkir Autonomous Republic 23.5 per cent Bashkirs, 39.9 per cent Russians and 17.3 per cent Tatars; in the Komi Autonomous Republic 92.3 per cent Komi, 6.1 per cent Russians. The development of coal mines in the Komi area by Russians, Ukrainians, and other Slavic labor has altered this balance to the detriment of the demographic position of the non-Russians.

In the Dagestan Republic, 64.5 per cent of the population consisted of 'peoples of Dagestan,' and 12.5 of Russians; in the North Osetin Autonomous Republic, 84.2 per cent were Osetins, 6.8 per cent Ukrainians, 6.6 per cent Russians; in the Kabardinian Autonomous Republic 60 per cent Kabardinians, 10.7 per cent Russians.

In the Buryat-Mongol Autonomous Republic, in Siberia, Buryats constituted 43.8 per cent of the population and Russians 52.7 per cent. This balance has since been drastically altered in favor of the Russians. The same is true of the Yakut Autonomous Republic, where in 1933 Yakuts constituted 81.6 per cent and Russians 10.4 per cent of the population.

Now we come to the pattern within the constituent republics. In the RSFSR, or Russian Republic, there were in 1933 73.4 per cent Russians and 7.8 per cent Ukrainians. In the Ukrainian Republic, 80 per cent of the population were Ukrainian, 9.2 per cent Russian, and 5.2 per cent Jews; in Belorussia, 80.6 per cent Belorussians, 8.2 per cent Jews, and 7.2 per cent Russians; in the Azerbaidzhanian Republic, 63.3 per cent Azerbaidzhanians, 12.4 per cent Armenians, and 9.7 per cent Russians; in the Armenian Republic 84.4 per cent Armenians, and 8.2 per cent Azerbaidzhanians; in the Georgian republic, for which 1939 figures are given, 61 per cent Georgian, 11.5 per cent Armenians, and 5.2 per cent Azerbaidzhanians; in the Turkmen Republic, 72 per cent Turkmen, 10.5 per cent Uzbeks, and 7.5 per cent Russians; in the Uzbek Republic 76 per cent Uzbeks, 5.6 per cent Russians; in the Tadzhik Republic, 78.4 per cent Tadzhiks, 17.9 per cent Uzbeks; in the Kazakh Republic 57.1 per cent Kazakh, 19.7 per cent Russians, 13.2 per cent Ukrainians. Caroe estimates that as of 1950 there were 3,400,000 Russians and 3,000,000 Kazakhs in Kazakhstan, out of a total population of 6,900,000. The Russians were the most numerous single people and had nearly achieved an over-all majority. In August 1955 Russians were elected to the two top posts in the Kazakh Party organization.[42]

As of 1933 Kirghiz constituted 66.6 per cent of the population of the Kirghiz Republic, and Russians 11.7 per cent. In 1939, Karelians constituted only 23 per cent of the population of the Karelo-Finnic Republic and Russians 62 per cent, although this was within the 1939 boundaries, before the Russo-Finnish war. No figures seem to be available for the Russian population of the Moldavian Republic. According to the latest Soviet statistics, Latvians constitute 75 per cent of the population of the Latvian Republic, Russians 12 per cent, and Jews 4.8 per cent. Most of the Jews fled or perished during the Soviet-German war. The only available data for Estonia indicate a 1941 figure of 90.8 per cent Estonians and 7.3 per cent Russians.[43] No figures appear to be available on the Great Russian population of Lithuania.

The figures above indicate the degree of penetration of the

non-Russian areas of the Soviet Union by Great Russians. It is apparently impossible to obtain up-to-date statistics on this pattern but a few additional facts and figures will help to indicate its intensification in the years since the Soviet figures cited above were compiled.

The movement of large numbers of Great Russians into areas in which they were formerly not numerous resulted in part from policies so drastic that they may perhaps deserve the name of genocide. Several groups of considerable size fell into the category of what Kolarz describes as 'liquidated' peoples, and others may have been partially liquidated as national entities. By decree of the Presidium of the Supreme Soviet of 28 August 1941, the whole population of German origin of the Volga German Autonomous Republic was ordered deported, partly to Siberia and partly to industrial areas in the Urals and the Kuznetsk Basin. The republic was abolished and its territory was divided between the Saratov and Stalingrad oblasts. About 400,000 people were involved in this action. Probably many of the million and a half persons of German culture living in other parts of the Soviet Union were also affected.[44] It is interesting, with respect to the fate of the Soviet Germans, and others who have become, in Bertram Wolfe's phrase, 'un-peoples,' that the table of nationality statistics contained in the USSR volume of the *Large Soviet Encyclopedia* contains an entry captioned 'others,' which makes no mention of Germans.

It also does not mention Chechens, Ingush, and other peoples known to have been eliminated as compact groups. The ominous nature of this caption is underlined by the fact that although Soviet Koreans were deported from the Soviet Far East in 1937, 180,000 Koreans are listed among the peoples of the Soviet Union. Germans, and several other peoples who have 'disappeared' were listed in the 1926 and 1939 censuses.[45] Next to be 'liquidated,' after the Chechen-Ingush unit, was the Kalmyk Autonomous Republic, located in the steppe region west of Stalingrad. The decree of 27 December 1943 which ordered the liquidation of this republic was never published, but it was indirectly referred to in a military order of 24 January 1944. The entire ethnic group was punished because a small minority voluntarily followed the German Army when it retreated from this area. Over 100,000 persons were affected by this action. It is interesting, incidentally, that several hundred Kalmyks made their way to the United States, and are now living in New Jersey.[46] Well over 500,000 persons were affected by the liquidation of the Chechen-Ingush Autonomous Republic.

A Chechen refugee scholar, A. Avtorkhanov, states that about a million persons, including not only Chechens and Ingush but Osetins and others, fell victim to this act.[47] Even before the war, in 1940, part of the population of this republic were deported because of doubts concerning their loyalty in the event of war with Turkey. The Balkarian Autonomous Oblast, which was a part of the Kabardino-Balkarian Autonomous Republic, and the Karachai Autonomous Oblast, also in the North Caucasus, were eliminated too. These peoples seem to have been deported, mostly to Central Asia. Avtorkhanov estimates that at least half of them perished of typhus, starvation, and hardship. Finally, the Crimean Tatars, who constituted about 25 per cent of the population of the Crimean Autonomous Oblast, were deported, apparently, to the Urals, where a majority reportedly died, because of hunger, slave labor, and harsh climate. Not until 1955 was it disclosed that Chechens exiled to Kazakhstan had been allowed to publish a weekly Chechen newspaper.[48] As of 1939, there were 75,737 Karachai, and 42,666 Balkars; the number of Crimean Tatars can be estimated on the basis of Soviet figures as over 200,000 at the time of deportation.[49]

The 'normal' operation of Soviet forced labor has brought similar experiences to Russians, Ukrainians, and to foreigners, such as Poles, Estonians, Latvians, and Lithuanians, and even to Englishmen, Frenchmen, and Americans, or, in the Soviet Far East, to Japanese, Chinese, and Koreans. The Baltic peoples were brought into this category in July 1940; immediately deportation of thousands of 'bourgeois' and other 'unreliable' elements took place. As a result of deportations, of flights to the West and other causes, the Latvian population of the Soviet Latvian Republic appears to have declined between 1940 and 1951 from about a million and a half to about 1,126,000.

On the other hand, the number of Russians, 233,000 in 1935,

has probably tripled. Russians, and members of other Soviet nationalities, now constitute about 25 per cent of the population of Riga.[50] Since the war there have been numerous reports, sufficiently persistent and well grounded to merit credence, though difficult to confirm, that Greeks, Iranians, Jews, Rumanians, and other non-Russian ethnic elements living in frontier areas, especially in the area near the Turkish and Iranian borders, have been deported by the thousands to the interior. A new wave of deportations of Rumanian-speaking people from Moldavia began in 1955. Tens of thousands of Russians have been settled on the land of the Chechens and Ingush, in the Western borderlands, and in newly acquired territories such as Southern Sakhalin and the Kuriles, as well as around the copper and nickel works of Petsamo and in Koenigsberg, renamed Kaliningrad. Kulischer, on the basis of Soviet sources, notes that Koenigsberg has become a Slavic city and that in the streets of Lwow the Russian tongue may be heard more often than the Ukrainian, the latter a statement confirmed to me by Ukrainian refugees.[51] Kulischer states that 'what is now happening at the new Finnish frontier and in the Baltic countries is but an acute aspect of the century-long retreat of Finnish and Teutonic peoples before the advancing Slavs.'[52]

The Soviet regime regards Great Russians as more reliable politically than non-Russians. This is indicated not only by Soviet sensitiveness about border areas, but by the fact that, as refugees emphasize, non-Russians account for a disproportionate share of political prisoners. One of the most objective Russian exiled scholars, the late G. P. Fedotov, acknowledged that 'among the formless oppositional mass mixed with the criminals, only the representatives of the small peoples of Russia stand out, even though labeled as spies.'[53] Walter Kolarz in his most recent book, *The Peoples of the Soviet Far East*, strongly emphasizes the Russian nationalist element in Soviet population and colonization policy in the Far East.[54] Ivar Spector writes that 'during World War II it became apparent that where settlements of Great Russians predominated the Germans met with fierce and implacable resistance.'[55] Perhaps actuated by a similar logic, the Chinese

Communists appear in 1953–5 to have sought to strengthen their border areas by bringing in 'pure' Chinese settlers.

Practices and methods of traditional Russian imperialism, perhaps borrowed from the Tatars, can be discerned in these developments. But there is a barbaric logic, not necessarily connected with nationalism, in the Soviet attitude toward non-Russian border peoples. Whenever it has felt that it could rely upon such peoples to serve its expansionist ends, the Kremlin has granted to them favors which, although illusory in operational terms, were designed to attract peoples on the other side of the Soviet borders, if they were related by language and culture to Soviet border peoples. But when it has been on the defensive, the Kremlin has not hesitated to ruthlessly uproot such peoples and to replace them by Russians drawn from the interior of the country and presumably less tainted by 'alien' influences.

Soviet Russification is the product of the material factors just discussed, plus basic features of Leninist-Stalinist doctrine. Soviet doctrines on Party, class, state, and nation impel the leadership to emphasize centralism, monolithism, and assimilation at the expense of other values. Ideological and power factors have tended to force the Soviet regime back toward nationality policies resembling the features of Tsarist policy regarded by Western and Russian liberals, and radicals, including the pre-1917 Bolsheviks, as extremely reactionary.

The combination of utopianism and demagogy in Soviet nationality doctrine makes it impossible for Soviet communism to achieve its professed goals. The utopian element in Leninism overlooked realities with which Lenin, and more particularly Stalin, were forced to compromise; in the long run recognition of necessity became a virtue. The demagogic element, a characteristic of Lenin's 'realism' from the beginning of his revolutionary career, fostered the habit of disguising real aims by promises which were designed to win the support of political groups, classes, and nationality movements destined for suppression or 'liquidation' after they had served the Bolsheviks' purposes. Even more than other revolutionaries, the Bolsheviks believed that the justice of their cause made it legitimate to use any available methods to win the struggle against their enemies. It is Soviet doctrine that 'forms of organization and methods of work are completely defined by the peculiarities of the given historical situation.' [56] One of the problems faced by the Bolsheviks was that of suppressing groups attracted by demagogic slogans but disappointed by failure to realize what had been promised. The result was the triumph of the most brutal forms of struggle for power, disguised and rationalized by 'revolutionary' slogans.

Stalin, as has been suggested in Chapter I, was to build his concept of the world role of the Soviet Union, the 'base' of the international revolutionary movement, on his interpretation of Lenin's doctrine. Lenin's concept of the Party was destined by an indirect logic to foster Soviet Russification. [57]

The most important feature of Soviet theory making for Russification is the insistence that the Party must be a unitary and not a federal organization. Insistence upon centralism is solidly rooted in Marxism and was reflected in the earliest period of Lenin's thinking on organizational matters. Lenin's anti-federalist views were adopted in 1903 at the crucial Second Congress of the Russian Social Democratic Labor Party. The vote on the position of the Jewish Socialist Bund in the Party caused the delegates of the Bund to leave the Congress, giving the majority to the supporters of Lenin, who subsequently became known as Bolsheviks. [58] In his important work, *One Step Forward, Two Steps Backward,* Lenin noted that the problem of the Bund had been discussed 'extraordinarily, excessively, thoroughly.' [59]

Lenin considered that the vote on the Bund was a vote against federation. [60] As Bertram Wolfe points out, if the demand of the Bund for autonomy in the handling of specifically Jewish problems, and its claim to represent all Jewish Socialists in Russia had been accepted, 'the Social Democratic Party would eventually have become a federated Party rather than a centralized one, with each nationality having its autonomous federation.' The state which would have issued out of the triumph of such a Party would have been a federalist rather than a centralized state. [61]

In Lenin's *One Step Forward, Two Steps Backward,* there is an interesting discussion of the debates and voting on the problem of 'equality of language' at the Second Congress, which sheds light on the roots of Bolshevik anti-federalism. Lenin denounced the demand for 'equality of languages' as 'fetichism.' Several Party members from the Caucasus, as well as representatives of the Bund, had voted for this principle. Lenin criticized 'laboring' elements who voted for it because they were afraid that people in the borderlands might think that the Social Democrats were in favor of Russification if the Congress rejected 'equality of languages.' In fairness to Lenin and the Russian Social Democratic Labor Party, it should be noted that the Party program adopted at the 1903 Congress included in points three, seven, eight, and nine a series of demands for use of local languages in educational, administrative, and other institutions of non-Russian areas, as well as the right to 'broad local self-government,' and the right of every nation to determine its own fate.

The pertinent articles of the program reflected the belief that 'final' solution of the national problem was impossible while political power remained in the hands of the *bourgeoisie*. According to Stalin, point nine of the program was designed to deal with the situation which would result if 'the advanced circles of the *bourgeoisie of* "foreign" nationalities demanded "national liberation." ' Such a movement might also be advantageous to the development of the class consciousness of the proletariat.[62] Stalin concluded that 'federalist Social democrats' would either have to give up the cause of the proletariat, or 'renounce any form of federalism in Party organization, and boldly raise the banner of destruction of national barriers and consolidate together with the all-Russian Social-Democratic Labor Party in a single camp.' [63]

This centralist conception of the Party became stronger with the passage of time. The Bund, which had originally raised the question in the Russian Party, opposed the Bolsheviks in 1917–18.[64] After the consolidation of the Bolsheviks, the Bund split into right and left wings. In April 1921, its left wing joined the Communist Party. Its right wing was outlawed and many of its leaders emigrated.[65] Stalin's final action against the Bund was the execution in 1942 of two of its early leaders, the Polish Socialists, Henry Alter and Victor Erlich.

Lenin's most important work on the nationality question, *The Right of Nations to Self Determination*,[66] devoted considerable attention to attacking Ukrainian and other federalist socialists.[67] In his article 'On the National Pride of the Great Russians,' Lenin again emphasized that 'we are not in any way champions of small nations; we are unconditionally, other things being equal, for centralization and against the Philistine ideal of federative relations.' [68] Here, and also in his praise of Engels' views on this problem in *State and Revolution*, Lenin discussed federalism not as a Party but as a state principle, and consequently took a much less unqualified position. As far as the Party structure was concerned, Lenin made only minor concessions, for example, granting the Poles the right to have their own Party organization; later he and Stalin temporarily, and for tactical reasons, made partial concessions to the Ukrainian communists in this question.

Lenin failed to realize that if such a Party as he had created were victorious, under Russian conditions, it might become an end in itself which would make impossible the realization of the goals of the revolution. Lenin wrote in *What Is To Be Done* that if the Party achieved 'strict conspiracy, the strictest selection of members and training of professional revolutionaries,' then it would be assured of something more important than 'democratism.' Such a Party would be assured of 'full, comradely trust among revolutionaries.' And such a Party would know that 'To eliminate a worthless member an organization of genuine revolutionaries does not stop at anything.' [69]

The centralist principles first formulated by Lenin are embedded in the concept of 'democratic centralism,' in the Party statutes. The most important of the four principles of democratic centralism states that 'the decisions of higher bodies are unconditionally binding upon lower ones.' [70] A typical Party commentary upon these principles asserts that 'the very construction of the Party makes it possible to guide all Party work from one center, and to realize, in practice, leadership over members of the Party, as well as planned distribution of Party forces.' The same document states 'The communist parties of union republics belong to our Party, but these communist parties belong to the all-union communist party, not as independent parties, but with the rights of oblast organizations of the all-union communist party. Our Party is not a federation of separate parties but a unified centralized party with a single central committee, in charge of all of the work of the Party on the territory of the USSR.' [71]

Since the majority of members of this monolithic organization were Great Russians from the beginning, its non-Russian members found themselves under heavy pressure to conform to Russian cultural patterns.

In the 'twenties, the Soviet regime published much statistical material on the ethnic characteristics of Party members. Statistical frankness ended with the beginning of Soviet industrialization. In 1922 Great Russians accounted for 72 per cent of Party membership. The Great Russian component was 65 per cent in 1927; less than 53 per cent of the total population at that time was Russian. As of 1927, Jewish, Latvian, Estonian, Polish, Armenian, and Georgian communists also had higher representation in the Party than in the total population.[72] Many of the Baltic and Polish communists were refugees who had opposed the establishment of the 'bourgeois' governments set up in their native countries after the latter had broken away from Russia. One thinks of Feliks Dzerzhinski, the famed and dread Head of the Cheka, or of Latvian secret police leaders such as Peters and Latsis. The Finn Otto Kuusinen is another communist refugee who made a career for himself in the Soviet Union.

For the year 1930, data is available on the nationality affiliation of the delegates to the Sixteenth Party Congress. Great Russians accounted for 57.4 per cent of the delegates, compared with 62 per cent at the Fifteenth Congress in 1927.[73] In areas economically less developed than central Russia, the percentage of communists of indigenous nationality has always tended to be considerably lower than the percentage of the local nationality in the total population. Party membership still is particularly low among the Turco-Tatar peoples. It has also tended to be low in Belorussia, and to a lesser degree in the Ukraine. One result of the purges appears to have been a loss of strength of the Jewish elements in the Party. The data revealed by the Nineteenth Congress, although it furnished only indirect indications, gave the impression that the Great Russian and the Georgian and the Armenian nationalities continued to be over-represented.[74]

Great Russian numerical predominance is intensified by the normal operations of the Party machinery. On the other hand, it should be noted that the Party authorities have consistently sought to develop Party 'cadres' among the non-Russian nationalities. The under-representation of the non-Russians reflects the fact that industrialization and urbanization are not so advanced among these peoples as among the Great Russians.

The factors discussed thus far might well be characterized as 'objective' prerequisites for Russification. Even the existence of these factors, given a strong desire to the contrary on the part of the supreme party leadership, might not have eventuated in the extremes of Russification which have occurred in the Soviet Union. As a matter of fact, up to about 1929, the Soviet regime attempted to hold in check the forces pushing toward Russification of the non-Russian peoples.

The Soviet Union's position in relation to the non-Soviet world played an indirect but powerful role in Soviet Russification. Such factors as the position of the Soviet Union in the world power constellation, the Kremlin's fear of 'alien' influences among the peoples of the Soviet Union, in particular on the non-Russians of the border areas, and the desirability of building a homogeneous bureaucracy and officer corps in the interests of military power, impinged not only upon Russian-non-Russian relationships inside the USSR but helped to shape the total pattern of Soviet Russian nationalism.

Some students of Soviet policies, perhaps especially anti-Russian refugees of Polish and Western Ukrainian origin, contend that Lenin was really a Russian nationalist in disguise. Roman Smal-Stocki writes: 'Lenin's internationalism was, in my opinion, only a theoretical camouflage for his deep Russian national feelings, which welcomed the Russification of the non-Russian nationalities.' [75] Although there is a measure of truth in this interpretation, it is essentially incorrect. Doubtless in his 'basic personality,' to use Kardiner's term, Lenin was a 'typical' Russian.[76]

Elements of Russian messianism can be found in Lenin's writings. *What Is To Be Done* contains proud references to the Russian tradition of terrorist revolutionaries. His statement that the 'immediate tasks' of the Russian proletariat were the most 'revolutionary' in the world [77] comes to mind. It seems clear, however, that the characteristic features of Lenin's political behavior reflected the attempt to apply Marxism to the unfavorable political and social situation of Russia. Lenin and Stalin were primarily Marxist revolutionaries who sought to harness the national sentiments of Russians and non-Russians, both inside and outside the Soviet Union, in the interests of communist power.

In works of Lenin and Stalin the phrase 'the peoples of Russia' is often found. Lenin, the Great Russian, referred throughout his major works touching on the nationality question, to the 'Russian proletariat' or the 'Russian working class.' He used the word Russki, which, strictly speaking, applies only to the Great Russian ethnic group. Stalin, more conscious of the point of view of the non-Russian nationalities—although far more brutal in his treatment of them—more often used the term *Rossiiski*. This word *Rossiiski* is roughly equivalent to 'all-Russian.' In a sense the term 'Soviet' is its modern equivalent.

Some Ukrainian socialist leaders considered that the Bolsheviks were continuing the old imperial policies of 'Russia one and indivisible' in a new form.[78] It is extremely difficult for the outsider to pass judgment on the claims of conflicting nationalisms within a foreign state. In general, the point of view of the extreme radicals, Lenin and Stalin, was similar on this matter to that of the leaders of most political parties in pre-revolutionary Russia, with the notable exception of the Socialist Revolutionaries, the peasant party, whose nationality platform was more liberal. Because of their radicalism, however, which required an efficient military type of party, and because they relied on the urban proletariat, the Bolsheviks were more centralist than most of the 'bourgeois' parties and less inclined to grant genuine autonomy to non-Russian groups. Instead, they offered the radical but illusory slogan of 'self-determination.'

Before analyzing, in the next chapter, the process and methods of Soviet Russification it may be helpful to introduce Karl

Deutsch's concept of 'mobilization.'[79] If I understand this concept correctly, Deutsch considers that in a multi-national state, the struggle for political power and for cultural influence tends, other things being equal, to turn in favor of large ethnic groups.[80] Of course, 'other things' are seldom if ever equal and are usually numerous and complicated. 'Quality,' in terms of skills, education, stamina, and traditions, can often more than hold its own against the sheer weight of numbers. But when as a result of the denser network of communications resulting from urbanization, the larger ethnic mass is 'mobilized' it becomes more and more difficult for the 'differentiated' groups to resist the pressure toward assimilation.

History suggests that if the several nationalities of which a multi-national state is composed differ considerably in culture and are all mobilized to a high degree, the state may explode into separate national entities. The disintegration, however, of the Dual Monarchy, the Ottoman empire, and the Russian Empire took place under the 'abnormal' conditions of international war. Perhaps, given time, and wise policies of adjusting competing claims the history of multi-national states in our era might have been different.

Russia of course differed from the Austro-Hungarian Empire in several ways, especially in the fact that a single nationality, the Great Russians, bulked so much larger numerically than the Germans or the Hungarians in the Hapsburg realm. And the cultural differences between the Great Russians and the second largest people within the Empire, the Ukrainians, were considerably less than those which distinguished Germans from Slavs or Magyars in Austria-Hungary. Such 'geopolitical' considerations give plausibility to the arguments of most Great Russian refugee scholars, however anti-Soviet, that all or most of the non-Russian peoples who were politically associated with the Great Russians in the Russian Empire belong in this association by virtue of overwhelming historical and social forces. On the other hand, as the Kremlin ruefully admits, the national consciousness of minorities is amazingly tenacious. This is true above all in the case of groups which have been humiliated, oppressed, or persecuted. A good case can be made for the proposition that cultural assimilation would have been much more successful if the peoples now under Soviet rule had been living during the last forty years under a regime less harsh and autocratic than the monopoly state capitalism imposed by the Kremlin.[81]

Indices and Characteristics of Soviet Russification

In Chapter III we distinguished between the relatively ineffective Tsarist policy of Russification and the more systematic Soviet assimilation policy. On the basis of available data it seems safe to predict that within a relatively short time, perhaps ten years, almost all Soviet citizens will have a good speaking and writing command of Russian. Language instruction is supplemented by ideological and administrative measures. These policies in combination seem to be intended to produce complete subjective Russification, which would increase Soviet power by enhancing the cohesion of Soviet society.

In 1951 the prominent Soviet philosopher F. V. Konstantinov made a contribution to the posthumous condemnation of N. Y. Marr by attacking the view of the formerly honored philologist that a society did not require a 'unified,' 'national,' language. This emphasis upon the need for linguistic social cement contrasts with the views of Lenin, who in one of his most important articles on the nationality problem, urged, as the program of workers' democracy, 'absolutely no privileges for any one nation, for any one language,' and contrasted the multilingualism of 'civilized' Switzerland with the cultural policy of 'frightfully backward' Russia.[1]

The results of Soviet cultural policy may be summed up in terms of a 'continuum of Russification.'[2] Our continuum resembles a rough sketch more than a map. We still need shelves of anthropological and sociological studies of the process of acculturation under Soviet conditions. Even had these studies been made, the well-known difficulties involved in the use of Soviet data would render them far less complete than studies of freer societies can be.

At one end of our continuum stand the two smaller Eastern Slavic peoples, the Ukrainians and Belorussians. The next most important, though not nearly so numerous, peoples, the Georgians and Armenians, are, in relation to the Russians, at least partly 'bi-national.' They can acquire Russian culture without losing their own. The two main Caucasian peoples have been more successful in achieving bi-culturality than the Ukrainians and Belorussians because of the intrinsic strength and distinctiveness of their antecedent cultural traditions. Somewhat similar to the Georgians and Armenians are the Osetins, who, as Kolarz points out, were set apart from the 'bad' Highland Caucasus peoples during World War II.[3] Ethnic affinity to the Great Russians, and a long history of Russian cultural influence help to explain the relative success of Russification among the Osetins.[4] Like the peoples mentioned above, the Osetins, before the revolution, were orthodox Christians.

The Jews might be placed still higher in the scale of Russification, although it is almost impossible to fit the Jews as a whole into even this framework. A distinction should be drawn between those Russian, Polish, Ukrainian, and other Jews who attempted to remain faithful to Yiddish culture, and those who readily, even eagerly, sought assimilation. It is important that the Jews, although not a 'nation' according to Soviet theory, nevertheless possess an unusually strong 'consciousness of kind.'

Association of the Baltic peoples with the Russians in the Empire gave them an intimate acquaintance with Russian culture, not entirely forgotten as the result of their inter-war experience as independent states. These countries had such large Russian *émigré* minorities that the link with Russian culture was never broken. On the other hand, Protestant and German influence in Latvia and Estonia, and a general Western orientation, militated against willing acceptance of the Russian pattern. Catholic and Polish influences had a similar effect in Lithuania. The subjection of these small, highly civilized peoples to 'Sovietization' aroused bitter hostility.

The small peoples of the Ural-Volga region, particularly those of Finnish background, probably rank next on our list. As Kolarz brings out in *Russia and Her Colonies,* most of these peoples have a history of susceptibility to foreign appeals, such as pan-Finnism. On the other hand, their relative numerical and cultural weakness makes them much easier to Russify than the larger, more anti-Russian Turco-Tatar peoples of Moslem culture.

We now reach a group of peoples a common trait of which has been bitter resistance to Russification. These peoples include various primitive groups which, according to Soviet sources, have 'skipped' the stage of capitalist development, as well as Poles and Germans, and, finally, Kalmyks, Crimean Tatars, Chechen-Ingush, and other 'liquidated' peoples discussed in the demographic section of Chapter III. As a result of dispersal, resulting from Soviet reprisals against their recalcitrance, the surviving members of these groups, about whom we have very little information, may be rendered helpless against policies of assimilation.

At present even the most Russified of the peoples ruled by the Kremlin, such as the Belorussians, still retain a consciousness of cultural differences between themselves and the Great Russians. The most convincing indication of this fact is the continual struggle of the Soviet authorities against 'bourgeois nationalism' among all non-Russian peoples. If present trends continue unaltered, national consciousness among the non-Russians may be a less serious problem for the Kremlin ten or twenty years from now than it is today.

Even now, from the standpoint of evaluating the political and social strengths and weaknesses of the Soviet system, the problem of non-Russian national consciousness may be a secondary one. It is less important than problems connected with the attitude of the Soviet peasantry, regardless of nationality, toward collective farms, of the Soviet factory workers toward low wages and long hours under heavy pressure, or the reaction of most Soviet citizens toward police terror and the constant pressure of propaganda.

But the problems posed by non-Russian national consciousness and 'national deviation' are important. National consciousness gives a special twist to social and political attitudes. A statement made in 1930 by a prominent refugee of Azerbaidzhanian origin retains considerable significance today. In a speech in Paris to representatives of the Caucasian, Ukrainian, and Turkestan emigration, M. E. Rasul-Zade said that, 'if "deviation" in Russia itself bears a purely social-class character, on the other hand in the non-Russian borderlands of the Soviet Union, it, for understandable reasons takes on a political-national character.' Some authorities, such as Richard Pipes, seem to think that among the Central Asian peoples national consciousness is still becoming stronger.[5]

One extreme view on Soviet politics is to dismiss the 'nationality problem' as insignificant. Another is to look hopefully to weaknesses connected with this problem for the 'key' to relations between the Soviet Union and the non-Soviet world. The facts which are available to us indicate that among most of the non-Russian peoples of the Soviet Union national discontent has limited political significance. It is most probable that a majority of the five million odd Estonians, Latvians, and Lithuanians and of the ten million or more Western Ukrainians still desire the restoration of their national independence, destroyed by the Kremlin.

Even the Baltic and Western Ukrainian peoples, however, have been living under Soviet rule for some ten years and politically conscious elements capable of resisting the Soviet policy of assimilation have been killed, or are in exile outside the Soviet Union, or in Siberia, or to a large degree convinced of the hopelessness of struggle against impossible odds.[6] For a few years after World War II, perhaps to the end of 1949, or even later, the hopes of resistance elements in these areas, as well as in the captive states of Eastern and Central Europe, rested in large part upon the belief that war was imminent between Soviet Russia and the United States. These hopes have faded, and the resistance groups have grown weaker. Latent and according to some reports even active resistance continues, and will be for years one of the important imponderables in the Soviet-Western equation, particularly in respect to the intensely nationalistic Western Ukrainians.

It is possible that the desire for political separation from the

Soviet Union, and perhaps for some sort of association with Turkey, is strong among the Turks of Soviet Central Asia, although it must be remembered that there are considerable cultural and linguistic differences among these peoples. Our information on this area is especially defective. There are relatively few recent refugees in the West from this part of the Soviet realm. However, the facts reported in Pipes's and Caroe's studies and conversations with knowledgeable Germans, lead me to believe that 'separatist' tendencies may still be rather strong in Central Asia.

The special position of the Turkic peoples in the Soviet Union is well summed up by an unusually objective Russian *émigré* scholar who states that these peoples 'have always formed an alien and unassimilated body within the empire, with their own historical and social trends, which differ greatly from those of the Slavs.' In contrast to the impact of Tsarist expansion on Ukrainians and Belorussians, or even on Georgians and Armenians, Russian conquest of Central Asia 'meant the subjugation of the native population by a people with whom there had never been any cultural or racial affinity.' [7]

It is extremely doubtful whether 'separatism' is more than a negligible factor among the Eastern Ukrainians, Belorussians, Georgians, or Armenians. These peoples were too long and closely associated with the Russians, and enjoyed too brief a period of national independence during the turbulent days between the seizure of power by the Bolsheviks in November 1917, and the snuffing out of their independent statehood by the Red Army to develop firm and lasting traditions of state sovereignty. This does not mean that we should 'write off' the national political potential of these peoples, but we must assess this latent force within a framework of realism.

Within the framework established, the 'objective' and 'subjective' Russification of the major non-Russian peoples will be discussed in some detail, with emphasis upon the linguistic factor. Language is a useful objective index of cultural assimilation and one which has great political significance. Linguistic Russification may be dealt with on two main levels. The first is knowledge of the Russian language among the non-Russian peoples. The second is the degree to which, as a result of the use of the Russian alphabet, and by lexicographical, orthographical, and other devices the non-Russian languages have been influenced by the language of the Great Russians.

Linguistic Russification advances with the march of the Soviet Union toward universal secondary education. When in the fall of 1938 the regime began to apply pressure systematically throughout the Soviet school system for the instruction of non-Russians in the Russian language, the majority of Soviet children were receiving, in the rural districts, in which well over half of the population still lived, only four or five years of elementary education. The fourth Five Year Plan, which began in 1946, provided for an increase to seven years in the rural areas. On 20 August 1952, the 'directives' for the fifth Five Year Plan were published. It was planned to complete, by the end of this Plan, the transfer from universal seven year education to secondary education, which in most parts of the Soviet Union means ten years, in the capitals of republics and in other specified large centers, and to prepare for adoption of universal secondary education by the end of the sixth Plan. Because tuition payments had been established in 1940 for the last three years of secondary school, it was difficult to see how this could be carried out until the Twentieth Party Congress disclosed in February 1956 that tuition payments were being abolished, except for special elite schools.

Since the end of World War II, and still more in comparison with 1938, the length of time spent by Soviet children in schools on the study of Russian has increased considerably.[8] Some of this progress exists largely on paper. The Soviet Press continues, as in past years, to complain about failure to enforce the compulsory education law. It is probably safe to estimate that even today perhaps 20 per cent of Soviet children do not get more than four or five years of schooling.[9] But especially in the cities the long-term trend is toward substantial lengthening of the time spent in school, although many factors, including a great deal of absenteeism, continue to plague Soviet schools, particularly in rural districts. This is particularly true with respect to girls in the Moslem republics, where a prejudice against secondary and higher education for women is still alive.

Since for non-Russian children, school instruction in the Russian language is the principal means of learning Russian—although in large industrial cities of mixed Russian and non-Russian population non-school contacts are also very important—it is clear that extension of time spent in school, together with increase of classroom time devoted to Russian language instruction, enhances the possibility that they will learn Russian well. Before 1938, there were apparently some Ukrainian schools in which as little as one hour a week was devoted to Russian, although as far back as 1926 Russian, as well as Ukrainian, was an obligatory subject in all schools of the Soviet Ukrainian republic.[10]

Beginning in 1938, there was a sharp increase in the number of hours per week devoted to the teaching of Russian in the non-Russian schools. In the Ukraine, for example, 240 hours were allotted to Russian in Ukrainian-language elementary schools in 1937, but by 1939 this allotment had increased to 390 hours in urban schools and to 429 hours in rural schools. In the ten year schools, the increase in time devoted to Russian was much greater, and a school program for 1939–40 showed that the study of Russian was allotted considerably more time in Ukrainian schools than was devoted to Ukrainian in Russian schools of the Ukraine.[11] Also, in schools for minority groups, such as Yiddish-speaking or Moldavian-speaking children, the study of Ukrainian had a position far below that of Russian.[12]

However, in terms of the major language of instruction, in the Ukraine, as of 1940–41, not including the Western Ukraine, the 18,634 Ukrainian schools far outnumbered Russian schools, of which there were 2,362. There were also 53 Moldavian, 19 'Jewish,' and 13 Uzbek schools in the Ukrainian republic at that time.[13]

These figures are somewhat misleading, because of course the Ukrainian schools, being mainly in the villages, were normally smaller than Russian schools. Subsequent to the reform of 1938, in the Ukraine teaching of Russian began in the second grade, with four hours a week, and with three hours of instruction in the third and fourth grades.[14]

In Uzbekistan, according to *Pravda Vostoka* for 20 March 1938,

2,159 out of 3,481 Uzbek elementary schools did not teach Russian, and most of those that did, taught it very poorly. The importance attached to the introduction of Russian throughout the country in the lower grades in 1938 is indicated by several paragraphs in Krushchev's speech at the Fourteenth Congress of the Communist Party of the Ukraine, in June 1938. Krushchev stated that 'now all the peoples will study the Russian language.' The enemies of the people, the 'bourgeois nationalists,' had driven the Russian language out of the schools because they knew that Russian was the language of Bolshevism and that it conveyed 'the influence of the teachings of Lenin and Stalin on the minds of the Ukrainian people.' In many schools Polish, German, or French had been the second language, not Russian.[15]

The decree introducing compulsory Russian in the Uzbek schools asserted that knowledge of Russian would promote greater unity among diverse nationalities, facilitate mastery of scientific literature, and help to prepare the Uzbeks for military service. The Soviet press during the summer and fall of 1938 reported the introduction of compulsory Russian in the lower grades of the schools of the other non-Russian republics. This development went hand in hand with the replacement of the Latin alphabet by Cyrillic in the languages of the Turco-Tatar peoples.[16]

The turmoil of war perhaps slowed the process of linguistic Russification in the schools, but war brought the powerful Russifying influence of the army to bear upon non-Russian soldiers. Scattered but illuminating references in Soviet publications reflect a vigorous campaign to overcome difficulties caused by ignorance of Russian on the part of non-Russian servicemen. *Red Star* for 2 June 1945, for example, stressed in an article on political education in the army that individual help was particularly important for men of non-Russian nationalities who had a poor command of Russian.

This subject was touched upon in a wartime Soviet publication entitled *Political Assurance of the Great Victory at Leningrad,* in a five-page section, on 'Educational Work among Soldiers of Non-Russian Nationality.' Political work among non-Russians was carried on mainly by Great Russians. 'The best agitators of non-Russian nationality took part,' however. There are indications that political officers had special difficulties with soldiers of Turkic stock. It may be significant, incidentally, that there is no mention of Jews in this section, although many other nationalities were mentioned. The study is optimistic about the success of language training among the non-Russians. It reports that 'the overwhelming majority of the troops began to speak Russian.' [17]

Lest the impression be created, by the foregoing references to Russian language instruction for Asian troops, that this policy involved solicitude for the welfare of Soviet Moslems, it is well to note the comment by Zaki Ali on the discrimination practiced in the Red Army against Moslems. Zaki Ali asserts that about 60 per cent of some five million Moslems mobilized during World War II into the Soviet forces perished because they were usually thrown immediately into the front lines.[18]

In the later stages of the Soviet-German war, the drive to expand and improve the teaching of Russian to non-Russian children was intensively resumed. A collection of 'guiding materials' published by the Administration of Elementary and Secondary Schools of the RSFSR, in 1944, directed the educational authorities to devote special attention to improving instruction, 'particularly in the Russian language.' The attention of The People's Commissariat of Public Instruction was directed especially to Russian language teaching in the non-Russian schools.[19] It should be remembered that there are some 30 million non-Russians in the RSFSR.

After the war, the Russification of non-Russian peoples proceeded with giant strides. The 1950 edition of *Pedagogy,* the official Soviet handbook for normal schools, used to train teachers for all Soviet schools, Russian and non-Russian alike, states 'it is essential that the children of non-Russian nationalities master the Russian language as early as possible so that they may be able to make use of the rich cultural values of Russian scientific and artistic literature.' [20] Somewhat vaguely, it is admitted that many non-Russian children are now receiving all but the first four years of their schooling entirely in Russian.[21]

The best source of information on Russification in the non-

Russian Soviet schools is *The Teacher's Newspaper,* the organ of the trade union of educational workers,[22] which, in March 1954, reported that five to six hours a week is devoted in each grade, beginning with the first, to the study of Russian language and literature in the schools of Azerbaidzhan. This is the same amount of time as is devoted to the study of the native language and literature. According to the Erevan newspaper *Kommunist* for 9 February 1954, preparations were being made in Armenian schools to begin the study of Russian in the first grade. *The Teacher's Newspaper* for 7 April 1954 reported that, beginning with the eighth grade, all instruction in a school in the Northern Osetin Autonomous Republic was already being given in the Russian language.

The authors of this article, both apparently Russians, did not make it clear whether or not this policy had yet been introduced in the entire autonomous republic, but judging by the editorial in the same issue, this is probably the case. An editorial noted that with the transition to general ten year education, preparation for which was ordered by the Nineteenth Party Congress, the significance of the Russian language in the education of non-Russian pupils had greatly increased. In many cases, pupils entered the eighth grade without sufficient knowledge of Russian to enable them to master the program of the last three grades of secondary school. As a result, many failed, or had to repeat a year, particularly in the national regions in which all instruction, beginning with the eighth grade, was being transferred to the Russian language.[23]

The extension of instruction in Russian in the Georgian Republic has apparently clashed with Georgian nationalism, judging by post-Stalin developments in the autonomous republic of Abkhazia, an administrative unit of the Georgian republic.[24] The Tbilisi newspaper *Zarya Vostoka,* for 20 October 1953, announced the revocation of a 1945 decree which ordered closing of elementary schools in which instruction was conducted in Abkhazian. Henceforth instruction in the first four years would be in Abkhazian and, from the fifth grade, in either Russian or Georgian, depending on the desire of parents and pupils.

Mgeladze, who headed the Party organization of Abkhazia

when this decree was promulgated, later became head of the Georgian Party organization but was removed on charges of 'nationalism.' Also, there were complaints, in connection with the revocation of the decree, that the Teachers' Institute of Sukhumi, the Abkhazian capital, lacked facilities for instruction in Abkhazian and Russian. In 1947, I stayed one night at the Hotel Ritsa in Sukhumi. The Georgian hotel manager spoke condescendingly of the Abkhazians, who, he said, lived 'in the hills,' and were descended from Arab slaves.

In February 1954 the Abkhazian language, written since 1938 in Georgian characters, was converted, by vote of the Party Central Committee of Georgia, to the Cyrillic script.[25] Demands appeared in *The Teacher's Newspaper* in 1954 that better facilities be provided for instruction in the Uighur language, for the benefit of the Uighur population of Kazakhstan. This may be related to the presence of Uighurs in Chinese Turkestan.

Besides increasing the number of hours devoted to Russian, the Soviet authorities have introduced many other measures to assure the success of linguistic Russification. One of the most important was the addition of an extra year to the program of the secondary schools in Georgia, Azerbaidzhan, and the Baltic countries. In its issue of 5 January 1954, *Kommunisti,* an organ of the Central Committee of the Georgian Communist Party, published an article entitled, 'Measures Necessary to Improve the Teaching of the Russian Language and Literature in the Schools of the Republic,' in which a pattern typical of all the non-Russian republics was discussed. The article stated that 'notwithstanding a whole series of measures such as for instance the introduction of an eleven year period of study; the foundation in Tbilisi of a Russian pedagogical institute, etc., the state of teaching of the Russian language and literature in the schools of Georgia is unsatisfactory.'[26]

Culture and Life stated in its issue for 11 May 1949 that serious attention should be devoted to checking up on the performance of non-Russian pupils in the study of Russian, and added that 'it is necessary to avoid a repetition of the mistakes of last year, when in many schools checking up on the knowledge of the Russian language was approached in a formal manner, and in some places it was even considered normal that pupils lacked literacy in the Russian language, and the ability to consciously read rapidly, and to write and speak correctly in Russian.' [27]

A number of important special publications designed to improve the teaching of Russian appeared shortly after Stalin laid down his rulings on linguistics in 1950. Among these was *The Russian Language Textbook for non-Russian Pedagogical Institutions*, published in 1951 by A. S. Bednyakov and A. S. Matichenko. The preface to this work seems to reflect a very practical approach, recognizing that sound teaching of Russian to non-Russians requires expert knowledge of the peculiarities of both of the languages involved in the teaching process. This sound principle is difficult to implement, as was indicated by an article complaining that the graduates of the pedagogical institutes of Uzbekistan have a very poor knowledge of the Uzbek language, and consequently are poorly equipped to teach the Russian language in Uzbek schools.[28] The author urged establishment of a special institute of the Russian language, which would unite all the best teaching cadres of Uzbekistan. A more optimistic note was struck by a 'methodologist' of the Ministry of Public Instruction of the Latvian Republic, in an article published in June 1954. This expert concluded that Latvian teachers 'honorably cope with the task assigned to them—to teach the younger generation of Latvians a perfect mastery of the Russian language, their second native language.' [29]

On the basis of the foregoing, certain conclusions may be drawn. The first is that as of today the teaching of Russian to non-Russians is still not satisfactory. Lack of sufficient knowledge of Russian by non-Russians is still a serious obstacle to the regime's program of training administrative, engineering, professional, and skilled labor cadres among the non-Russian peoples, particularly in Central Asia. A second conclusion is that, beginning on a systematic scale about 1950, and with increasing emphasis from the spring of 1954, the Soviet government has adopted an effective program for the achievement of bi-lingualism among the non-Russians now entering, or now in the lower grades of the schools.

Some revealing information on linguistic Russification in

Latvia was contained in the magazine *Bolshevik of Soviet Latvia* in 1945 and 1946.[30] An indication of demographic Russification was furnished by the statement in the December 1945 issue [31] which reported that more than 430 communists had been sent to Latvia from the Soviet Union as local Party organizers. 'Most of them had lived and worked in the old republics of the Soviet Union and entered the Party before the war.' [32] The publication urged the establishment of 'circles' for the systematic study of both Russian and Latvian.[33] Probably some Soviet Latvians brought up in Russia had a very poor knowledge of Latvian.

Recent refugees from Latvia report that in the factories of Riga the language used is Russian, and that the same is true on the Riga telephone system. A similar pattern is reported from Estonia.[34]

So much attention has already been devoted to the problem of Russian language teaching that other pertinent aspects of the language problem must be treated rather briefly.[35]

There is a considerable Soviet program of adult education in Russian for non-Russians.[36] The invasion of non-Russian languages by Russian words and forms continues, although on a more rational and skillful basis since 1950. Before examining this problem, and the question of alphabets, one point which is often overlooked in discussion of Soviet language policy should be stressed.

This is the fact that many non-Russian children, whether 'pure' non-Russians or of mixed marriages, attend Russian elementary and secondary schools, and thus get a completely 'Russian' education. This process can result in failure of such children to know more than a mere smattering of their 'native' language, if any at all. During my own experience in Moscow from 1942–7, I knew a number of Soviet people of non-Russian background who seemed largely ignorant of the cultural traditions of their ancestors and of the languages of their parents.

It is likely that those who are completely assimilated are more fortunate, or more contented than non-Russian children who know both their native language and Russian, but speak the latter with an accent or with insufficient mastery to successfully compete with Russian and Russified youths in the upper grades of secondary schools or in the higher educational institutions.

This possibility may explain the fact reported by some refugees that parents of non-Russian children in some cases desire that their children go to Russian schools in order to attain the advantages of full participation in the dominant culture. In connection with this phenomenon, it should also be noted that even in emigration many Soviet Ukrainian refugee couples use Russian as their spoken language at home, something I have observed, and which has been confirmed to me by several informants. On the other hand, Central Asian refugees, Pipes found, speak no Russian in the family circle.

Scattered data indicate that the type of assimilation referred to above continues to occur on a considerable scale. In 1949 there were 47,800 Russians, 46,200 Azerbaidzhani, and 19,000 Armenian school children in the oil city of Baku. But Russian was the language of instruction in 78 schools and Azerbaidzhanian in only 58, and there were only 4 Armenian schools, an indication that most of the local Armenians received their schooling entirely in Russian.[37]

Some Georgian and Ukrainian refugee sources insist that in many cases Great Russians are assimilated into these non-Russian cultures. Tamburek Dawletschin maintains in his study, *Cultural Life in the Tatar Autonomous Republic,* that 'there is every basis for believing that the policy of Russification among the Tatars will not be successful. The history of 400 years has shown that the Tatar people is immune to Russification.' [38] Dawletschin is probably over-optimistic, but his statement may be substantially correct with regard to the rural masses of his own and other non-Russian peoples. Pipes, somewhat more cautiously, confirms this finding with respect to Central Asia. In my own experience in Georgia in February 1947, I found that the Georgians with whom I dealt in Tbilisi, in my hotel, and in the University, and other public institutions, spoke perfect Russian. On the other hand the peasants in the countryside seemed to speak only Georgian, and I was even arrested by a Georgian railway policeman who had a very limited knowledge of Russian and who released me after a Russian soldier read my identity card and explained it to him.

Scholars have coined the expression 'alphabetic revolution' to refer to the conversion from Arabic to Latin script effected by the Soviet authorities for the Turkic languages in the 1920's and the early 1930's, and the subsequent 'second alphabetic revolution' which took place in the middle and late 1930's and in the 1940's and in which the Cyrillic alphabet was adopted. It is interesting to compare the official Soviet views on alphabets for the Turkic peoples at various periods. Since the introduction of the Russian alphabet for these languages, the official position has been that advocates of other alphabets were enemies of the Soviet regime. Yet, in 1926 at the first Turcological Congress in Baku, speaker after speaker hailed the Latin alphabet as an aid to enlightenment because its adoption would facilitate, for the Soviet Turkic peoples, mastery of their own languages, and access to Western languages.[39]

The final result of the 'second alphabetic revolution' is that today all of the languages of the Soviet Union are written and printed in the Cyrillic, or Russian, alphabet with the exception of the Baltic languages which still use the Latin script, and Georgian and Armenian, each of which has its own ancient, highly distinctive, and beautiful alphabet. Both Latinization and Cyrillization were intended to combat foreign influences, especially Turkish influence upon the Soviet Turco-Tatar peoples, and to strengthen Russian influence. And as Dawletschin, Weinreich, and others emphasize, these measures were also directed against the Moslem religion.

These measures and the accompanying spelling and vocabulary policies aroused bitter resentment among non-Russian intellectuals. This resentment was met with accusations of 'bourgeois nationalism' on the part of the Soviet authorities. Ideological sins on the 'language front' resulted in the arrest, deportation, or even execution of many non-Russian linguists.[40] The introduction of Russian words into non-Russian languages is defended on grounds of 'socialism' and 'internationalism.' In many cases, these are Russianized forms of English, German, or other Western European 'international' terms. Such words are forced upon the non-Russians, despite the fact that in many cases perfectly good native terms are available in these languages.

The result of this policy of 'Russification' of non-Russian languages is to limit their development and weaken them, thus facilitating the long-range goal of over-all Russification and cultural assimilation. To this picture should be added the virtually complete suppression of German, Yiddish, and several other languages.

The meaning to the non-Russians of Moscow's spelling and script reforms is illuminated by a great anthropologist's statement that 'specific forms of writing, conventionalized spelling, peculiar pronunciations, and verbal slogans,' become highly important as 'substitutive forms of emotional expression.' [41]

No Soviet citizen can achieve a career of any distinction without a thorough knowledge of the Russian language. Let us consider briefly the preference given to a person with a good knowledge of Russian in terms of access to Soviet higher education. In the Soviet Union, as in no other country, higher education is an indispensable prerequisite for advancement. Without higher education a Soviet citizen cannot rise far above the level of a collective farmer or factory worker. Therefore, the fact that passage of an examination in the Russian language is one of the entrance requirements of most Soviet higher educational institutions, and that most instruction in such institutions is in Russian, takes on great social significance. [42]

The Ministry of Higher Education of the USSR and other Soviet educational agencies publish very interesting handbooks for students entering higher educational institutions. [43] These handbooks, as well as the syllabi for secondary schools and higher educational and pedagogical institutions, shed considerable light on Soviet cultural policy. A search of issues of *Handbook for Persons Entering Higher Educational Institutions of the USSR* for 1942–7, and for 1950 and 1954, reveals that satisfactory passage of an examination in Russian language and literature is among the entrance requirements of universities, scientific and technical institutes, and other higher educational institutions.

In most fields, these entrance examinations are oral, but in the Russian language both a written and an oral examination was compulsory until 1955. It should be noted that students entering

higher educational institutions in which the language of instruction is not Russian, must take an examination in the language
of instruction of the given institution.[44] It is instructive to examine the pattern of languages of instruction in the various
types of educational institutions. Let us consider first the 33
Soviet universities, including those of the non-Russian republics.
Russian is used as the language of instruction in non-Russian
universities only in the Russian 'historical-philological' faculties,
and in a few other specialties. On the other hand, in the Russian
universities, with the exception of a few of the largest, such as
Moscow and Leningrad, the languages of the non-Russian peoples
of the USSR are not included as specialties. At the University of
Leningrad, 'literature of the peoples of the USSR' is one of the
specialties included in the philological faculty. Since the Handbook does not specify in what language these literatures are
taught, we assume that it is Russian.

In a considerable number of Ukrainian institutions, such as the
Odessa University, the philological faculty offers both Ukrainian
language and literature and Russian language and literature.
Similarly, the Tbilisi University offers in its philological faculty,
the Georgian language and literature, the Russian language and
literature, and the languages and literatures of the peoples of the
Caucasus. The latter is probably given in Georgian, since according to the Rector of the University with whom I talked for two
hours in February 1947, the language of instruction was Georgian
throughout the University, with the exception of the Russian
Philological Faculty.

In 1954 the Pushkin Pedagogical Institute was incorporated
into the Tbilisi University, and as the language of instruction in
this institute is Russian, more Russian is perhaps now used, even
in Tbilisi University, than formerly. Also, the number of dissertations presented at Tbilisi in the Russian language has increased
greatly. Until quite recently, all dissertations at this institution
were presented in Georgian. Judging by announcements in *Kommunisti* of 20 March 1954 and subsequently, that the Tbilisi
University was in need of new instructional personnel, it is
possible that in connection with the new wave of Russification in

1954, some Georgian academic workers were dismissed, and possibly replaced by Georgians trained in Russian universities.

In addition to the specifically 'national' universities, particularly those of Erevan and Tbilisi, Kiev and Kharkov, and a few others, another major stronghold of academic instruction in non-Russian languages above the level of the secondary school is the network of non-Russian Teacher Training Institutes. Although the role of these institutions in keeping alive the non-Russian languages and non-Russian culture in general should not be minimized, it bulks rather small in the total Soviet pattern of higher education. Most Soviet higher educational institutions are not universities but highly specialized institutes, which train engineering, medical, scientific, and other specialists. The various industrial ministries have from time to time operated most of these institutes. After World War II, direct administrative control over them was assigned to the All-Union Ministry of Higher Education, but the industrial ministries still influence them. Since the ministries need personnel who can operate throughout the entire Soviet Union, the language of instruction of most of these institutions is Russian. In some of the technical secondary schools, however, non-Russian languages are used.[45]

This sketch of linguistic Russification in the Soviet higher educational system may be concluded by reference to Russian language requirements in the political education system of the Communist Party of the Soviet Union. The highest Party educational institution is the Higher Party School, reopened in August 1946. Passage of an examination in the Russian language is required to enter this institution and its branches on the oblast and republic level.[46]

The Russian character of Soviet higher education derives not only from language but also from the predominantly Russian content of instruction in history, folklore, literature, and 'history of the peoples of the USSR'; on these subjects entrance examinations must be passed for admission to higher educational institutions. Secondary and higher educational syllabi indicate that Soviet citizens receive in the last years of secondary schools and in the Soviet equivalent of American colleges and universities, a highly nationalistic and heavily factual training based, in so far as the humanities are concerned, almost entirely on the Russian cultural heritage, interpreted from the Kremlin's point of view. The 1947 issue of the handbook already referred to listed, under 'Program in the History of the Peoples of the USSR,' Professor A. M. Pankratova's highly nationalistic textbook, *The History of the USSR*, the constitution of the USSR, and Stalin's book *On the Great Fatherland War of the Soviet Union*. The 1954 edition lists no textbook, but stresses the 'world significance' of Soviet victory in the 'Fatherland War,' and the struggle of 'two camps' in the international arena, as well as the 'leading role of the Russian people.' An article in *The Teacher's Newspaper* for 17 March 1954 referred to Pankratova's book as 'standard' for the whole country and criticized its poor translation into Uzbek, thus indicating continued union-wide use of a basic text. In literature, students must pass an examination on, for example, *The Tale of Igor's Armament* and on numerous patriotic works by Lomonosov, Karamzin, and other classical Russian authors.

The centrally controlled Ministry of Higher Education of the USSR and, on the elementary and secondary levels, the formally decentralized Ministries of Education of the constituent republics, through an elaborate system of inspectors and agents, make certain that the same syllabi, textbooks, and methods are used throughout the entire system. The textbook *Pedagogy* is used to train all Soviet teachers. The 'general line' on the elementary and secondary school level is laid down by the Academy of Pedagogical Sciences of the RSFSR in Moscow.

Numerous patriotic brochures and handbooks carry the same Russia-centered emphasis as do the more formal basic texts. For example, in M. Morozov's long pamphlet, 'National Traditions and the Inculcation of Soviet Patriotism,' more than 90 per cent of all material dealing with political, military, literary, and other achievements of the various peoples of the whole world, is devoted to the Great Russians.[47]

The foregoing indicates gradually increasing Russification of Soviet education. Refugee testimony gives the impression that official pressure bulks large in this pattern. Refugee opinion regarding this question, however, is influenced by ethnic background. Russians tend to report that the spread of Russian culture is welcomed by the non-Russian peoples. Some Ukrainians assert that while they were in the Soviet Union they were, under certain situations such as performing teaching duties in institutions in the Ukraine in which the language of instruction was Russian, physically afraid to speak Ukrainian. The general pattern appears to be one in which Russian is, as Soviet sources ceaselessly emphasize, the 'language of communication' among the peoples of the USSR. The non-Russian languages occupy a subordinate, local, and in a sense a private position. They convey a content prescribed in Moscow, in which Russian traditions and Kremlin-approved ideas are dominant.

A similar pattern prevails in the press, in publishing, and in many other fields. The major exceptions are the training of teachers, the actual teaching process on the lower levels in non-Russian political units, and the lower levels of administration including the courts and police and the republic branches of the agricultural administration among the non-Russian peoples.

Predominantly Russian though it is, the Soviet language pattern continues to present important elements of bi-lingualism. It is a significant fact, constantly emphasized in Soviet articles on the nationality question, that before the Soviet revolution there were no universities even in Tbilisi or Erevan, and of course none in the then extremely backward Central Asian region. Even in Belorussia there were no higher educational institutions.[48] There were also very few non-Russian schoolteachers, whereas, according to Hans, in 1941 45 per cent of Soviet teachers were non-Russians, teaching in their native languages.[49]

In the press, too, the Soviet regime created new outlets for the use of non-Russian languages. In 1913, only 84 newspapers were published in non-Russian languages. This figure had risen to 2,294 by 1939, although it dropped to 1,959 by 1947. 'The non-Russian newspapers published in 1939 accounted for only about one fourth of the total circulation, although the non-Russian peoples represented more than 42 per cent of the total population.'[50] As Inkeles observes, the nationality press serves as a symbol of group status for non-Russian nationalities, and as a mobilizing agent for carrying to these groups the total policy of the regime.[51]

According to the *Large Soviet Encyclopedia,* as of 1940–41, 91 of the 137 newspapers published in Georgia were in the native language. In Kazakhstan, 421,000 of the total newspaper circulation of 945,000 were in Kazakh language papers. In Uzbekistan, 225 newspapers were published in 1941, 135 of them in Uzbek. In the Turkmen republic, in 1944, 43 of a total of 63 newspapers appeared in Turkmen. In Kirghizia, in 1940, 42 of 69 newspapers were published in Kirghiz. No figures were given for Belorussia or the Ukraine.[52]

In radio broadcasting, also, non-Russian languages are used. As of 1948, the Ukrainian branch of the All-Union Radio Committee was doing about 80 per cent of its broadcasting in Ukrainian.[53]

If it is difficult to obtain accurate information about the Soviet linguistic pattern, it is much more difficult to chart the course of cultural assimilation in less obvious areas such as the creation of a pattern of daily life, customs, and sentiments common to Russians and non-Russians. The available evidence indicates that the tendency toward standardization of the physical environment, social relations, customs, and perhaps even of sentiments, which has accompanied industrialization everywhere, has made considerable progress also in the Soviet Union. As in other societies, this process affects the elite more than the masses and the urban population more than the rural.

Malenkov in his address to the USSR Supreme Soviet on 8 August 1953 gave a figure of 80 million for the urban population.[54] To this figure must be added at least part of the rural population, including skilled workers on Machine Tractor Stations and the rapidly developing 'rural intelligentsia' of the collective farms. A. Poplyuiko, a refugee economist, estimates that by the end of 1955 almost 42 per cent of the Soviet population will be living in cities and that after 1955 a drop in the absolute number of rural inhabitants can be expected.

The rural intelligentsia, with higher or intermediate specialized education, is taking over the managerial and administrative functions in the countryside. Poplyuiko refers to this process as the 'proletarianization' of the village. The American sociologist Vucinich more cautiously concludes, on the basis of the meager information available, that the Soviet village is gradually becoming urbanized 'not only in terms of officially postulated *desiderata* (that is, in terms of socialist consolidation) but also in terms of a normal diffusion of urban traits.' [55]

Urbanization affects the life and attitudes of the non-Russians in a contradictory fashion. It is a force for assimilation. The non-Russian areas are less urbanized, on the whole, than is Russia. But within them, the large cities, especially in Central Asia, were, even to a considerable extent before the Bolshevik revolution, centers of Russian population. Even before the revolution, 29 per cent of the industrial workers of Uzbekistan, for example, were Russians.[56] As Russians pour into cities like Karaganda, Tashkent, Namangan, and other Central Asian industrial-administrative centers, and as local peasant boys are drawn off the farms by the planned Soviet program, the Soviet 'melting pot' boils. A striking example is the vast Ust-Kamenogorsk project on the Irtysh River in East Kazakhstan, on which Russians, Ukrainians, Uzbeks, Kirghiz, Kazakhs, and Georgians are working together. Reports on this enterprise have stressed its all-Union significance.[57] In view of the role of exile and forced labor in building up Central Asian cities, such as Karaganda, which today has a population of more than a quarter of a million, from a village of 150 inhabitants in 1926, one wonders what role forced labor plays in the Ust-Kamenogorsk, Farkhad, and other great Central Asian projects.

Occasional press items report an allegedly receptive attitude of non-Russians toward the diffusion among them of Russian ways and customs. One of the most interesting appeared in 1953 in the academic journal *Soviet Ethnography*. S. M. Abramzon, a member of a team of anthropologists, summed up the results of two years of study in 1951–3 of conditions on collective farms in Northern Kirghizia. He reported a striking extension of Russian influence on the agricultural practices, diet, music, attitudes toward women, leisure-time activity, and other aspects of life of the Kirghiz population. Summing up, Abramzon concluded that 'the cultural life of the Kolkhoz *ayil* [58] is unfolding under the ever-increasing influence of all that is best in Russian culture.' As the *Central Asian Review* drily notes, such a picture presented in all-Union publications is not reflected in the local Central Asian press.[59]

The cases of the Chechen-Ingush, the Kalmyks, and other peoples mentioned in Chapter III, show that the policy of assimilation has in some instances been a dismal failure. Avtorkhanov stresses the bitterness aroused among the Chechens, a Moslem people, by the regime's attempt to introduce pig breeding, and to deprive the proud mountaineers of the right to maintain ancient customs such as the wearing of daggers. While in Germany interviewing Soviet refugees I received confirmation of the correctness of Avtorkhanov's position from several Soviet escapees, including a Russian originally from Central Asia who had witnessed savage fights between dagger-wielding Chechens and pistol-toting Russian airmen, and a former MGB officer who described tricks such as the use of poisoned meat, employed in the struggle during the 1930's to break the spirit of the Chechens.

The Soviet press, especially since the wartime influx of Russians into Central Asia, has published hundreds of items complaining about the persistence of 'feudal' practices. These include a wide range of customs inherited from the patriarchal, and in some areas, nomadic, culture common to most of the Soviet peoples of Central Asia prior to the revolution. A frontal assault was not made on this ancient culture, including the Moslem religion, until about 1928. It is interesting, in this connection, that perhaps the first communist leader to be executed—in 1929—for 'national deviation,' Sultan Galiev, was a Tatar. As Tatar refugees stress, the Tatars held intellectual pre-eminence among the Soviet Moslems, and have thus been kept under particularly close ideological control because they might be potential leaders of 'Pan-Turanianism.' [60]

Post-war criticism of kidnapping of women, polygamy, wearing of veils, and other 'feudal' practices indicate that such customs did not die out in the 'twenties and 'thirties as might have been thought from reading the numerous books by Westerners in those years which hailed the 'modernization' of the Soviet East.[61] Reviewing a mass of reports on these problems, *The Central Asian Review* concludes that 'These practices still persist —and in the homes of men and women who are considered prominent public figures, as well as in the old and less advanced town and country areas.' [62]

During two weeks in Georgia and Armenia in 1947 I talked to many Georgians and observed the manners and customs of the population. Certainly the Georgians are more 'Western' than the Moslem and formerly-Moslem population of Central Asia. Indeed, in their political and intellectual sympathies, many Georgian intellectuals, I would judge, are more 'Western-oriented' than are the Russians. Several cultivated Georgians with whom I talked spoke rather wistfully of the 'old times' when it was possible to study in Europe, and young people were reading Russian translations of American books—Ernie Pyle's *This Is Your War* was one of them—or were thrilled by Deanna Durbin movies.

But Georgians—and this is, I believe, also true of Armenians—had at the same time some 'Eastern' traits. They regarded Russian women, I was told, as 'aggressive' and 'loose.' Something of the old, patriarchal attitude, fostered in Georgia by several centuries of Arab and Persian rule, still persisted. A certain courtliness of manner could be observed here, and a degree of self-respect several notches above that of most Russians. Space is lacking to present many of my observations of Georgia, the 'Russian Switzerland,' as one Georgian described his country. This beautiful and exotic country struck me as an island of relative plenty and gaiety in the somber gray sea of Soviet Russia. People seemed to be enjoying themselves in the restaurants and wine cellars—an institution with no Russian counterpart. The local mood, though not free of the oppressive Soviet atmosphere, was livelier than that of Moscow.

A Caucasian trait that was stressed on my 1947 trip, and by an Armenian with whom I had long discussions in Moscow, was intense national consciousness and family loyalty. Caucasians claimed that such loyalty did not exist among Russians. That they may have been stressing an important culture trait is indicated by the fact that many Great Russians also told me that Jews and Caucasians possessed a degree of family and national solidarity which was lacking among Russians. The existence of a rather strong concentration of this trait among peoples, part

of which consist of mountain clans among whom customs such
as the blood feud prevailed until recently, is not surprising. As
Grigolia remarks, 'a clearly marked group solidarity, expressed in
reciprocal assistance and co-operation,' is characteristic of all
groups of the Georgian nation.[63]

In Georgia also, as in Central Asia or the Ukraine, architectural
and other physical features of culture keep national consciousness alive. Tbilisi, as I saw it, was really three cities: the oriental
Near Eastern town of stucco and clay, the nineteenth-century
Russian imperial city, to which belonged the main street, renamed by the Bolsheviks after Rustaveli, the famous Georgian
poet, and the Soviet city of large, imposing but drably functional
office buildings. How could any Georgian with a trace of imagination fail to respond to the historical meaning of the ancient castle
of Queen Tamara in Mtskhete?

In the Ukraine the traditional white cottages [64] of the peasants,
and the special design of the peasants' embroidered blouses,
which differ from those of the Russians, keep alive 'consciousness
of kind.' These and other symbols, too numerous to mention here,
help to preserve the national consciousness of the non-Russian
peoples.[65]

It should also be remembered that ancient customs and local
differences persist among the Russian peasantry also. Reporting
on a trip to the Volga, Harrison Salisbury noted that the Soviet
Union has jet planes that can take off from a base in the Southern Ukraine and fly to Moscow and back before a peasant on
a near-by collective farm can drive his ox team fifteen miles to
town and back. And within half a mile of up-to-date farm machines peasant women were flailing grain in the courtyards of
the mud-walled *izbas,* or peasant huts, as had their ancestors 500
years before.[66]

Local and national differences, ancestral customs, and inherited
attitudes survive tenaciously in the Soviet Union. But the influence of industrialization, especially within the context of Soviet
policy, fosters cultural homogeneity. I would venture to guess
that today some sort of 'non-Russian national consciousness' is a
significant factor in the mental and spiritual make-up of 40 to 50
per cent of the Soviet population but that twenty years from

now this percentage will be lower, assuming a continuation of present trends. The significance of the national consciousness of the non-Russians is considerable and must not be dismissed as a figment of the refugee imagination, but at the same time it is difficult to see how national differences can fail to diminish gradually, given the demographic pattern discussed in Chapter II, combined with the resources of a totalitarian industrial society.

As Kurganov points out, the removal of 24 million peasants from the soil cannot fail to weaken traditional culture patterns, since the peasant has always been the bearer of national peculiarities. A Kirghiz, placed at a Moscow conveyor belt, has ceased to be a 'full blooded' Kirghiz.[67]

Thus far we have made only incidental use of data obtained from Soviet refugees on Soviet Russification. I spent a total of almost two years in Germany interviewing recent Soviet escapees during the period 1949–52, and have attempted to keep abreast of developments in this rather obscure field since 1952. I am familiar with the major findings of the various refugee interview projects, including the largest and most systematic, which was carried out by the Russian Research Center of Harvard University in 1950 and 1951. The data obtained by systematic interviewing of Soviet refugees, although extremely valuable, must be used with great caution. As far as the nationality problem is concerned, it appears that the principal weakness of the sample of refugees available is in the Central Asian area, an area in which, judging from other data, national discontent is relatively sharp.

In addition, the flow of refugees has been very thin during the past two or three years, and therefore may be inadequate to give even an approximate indication of developments since 1951 or 1952.

With the above qualifications in mind, let us survey the Soviet nationality picture as revealed by available refugee evidence. The most cautious interpretation of the available refugee data would be that it gives a fairly satisfactory picture of nationality attitudes up to the outbreak of World War II, and useful hints on subsequent developments. Some readers may be dismayed by these qualifications, but in this, as in most areas of Soviet life we know far less than we should like to know or need to know.

Nationality attitudes are, on the whole, subordinate to social position. As a rule, people in the same social group have basically similar value and attitude patterns regardless of nationality.[68] These findings of one of the major research studies on Soviet refugees tally with the position long held by this author.[69] In my own experience in Moscow, and on trips to Vladivostok and back, and to the Caucasus and the Ukraine, I cannot recall any expressions of strongly anti-Russian sentiments on the part of members of any Soviet ethnic group with the exception of some Soviet Jews, and their resentment was directed not against the Russians as a people but against the Soviet system. I heard a great deal of resentment against the system in general from Russians too, but we are not here concerned with general anti-regime sentiments. The ethnic group most disliked by most Soviet people with whom I discussed such matters in the USSR, and also by the refugees whom I interviewed, was the Jews. There was general agreement that the sorest point of nationality relations was anti-Semitism. Russians and Ukrainians whom I knew took a slightly humorous, condescending attitude toward Central Asians.

During my refugee interview work, I sometimes heard Great Russian refugees refer to Central Asians as 'eldashi,' the Tatar word for 'comrade,' which has acquired depreciative connotations. Russian acquaintances regarded the mountain peoples of the Caucasus, and to a lesser extent the lowland Georgians, with a mixture of romantic idealization and respect for their hot tempers and skill in the use of daggers. There was, so far as my observations go, a good deal of irritation with, perhaps even dislike of, Armenians. Armenians and Jews were often characterized as 'commercial' peoples. But Russians often indicated considerable respect for the family life and solidarity of Jews and Armenians.

Alexander Werth, in his illuminating book *The Year of Stalingrad*, reported a very interesting conversation with Konstantin Umanski, who later died under mysterious circumstances as Ambassador to Mexico. Umanski told Werth that Moscow was worried about the Caucasus and trusted none of the peoples there, except the Armenians. When Werth asked whether this applied to the Georgians, in view of Stalin's nationality, Umanski replied in the affirmative and characterized the Georgians as 'a lazy, wine-drinking, pleasure-loving bunch.'

In view of the fact that the foreign colony in Moscow regarded Umanski as a high-ranking member of the secret police, this is an interesting indication of sentiment in higher spheres toward the Georgians, and perhaps helps us to understand to some degree the loss of power of Georgians, now that their protector—in some degree—Stalin, has disappeared.[70]

Umanski's attitude reflected the annoyance and fear felt in high elite echelons regarding attitudes and traits of non-Russian peoples which made them less useful—certainly as military raw material—than the Great Russians.

The Georgians, at least, retained a position substantially preferable to that of most other non-Russians, however. The regime even made some concessions to Georgian expansionism by granting to the Georgian republic about 2500 square miles formerly within 'liquidated' autonomous units of the RSFSR, and by other gestures.[71] And in 1943, as reported in the *Journal of the Moscow Patriarchate* of March 1944, the autonomy of the Georgian Orthodox Church was recognized.

A bit of evidence which came to the attention of the writer in the winter of 1954–5 is pertinent here. A Soviet diplomat indicated in a conversation with an English-speaking foreigner that 'traitors' who defected to the Americans were largely Ukrainians. During the summer of 1954 the Soviet secret police began an intensified campaign to persuade or lure Ukrainian and Georgian Soviet *émigrés* back to the 'homeland.'[72]

The revival of old Russian imperial attitudes toward the national minorities may have been fostered during the 1930's and 1940's by renewed interest in classical Russian literature. Pushkin, Lermontov, Gogol, and other Russian writers on whom Soviet youth has been brought up since the early 'thirties contain, in addition to their broad humanitarianism, a strong vein of violent irrational Great Russian chauvinism, directed mainly against the West, but sometimes manifested in expressions of condescension or contempt toward non-Russian peoples of the

Russian Empire. An example is the description of the filthy and savage 'Asiatics' of the Caucasus mountains contained in Lermontov's *A Hero of Our Time,* a work read in all Soviet schools.

With the possible exception of anti-Semitism, the picture of nationality relations as seen by this writer and his colleagues during four years in Soviet Russia was not one of bitter conflict or antagonism. There was, however, widespread resentment among Russians of the fact that they were ruled by the Georgian Stalin. Also, the attitude of Russians and Russified non-Russians contained an element of ethnocentrism with respect to 'backward,' 'dirty,' or 'wild' non-Russians. I often heard criticism of Asiatic Soviet troops for deserting to the Germans, and humorous remarks about the minor role of the Georgians and other Caucasians in the war effort.

I recall also one conversation with a Soviet girl, long before it was officially revealed that the Crimean Tatars had been banished, in which she told me about the 'treason' and pro-German behavior of the Tatars. Finally, during travel in the Ukraine and the Caucasus, I detected, I thought, some covert anti-Russian attitudes. For example, a Ukrainian woman in a church in Kharkov told me that the churches in the city had only been opened after the 'Reds' had left and the Germans had entered the city, but this remark, again, could be considered purely anti-Soviet and not necessarily anti-Russian. Remarks of this kind, which I heard from time to time while I was in the Soviet Union, could be interpreted as expressing a 'national' form of anti-Bolshevism.

During my work in Germany I received a somewhat sharper impression of national tensions than while I was in the Soviet Union. This probably, in part at least, reflects the fact that Moscow, where I spent most of my stay in Soviet Russia, is naturally a highly Russified center. It also reflects the inevitable intensification of national prejudices under the stress of exile. The impressions based upon my German experience do not, however, differ essentially from those derived from direct observation in the Soviet Union.

As far as can be determined, although there is considerable

anti-Russian sentiment, the grievances of non-Russians are directed mainly against the Soviet system as a whole, or more usually against specific features of the system which have impinged upon them as individuals. I am inclined to agree with the statement sometimes made by anti-Soviet refugees that since all nationalities are equal in misfortune under Bolshevism they hate one another far less than they hate the Kremlin. The national consciousness of Ukrainians and Belorussians is, I think, more highly developed than some Great Russian refugees admit. Great Russian escapees often say that 'all Eastern Slavs are the same people' or refer to the Belorussian language, for example, as a 'Village Russian.' There is evidence that most Ukrainians continue to speak Ukrainian within the family circle. The majority also read Ukrainian newspapers. With respect to the latter question, however, it is surprising that a great many refugees of Ukrainian origin report that they read Russian newspapers at home.

A very large percentage of Ukrainian refugees have reported that while in the Soviet Union they were unaware of the identity of men such as Skrypnik, Shumski, or other famous Ukrainian leaders of the 1920's and early 1930's.[73] This kind of ignorance is not so surprising, given Soviet conditions, as it might appear at first sight. A regime which can completely remove the figure of Trotski from the Museum of the Revolution in Moscow—I looked in vain for him myself in this museum—has unusual ability to blot out from the popular mind symbols and figures it considers best forgotten. In the initial stage such enforced forgetting probably causes bitter resentment. As noted earlier, Ukrainian refugees report that they were even, at times, afraid to speak Ukrainian. Refugees also report concealment of their ethnic origin on grounds of prudence. In the long run, however, suppression of national identity and its normal outward manifestations may, if practiced as systematically as it can be in a totalitarian state, tend seriously to weaken the national consciousness of the group or groups against which it is directed.

It seems most unlikely, however, that a nationality as large as the Ukrainian can be completely assimilated, at least for some years. The splitting and assimilating tactics of the Kremlin have probably already effectively eliminated some smaller Soviet nationalities and may eventually do the same to the Jews and even the Turkic peoples, although the process will require several generations. But to eliminate the 'consciousness of kind' of an ethnic group numbering some 40 million is probably impossible, at least without substantial support from members of the affected group. It should be noted, however, that a French citizen of Ukrainian origin Jurko Turkevich, who visited the USSR in 1954 reported in the newspaper *Vpered,* in 1955, that Ukrainian children, in the big cities, were not even learning the Ukrainian language.

Let us now examine another type of data which sheds some light on Russification, namely the record of armed resistance against the Soviet regime by Soviet citizens, particularly in World War II. Here again the data are scarce and difficult to evaluate. The most complete and thorough study in this field is George Fischer's *Soviet Opposition to Stalin.* On the basis of extensive study of published sources and of interviews, Fischer concludes that non-Russians were not more hostile to the Stalin regime than Russians. Among other things, all six of the top leaders of the Vlasov movement were of Great Russian origin. Non-Russian Soviet individuals did not emerge anywhere as outstanding opposition leaders either during or after World War II, although one might cite secondary leaders among Ukrainians, Tatars, and Caucasians.[74] Fischer also notes that between one-third and one-half of the members of the KONR,[75] the top directing body of the 'Vlasov movement,' were non-Russian.[76]

While I was in Germany, I talked to a number of former German intelligence officers who, during the war, had been concerned with organizations or leadership of military formations composed of Soviet defectors. The well-informed Germans with whom I talked agreed that the ethnic stock that fought hardest against the Soviets was the Turkic. Although presenting the picture from a slightly different angle, the observations of these German experts do not necessarily contradict Fischer's findings. The majority of Soviet defectors ranged against the Soviets, and in the fighting in 1944 against the allies in Normandy, were probably Turks. These Turkic and other non-

Russian troops fought as members of German units. They did not enter into the so-called 'Vlasov army,' which, as is now well known, hardly saw any military service because of Hitler's fear that the Vlasov forces might become politically dangerous. Caroe emphasizes the good fighting qualities of these Soviet Turkic troops, and also the shabby treatment which they received at the hands of the Germans.[77]

An offset to Caroe's view regarding German treatment of Turkic units is the statement made to me by a Soviet refugee in Germany that because of good German treatment, including much better food than they received in the Red Army, these troops fought 'ferociously' against the Soviet army.

In his excellent and thorough study, *Ukrainian Nationalism, 1939–1945,* John Armstrong expresses the opinion that during World War II, Ukrainian nationalism attracted a large proportion of the intellectuals and teachers in the area under German occupation and that a section of the Ukrainian elite desired national independence based on cultural distinctiveness. Armstrong also appears to have reached the conclusion that there were no significant ethnically Russian anti-Soviet forces in the Ukraine during World War II. The Ukrainian national movement might have been a much more powerful force, Armstrong indicates, if it had not been for the ill-concealed determination of the Nazi leadership to convert the Ukraine into an exploited colony.

Armstrong takes a more positive view than that presented by previous writers on what was, until his work was published, a largely unexplored subject. His interpretation tallies closely with most other expert opinion, however, when he places 'national expression in culture and perhaps in government' fifth on the list of desiderata of the population in German-occupied Ukraine during the war. Under the frightful conditions of those days physical survival had first priority and 'equality of persons' was fourth on the list.[78]

The subject of armed resistance to Soviet authority is still virgin territory. Much interesting material, presented in a lively fashion, is contained in *Our Secret Allies: the Peoples of Russia,* by Eugene Lyons.[79] Most of those who have ventured into this vital, and largely unexplored field, agree that on the whole the nationality factor was not decisive.[80]

It is possible that as time passes the 'national form' of the attitudes of Soviet people, although it will continue to be important and complicated, may gradually diminish in significance, yielding to new factors as social relations and group attitudes develop and evolve.[81]

The Dynamics of Sovietization

Soviet Russification, or 'Sovietization,' is an unique phenomenon. The attempt is made by a totalitarian state, exploiting its monopoly of the formal communications system and employing a centrally administered arsenal of reward and punishment, to amalgamate diverse ethnic and cultural elements into a new homogeneity. Both synthetic and analytical methods are employed. By 'synthetic' we mean organization, training, and education which induce non-Russians to adopt the pattern of Soviet Russian culture. These positive, or synthetic, techniques might also be called 'integrative.' By 'analytical' techniques we mean actions which deprive, or even disintegrate, ethnic or national groups to force them into officially approved patterns. Although the disintegrative techniques are more terrifying, they are probably less important in the long run than the integrative ones. Hence, we describe them first.

Soviet negative cultural techniques range from relatively mild exertion of social pressure through mass communications media, and oral agitation, the educational system and 'voluntary' organizations such as trade unions or professional groups of scientists and scholars, to arrests, deportation, and even 'liquidation.' In the short run, the objective of negative methods is to silence hostile, 'harmful,' or 'alien,' individuals and their views. The ultimate objective is to eliminate alternatives to official patterns of belief and identification.

In the early days of the regime the first of these objectives was the more important; today the struggle against a more diffuse, and perhaps more widespread, pattern of disaffection and apathy

—in George Fischer's term, 'inertness'—is more important. As long as the Soviet system remains totalitarian and as long as there is a single powerful free country outside its borders, this struggle will continue. And as long as group sentiments other than the official Soviet Russian nationalism exist in the Soviet Union, prophylactic measures will be employed.

In the nationality field, preventive measures find expression in, for example, the prohibition of the study of Hebrew and Yiddish. By depriving Jews of distinctive modes of cultural expression, it is hoped to destroy 'Jewish' group consciousness. Measures of this kind go a step beyond attacks on 'cosmopolitanism.' Press attacks on disapproved attitudes deal with present problems. Linguistic and other cultural prohibitions and acts of violence such as deportations, look to the future. As Avtorkhanov points out, it is possible that the Chechen-Ingush people were removed as part of a program of preparation for World War III.[1] There is little reason to question his statement that 'if Soviet material interests require a radical solution of the Caucasian question in a future war, the Caucasus may be without a single Caucasian.' [2]

Within this framework, any attempt at 'proselytizing' on the part of any non-Russian ethnic or national group is nipped in the bud by the Soviet authorities. Khrushchev in 1946 spoke of the 'perversion' of nationality policies in the Western Ukraine, where, he declared, there was an unjustifiable tendency to turn Russian schools into Ukrainian schools. 'Harmful' decisions made in this field by the Ukrainian Ministry of Public Instruction, were 'annulled' and those responsible severely punished. This situation showed the need for constant vigilance, Khrushchev maintained.[3]

The process of Soviet revolutionary Russification can be summed up in terms of several main stages. In the first stage, non-Russian, or perhaps it would be more accurate to say non-Slavic groups, such as the Central Asian Turks, are divided into the smallest possible segments. This splitting tactic is an application in the nationality field of general Soviet tactics of analyzing social forces in 'enemy' groups into elements with which temporary alliances can be made, elements which must be annihilated immediately if possible, and an intermediate mass which can be neutralized or temporarily disregarded.

This first stage of 'Sovietization' involves maximum use of deception, by which the affected people are disunited. Disintegration is applied horizontally, as in the splitting of the Central Asian Turks into separate 'nations,' and vertically, as in the making of temporary alliances with Turkic and Ukrainian nationalist leaders. The Ukrainian Skrypnik, the Tatar Sultan-Galiev, and the Uzbek Faizulla Khodzhaev are three of the best-known victims of this tactic.[4] If, as was the case in the Ukraine and Belorussia, sentiment can be aroused, mainly in the still 'unliberated' area, for 're-unification,' in order to bring into the USSR suffering 'blood brothers' beyond the borders, the tasks of deception may be rendered easier.[5]

Sometimes a specious irredentist claim has been employed to press Soviet demands on neighboring states. An outstanding example is afforded by the post-World War II demands that Soviet Armenia and Georgia be given Turkish territories allegedly inhabited in remote ages by Georgian-speaking tribes. This demand was voiced by three leading Georgian historians in a sensational article published in *Pravda* on 20 December 1945. The areas discussed in this article comprised about one quarter of Turkey.

Of course, from the point of view of continuity of Tsarist and Soviet state interests, Moscow did have an arguable claim to part of this territory, namely, the provinces of Kars and Ardahan, ceded to Turkey in 1921 and historically largely Armenian in population. The Kremlin sought to mobilize Armenian opinion throughout the world in support of this claim. It also successfully exploited Armenian nationalism in persuading tens of thousands of Armenians to resettle in Soviet Armenia. It is likely that post-Stalin renunciation of Soviet demands for Kars and Ardahan may have shocked pro-Soviet Armenians abroad. As for the hapless resettlers, they have long since undergone the disillusionment which 'Sovietization' holds in store for those who accept at face value the promises held out by Soviet nationality policy.

One cannot generalize easily about Soviet tactics toward irredentas, which are adjusted flexibly in response to shifts in the international situation. Thus at times Polish minorities in Soviet Belorussia were favored, as in the 1920's, when it was thought that they might be useful in a revolutionary advance against Poland. On the other hand, during the 1930's when Poland was feared as an ally first of France and later, potentially, of Nazi Germany, savage purges and deportations were visited upon the Polish frontier communities.[6]

In the first stage of 'Sovietization,' generous grants of 'self-determination' and local cultural 'autonomy' are usually made. These have never had much significance so far as the substance of political and economic power is concerned. As Lawrynenko and Majstrenko point out, the Ukrainian communists were from the beginning helpless in their struggle against the Kremlin because they had no army, no police, or other sinews of political power. The early, consequently relatively frank, Soviet *Encyclopedia of State and Law,* referred to in Chapter I, contains an article entitled 'Oblasts,' which shows that the police power in the hands of the Kremlin from the very earliest days of the establishment of Soviet power in non-Russian areas made it impossible for these areas to enjoy self-government.[7]

Referring to 'national oblasts,' this *Encyclopedia* states that 'subordination [on strictly defined principles] of the national oblast organs to those of the territory proceed along the line of the unified peoples commissariat [of Internal Affairs] and the general principle of the Soviet system of dual subordination with respect to the relation between oblast territory and the center of the entire state.'[8]

The emphasis in the article above is on the 'rapid, unconditional execution of all plans of the central Soviet authority.' Up-to-date information on Moscow's control of non-Russian political units and of local government is contained in a work entitled *The Soviet State Apparatus,* which emphasizes that the Council of Ministers of the central government may cancel orders and regulations of the constituent republics. Referring to the earlier period of Soviet rule, it declares that 'by establishing the RSFSR the Bolshevik Party laid a firm foundation for building the other Socialist republics.' This standard text, incidentally, declares that 'Anglo-Saxon racism' attempts to liquidate the national statehood and culture of peoples who do not speak English.' [9]

An important weapon for disintegrating non-Russian national groups in the first phase of Soviet Russification is the practice of gerrymandering. This was applied with particular force in Central Asia. As Caroe and Kolarz demonstrate in detail, the 'national' boundaries of the new nations formed from the population of Turkestan did not correspond to ethnic lines. Populations overlapped, with the result that the regime could set one group off against another. Other applications of this process include the establishment of capital cities of 'national' units in cities in which the majority of the population are Great Russians.

Such manipulations have often been applied with particular skill in border regions when the Kremlin was seeking to influence people of similar national origins across Soviet frontiers. It should be noted, incidentally, that communists in countries such as India have been attempting in the post-war years to manipulate linguistic and other cultural differences with a view to weakening the unity of the Indian state.[10]

It would be a mistake to dismiss as unimportant gestures the semantic manipulations of national symbols employed in the first stage of 'Sovietization.' In this stage, and to a lesser degree throughout the later stages of development of a Soviet 'republic,' manipulation of symbols of nationalism serves important psychological purposes.[11] The verbal substitutes for sovereignty to which Soviet propaganda devotes so much attention, may appeal to peoples who before the Bolshevik revolution did not receive even token recognition of their developing group consciousness. The persistent attention devoted to this theme is impressive; even discounting for its very important role in foreign propaganda it is difficult to doubt that the Kremlin appraises shrewdly the value of frequent gestures of recognition of group identities. Thus in connection with the 1955 session of the RSFSR Supreme Soviet *Pravda* for 25 March asserted that 'The composition of the deputies of the Supreme Soviet of the RSFSR is a shining

example of the friendship of peoples of our multi-national republic; the deputies represent twenty-six nationalities.'

These observations apply with even greater force to the arts.
The often commented upon establishment of 'national' theaters,
dance groups, ballet and opera companies, and other outlets for
the expression of national cultural impulses has been a source of
some satisfaction to the non-Russian peoples of the Soviet Union.
The Kremlin has shown considerable skill in fashioning a pattern of synthetic identities, in which the general policy of the
regime is expressed in the local cultural idiom.

This policy contains, to be sure, inherent contradictions. When
a tendency develops to infuse non-Soviet content into local cultural forms, drastic punitive action is taken. Since the purges of
1936-8 and especially since World War II, more and more of the
local content has been replaced by a 'universal,' Soviet content.

Soviet sources indicate that progress in the displacement of
national customs by 'socialist' patterns is a source of satisfaction
to the regime. Thus, the article on Georgia in the second edition
of the *Large Soviet Encyclopedia* notes that the Georgian national costume has been fully replaced by city dress, the folk
costumes being retained only for holidays, and that native art
forms flourish in the villages for the most part. As a work on the
judicial system of Kazakhstan points out, 'Respect for national
peculiarities in no way signifies protection by the Soviet courts of
those customs of the peoples of the USSR which give expression
to patriarchal-feudal relations prevalent before the revolution
and which, in Kazakhstan in particular, were supported by the
shariat and the adat.' [12] And yet it will be a long time before the
embodiment of local cultural individuality in such forms as
national representation in the annual Moscow sports festival or
in the agricultural exposition, held in 1939, and, according to
Pravda for 1 August 1954, reopened, with special emphasis on
the exhibits of the non-Russians, can be disregarded as instruments by which the Kremlin provides a substitute for genuine
self-government and real cultural autonomy.

Soviet cultural concessions paid big dividends, in the Ukraine
and elsewhere, in the 1920's. They won the enthusiastic support
of men like Skrypnik who were both sincere nationalists and

loyal communists. They attracted patriotic scholars such as the great historian, Hrushevsky, who returned from emigration, only to end his days in disgrace following the adoption of repressive policies after 1930. They won support among many members of the Ukrainian and Belorussian minorities in Poland and other countries, and this was a valuable asset to Moscow.

The relationship between Muscovite centralism and local nationalism involves a dilemma. Soviet power means industrialization, literacy, and mass education. These forces create the need for administrative standardization and cultural homogeneity. They also awaken the hitherto latent national consciousness of 'historyless' peoples. An awakened sense of a national past can lead to indignation against Muscovite violations of national identity.

The dislocations of early industrialization exacerbate tensions and insecurity. Individuals turn to deeply buried group memories for compensatory solace and support. But this psychological refuge is denied to non-Russians, except within prescribed limits. The only legitimate form of cultural nationalism is Great Russian.[13]

The second phase of Soviet Russification is one in which deprivation of non-Russian peoples of administrative direction in all important areas is carried to its completion. Several aspects of the 'denationalization' of administration have already been touched upon. Others are discussed in the last pages of this chapter. Suffice it to remind the reader here of the well-known Soviet combination of administrative centralization and police and other controls by which the formation of homogeneous power clusters outside of the centrally controlled all-union administrative mechanism is combatted. If, as was true in the case of the Chechen-Ingush, these methods fail, persecution may follow. Kazakhstan apparently entered the second stage of Russification in 1954–5.

A third general characteristic of Sovietization is the employment of various techniques of discrimination, short of the most drastic methods, such as deportation, against elements that prove resistant to assimilation. These techniques are numerous but they can be summed up as the establishment of favorable life chances for conformists and the opposite for nonconformists. The Russified segments of ethnic groups to whom this process is applied are favored, and when they start to approach a numerical majority, measures are taken to suppress or, in extreme cases, to liquidate the non-Russian elements, their institutions, their customs, and even their language. In the final stage of this operation the non-Russian components are eliminated and the complete assimilation of the group to Russian culture takes place.

The combination of disintegrative measures, which have been emphasized thus far, and integrative techniques has probably been most successful with regard to the Jewish population of the Soviet Union, although it will be several generations before the Soviet Jews are completely Russified. It may also be predicted that within thirty or forty years, unless new factors supervene, the Soviet Turks will, to a great degree, have lost their cultural distinctiveness and perhaps even their language. These 'predictions' are tentative. It is well, however, to realize the power of the unusually systematic assimilation process carried on in the Soviet Union today.[14]

Lest the reader feel that excessively sweeping conclusions are being drawn, he might turn, with regard to the Jews, to Peter Meyer's article in the July 1954 *Commentary*. Meyer expresses the opinion that the Jews have become a group to be isolated, 'rendered harmless,' and finally 'liquidated.' The basic work on Soviet anti-Semitism, Solomon M. Schwarz's *The Jews in the Soviet Union*,[15] does not draw such a decisive conclusion but its wealth of documentation on the surreptitious anti-Jewishness which for years has been penetrating many spheres of Soviet society leads to similar conclusions.[16]

The suppression of the Yiddish press, Jewish theaters, and other Jewish cultural activity has been carried so far that even in the Jewish Autonomous Oblast of Birobidzhan, there was, in June 1954, only one newspaper, with a circulation of 1000, for the approximately 100,000 Jews of the area. Local Jewish officials explained to Harrison Salisbury that the Jews, being an 'advanced' people, did not require the protection and development of their native language needed by such peoples as the Yakuts;

he was assured that the Jews for the most part preferred to speak and read Russian.

The vestiges of Jewish cultural life which have survived in Birobidzhan seem to be almost unique. Since 1948, when the Yiddish publishing house Emes, and the Jewish Anti-Fascist Committee newspaper, *Einikait,* were closed, there has been no central Jewish periodical press or publishing activity. Jewish theaters were also all closed in 1948, despite the fact that the Moscow Jewish Theater, in particular, was outstanding, especially in Shakespearian productions.

Cultural suppression probably affected mainly the minority of Soviet Jews who still cherished some elements of 'Jewish' culture even though they might have been largely Russified. The policy of discrimination against Jews in educational institutions and in 'sensitive' government agencies which accompanied it must have been a heavy blow to many loyal Russified Jews. These developments, together with the campaign against 'cosmopolitanism' and the 'doctors' plot' accusations, may well have left most Soviet Jews uneasy. At the time of writing it is too early to appraise the sincerity or the chances of permanence of post-Stalin denunciation of anti-Semitism and partial undoing of harm done to Jews and Jewish culture under Stalin.[17] The articles published by Harry Schwartz in *The New York Times* after his return from the Soviet Union in November 1955 tend strongly to confirm the generally negative conclusions which I have reached.

The Jews as a cultural group represent the most conspicuous—certainly the most studied—target of the curious combination of assimilation and discrimination toward which Soviet nationality policy has evolved. Yet if their fate reveals many of the weaknesses and injustices of this policy, it also shows clearly the tremendous power of Soviet planned assimilation. I would guess that Soviet Jews include some of the most dissatisfied elements in the Soviet population but that within another generation or two intermarriage and other forces making for assimilation will have greatly reduced both the qualitative and quantitative aspects of Jewish group consciousness.[18]

This brief survey of the application of Soviet assimilationist policy to the Jews could not be concluded without emphasizing that despite its many negative features, official Soviet policy has made no major overt concessions to 'racial' prejudice. Official policy has sometimes flirted with Ukrainian and Russian popular anti-Semitism. Legal prohibitions against incitement of racial hatred, and official denunciations of anti-Semitism remain, however.

The very considerable success of the assimilation policy so far as Soviet Jews are concerned, is probably largely a result of this absence of 'racialism.'

Bernard Choseed in an objective study concludes that in terms of cultural adjustment Soviet Jews responded positively to their situation. 'Although the agitation for . . . Birobidzhan was often framed in terms of developing a Soviet "national" Jew, in effect this did not take place.' Choseed discerns a 'pattern of gradually lessened national consciousness.' [19]

Recent tendencies to reduce, by conscious official policy, the percentage of Soviet Jews in many vital fields of activity perhaps render Choseed's views somewhat obsolete. Increasing pressures were applied to Soviet Jews after 1948, and their situation steadily worsened. As recently as 1939, however, approximately 10 per cent of the entire Soviet intelligentsia, 17 per cent of all doctors, and 10 per cent of students in higher education had been Jews. Choseed asserts that the majority of Jewish writers were not touched by the campaign against 'cosmopolitanism' and furnishes other data demonstrating continued participation of loyal Jews in Soviet cultural life.[21]

Perhaps the greatest significance of such studies as that of Choseed is as a reminder that probably most Soviet Jews desired assimilation, and responded eagerly to the opportunity to participate in the Soviet Russian pattern. After the war, the Kremlin's fear that Jewish assimilation was not complete, and that knowledge of and a certain sympathy for the 'capitalist' West, and keen interest in Israel was a part of the mentality of many Soviet Jews, drastically and unfavorably altered the government's attitude toward Jews. Yet as long as Jews such as Ilya Ehrenburg, Lazar Kaganovich, and others occupy prominent positions in Soviet life, we must admit that fully assimilated Jews who are useful to the regime are treated like similar Soviet citizens of other nationalities. The Kremlin, of course, decides whether or not a Jew or any other Soviet citizen is to be trusted, and changes its mind frequently, often with fatal consequences for suspected individuals or groups.

The Jews, more than any other element of the Soviet population, may actually have derived benefit from the earlier stage of the revolution, provided they conformed to Party norms.[22] Their urban-literary traditions enabled them to offer needed skills. But, as Russians were educated in the new Soviet schools and universities, the need for Jewish skills diminished, while lingering remnants of Jewish distinctiveness, stimulated to new awareness by the war and by Soviet anti-Nazi propaganda, became a threat to the extreme homogeneity demanded by the Kremlin.

Some of the major 'positive' techniques of Soviet totalitarian Russification remain to be considered. Here, only aspects of Soviet policy specifically related to Russification will be dealt with, to avoid duplication of material in standard works on Soviet government.[23] Assimilation by organization, assimilation by instruction, and assimilation by 'exposure' will be discussed here. Perhaps these aspects of cultural assimilation in the Soviet Union might be summed up in the term 'assimilation by participation.' We must recognize that despite its brutality and disregard for human rights, Soviet revolutionary Russification has much positive strength. Its appeal is suggested by the word 'participation.' Soviet Russification is totalitarian assimilation, and history has shown that assimilation without political and legal safeguards for the rights of minorities can become the worst form of 'discrimination.'

Yet in the sense in which 'discrimination' is understood by most Americans, Soviet policy is not highly discriminatory.[24] Westerners and, in some cases, Asians who have traveled in Soviet Central Asia have correctly reported that 'Russian' and 'native' sections still exist in the cities of that region. Yet, it is safe to say that there is little or no compulsory 'segregation'—that most extreme form of discrimination—in the Soviet Union. On the contrary, in the terms used by Lenin at the height of the revolution, Soviet policy may be summed up under the slogan

'Come unto us!' although this receptiveness is sharply qualified by military-political considerations. But those individuals and groups which are not considered to be under the influence of the foreign 'imperialist' enemy and are able and willing to pay the price of conformity are readily assimilated. The Soviet non-Russian who is willing to renounce 'feudal' practices and 'bourgeois-nationalist' attitudes—and to become a Russianized 'Soviet' person—can go far. He may even become an official in Moscow.

As Lowie points out, there are two basic questions for minority groups. One, do they wish to be assimilated? And, two, does the majority welcome assimilation to its norm?[25] It seems likely that Soviet Jews in particular tended to welcome assimilation to the Soviet Russian pattern, especially in the earlier phases of the revolution. Probably many members of the relatively small intellectual groups of the more 'backward' Soviet peoples experienced, and still experience, satisfaction and gratification from inclusion in the over-all society from which they were largely excluded before the revolution. On the other hand, one reason for post-war national discontent is the fact that Great Russian chauvinism has partially reverted to exclusionist policies, of which the Jews have been the major victims.

The Soviet state is lavish, even cannibalistic, in its use of human resources. Offsetting its frightful negative consequences, this habit has the advantage of fostering a high degree of social mobility, which combined with administrative centralism has led to the development of one of the many unique characteristics of the Soviet system. This is the development of the closest approach in history to a unified, homogeneous national personnel pool. The major agencies, such as the political police, the great industrial ministries, and the armed forces, are national organizations composed of highly transferable individuals and units.

Not only linguistically but in myriad other ways, the Soviet army is probably the most thoroughly, and traditionally, 'Russian' agency of the whole system. Its instructional and disciplinary manuals, and its propaganda literature, are impregnated with Tsarist Russian traditions and images. For example, the Soviet army garrison service regulations manual contains, in its sample lists of forms and names, only Russian names.[26] In 1945, the army publishing house put out a new edition of a famous Tsarist military manual entitled *The Commander and the Subordinate,* which stressed a traditional Russian conception of stern, patriarchal authority.[27]

Obviously, in order to function in such a system it is necessary to learn the Russian language well, and to acquire the other cultural traits which facilitate operation of these agencies. The Communist Party of the Soviet Union, the seven million man political army which gives direction and cohesiveness to the vast mechanism, possesses in the highest degree the characteristics of unity, centralism, and homogeneity. Its apparatus is truly 'international,' in the Soviet sense, and possesses to an even greater extent than the armies of non-Soviet states cohesion and discipline.

This Party-state machine transcends nationality. It draws, if not always the ablest, at any rate the most aggressive, forceful, and ruthless individuals out of all parts of the country into a mechanism whose center is the ancient Russian city of Moscow. Ambitious Party careerists, rising young engineers and industrial executives, promising young army officers, and also of course aspirants for artistic and literary careers, are drawn to Moscow. Certainly Moscow training and the habit of adjusting one's conduct to the Moscow-ordained pattern is a powerful force for Soviet Russification. More than Paris or London, more than New York, Chicago, and Washington combined, Moscow sets the pace of Soviet life.

To what extent do the non-Russians 'participate' in all-Union affairs? Certainly to a far greater extent than before the Soviet regime was established. In my opinion, this fact, far more than the sham 'sovereignty' of the non-Russian political units, has gained support for the regime from many non-Russians. In Chapter III we discussed the over-all pattern of Russian and non-Russian Party membership. Here we consider the problem of representation of the non-Russians in the top echelons of the Party and other leading organs, and also the closely related question of the availability of education and other advantages to the non-Russians.

Schueller notes that 'in many ways the Politburo is not at all

representative of the population of the Soviet Union.' No Politburo or Presidium members or alternates with the exception of
Bagirov, removed in 1953, have been drawn from the Turco-
Tatar group. The trend has been toward domination of the
Party summit by Russians and Russified members of the Ukrainian, Belorussian, Jewish, or Caucasian nationalities. The earlier
over-representation of Jews and Caucasians appears now definitely to be at an end. As Schueller remarks, with respect to the
Jews, their over-representation belonged to the period when
urban intellectuals predominated in the Politburo.[28] One Jew,
Kaganovich, remains in the Presidium, however. No Jew held a
comparable position in the Tsarist regime.

The most recent information on Russification in the top circles
of the Soviet regime has been assembled in a recent careful survey. Nearly 60 per cent of the 236 members and alternates of the
Central Committee elected at the Nineteenth Party Congress in
October 1952 represented all-Union Party and Soviet organizations. Of the remaining 103 members and candidates 55 represented the Russian Republic. Only 44 out of 167 regional Party
organizations were represented, and of these a total of 40, mostly
Russians, derived from the RSFSR. Summing up, Towster points
out that the Russian ethnic group predominates in the total
membership of the Central Committee elected in 1952, which
comprises the most important part of Soviet officialdom, the all-
Union bureaucracy.[29]

Great Russian predominance is not so clear of course at the
level of republic and other national Party units. Here Muscovite control is often masked by giving the nominally top positions
both in the Party and in the governmental organizations to local
men, while the second in command is usually a Russian or other
non-local man. The vast majority of commanders of the 23 Military Districts of the Soviet Union are Great Russians.

On the intermediate and local level in the non-Russian republics the pattern is reversed. Here, as a rule, the majority of party
and government officials, particularly in the fields of education,
justice, and the non-political parts of the police administration,
and agriculture, are non-Russian. This pattern has been reason-
ably well established by Western scholars for the Ukraine, al-

though the tedious biographical research which would be necessary for a comprehensive and detailed study, even of the Ukraine, has not been done.[30]

Recently evidence has appeared in the Soviet press indicating that the strength of the Soviet Ukrainian civil service, Party cadres and economic officials, vis-à-vis Russians and members of other nationalities in the Ukraine, has increased considerably. Among possible reasons for this development are the departure from the Ukraine of Khrushchev and members of his entourage, and the decimation of the Jewish population during the war.[31]

In Belorussia, according to testimony before a Congressional committee in 1954, only 7 out of 26 ministers of the republic government were Belorussians. Of the remainder, one was a Georgian, one a Jew, and the rest were Great Russians. Eighty to 90 per cent of oblast and rayon Party leaders were Russians.[32]

By contrast, in Georgia, as of April 1955, all of the ministers of the republic government were Georgians, although one Russian and one Armenian belonged to the seventeen-member Presidium of the republic Supreme Soviet.[33] In Georgia, however, the other Caucasian republics, and Kazakhstan, a drastic turnover is apparent in the ranks of deputies to the USSR Supreme Soviet.

In the central Asian republics, the representation of indigenous elements in the Party, the civil service and the professions appears to be lower than in the Ukraine, and far lower than in Georgia. According to one account, based on the observations of a Polish exile in Turkmenia, when Turkmen clash with the authorities, they have to deal with Russians; even relatively low ranking, semi-skilled jobs, if they have any security significance, are usually held by Russians, because Turkmen are not trusted.[34] A less extreme but similar picture emerges from reading the carefully prepared material on Central Asia contained in *Central Asian Review*. But it should be borne in mind that before the revolution there were infinitely fewer educated persons in Central Asia and virtually no Kirghiz, Kazakh, Turkmen, or other Turkic officers or officials. Military service was not even required of these peoples and when the Tsarist government attempted in 1916 to impose it, the resulting uprising led to the loss of more than 100,000 lives.

In education the situation is on the whole similar to that
which prevails in the bureaucracy. The Russians and, to a lesser
extent, the other Slavic peoples, enjoy certain advantages in
comparison to most non-Russian peoples. In terms of persons
with higher education, however, per one thousand of the population, according to the 1939 census, the Georgian Republic with
11.2, was far ahead of the Russian Republic with 6.5, the Ukrainian Republic with 7.2, the Belorussians with 4.5, or the Central
Asian Republics which, with the exception of Kazakhstan, had
two or three such persons per thousand.

The relatively favorable position of Kazakhstan probably reflected the large percentage of Russians and Ukrainians in its
population.[35] More recent data indicate some improvement in
the relative position of Central Asia, but it still lags far behind
Georgia, Armenia, and the Russian Republic. Soviet sources have
published many individual items which bring out strikingly the
continued backwardness of Central Asia in education. Usually,
however, statements of this nature appear in publications seldom
read by foreigners. On the other hand, the fact that they appear
at all indicates Moscow's desire to correct such defects.

The Central Committee organ *Party Life* stated in 1947 that
there was an acute shortage of 'national' engineering and technical cadres in Uzbekistan and Kazakhstan, and that 'in particular' there were very few students of the native nationalities at
the industrial institutes and technical schools of Central Asia.[36]
According to *Kazakhstanskaya Pravda* for 16 December 1951,
the higher educational institutions of Kazakhstan graduated
7,040 women in the four years from 1947 to 1951, of whom 1,380
were Kazakhs. It is significant that the Party has special sections
for work among women in the Central Asian Republics.[37]

It is also significant that non-natives, largely Russians, constitute about 90 per cent of the population of Alma-ata, capital
of the Kazakh republic. The agricultural resettlement program
of 1954–6 brought an additional influx of non-Kazakhs, especially Great Russians and Ukrainians, to this republic. Apparently, between one and two million persons will be needed for
the total resettlement program, and Kazakhstan's share is about
one half. An indication of the polyglot pattern of settlers on

the 'new lands' was given on 14 January 1955 by the Soviet newspaper *Agriculture,* which reported that in one new state farm persons from 20 oblasts of the Soviet Union, representing 12 different nationalities, were present.[38]

The Volga Tatars have always been perhaps the most 'advanced' of the Turco-Tatar peoples of the Soviet Union. That this is still the case was indicated by the fact that the only speaker from the Volga-Ural or Central Asian areas at the Nineteenth Party Congress in October 1952 who gave any statistics regarding education was Muratov, the first secretary of the Party organization of the Tatar Autonomous Republic, who stated that of 21,912 students in the higher educational institutions of the republic, 6,866 were Tatars. Of the 1,904 scientific workers in Tataria, 400 were Tatars. In proportion to the nearly 50 per cent of the republic's population represented by Tatars, these figures are not high, but they are undoubtedly far more favorable than those of the Central Asian region as a whole.[39]

Central Asia, like the North Caucasus, the Soviet far north, and much of Soviet Siberia, is still backward, both relatively and absolutely. Soviet propaganda, and the accounts of this area written by enthusiastic foreigners without knowledge of the Russian or local languages or any other expert knowledge, have presented a fantastically exaggerated picture of the 'progress' made here. On the other hand, there has been progress in industry, education, literacy, sanitation, and other aspects of modern industrial civilization.

In formal education, progress in the non-Russian areas has been extremely rapid since the end of World War II. Between 1949 and 1953, enrollment in Central Asian higher educational institutions increased by 47,000, and in the three Caucasus republics by 38,000.[40] There is every indication that this progress is continuing. As a matter of fact, the material, technical, and educational progress of the more 'backward' parts of the Soviet Union has been much more rapid than that of the central Great Russian area. The result has been to increase the power of the Soviet Union as a whole and of its Moscow rulers, rather than to foster local interests and welfare. Nevertheless, and particularly in view of the underdeveloped condition of most of the non-European world, the results must seem impressive to many Soviet Asians, especially if they have come to identify not with their nationality but with the Soviet Union as a whole.[41]

There is little doubt that some Central Asians, probably including some of the most effective human material among Soviet Asians, have become 'Soviet men' and have perhaps irrevocably severed their ties with their national-cultural and religious heritage. It is equally likely that completion of this process, if it can be completed at all may require decades. It is especially difficult among peoples with a Moslem background and non-European physical characteristics, because of tensions engendered on both the Russian and the non-Russian side by increasing interaction under the unfavorable conditions of excessively rapid and centralized economic development. The Central Asians, like the Ukrainians, will long hold, in the recesses of their minds, dark memories of collectivization, although this is a factor of diminishing significance to the younger age groups.

It should be borne in mind that, on the whole, collectivization affected non-Russians more adversely than it did Russians. The Ukrainians had a stronger tradition of individual peasant farming than the Russians, among whom communal land tenure was widespread. Central Asians were to a large extent not even settled agricultural peoples. The Ukrainian peasantry formed a disproportionate part of the 'kulaks' exiled to Siberia and Kazakhstan.[42] This fact may have cast a somber hue on the attitude of many Ukrainian 'volunteers' in the Khrushchev resettlement program.

Among non-Russians in general the aspirations generated by the sham Soviet 'federalism,' to which we have already referred, may tend to generate discontent among some who, despite the fear inspired by past purges, feel a sense of frustration because the nationality provisions of the Soviet constitution mean so little in practice.

There is a contradiction between all-Union 'Soviet patriotism' and part of the Soviet doctrine which acclaims the values of 'sovereignty' of the sixteen Soviet 'republics.' Probably it seems less acute to most Soviet people than it does to us. The claim of 'sovereignty' of the national units, like the propaganda of 'Soviet Democracy,' is intended for the masses, not for the communist elite. The members of all nationalities who master the esoteric doctrines of Marxism-Leninism and, far more important, the Soviet techniques of power, in Party work and by study in Party training centers, are not as likely as are the non-Party masses or the relatively unpolitical intelligentsia, Russian or non-Russian, to be influenced by 'survivals of the past' in the form of religious and national sentiments.[43] Some of the ablest Western students of Soviet affairs and many well-informed Soviet refugees believe, however, that a kind of 'nationality frustration' is still an important factor in Soviet politics.[44]

Both politically and economically, Soviet 'republics' enjoy far less self-rule than an American state or a city such as New York. Even a critical examination of the Soviet constitution, with little reference to the real sources of power in the Party-police mechanism underlying the constitutional facade, reveals that this is the case. On the basis of examination of articles 14 and 19 of the Soviet constitution, K. C. Wheare, the leading authority on federalism, correctly, but with extreme restraint, concludes that the Soviet government is 'highly centralized,' and cannot be regarded as federal.[45]

Budgetary practice reflects extreme centralism. Not only the invariably unanimous vote on the All-Union budget, indicating the purely ceremonial character of Soviet 'legislation,' but the fact that the federal budget constitutes about 80 per cent of the total national revenue, confirm this conclusion. Moreover, the central government not only fixes the total sum allotted to the republic budgets, but also prescribes the distribution of expenditures among various republic activities. This pattern leads one student to observe correctly that 'The Soviet system does not offer economic nationalism to its constituent units.' [46]

The foregoing conveys only a feeble sense of the Kremlin's arbitrary and detailed intervention in local affairs. Until 1949 one of the best sources of information on this subject was the periodical which publishes official decrees of the Soviet Government, but this has now been denied to foreigners. A search through issues for the late 1930's revealed that the central government ordered the republics to grow fixed areas of crops, and even fixed the numbers and kinds of livestock allotted to each region. The central government also expands or contracts the area, fixes the boundaries, and determines the names of nationality and other local administrative units.[47]

Special Moscow controls supplement the 'normal' functioning of the centralized Party-state mechanism described earlier. Attentive readers of the daily press are aware that the Party Presidium member P. K. Ponomarenko was, in 1954, made head for a time of the Party organization of Kazakhstan and that Semen Ignatev, recovering in part from the eclipse into which he fell in connection with his dismissal by Beria from the post of Minister of State Security in April 1953, became head of the Party organization in Bashkiria.

Not so well known is the way in which men like Ignatev act as Moscow's watchdogs over local Party organizations. For some years, in the late 1940's and early 1950's, Ignatev was Moscow representative to the Central Committee of the Communist Party of Uzbekistan. Under his eye worked the First Secretary, the Kazakh, Niyazov, and the Second Secretary, Melnikov, judging by his name a Russian, like Ignatev.[48] Earlier, in the 1930's, Ignatev had supervised the deportation of Koreans from the Soviet Far East. [49]

Revealing data on the machinery of the continuous Soviet cultural purges in the non-Russian republics may be gleaned from the press. According to a report in the Russian-language newspaper *Soviet Latvia,* for 6 January 1952, Kalnberzin, one of the Latvian Party secretaries, expressed gratitude to the Moscow Central Committee for sending to Latvia a 'brigade' of Party experts who unearthed 'defects' in Latvian educational, scientific, and propaganda work.

Kazakhstanskaya Pravda for 16 December 1951 reported a speech by Shayakhmetov, head of a section of the Kazakh Party Central Committee, on problems of Marxist-Leninist training, the work of the Kazakh section of the Institute for the History of the Communist Party, and kindred topics. The tone of the speech is indicated by the fact that Shayakhmetov began most of its sections with the assertion that Kazakhstan was 'carrying out the historic decisions' of the Central Committee.

The Party-state machine defines and checks on the policies of non-Russian political, educational, artistic, literary, and communications organizations. The Party organizations, at each territorial level and within each functional group, are the heart and brain of this system. It is the duty of these bodies to guide and manipulate the local governmental, public, and professional organizations so as to fulfill the directives of the Central Committee. Thus the Party Presidium with the aid of Central Committee experts, drafts a policy on the teaching of Russian, for example, and it, or a top leader such as Zhdanov, Stalin, or Khruschchev, may announce the policy. The mechanism of central scientific bodies such as the Academy of Sciences, and of their local branches, as well as of the new USSR Ministry of Culture, may be utilized to promulgate and disseminate the new doctrine. Down it goes via the republic, oblast, city, rayon,[50] and finally village, Party and Komsomal channels, to the teachers in every schoolroom in the land.

Into this machine of exhortation, indoctrination, and instruction the demands, images, and symbols of Soviet revolutionary Russification have been poured for some twenty years, with vastly increased pressure since 1945. Language, literature, folklore, and songs have received a heavy Russian injection.[51]

A few examples may serve to illustrate the penetration achieved by this program. A directive of 7 May 1947, of the All-Union Central Council of Trade Unions, whose 30-odd million members include almost all Soviet industrial, clerical, and even professional workers, ordered that all trade-union libraries feature material on 'the revolutionary traditions of the Bolshevik Party and the patriotism and heroism of the Russian people.'[52] In this way trade-union libraries could play their part in implementing the Central Committee decisions on ideological work.[53]

The Program for Pre-Mobilization Training for pupils, including girls, of the eighth, ninth, and tenth classes of secondary schools featured, in its section on 'Readings and Lectures on the Red Army,' outlines for talks on the military art of Suvorov, on Kutuzov, the Crimean War, the defense of Port Arthur, and the 'military heritage of the Russian people.'[54] Similarly, the

Bibliography of Soviet Bibliography, 1939, contained a host of items on the benefits to the Ukraine and Belorussia of 'adherence' to Russia, and on the past wars and present glory of Russia.[55]

Such guides and materials are used by the political workers and agitators in the Soviet armed forces, whose personnel are required to listen to daily talks on 'current events' and to 'political chats' and lectures. The army, the trade-unions, and agitators in factories and on farms thus continue the work begun in the schools. The propaganda of assimilation is thus brought down to the small group level where it can achieve the maximum effect.

The description of results and methods of Soviet revolutionary Russification given in this chapter will have served its purpose if it sheds light on the special characteristics, strengths, and weaknesses of the Soviet Russian pattern of cultural assimilation. The mistake which most Americans, and perhaps also most citizens of other 'great' Western countries are likely to make in this area is to lump all of the population of the Soviet Union under the heading of 'Russians.' The Soviet leadership does not make this mistake. It presses for homogeneity, but with a shrewd eye on the cultural diversity with which it must contend. If the non-Soviet world is to match the Kremlin's awareness of the cultural facts of life on the level of practical politics, a great deal of research and analysis remains to be done.[56]

Another extreme is to believe that a program of 'Balkanization' could gain support among the peoples of the Soviet Union. Family solidarity, memories of cataclysmic events and negative reactions to policies which seem to members of non-Russian groups to threaten ethnic survival can delay and in some ways defeat the assimilationist efforts of the Kremlin. But the common experience, if you will, the common misfortune, of Soviet life works constantly to create a common Soviet consciousness. This does not mean that the Kremlin will ever be successful in creating the 'new Soviet man.'

It does, however, probably mean that much of the pattern of Soviet Russian culture, particularly in science and technology, has been incorporated into the thinking of most Soviet people, Russian and non-Russian alike. Ability to communicate effectively with the peoples under Kremlin control will not be facilitated by archaic concepts.[57] A balanced approach must be sensitive to the non-Russian, the Great Russian, and the new, Marxist-Leninist-Stalinist elements in the total pattern of sentiments of the Soviet population.

Traditional and Revolutionary Factors
in Soviet Russian Nationalism

The term 'traditional' here refers to pre-Soviet Russian ideas, symbols, customs, and other elements of Great Russian culture which persist under the Soviet regime. By 'revolutionary' we mean symbols, attitudes, and institutions created by the Bolsheviks. We are concerned with significant Russian cultural traits incorporated into the Soviet pattern or exploited by the regime.

It should be emphasized again that in our view Soviet Russian nationalism is not a mere continuation of the Tsarist tradition which it exploits. We are skeptical regarding extreme 'psycho-cultural' interpretations which tend to derive Bolshevism mainly from 'Russian national character.' Apart from the prominence of non-Russians in the Bolshevik revolution and in building the Soviet state, we are impressed by the fact that Soviet totalitarianism is to a greater degree the product of the Stalinist economic program begun in 1928–9 than it is of the pre-revolutionary culture pattern or of the 'Russian' personality of Lenin.

A major component of the pre-revolutionary political-cultural pattern was the Byzantine-Russian absolutist heritage, which Thomas G. Masaryk called 'Caesaropopism,' and which as a ruling system finally collapsed in 1917. A second major element was the revolutionary-utopian current represented by eighteenth- and nineteenth-century radical intellectuals and culminating in Lenin, aptly characterized by Waldemar Gurian as 'the product and nemesis of the Russian radical intelligentsia.' Finally, there was a liberal-constitutionalist trend, weaker than the other two though growing in strength in the last decades of imperial Russia, brilliantly represented by Paul Milyukov.[1]

The first tradition furnished the model for many of the techniques of Soviet totalitarianism. The second supplied Bolshevik faith in science, organization, and the possibility of transforming the whole world into a 'socialist' and eventually a 'communist' paradise by scientific planning and organization. The third has survived precariously—to a limited degree and under frequent attacks—in the 'cosmopolitanism' of some Soviet intellectuals.

Other elements of traditional Russian culture have retained sufficient relevance to deserve mention. One is the primitive anarchism of Russians of humble rank, manifested sometimes in apathy, evasiveness, or passive resistance, occasionally in flight, rarely, though explosively, in outbursts of resistance to authority. Another is the tender, lyrical, and 'feminine' aspect of the Russian character, seemingly incompatible with its more brutal aspects, yet still alive. It is expressed, among other ways, in the Russian tradition of great freedom of expression of personal feelings and a more tolerant attitude toward personal weaknesses than is permitted by Western, particularly Anglo-Saxon, culture. These qualities are sometimes referred to by the vague and unsatisfactory expression 'the Russian soul.'

Perhaps an even older aspect of the Russian tradition, a wild pagan naturalism, should also be mentioned. It is of course easy to get lost, as Germans sometimes have, in vague discourses on the Russians as '*Naturmenschen.*' Yet unusual vitality and simplicity are striking Russian characteristics. These perhaps reflect effects of the biological struggle for survival under unusually severe conditions, and Russia's isolation from the relatively sophisticated cultures of East and West.

Fedotov stressed in Russian paganism veneration of nature and the 'dionysiac,' or 'orgiastic,' element. The Russian 'wild debauch of popular feasts' has been described by travelers and by natives from the thirteenth century to our own times. Fedotov noted that the 'orgiastic' element had surged to the surface 'every time a political or cultural outburst freed the chained chaos of the Russian soul.'

With regard to the Russian cult of nature, Fedotov wrote that

'Russia, taking over Byzantine Cosmology, imparted to it warmth, spontaneity, and even poignancy which went far beyond the Western medieval sense of nature.' [2]

Again, Fedotov here seems to have put his finger on a persistent Russian trait, which is undoubtedly a factor in the primitive patriotism, devoid of full-fledged 'state consciousness,' of the Great Russian peasants even in our time. Unusually intense attachment to the native soil has been attributed to the Russians by most students. The Polish scholar K. Waliszewski suggested in this connection that the Russian's life is so lacking in happiness, that he 'has been constrained to idealize the object of his love.' [3]

Love for immediately known hearth and haunts, for land and landscape, expressed with a freedom not permitted by our more reticent culture, is a vital ingredient of Great Russian culture. Edward Crankshaw tells of a conversation with a Soviet woman who bitterly hated the Soviet order but told him she would nevertheless not leave Russia, even if she could. Asked why, she replied 'But how could I leave the birch trees?' [4]

During World War II when restraint on expression of personal feeling in print was partially relaxed, patriotic poetry featured such themes as the Russian snow-covered fields, the Russian pine, fir, and birch. *Leningrad*, the literary magazine banned in 1946 for its alleged ideological mistakes, featured the Russian fighting man, and the Russian landscape.

The Bolsheviks have sought to make all Russians disciplined citizens, to exploit Russian idealism, and to equip 'Soviet man,' their somewhat mythical construction, with an idealized version of the cunning of the Muscovite who outwitted or out-fought Tatar, Turk, and Pole.

The attribution, whether 'spontaneously' or by deliberate official policy, of national characteristics to a wide range of objects and symbols not necessarily or primarily national in origin or relevance is a major characteristic of modern nationalism. Thus, we speak of 'American know how,' 'the American girl,' and, in more general terms, of 'the American way.' Recently universities have inaugurated programs of 'American studies.' This 'nationalization' or 'politicalization' of social symbols is more highly developed in the Soviet Union than in 'liberal' societies. A flood of books on Russian folklore, art, literature, science, geographic exploration, and technology poured from Soviet presses after 1934.[5]

These works, however, usually interpreted cultural elements out of context and often in a manner alien to the spirit of their originators. Russian traditions and achievements became evidence of the merits of Soviet policy. As the preface to an excellent work on Russian wooden architecture pointed out, the study contributed to the 'world reputation of Russian culture.' This neopatriotic literature often expressed a narrowly ethnocentric point of view regarding the uses of culture and the social roles of its creators. One work, for example, quoted a Russian scientist as saying: 'I am a Russian and it is only to my motherland that I have the right to give my knowledge, toil and achievements.'[6]

Because of an unusually high degree of manipulative use of old forms with a new content, Soviet Russian patriotism often appears to have an 'artificial' character.[7] A leadership group, however, which on the conscious level may be highly rationalistic and manipulative, may at the same time unconsciously cling to historically determined attitudes of which they are not fully aware. Eventually their formal doctrine can relapse into a pattern of rationalization for actions determined by factors not consistent with their ideology.

Perhaps for this reason those who emphasize unconscious and irrational factors in politics are inclined to stress the elements of continuity between old and new Russia. For quite different reasons some members of nationalities such as Poles or Ukrainians who have suffered at the hands of Russians tend to regard Soviet terminology as a mere cloak for traditional Russian imperialism. Such a view can be confusing because it may obscure our view of the totalitarian innovations of Soviet policy.

Another difficult problem is the relationship between 'official' and 'popular' elements in Russian and Soviet thought. A fact, which is often overlooked, is that while there was a flourishing unofficial intellectual life in pre-revolutionary Russia as far back as the early nineteenth or even the late eighteenth century, nothing comparable has existed in Russia since the consolidation of Soviet power about 1930. Although, as Alexander Herzen expressed it, the history of Russian literature in the first half of the nineteenth century was a 'martyrology,' the light of the spirit glowed even in the darkest periods of nineteenth-century Russia. In the Soviet period, there has been a massive development of rigidly patterned official doctrines but we cannot do much more than intelligently guess about the content of non-official thought.

Among the oversimplifications by which the study of Soviet thought is plagued is the belief that there is an absolute antithesis between official and non-official sentiments. It is more sensible to assume that official and unofficial beliefs, especially in a totalitarian society, are always somewhat at variance, but that the gap between them narrows and widens with changes in official policy and shifts in foreign and domestic situations.

Some elements of traditional culture such as religion have been and still are so tenacious that the regime has been forced to compromise with them, although it has often employed strenuous and even sanguinary measures to destroy them. In the case of religion, the regime embarked on a new campaign of vigorous but non-violent 'enlightenment' in the summer of 1954.[8] As John Shelton Curtiss brings out, however, in the last chapter of his definitive study, *The Russian Church and the Soviet State*,[9] ideological opposition to religion and the Russian church, although at times restrained, has always remained a constant element.[10]

In times of crisis, when the regime has desperately needed popular support, it has made concessions to traditional values and beliefs. When, as has been true since the end of the Korean War, international tension has been somewhat eased, the regime has tended to move forward more rapidly toward revolutionary goals. Tentatively, it might be said that traditional beliefs, including traditional nationalistic attitudes, religion, and other still widely popular survivals of the pre-revolutionary past, benefit from a relaxation of official anti-traditional policies during periods when the regime feels menaced by threats, particularly external threats. This statement applies primarily to Soviet domestic policy. Abroad, quite different factors may operate. For example, 'internationalism' in current Soviet foreign propaganda may represent a concession to Chinese nationalism.

It must of course be borne in mind that the Soviet population, like that of any other modern industrial society, is not homogeneous. At the risk of some oversimplification, it can be stated that elite elements tend more to support the regime and its revolutionary policies than do the worker and peasant masses. Traditional patriotism, a simple, inarticulate and not very intense ethnocentrism, and religion, are certainly strongest among the peasants, particularly among persons of advanced age. On the other hand, these attitudes are probably weaker among the skilled factory workers who are, nevertheless, among the elements most critical of official policy. These elements, the most 'proletarian' of Soviet society, tend more than others to be disillusioned about the degree to which the Soviet leaders live up to their Marxist ideals.

By far the most complex stratum of Soviet society is the intelligentsia. This is, I believe, reflected in its attitude toward revolutionary and traditional elements in Soviet culture. As a part of the privileged class, the intelligentsia is less anti-regime in its attitudes than the workers and peasants. On the other hand, it probably shares with the peasantry a high degree of attachment to many traditional Russian attitudes, values, and customs. To a considerable extent, this attachment is to Russian traditional habits of speech, personal relations, dress, food, drink and traditional customs with regard to marriage, birth, death, and the other major events of individual life. Ancient Russian units of measurement, such as the pood, are still used. And even in 1956 returning travelers were still reporting that the abacus was used to reckon sums in Moscow shops.

The Party has succeeded in wholly or partially eliminating some Russian customs. In some cases, substitutes have been offered, as in the case of 'New Year's trees' substituted for Christmas trees, and in the substitution of the legendary Russian 'Father Frost' for 'Santa Claus.'

It seems probable that, especially in the rural districts, inherited patterns of life and custom, as distinct from technological, administrative, political, and overt ideological factors, have remained largely intact under the Soviet regime. In fact, Soviet Russia is, in this respect, far more conservative than the United

States. Peasant cottages have the same external appearance as they had a hundred years ago. They also provide an almost equally miserable standard of housing; the average peasant family lives in less than two rooms, which usually do not have glass windows. Clothing changes much more slowly and displays much less variety than in the United States or Western Europe.

Eating and drinking habits, especially the latter, with the well-known profusion of toasts, seem to be identical with those of Gogol's time. Many traditions that the Kremlin has felt were not dangerous have been officially approved. Contemporary Soviet architecture is heavily influenced by the Russian eighteenth-century aristocratic style. Workers' clubs are designed like noblemen's palaces or eighteenth-century government buildings.[11]

At the same time, the regime encourages return to a still more distant past in erecting on one of the main squares of Moscow a huge statue of Yuri Dolgoruki, the legendary founder of Moscow. This official cult of the archaic is intended to strengthen Soviet national pride and to heighten the population's sense of distinctness and difference from the 'capitalist,' and non-Russian, world.

Probably the social elements most critical of this type of traditionalism are the factory workers, particularly the skilled workers, and the convinced Marxists among the Party members. This conclusion is suggested by my experience in the Soviet Union. Concessions to religion and the revival of military epaulettes and decorations aroused the suspicion or scorn of some of my Soviet acquaintances who were Party or Komsomol members. Some of them were particularly scornful of Stalin's assumption of the title of Generalissimo, which elicited ironic comparisons with Franco and Chiang-Kai-Shek. It is interesting in this connection that the post-Stalin regime, which in some ways is returning to Leninist doctrine or at least seeks to create such an impression, reversed the post-war trend toward equipping the Soviet civil service with uniforms.[12]

The Soviet intelligentsia, particularly its non-Party segments, is probably not hostile and may even be strongly favorable to retention of Russian traditions which emphasize the importance of rank, status, and national service. In these respects the attitude of the intelligentsia may be closer to that of the peasantry than to that of the urban working class. At the same time, among some elements of the Soviet intelligentsia some of the attitudes of the old pre-revolutionary Russian radical intelligentsia seem to survive. In sharp distinction to the somewhat 'dionysiac' and 'orgiastic' culture of the peasants, the mentality of the pre-revolutionary radical intelligentsia was guilt-ridden and ascetic. It was also anti-capitalist, socialist, materialist, and 'populist.' Its central conviction was that the educated classes were under obligation to dedicate themselves to overcoming the backwardness of Russia in order to pay their debt to the long-suffering people.[13]

Let us now proceed to a brief comparative survey of Russian and Soviet ethnocentrism. Our purpose is to identify elements of the traditional Russian self-image and the concomitant image of foreigners which helped to shape the Soviet mentality and provided patterns for the Kremlin to exploit in the interests of Soviet power.

William Graham Sumner's theory of 'ethnocentrism,' like Karl Mannheim's concept of 'ideology,' was highly relativistic. It emphasized the inability of a social group to perceive reality except in terms of its own experience and of its own selfish interests.[14] Although relativistic in emphasizing group-boundedness, Sumner's theory was absolute in asserting that all groups had the same kinds of sentiments about themselves and other groups. According to Sumner, ethnocentrism is the view of things in which one's own group is the center of everything, and all others are scaled and rated with reference to it. Sumner, incidentally, wrote that in Russian books and newspapers 'The civilizing mission of Russia is talked about just as in the books and journals of France, Germany, and the United States, the civilizing mission of those countries is assumed and referred to as well understood. Each state now regards itself as the leader of civilization, the best, the freest, and the wisest, and all others as inferior.'[15]

The value of this concept is that it helps us to overcome the attitude that it describes, and thus facilitates international understanding. It applies not only to national sentiments but to class and other group sentiments. Certainly leaders of class movements, such as Marx or Lenin, can be better understood with the aid of Sumner's concept. The relativistic approach, to which Sumner's concept was an important contribution, may also have serious defects. It is arguable that the ethnocentrism of some leadership groups is more intense and perhaps qualitatively different from that of other regimes. Historical experience, particularly war, contact or lack of contact with other peoples, and political institutions, are among the factors that seem to affect the patterns of attitudes of any given people toward foreign peoples.

Russian conditions fostered the development of unusually intense negative attitudes toward foreign states. Subsequent to the Bolshevik revolution, conditions which generate extreme fear, hostility, and suspicion of the outside world have grown even stronger than they were in pre-revolutionary Russia.

Since the reign of Peter the Great Russia had been moving from extreme isolation and despotism toward a closer relationship with the world of constitutional governments.[16] Incomplete as this process was by 1914, it had brought a growing community of interests, concepts, values, and tastes between Russia and the West. By reversing this trend, Bolshevism plunged Russia, in some ways, back into the pre-Petrine period. The post-1917 contrast of institutions, and opposition of interests, between Russia and the West has been accompanied by the well-known ideological schism.

With the full development of Soviet totalitarianism came a revival of interest in the Muscovite period of Russian history. In many ways the foreign relations and the internal situation of Stalinist Russia resembled those of the Russia of Ivan the Terrible.[17] Certainly Stalin himself must have felt that this was the case, for otherwise he would not have encouraged the veritable cult of Ivan the Terrible which flourished during his regime. Probably as a reflection of the post-Stalin emphasis upon the 'role of the people as the creators of history,' and the accompanying playing down of the cult of personalities, there has been some criticism of this emphasis upon Ivan the Terrible, Peter the Great, and other outstanding individuals.[18]

This does not signify, however, any fundamental revision of the peculiarly exclusive Russian nationalism characteristic of the

Soviet regime. One of the leading Soviet learned journals reported in March 1954 that problems of the formation of the Russian nationality and the Russian nation are at the 'center of attention' of Soviet scholarship. In 1955 Moscow University and the Soviet Academy of Sciences called a conference to plan a study aid for universities on 'the history of Soviet society,' at which the concepts of the uniqueness of 'Soviet culture' and the role of the Russian people in 'overcoming the economic and cultural backwardness of other peoples' of the Soviet Union were stressed.[19]

Our survey of the roots of Russian and Soviet ethnocentrism must consider military-political, religious-cultural, and social-economic factors. Influencing all of these was an unfavorable geographic environment which made the struggle for individual and national existence unusually severe.[20]

Largely because of disadvantages involved in the location of the Russian people on the Eurasian plain, the official image of the foreigner as a cunning and implacable enemy has bulked unusually large in the Russian political mind. The immensity of the plain, its vast resources, and its proximity to so much of Europe and Asia contained the promise of power, but poverty and lack of defensible frontiers tended to make military strength and political centralism necessary for national independence. Although biased, perhaps partly because it was written during the Crimean war, Thomas Henry Buckle's appraisal of Russian civilization contained elements of truth. According to Buckle, in Russia all ability 'is estimated by a military standard,' and 'to win a battle or outwit an enemy, is valued as one of the noblest achievements of life, and civilians, whatever their merits, are despised by this barbarous people, as beings of an altogether inferior and subordinate character.[21] Buckle's anti-Russian prejudice was balanced by his characterization of Turkey, the ally of his own country, as 'barbarous,' and 'uncivilized.'

Among Russian intellectuals, only a few extremists fully shared Buckle's negative appraisal of Russian civilization. Many passages in the writings of nineteenth-century Russian thinkers, however, stressed the role of the military factor in awakening and forming Russian national consciousness and in debasing Russian civilization. Alexander Herzen wrote that the true history of Russia began only with the war of 1812.[22] It is interesting that while stressing the military nature of Russian civilization, Herzen unfavorably contrasted the Great Russians with the more liberty-loving Ukrainians, who, he said, have been submerged under the Russian 'glacier' which brought with it the 'enslavement of the ice age.' [23] The Russian anarchist Bakunin summed up the hatred of many nineteenth-century Russian radicals for the militaristic Tsarist regime in his expression 'the knouto-Germanic empire.'

Many Russian intellectuals, to be sure, regarded militarism and bureaucracy as foreign importations imposed upon the Russian people as a result of Tatar and Prussian influences. However, while they hated the Tsarist regime and its ideology of 'official nationality' many, probably most, pre-revolutionary intellectuals shared with other elements in the population the fanatical patriotism which was in large part the product of Russia's many wars. Traditional Russian images of foreigners in general, and of particular foreign nations, took form as the result of wars for national survival. One indication of the strength of such traditions is the fact that the Soviet government fought the war against Nazi Germany in 1941–5 as the 'Fatherland War,' the term applied since 1812 to the war of that year against Napoleonic France.

Russian national consciousness, based upon the need to unite in the face of external danger extends to some degree even as far back as the eleventh century. As Sergius Yakobson puts it, 'the geographical environment, the life between Europe and Asia in the Eastern European plain in constant direct contact with peoples of strange blood and culture, the incessant danger of being overthrown by Asiatic nomads, demanded the emergence and development of these first elements of a national consciousness.' [24]

In 1946 a Soviet Russian scholar, G. Samarin, published a very interesting book entitled *The Patriotic Theme in the Choral Art of the Russian People*,[25] one of many works of Soviet scholarship which, although they exaggerate, are nevertheless correct in emphasizing the wealth of reflections in Russian culture of defensive reactions against foreign threats. Among the most interesting parts of Samarin's book are those dealing with the ancient Russian Byliny, or sagas, bringing out the vivid imagery in which descriptions of Russian warriors and their heroic feats were expressed. The publication of Samarin's work, as well as the profusion of patriotic folk songs and Soviet war songs, incidentally furnishes interesting confirmation of the theory set forth by Robert Michels on the high degree of significance for nationalism of popular songs.[26]

Russian patriotism, in terms of popular support of the Tsarist government, was gradually weakening during the last sixty or seventy years of the empire. Social tensions and the revolutionary movement sapped popular support for official nationalism. Nevertheless despite the inefficiency of the Tsarist regime, and the poor showing made by Russian generals in the Russo-Japanese war and the First World War, Russian soldiers and officers continued to fight with great bravery and loyalty.[27] Especially among the upper classes, the medieval Russian psychology of encirclement was gradually dying out in the last hundred years of the empire. It is interesting to note, however, that the greatest of Russian historians, V. O. Klyuchevski, concluded the first chapter of his famous *Course in Russian History,* written before World War I, with a statement comparing the hardships faced by the Russians, in their medieval struggle with the steppe nomads, with the much more advantageous situation of the peoples of Western Europe.

Internal unity and political centralism are natural answers to external dangers. The Russian mind early developed an image of the ruler as first soldier of the land and as defender of national political unity, if need be by the sternest measures. Nikolai Chernyshevski, the most influential of Russian nineteenth-century pre-Marxist revolutionaries, summed up the Russian tendency to political unity very well when he wrote, in 1856, that 'among us the consciousness of national unity has always had a decisive preponderance over provincial strivings.' People of various provinces, said Chernyshevski, knew only one thing: that they were Russians.[28]

Chernyshevski foreshadowed much of Soviet propaganda of 1941–5, when he wrote that 'the Russian people and the Russian armies, and not only cold and hunger, defeated the French in 1812.' [29] In terms of national power, absolutism and autocracy certainly paid dividends, both in medieval Russia and in Soviet Russia, although to the detriment of other values. It is well to remember that Muscovy was a far weaker power than Poland in the sixteenth or even in the first half of the seventeenth century. And well into the second half of the seventeenth century the Muscovite state suffered from devastating Tatar raids.[30]

The militarized Russian state developed methods of government and diplomacy which became tenacious traits of the Russian cultural heritage. Many students of history are familiar with the brilliant although somewhat one-sided account of some of these methods in their nineteenth-century form in by far the most influential travel book on Russia ever published, the Marquis de Custine's famous work, *La Russie en 1839*. Custine wrote 'here in Russia friendship itself partakes of police surveillance. How is a man to feel at ease with people so circumspect, so discreet in whatever concerns themselves and so inquisitive in what concerns others?' And he added 'this Byzantine government and indeed all Russia, have always looked upon the diplomatic corps and Westerners in general as envious and malevolent spies.' [31]

As late as 1930, before the Soviet regime had fully embarked on its program of openly encouraging extreme nationalism and xenophobia, a Russian translation of Custine's book was published in Moscow. Its uncompromising criticism of Russian despotism aroused the bitter hostility of nineteenth-century Russian nationalists, but liberals such as Herzen considered it the best description of the regime of Nicholas I. Valuable material on the political mentality which shocked and terrified Custine is available in the works of Russian and non-Russian historians.[32]

Suspicion of foreigners and foreign influences was inherent in Tsarist despotism. This system was modified by the great reforms of the 1860's during the reign of Alexander II and still more as a result of the concessions forced upon Tsar Nicholas II by the revolution of 1905. Yet Russia on the eve of World War I was still, in comparison with Western Europe and the United States, a despotic country. Symbolic of the distance which still separated the Russian political system from the constitutional regimes of the West is the often noted fact that in 1914 an American or European traveler could proceed freely to any country without a visa, except to Russia and Turkey. Another notorious feature of this pattern was the internal passport system, one of the targets of Lenin's criticism, but which the Soviet government, beginning in 1932, restored.

This was a political order in which the normal operation of law was often capriciously suspended by arbitrary action of the government, in which Jews, unless they were influential, were required to live within a pale stipulated by the government and in which as late as 1913 the Duma [33] debated the government policy of permitting only politically safe students to study abroad.[34] But, the 'despotism tempered by inefficiency' of old Russia was being gradually dissolved by the growing forces of foreign trade and contacts, and by capitalism and liberalism. There is a sharp contrast between a Russia in which it was a commendation to say of somebody that 'he is a European' and in which America was synonymous with liberty and progress, and the Soviet Union, in which 'European' and, to a still greater degree, 'American' civilization are depicted in official sources of information as decadent, putrid, and malevolent.[35]

Muscovite statecraft, particularly in its methods for conducting foreign relations, has never been described more brilliantly than by Vasily Osipovich Klyuchevski, Russia's great historian, in his *Accounts by Foreigners Concerning the Muscovite State*. Since this Muscovite system for dealing with foreigners, and its accompanying attitudes, seems to have been taken over in its essentials by the Soviet regime, it will be worth our while to devote several pages to summarizing Klyuchevski's description.[36] Russia attracted foreign attention only after about 1450 when she began to consolidate internally and to expand rapidly. Many of the visitors during the period covered by Klyuchevski, from the fifteenth through the seventeenth centuries, were impressed by the tendency of Russians to think and act communally, in groups or crowds. Most foreigners were depressed and awed by the long and dangerous journey to Moscow, which had to be made through primeval forests and treacherous swamps often infested by robber bands.[37]

From the moment a foreign ambassador crossed the border of the Muscovite state, he was under vigilant surveillance and was required to comply with the most elaborate and exacting protocol. For example, every effort was made to force the foreign diplomat to remove his hat first and put his hat back on first when he met the agent of the Tsar who had been sent to meet him at a point quite far from the capital. The Tsar provided for the subsistence and transportation of the foreign envoy, but the horses were frequently stolen and the food was so highly seasoned with garlic, pepper, and vinegar that foreign envoys often had difficulty in deriving any nourishment from it. One such envoy, Herberstein, became on one occasion so enraged that he threatened to crack the skull of the agent in charge of him if he did not permit him to purchase food from the local markets. An extremely interesting touch noted by Klyuchevski was the fact that by order of the Muscovite rulers, crowds dressed in their best clothes gathered along the roads traversed by foreign envoys in order to impress upon the latter the density and prosperity of the population.[38]

This indicates that the well-known Potemkin village technique was standard practice in Russian statecraft long before the reign of Catharine the Great. It has remained standard practice down to our own day. In fact so skilled are Soviet Russians in political stage management that they often succeed in concealing their intentions even from highly trained and experienced foreigners, or in creating impressions of either strength or of weakness quite out of line with reality, depending upon their purpose at a particular time. According to Eleanor Lipper, when Vice President Wallace in 1944 visited the town of Magadan, in an area in Siberia controlled by the secret police, in the economy of which slave labor played a preponderant role, he saw surprisingly fine, well-stocked shops, a theater, and other evidences of popular welfare. By such scene-shifting as removal of the prison watchtowers, the secret police had temporarily transformed the slave labor city into a model of cultured progress.[39]

Those who have read books by British and American diplomats and military and naval personnel who have been stationed in Soviet Russia will recognize many parallels.[40] In four years in the Soviet Union during which time I had the good fortune, in 1946, to make a journey to visit the American Consulate in Vladivostok,[41] where I spent three weeks, I had occasion to observe that in almost every way Soviet treatment of foreigners, on both the negative and positive sides, remained, in 1942–7, essentially true to the system described by Klyuchevski. In Vladivostok, for example, the American building in which I stayed was bathed at night in the brilliant illumination of a searchlight, so that the guard who sat across the street could report the movements of the Americans and of any Soviet citizens who might, in a spirit of foolhardy adventure or with treasonable intent, venture to enter the building. None did while I was there. It is perhaps too early to say whether or not the slight relaxation of surveillance over foreigners in Russia by the post-Stalin regime represents more than a minor change of decorations.

Klyuchevski's description of the conduct of negotiations by the Muscovite Russians is exceptionally interesting. He writes: 'The diplomatic methods of the Muscovite boyars often threw the foreign envoys into desperation, particularly those who wanted to carry on their business forthrightly and conscientiously.' He adds, 'in order not to fall into their nets it was not enough to make certain that they were lying; it was also necessary to decide what the purpose of the lie was; and what was one to do then? If someone caught them lying, they did not blush and they answered all reproaches with a laugh.' [43] There is a striking resemblance between these Muscovite diplomatic methods described by Klyuchevski and the prescription for conducting a case given by the lawyer in Gogol's *Dead Souls*. 'Tangle everything up, and that's all there is to it. Bring into the case other extraneous circumstances, side issues which may implicate other people in their turn; make the case complicated, and that is all.'

Karl Marx presented a more lurid, if less scholarly, picture of Russian diplomacy than Klyuchevski.[44] These methods, and many other aspects of old Russian political behavior, were continued by the Soviet regime. It is difficult to trace the process by which Bolshevism reclaimed parts of the Muscovite heritage. One way was by substitution of new external forms of belief and behavior for old, leaving content relatively unchanged.

We know from the abundance of complaints in the Soviet press over a period of many years that attitudes and practices carried over from the past have remained strong in many segments of the Soviet population. During the anti-religious drive in 1937, the Central Committee magazine *Bolshevik* published an article entitled 'Down with an easy-going attitude in anti-religious work,' in which it was asserted that many Communist Party members were still hanging ikons in their homes.[45] In the renewed anti-religious drive of the summer of 1954 similar charges were made.[46] Since Russian concepts of authority were closely associated with religion, one can surmise that while the Soviet regime has always fought against religion, the Party's ranks included many whose political attitudes had been shaped by pre-revolutionary models, in which authoritarian political concepts were legitimized by authoritarian religious images. Soviet political iconography was a substitute for its pre-Soviet religious equivalent.

A very important factor was the destruction or intimidation by the Bolsheviks of the sophisticated cosmopolitan elements of the population. Such elements, including some within the Party, had difficulty surviving in the turbulent Soviet situation. From the beginning the Party included many tough, gangsterish types; one factor in Stalin's rise was his ability to harness these tough operators to his purposes. But he had to reward them with power and prestige. Their mentality was more 'Muscovite' than 'European.' A 'European' outlook had, since the 1860's, been growing up in the universities, in business, especially those branches controlled by foreigners, in the bureaucracy, and in the zemstvos.[47]

The Party as a whole was very small. During the 1920's less than one Soviet citizen in a hundred belonged to it. As it recruited new members, particularly after the great industrialization drive which began in 1928, it was forced to enroll many who were unable to master Marxist doctrine. Doctrine was interpreted more and more crudely. Strict loyalty and unquestioning obedience were, in essence, all that were required of a Party member, provided he was energetic and efficient. One of the best descriptions of the modern Soviet leadership type was made by Fedotov: 'He is robust, physically and mentally; he . . . dislikes thought and doubt and appreciates practical knowledge and experience'; his characteristics 'are reminiscent of the ruling class of Muscovy in the XVI century.' [48]

Trotski in his posthumous biography of Stalin offers an explanation of the 'degeneration' of the Party, which sheds light on the covert survival of old Russian political attitudes. He argues that 'by 1923 the Party had been pretty diluted by the green and shallow marsh which was rapidly being molded into shape to play the role of snappy yes-men at a prod from the professionals of the machine.' [49] He adds that 'the army of the Soviet Thermidor was recruited essentially from the remnants of the former ruling parties and their ideological representatives. Members of the old classes were taken into the State machine and quite a few even into the Party.' [50]

Trotski also stresses that 'Stalin like many others, was molded by the environment and circumstances of the Civil War.' [51] In such factors Trotski perceived major elements of continuity between the old regime and the new. [52]

A recent writer questions whether Tsarist Russia was ever a 'capitalist state' in the Marxist sense. [53] But if Russia was not a capitalist country, it should not have had a 'proletarian' revolution. This, of course, was the point of view of Russian Mensheviks such as Martov—although Martov attempted for a time to collaborate with the Bolsheviks until he was eventually forced into emigration—and of Western European Socialists such as Kautsky and Bernstein. [54] The essence of the position of the Mensheviks and the non-communist Western European socialists was that the attempt to establish socialism in a country as backward as Russia would lead inevitably to a reactionary, nationalist regime based upon a kind of state capitalism. Bernstein gave expression to this attitude when he said 'in their lust for power they [the Bolsheviks] had barbarized Marx's evolutionary teachings; what is more they ignored Marx's economics in jumping to socialism in Russia, a country whose capitalist development was on a far lower level than that of any Western country.' [55]

The Soviet regime found itself in a somewhat paradoxical position with respect to the surviving remnants of the old intelligentsia. Because of the passions aroused by civil war, foreign intervention, and other factors, it regarded the 'bourgeois' intelligentsia with suspicion and bitterness. On the other hand, the economic and social backwardness of Russia made it necessary to use 'bourgeois' specialists to help, first to reconstruct, and then to expand the economy. A process occurred which is described as follows by an American sociologist in referring to surviving members of the pre-revolutionary intelligentsia.

Therefore, during this period, despite a relatively or even absolutely depressed standard of living, a lowered official, and to some extent unofficial evaluation of their status, and numerous legal obstacles which the regime placed in their way, these persons were able not only to hold their jobs but also to maintain the type of sociocultural environment in their homes and, perhaps, the informal occupational connections as well which gave their children advantages with regard to status aspirations that they themselves had had.[56]

As a result, many members of the old Russian intelligentsia, with its good and bad traits, characteristics, and attitudes, survived into the new regime.[57]

Concepts of extreme centralism and absolutism, although undergoing some modification in the last years of the empire, played an unusually large role in pre-revolutionary Russian thought. The Bolshevik regime intensified these characteristics. Opinions differ as to why this reversion occurred and as to the justification of the Soviet behavior which caused this ideological relapse. The conviction of Lenin and his followers that the 'capitalist' world must, because of the internal 'laws' governing it, seek to destroy the Soviet Union has in any case proven to be very tenacious.

There is similarity between the Soviet view that capitalism breeds aggression and the Western view that Soviet internal tensions force the Kremlin to focus internally generated aggression on foreign enemies.[58] No doubt both sides to a considerable extent project their own aggressive impulses on to external opponents. It seems clear, however, that a prosperous parliamentary democracy, with relatively free play of political competition and better conditions for the development of social science and the 'scientific spirit,' can avoid such violently irrational attitudes toward the outside world as tend to color the outlook of the leadership elements in a totalitarian state.

There are of course, both 'rational' and 'irrational' elements of great importance in Soviet thinking which have helped to enhance the role of military factors in Soviet society. Among the irrational factors are those generated by the long underground struggle of the Bolsheviks against heavy odds and the subsequent struggle of the Soviet regime for survival. These have been incorporated into Soviet thinking in the form of political maxims strewn throughout key works of Lenin and Stalin which Soviet leaders study in school and then re-study in special Party educational institutions. Thus they become steeped in them.[59]

But even if super-rationalists made policy in Moscow, London, and Washington, Russia and the Atlantic powers might well, given the present state system and the power of modern superweapons, fear and suspect one another. Certainly some features of Soviet policy make sense from a geo-political point of view when related to basic factors in modern international relations.[60]

The Soviet leadership has always been conscious of the domestic unpopularity of many of its policies. It has also tended to exaggerate foreign hostility. Soviet doctrine, reinforcing political absolutism and extreme concentration of authority, has acted to inhibit exchange of ideas with non-Bolshevik sources, as well as fundamental criticism at home of official dogma.

Hence the Soviet 'peace' propaganda. Where there is so much emphasis upon peace there must be some genuine fear of war. Of course in Soviet tactics, peace is a multipurpose weapon. By preparing for war, the Soviet leadership also creates a condition in which it can exploit the yearning of the peoples of the world for peace. Because of its control of communications, it can make certain that statements emanating from Soviet communications media uniformly praise peace and condemn war. Public saber rattling such as the Nazis indulged in, and such as occasionally embarrasses the leadership of democratic states when indulged in by distinguished military personalities, is strictly controlled. But making due allowance for the tactical manipulation of the peace theme, it is also plausible that the calls for relaxation of 'international tension,' and for the 'struggle for peace,' which year after year are among the most prominent themes in the May Day and 6 November slogans and in other Soviet key statements, also express fear of war on the part of the Soviet leadership.

This in turn has led to the pursuit of policies which aroused similar fears abroad. Caught in this vicious circle, Soviet culture became a more military culture than that of imperial Russia. This explains how a 'socialist' state can glorify generals like Suvorov, who not only served the Tsars, but crushed the revolutionary democratic movement of the Poles.[61]

The military-political factors which we have briefly surveyed are perhaps the most important foundations of Soviet nationalism. We can also perceive links, however, between pre-revolutionary religious, social, and economic concepts, and those of the Soviet period.[62] In some ways, it is paradoxical to seek a link between the Russian Orthodox religion and atheistic Soviet communism. However, one of the most original of Russian philosophers, Nicholas Berdyaev, sought to establish such a link in many works, of which *The Origin of Russian Communism* is the best known.[63] Berdyaev traced the fanaticism, single-mindedness, and intolerance of the Russian radical intelligentsia to equivalent traits of Russian Orthodox religious believers. Although he was anti-communist, Berdyaev admired the striving for social justice which he considered to be a link between Russian Orthodoxy and, through the nineteenth-century radical intelligentsia, Bolshevism.

In various ways, other interpreters of Russian Bolshevism have seen connections between it and certain features of Russian Orthodoxy. Paul Milyukov emphasized in Russian Orthodoxy ritualism and failure to understand the intellectual heritage of Christianity. He stressed especially the failure of Russians to develop the habit of critical comparison and analysis.[64] Rather similar to Milyukov's point of view on the social and intellectual significance of the Russian church was that of Thomas D. Masaryk in his two volume work *The Spirit of Russia*. Masaryk stressed the 'uncritical objectivism' of the Russians.

This he attributed in large part to the heritage of 'Caesaro-Papism.' Milyukov and Masaryk both stressed the tendency of Russians to 'mythical' thinking.[65]

These scholars, and others, too numerous to mention, who came to more or less similar conclusions, help us to understand some features of the Russian mentality which played a part in shaping and keeping alive absolutism of rulers and passivity of the ruled despite a fundamental revolution. In general, the pre-Soviet political Russian mentality, and to a considerable extent the Soviet mentality, too, might be characterized as 'pre-scientific.' Bertrand Russell, with a keenness of perception rare among Western intellectuals, was shocked in 1920 by Bolshevik political fanaticism. Commenting on it, he wrote, 'This habit of militant certainty about objectively doubtful matters, is one from which, since the renaissance, the world has been gradually emerging, into that temper of constructive and fruitful skepticism which constitutes the scientific outlook.[66]

The dogmatism of the Russian intelligentsia was, however, diminishing in the immediate pre-World War I years. A more cosmopolitan, sophisticated, and self-critical spirit was gaining strength. The only important radical group among whom the old dogmatism survived intact was Lenin's Bolsheviks. The Bolsheviks, too, underwent changes and suffered serious defections, including that of Plekhanov, who after close association with Lenin, broke away, devoted the last years of his life to the study of Russian intellectual history, and died a 'defensist.'[67] The trend toward greater liberalism and away from dogmatic radicalism is exemplified in two very interesting books published, respectively, in 1909 and 1910. In *Landmarks*, Berdyaev, Bulgakov, Peter Struve, and four other brilliant thinkers who had rejected Marxism, called for a return to religious, aesthetic, and spiritual values which had been anathema to earlier generations of the radical intelligentsia. Members of another group of the liberal intelligentsia, headed by Milyukov, criticized the views of the *Landmarks* group, in *The Intelligentsia in Russia*.[68]

Berdyaev considered the influence of men like Chernyshevski to have been very harmful. Because of it, the spiritual values contained in the works of Tolstoi and Dostoevski were ignored by Russian intellectuals. Berdyaev's statement regarding Dostoevski puts us on guard against the tendency of some scholars to regard him as representative of Russian thought. Marxism, according to Berdyaev, caused the Russian intelligentsia to 'put on a European costume,' but its underlying attitude remained unchanged. Berdyaev also observed that scientific positivism was accepted by the Russian intelligentsia in a highly perverse fashion.

The attitude of the Russian intelligentsia toward science was one of 'idol worship.' In the West, the spheres of science and religion were quite properly kept separate, but the Russian intelligentsia had no use for a scientist, or a scientific theory, unless the scientist and his theory were politically 'correct.' Berdyaev stated that 'under the concept of scientific spirit we always understood political progressiveness and social radicalism.' Consequently, Dostoevski and the great philosopher Vladimir Solovev were not read. They were regarded as 'reactionary.' [69]

Milyukov defended the Russian intelligentsia against the criticisms leveled by Berdyaev and his associates. The essence of Milyukov's position was that Russia was following in the footsteps of England, France, and other advanced countries. The characteristics of the intelligentsia described by Berdyaev reflected, in the opinion of Milyukov, Russian cultural immaturity. In earlier centuries, in Western countries also, the intelligentsia had lacked organic connections with society as a whole, and consequently tended to be sectarian and to feel frustrated.

Russia had entered this stage more recently. With emergence from it and the development of greater specialization and a more practical spirit, constitutionalism, liberalism, and a sense of law were developing. Legal and constitutional concepts were still poorly developed, however. Milyukov accused the *Landmarks* group of a futile attempt to return to the reactionary religious nationalism of the mid-nineteenth-century Slavophiles. [70]

An interesting point made by Milyukov was that nationalism in Russia was weak, because symbols of all kinds were not well defined among the Russians. [71] Criticizing what he considered to be the fatuous desire of the Berdyaev group to revive archaic Russian traditions, Milyukov asserted that political ideas of the pre-Petrine period had completely died out in the consciousness of the Russian people. Milyukov's opinion on this point suggests the hypothesis that Stalin's cult of Ivan the Terrible was a device for the glorification of the dictator in which he deliberately made use of the historians under his command.[72] The effective use made of 'archaic' traditions by Stalin indicates that Milyukov evaluation of their vitality was in error.

Let us turn now to a brief discussion of the connection between the heritage of pre-revolutionary and in particular, pre-Marxian, Russian social thought, and Soviet nationalism. Here we must stress the Russian heritage of anti-capitalism. Some scholars have even viewed Bolshevism as a form of Russian anti-capitalist nationalism.[73] There was widespread antipathy toward capitalism and 'bourgeois' civilization. This statement applies, of course, most fully to the Marxist parties and to other radical parties such as the Socialist-revolutionaries. But it applies also to conservatives and reactionaries. Even at the level of the imperial court and the highest military and bureaucratic circles there were, during World War I, anti-capitalist pro-German elements. This pro-Germanism may be regarded as in part at least an expression of the hostility felt in conservative circles against Russia's Western capitalist allies.

As was true of many of the other attitudes discussed in this chapter thus far, Russian anti-capitalism was probably declining before 1914. The middle class and the technical intelligentsia, although still relatively small, were growing, and these classes saw in the expansion of industry and commerce the path to a brighter future for Russia. Liberals of the Milyukov type gave ideological and political expression to the views and aspirations of these classes. Russian liberals included some of the ablest and, in the best sense, cosmopolitan, intellects of Europe.

On balance, however, most elements in Russian society even in 1914 were anti-capitalist and relatively indifferent to ideas of constitutional government. The middle class was weak, and Stolypin's 'wager on the strong,' the policy of attempting to build up a class of prosperous individual farmers by encouraging peasants to claim as individual property their shares of the village land communes, had not had time to produce substantial results.[74] Among the most important factors in this complex situation was the large role of foreign capital in some of the most important branches of Russian industry. The prominence of foreigners in the more advanced fields of industry aroused resentment not only among radicals, whose hatred of the native *bourgeoisie* was intensified by a tendency to regard it as a tool of foreign interests, but also among Russian engineers and technical men who often found foreigners difficult, and at the same time somewhat condescending, competitors.[75]

Since capitalism, constitutional government, and the sense of law were all relatively alien to Russia and in greater or lesser degree identified with things foreign, it was logical that those who wished to revolutionize Russia were hostile to these aspects of 'bourgeois' civilization. Russian radicals fought against the nobility because it was the ruling class, and against the middle class because it would introduce capitalism as the dominant factor in Russian life if it gained political power. But in different ways both the nobility and the middle classes were Europeanized. As early as 1836, Chaadaev wrote to Pushkin that 'only Russia's government is Western.' [76] This was something of an exaggeration even in 1836, and was much less true in the second half of the nineteenth century, but the statement does contain an element of truth that sheds light on the anti-European attitude of many Russians.

Discontented Russians identified themselves with the tendencies in European thought which rejected the dominant middle-class civilization.[77] Perhaps some of the Russian radicals felt that since the West had failed to follow the teachings of its own prophets, Russia fell heir to them. This is suggested by Herzen's and Chernyshevski's disillusionment with the West after the abortive revolutions of 1848, which deeply influenced the thinking of Lenin, who in turn was to suffer a similar emotional shock in 1914 when German and other Western European social democrats committed 'treason' by voting credits to support their governments in the 'imperialist' war.

Another significant feature of the Russian attitude toward foreigners which has continued into the Soviet period and which disturbs the Soviet regime deeply, is the tendency of many

Russians to be fascinated by foreign ways and ideas. On the basis of my own experience in Soviet Russia I am deeply convinced that foreigners, particularly Americans, seem more exotic, exciting, and interesting, and have much more power to exert influence as individuals upon the Soviet people than have Soviet people to influence individual Westerners, especially Americans.

In many cases, when Soviet citizens have come into personal contact with foreigners, particularly if the latter were relatively sympathetic, intelligent, and decent individuals, the foreigners have seemed to embody in their attitude and conduct values familiar to Russians from tradition and from their great literary classics, and professed but not practiced by their own government. Much has been written on this general subject and we cannot deal with it in detail here, although it is very important that we in the West should never lose sight of the fact that there are powerful submerged cravings among the Russian people, and the other peoples of the Soviet Union, for normal friendly personal relations with foreigners.[78]

Detailed comparison of pre-revolutionary and Soviet obstacles to international communications would require many pages, but an indication of intensification of anti-foreign practices by the Bolsheviks may be gained by comparing their policies with those in force during one of the most reactionary nineteenth-century reigns, that of Tsar Nicholas I. Despite the least liberal passport and visa regulations in Europe, dozens of Russians received permission to travel abroad, including the revolutionaries Bukunin and Herzen, the famous writer Gogol, and the radical critic Belinski. The great and unfortunate poet Pushkin was not allowed to go abroad, however, and was subjected to personal censorship by the Tsar. Some Russian travelers became acquainted with Karl Marx during the 'forties and exchanged many letters with him. Even during the West European revolutions of 1848, which frightened Nicholas into a paroxysm of increased repression, French newspapers lay on the tables of St. Petersburg cafes. Some 700,000 foreign books were imported into Russia in 1845. In 1849, a police search of St. Petersburg bookshops revealed the presence of 2,581 'forbidden' books in one store.[79]

In contrast, Soviet border guards search even high ranking Russian army officers returning home from abroad and confiscate such foreign publications as they may have in their luggage. While I was in Moscow, even during the period of the Anglo-Soviet-American 'coalition' one could search that city of some six million inhabitants—its exact population was and remains a military secret—in vain for any copies of the newspapers and magazines which Americans, Englishmen, or Frenchmen regard as necessities of life.[80] It is difficult to disagree seriously with the estimate of the effects of this system made by an able young British diplomat: 'The new Soviet Man sees the world through Lenin's eyes: He reads about the outside world in terms formulated by Lenin and this picture is (1) out of date; (2) constant; and (3) losing out to the living and the moving Soviet reality, to the insulated Russian context.' [81]

The only critical comment that I would make on Mr. Watson's statement is that this system of controls produces frustration as well as indoctrination, and curiosity as well as animosity. But, of course, to influence from the outside those who have been conditioned by this closed intellectual system it is necessary to establish communication with them, and that is precisely what the system is so carefully designed to prevent.

Russian history furnishes abundant evidence that susceptibility to foreign influence, the reverse side of Russian xenophobia, has very deep roots in the past. As far back as the sixteenth and seventeenth centuries, individual Russians such as Ordin-Nash-chokin, Kotoshikhin, and many others who had come under the influence of foreign ideas attempted to flee from their native land or in other ways to express their craving for an alternative to the stifling despotism of Russia.[82] The importance of foreign travel and political emigration for pre-Soviet Russians are well known. And defection from Soviet rule, including the greatest rate of military and civilian flight in time of war ever experienced by any modern nation, far exceeding anything comparable in the days of the Tsar, has been a conspicuous feature of international political life in our time.[83]

There is considerable evidence, even in Soviet sources, that continued Russian susceptibility to foreign influence, which has often led to sudden disillusionment with native political authority and ideology, is still very much alive. During the war and the early post-war years, the Soviet press contained tantalizingly cautious but telltale admissions that Soviet citizens in areas occupied by the Germans, or carried into captivity inside Germany, were often deeply impressed by German culture. *Komsomolskaya Pravda* for 9 December 1945 published an item by A. Tselikova entitled 'They have returned to their Fatherland,' noting that some Soviet girls who had come back from Germany wore trinkets and cheap bracelets, and arranged their hair in a peculiar way. They had, she said, been in Germany for such a long time that they had assumed some of the external aspects of the 'notorious' German 'culture.' The situation was being remedied, according to Tselikova, by Soviet agitators who explained the speciousness of German culture and the genuineness of Soviet culture.

Perhaps the most interesting item of this tenor was an article entitled 'On Poetry, on the Education of Youth and on Culture' by the outstanding Soviet poet, Pavel Antokolski, in the literary monthly *Znamya* for January 1947.[84]

Antokolski complained that many Soviet youths who had been in central Europe on military or other service idealized Western culture. They said 'What wonderful roads they have there! What bathrooms! bicycles! cameras! brushes!' He was indignant because 'the word "culture" is applied to face powder, cigarette lighters and stockings.'[85] Actually, Antokolski contended, Soviet people were much more cultured than the Germans, who knew Goethe's name but had never read his poems. Soviet life was often uncomfortable, but culture and education did not consist in the use of toothbrushes and in good table manners.

Too often, Western culture was only a superficial veneer. Real culture was the creation of values. The renaissance knew this, and so did Soviet society, which was creating new values and new cadres. Soviet people must not succumb to the deadly odor of false 'prosperity,' but must press on with the struggle to build a better life. One should not settle for such cheap satisfactions as fox trots and light opera.

Even the highest Soviet leaders, on several important occasions in the post-war period, felt constrained to express concern regarding the tendencies criticized by Antokolski. In his speech at the founding of the Cominform in September 1947 Georgi Malenkov had this to say: 'The agents of foreign intelligence services search diligently for soft spots among certain unstable strata of our intelligentsia, who bear the mark of the old lack of confidence in their own strength and suffer from the disease of kowtowing before everything foreign.' [86]

The continued existence of a consumers' goods shortage and the apparently very acute agricultural situation which has been the main preoccupation of the post-Stalin regime on the domestic front, are among factors which make one doubt whether the susceptibility of the Soviet peoples to foreign influences, in so far as it springs from material causes, has been fundamentally altered. Some of the regime's difficulties result also from the isolation of its citizens from foreign contacts, which makes them seem all the more interesting and even enticing. Discerning travelers are agreed that intense, to Western eyes almost abnormal, curiosity about foreign ways and wares are outstanding Russian traits. What foreigner has not had his shoes stared at or his clothing fingered? [87]

These tendencies would seem to reflect two main aspects of the Russian situation. The first is the fact that national consciousness, although it probably is stronger, at least among the elite elements, than it was before the revolution, is still relatively weak among the rank and file of the Soviet population. The second is that government is still, to a certain extent an 'alien' element in Russian culture. Many students of Russian history, including some of the greatest Russian historians, have stressed the fact that, to the Russians, government and state power were not 'organic' parts of the indigenous culture. There was a great gulf, which to a considerable extent still seems to persist, between 'state' and 'society.'

This writer observed in his contacts with Soviet people in four years of life in Moscow, a sharp contrast betwen the very 'personal' view of human relations taken traditionally by Russians and the cold, impersonal efficiency which is the ideal of the Soviet elite. This party ideal is formalized in the concept of the 'new Soviet man,' the model of behavior for Party and government officials, and even for Soviet people in general. A minority of authoritarian personality types who can easily conform to this official norm rise to the top in such a system and a tiny group of exceptionally ruthless and able men operate it, but to many, the shock of coming from the relatively warm and affectionate atmosphere of the Russian family into the harsh competition and regimentation of Soviet life leads to bitterness or to apathy.

Some Soviet refugees present a very pessimistic picture of the breaking down of what they consider to be the normal and traditional Russian family and its values under the pressure of Soviet agencies of indoctrination and personality formation. The highly 'personal' approach of the Russians to problems of government, however, and their tendency to what psychologists call 'affect' behavior, are among many indications that some of the basic and politically relevant attitudes and traits traditionally characteristic of Russians, and, indeed, of human beings in general, are still living forces in Soviet Russia.

What can be said about the comparative intensity, similarities, and dissimilarities, of Russian national consciousness before and since the Bolshevik revolution? Of course it is impossible to answer such questions with any degree of certainty. Even to begin to give 'scientific' answers it would be necessary to set up a large research project on comparative ethnocentrism, nationalism, and related topics, studying individual countries at different historical periods, and several countries at the same period.[88]

We need only to provide sufficient background for topics treated in subsequent chapters. With regard to the comparative strength of nationalism in pre-revolutionary and post-revolutionary Russia, available evidence points strongly to the conclusion that the 'internationalist' and 'socialist' Soviet Union is a much more nationalistic state, with far more ethnocentric attitudes, than was imperial Russia. This, however, does not mean that the mass of the Soviet population is necessarily more patriotic, or more hostile to foreigners, than were the masses in the Russian Empire. It is even possible that the Soviet 'lower classes' are more susceptible to foreign influence, and more opposed to, or at least more apathetic about the political authority which governs them, than their counterparts in imperial times. The explanation of this apparent paradox might be that nationalism, and, in particular, the sense of statehood [89] have been intensified in a small ruling segment of the Soviet population, while political indifference and apathy have increased among other segments, perhaps a majority of the people.

Let us return for a moment to the appraisal of Russian nationalism made by Milyukov in 1910. According to Milyukov, in Russia social differentiation and symbologies of all kinds, including 'national-historical' symbols, were very poorly developed. This situation reflected the 'elementariness' of Russian culture. The network of human relations had not developed to the point of generating a strong and articulate nationalism. According to Milyukov, 'our nationalists made out of this defect in social solidarity a special Russian virtue.' [90] Dostoevski stressed the 'unlimited plasticity' of the Russian nature. The Slavophiles of the mid-century exalted the 'breadth' of the Russian character. But, maintained Milyukov, in this 'broad nature' [91] there was no basis for a 'stubborn, conscious and self-valuing nationalism.' [92]

Nikolai Bukharin, despite the chasm which separated the Bolshevik from the liberal, agreed with Milyukov on the relative weakness of pre-revolutionary nationalism among the Russian masses. Bukharin even attributed the success of the Bolsheviks, in large measure, to this fact. He referred to the 'mighty masses of peasantry, not yet awakened to patriotism,' but full of hatred for the landlords.[93]

Milyukov believed that the foundations of Russian religious nationalism and messianism had been destroyed by the reforms of Peter the Great. In a discussion of the Muscovite 'third Rome' ideology Milyukov referred to Ivan IV [94] as the first representative of 'demagogic absolutism,' who had promised to 'uproot treason from the Russian land.' [95] Since the subjection of the church to rigid state supervision by Peter, Russian nationalism had had only a negative program. Its program was one of defending the 'Russian way of life' and it lacked a 'sacred Russian mission.' [96] In the nineteenth century the Slavophiles, appropriating the ideas of German romantic thinkers, had attempted to elaborate a new Russian religious messianism. Subsequently, philosophers such as Vladimir Solovev sought a 'universal human principle' in the form of a cosmopolitan religion.

All such attempts failed, 'probably because among the great majority of our intelligentsia there was sufficient common sense and self-criticism so that they did not want to satisfy themselves, but arouse the ridicule of others by displaying national-messianic attitudes.' [97] Milyukov accused the *Landmarks* group of attempting to repeat previous attempts to create a Russian 'nationalism' which could only be artificial. But, he maintained, national consciousness could only appear if it reflected the consciousness of the 'thinking and feeling apparatus of a nation, which is known as its intelligentsia.' [98] The *Landmarks* group stood in the path of the progress of Russia toward a growing social conscience, religious tolerance, and national-cultural equality. If they were successful, they would lead the way back to Muscovite Rus and the nineteenth-century doctrine of so-called official nationality. Of course this path was a reactionary one, contrary to the interests of Russians and non-Russians alike.[99]

Milyukov's estimate of the state of Russian national consciousness on the eve of World War I may seem naïvely optimistic today. It probably reflected, in part, the inability of the Western-oriented liberal scholar and politician to appreciate fully the significance of many latent irrational currents in the Russian mind. However, Milyukov of course was keenly aware of, and bitterly opposed to the chauvinism of notorious demagogues and reactionaries such as Purishkevich and Markov.[100]

Milyukov's appraisal also serves as a valuable reminder that pre-Bolshevik Russia was probably less chauvinistic than most other European countries.[101]

We have cited Milyukov extensively to indicate the relative weakness of Russian nationalism before World War I, if contrasted with that of the Soviet elite, or at least its policy-making core, today. The probability should be recognized, however, that even had there been no Bolshevik revolution, Russia today would have been a more nationalistic country than it was in 1910 or 1914. Unfortunately, industrialization has everywhere been accompanied by a dangerous intensification of national consciousness. This applies to the situation within nations, as well as to relations among nations.[102] The effects of such a development might not have been overly harmful, however, if the economic and cultural links which were increasingly binding Russia to the West had not been severed by the Bolshevik revolution.

It must be admitted that Soviet people have legitimate reasons for national pride. Not to recognize this fact would be ungracious and politically unwise. Immense progress has been made in the quantitative, and to some extent in the qualitative, aspects of civilization. Tremendous effort and heroism has been displayed in carrying out many vast construction projects. Individuals have derived deep satisfaction from participation in these projects. Tens of thousands of Soviet engineers, technicians, and administrators are the children of illiterate peasant parents. Such a process of social mobility naturally generates an inflation of ego.

Accompanied as it is by the insecurity of the new elite, it can easily generate national chauvinism. This is all the more understandable when it is recalled that the West has, by and large, tended to regard Russia as at best an exotic, at worst a barbaric, country. Add to all this the national pride resulting from victory in the greatest and cruelest war in history, and many of the objectionable characteristics of post-war Soviet nationalism become somewhat more understandable.

It is not these sentiments alone, however, difficult though they might be to deal with, that have aroused fear of Soviet power and intentions. It was rather their manipulation by a regime which exploited them, together with the aspirations of foreign communists and nationalists, that has made the new Soviet nationalism a disturbing factor in world politics.

The fact that such a frank and vigorous exchange of views as that between Milyukov and Berdyaev could take place in pre-Bolshevik Russia is not the least of the many indications that national exclusiveness and boastfulness was weaker in old Russia than it is in the 'socialist' Soviet Union.

One of the salient characteristics of totalitarian nationalism is that it does not permit critical discussion of political, cultural, or philosophic issues. On the contrary, and in this respect its tyranny far exceeds that of Nicholas I at its worst, it demands that intellectuals devote their full and enthusiastic efforts to justification and exaltation of official policy.[103] This abolition of even the privacy of one's thoughts is perhaps the most disturbing feature of totalitarianism. The military draft of intellectuals produces some of the most ludicrous yet tragic manifestations of Soviet chauvinism.

Basic to Soviet nationalism is the concept that all values and traditions must be judged according to their usefulness to the political leadership of the country. The following quotation from an article by a distinguished Soviet educator, A. S. Makarenko, suggests the official Soviet attitude: 'The history of mankind is divided into two periods: before the Stalin constitution and after the Stalin constitution.' [104] Such fanatical assertions are accompanied by claims that the 'progressive' aspects of pre-revolutionary Russian culture assured it of superiority to the culture of any other country. Complete self-sufficiency is claimed for 'progressive' Russian culture, and any genuine discussion of external influences, or of historical parallels is banned.[105] The editors of the new edition of the *Large Soviet Encyclopedia* have been instructed to 'demonstrate the superiority of socialist culture over the culture of the capitalist world with exhaustive thoroughness.' [106]

As Dicks has pointed out, the official ideology bears traces of paranoid mentality.[107] Some of the ablest Soviet refugees express the opinion that Soviet imperialism, while it oppresses even high-ranking members of the elite, compensates for this by giving the individual in the upper echelons a sense of freedom in the form of abstract impersonal fulfillment of his hamstrung will to power. It also directs feelings of persecution and inferiority against outgroups. Apparently still alive are those reactions to despotism noted by Custine, who perceived in the Russian the inordinate ambition and vanity of the slave. Many statements by Soviet leaders seem to reflect a perhaps unconscious craving for the achievement of individual immortality through the success of the state.

For example, Peter Pospelov one of the highest ranking interpreters of official doctrine, made the following statement in his speech on January 1951, on the twenty-seventh anniversary of the death of Lenin, 'The future belongs to the advanced ideas of our century, which no "world policeman" (to this role as is well known, the United States aspires) will succeed in putting behind bars.' [108] Similarly grandiose was the neurotic statement which appeared in *Pravda* ten days after the death of Stalin. 'The beacon of the new era brightly shines to all the world. And the stormy waves, no matter how frenziedly they dash, do not have the strength to crumble even one particle from the granite rock.' [109]

Sometimes there appears in statements of Soviet leaders a note of indignation because the people they rule do not seem to appreciate the blessings of the system which their leaders provide for them. In his well-known castigation of the writers of Leningrad in August 1946, Andrei Zhdanov asked: 'Is it up to us, representatives of advanced Soviet culture, and Soviet patriots, to assume an attitude of subservience to bourgeois culture, or to act as if we were students?' Zhdanov emphasized that the Soviet people owed their stature to the policy of the Bolshevik Party. He said, 'Today we are not the Russians that we were before 1917 and our Rus already is not the same as yesterday. Our character is also not the same.' [110]

Soviet nationalism, although it has many important links with the Russian past is not a purely 'Russian' product. The development of what seems to be an even more fanatical communist Chinese nationalism indicates this. Neither, in my opinion, can this new communist nationalism be considered the necessary embodiment of Marxism in action. Soviet nationalism represents the ideology of a new, totalitarian ruling class. The 'state *bourgeoisie*,' to borrow an apt phrase from Hugh Seton-Watson, is both more powerful as a class, and more insecure as individuals, than the elite strata of traditional monarchies or of capitalist democracy. Social tensions are probably more acute than in constitutional states. To a much greater extent than in freer societies there is a compulsion to direct the aggressions generated by these tensions to out-groups.

Two Cultures in Rivalry

Some of the most important characteristics of the ideologies of nations, states, and empires are revealed in basic doctrines regarding international and intercultural relations. It is customary to describe as 'imperialistic,' 'messianic,' 'xenophobic,' 'ethnocentric,' and 'chauvinistic,' minatory, depreciative, and destructive attitudes of other countries toward one's own. Unfortunately, governments often fail to apply in their own conduct norms by which they appraise the behavior of other states. Only if we employ, at least by implication, a comparative method can we approach objectivity in studying political attitudes and behavior. We have attempted in this study to avoid absolutist attitudes.

Soviet thought tends to be absolutist in the attribution of positive qualities to Soviet intentions, actions, and achievements and in the imputation of evil motives and pernicious actions to the representatives of the non-Soviet world. Soviet thought has been difficult to understand and Soviet behavior difficult to deal with because they seem to be based on denial of the right of alternative patterns to exist.

In earlier chapters we indicated the intensity of Moscow's intolerance of domestic ideological and cultural pluralism. Exceptional intolerance has usually been displayed also toward the 'capitalist' institutions and the 'bourgeois' culture of the non-Soviet world.

As a distinguished French scholar has emphasized, Soviet thinking on international relations has been based on a 'Manichaean' division of the world into capitalist and socialist countries and political movements. Communist parties, in this pattern, represented the only possible incarnation of 'socialism.' Truly peaceful co-existence requires the alteration of this pattern, which is dominated by the expectation of conflict.[1] We hope that this pattern will change, and we believe that the Western nations should go more than halfway in responding to genuine Soviet efforts to change it, but as we seek to demonstrate in this chapter this is a deeply rooted, change-resistant complex. Generations may be required before it can be altered fundamentally.

In the by now traditional Soviet view, the culture and civilization of the two antagonistic 'camps' into which the world is divided are determined by the political and economic institutions dominant in each. While the socialist camp is internally united, however, the one ruled by capitalists is rent by struggle between the forces of 'reaction,' and the 'progressive' allies of the Soviet Union. The struggle between the two camps will inevitably end in the complete triumph of the socialist forces and the universal extension of 'socialist culture.'

It will be instructive to illustrate these points by reference to a review article on 'Soviet culture' in an authoritative theoretical journal of the Central Committee of the Soviet Communist Party.[2]

According to this article, 'The essence of the theory of socialist culture and the cultural revolution can be understood only in the closest connection with the Leninist theory of socialist revolution.'[3] With the victory of the proletarian revolution, the cultural revolution begins. Some elements of socialist culture are struggling to take shape in capitalist society, in the course of the revolutionary movement. But the major part of the task of creating the new culture can be carried out only after the revolution, under the direction of 'the proletarian state power.'[4] The author, in keeping with the tendency of Soviet thought since Stalin's pronouncements on linguistics in 1950, also points out that culture is not entirely class-determined. Some elements of the cultural legacy of each people form a part of 'general' human culture. This minor modification of Leninist doctrine enables Soviet propaganda to appeal to nationalism in non-Soviet countries, particularly in countries such as India, in which there is a tradition of anti-imperialism and 'anti-cosmopolitanism.' It also reflects the gradually increasing significance of national tradition in Soviet culture.

Perhaps the most significant statements in the above article are the following: 'Only socialist culture can furnish the basis for a unified world culture.' And, 'The idea of a "unified" culture preached by American and other cosmopolitans signifies the desire of the imperialistic *bourgeoisie* to extend throughout the world its rotten, anti-people's culture, which is a weapon of struggle against the culture of the socialist, anti-imperialist camp.' [5] A similar view is found in the second edition of the *Great Soviet Encyclopedia,* according to which Lenin and Stalin set forth the 'prerequisites for the creation in the future of a communist culture, unified both in form and in content.[6]

Russian cultural imperialism is a tool of Soviet political expansionism. The encyclopedia article cited above states that 'Advanced Russian culture exercises an enormous influence on the culture of the peoples of the Soviet Union, the countries of people's democracy and the progressive culture of the other countries of the world.' According to the same source Soviet culture, 'permeated with optimism,' defends the right of 'people' everywhere to a 'bright future.' Here we are in the presence of a mixture of chauvinism, imperialism, and messianism. To the extent that such attitudes shape Soviet foreign policy, the whole world, and not merely that part of it already under communist rule, is threatened with—or promised, depending on one's point of view—Russification and Sovietization.

Within such a framework, the logical pattern of cultural policy is a combination of insulation against foreign influences and export of Soviet patterns. As long as such attitudes prevail, we may expect the Kremlin to limit contact between Soviet citizens and representatives of the 'capitalist' world for the most part to controlled interactions among carefully selected individuals, although the illusion of spontaneity may be created by skillful staging and reporting. We may also expect that the Soviet communications system will project to the outside world an attractive image of Soviet life but that it will not make an adequate corresponding effort to alter the bleak picture of 'bourgeois' civilization which it has traditionally presented to Soviet citizens.

This pattern rests partly upon intellectual conviction, bolstered by ignorance, and partly upon irrational fear, hostility, and aspiration for unlimited power. In this mentality, menacing and sinister though it is, fear of opponents with the power and resolution to resist has tended to overbalance adventurous expansionism. This is the mentality of a leadership which feels threatened but is, at least in terms of its official, systematic political education, confident of ultimate success. Such confidence, combined with the old Russian tradition of patience, circumspection, and deception, fosters the choice of indirect rather than direct, 'adventurous' techniques in international relations.

Since the 'masses' in 'capitalist' countries are regarded as instruments in the hands of ruling classes who would destroy Soviet power if they dared, it is considered necessary, in domestic propaganda, to play upon fear and hatred of the foreigner. In this process, traditional images of foreign enemies, invaders, and heretics, are exploited. To be sure, maintenance of the structure of Marxist ideology requires that the 'simple' working people be carefully distinguished from their evil rulers. Thus a secondary alternative is provided to the predominantly evil image of the foreigner. This distinction is ideologically orthodox and psychologically comforting, and the Soviet leadership undoubtedly regards it as politically shrewd. One of the main features of the period since the death of Stalin has consisted in a renewed emphasis in Soviet propaganda upon 'proletarian internationalism.' [7]

In keeping with re-emphasis upon 'internationalism,' Soviet historians were urged in 1954 to produce works directed against 'the present ruling circles of the United States, who act contrary to the true national interests of the American people itself.' [8] In Soviet terminology 'ruling circles' denotes not merely the administration in office, but any government not controlled by communists. Those who regard this as an extreme interpretation should consult Stalin's farewell speech of 14 October 1952, in which he asserted that the 'banner of national independence and national sovereignty' belonged in the present era to the 'representatives of communist and democratic Parties.' These parties must carry this banner forward if they wished to be 'patriots of their countries' and to become 'the ruling force of the nations.' [9] Much in post-Stalin policy represents, in essence, an attempt to implement this Stalinist directive. The purpose of this new version of the old communist 'united front' is probably to overcome the isolation which has increasingly threatened foreign communist parties, especially in Europe, as their anti-national character was increasingly revealed. As early as 1951, when Jacob Malik proposed negotiations to end the Korean war, the policy that led to the Geneva 'summit' meeting of 1955 was probably under preparation in the Kremlin.

Doubtless the appreciation in Moscow of the power of atomic and hydrogen weapons also played a major role in the choice of this policy. On the one hand, it was realized that a new war might render old political conceptions obsolete, along with those who clung to them. On the other, it was felt that Western fear of super-weapons surpassed even that of Moscow and that much could be gained by a policy of promising relief from this fear.

While holding fast to what is, ultimately, the pre-World War II doctrine of world revolution adapted to contemporary conditions, the Soviet leadership at the same time carried on nationalistic propaganda against the United States which was calculated to make the average Soviet citizen suspicious of non-communist Americans. Propaganda against the United States and its friends and allies has, under the post-Stalin rulers, been carried out under the over-all slogan of a campaign for the 'relaxation of international tensions.' The Soviet 'negotiations' campaign is the newest version of the old but powerful Bolshevik strategy of attempting to pin the onus for aggression on the leaders of the 'capitalist' world.[10]

In terms of formal categories, the Soviet indictment of 'capitalist' governments continues to rest on a Marxist basis. This indictment charges that 'private' property breeds exploitation, cultural decay, and war, while 'public' property, under the management of the Soviet Communist Party, fosters the highest form of democracy, social harmony, and a new and higher type of culture. According to this argument, the rulers of the disintegrating capitalist society cannot permit the peaceful development of socialism and would intervene against it by force if the 'socialist camp' were not sufficiently armed, astute, and alert. The other side of the medal is that the rulers of the realm of harmony are in duty bound to extend it to encompass the world. Rarely is this thought expressed in other than veiled terms, but occasionally Soviet writers have gone so far as to depict 'the last execution on earth,' that of the American 'war mongers.' [11]

We need not here develop in detail the major propositions of Soviet anti-capitalist propaganda.[12] It may be well, however, to refresh the reader's memory by referring briefly to the major themes calculated to keep alive suspicion of the non-Soviet world. Soviet propaganda usually presents the capitalist countries in general, and the United States in particular, as compulsively striving for economic expansion.

The post-war return to the doctrine which sees the chief danger to world peace in capitalist 'imperialism' was first signaled dramatically in Stalin's crucial speech of 9 February 1946. Applied to the contemporary situation in his article 'Economic Problems of Socialism in the USSR,' published on the eve of the Nineteenth Party Congress, it remains an important part of the framework of Soviet foreign policy analysis. Stalin emphasized that the basic 'law' of modern capitalism is the struggle for maximum profits. He underlined his claim that capitalism was doomed, by asserting that it was no longer capable of achieving even temporary 'stabilization.'

The search for profits allegedly forces capitalist countries to invest capital in all parts of the world where this is still possible. The 'socialist' part of the world is now closed to capitalist exploitation. Investment is accompanied by pressure for political control. One aspect of propaganda against Western 'imperialism,' which may be more effective in underdeveloped countries than we think, is the accusation that capitalist powers wastefully exploit natural and human resources. In pressing this charge, the Kremlin has been restrained only by the capabilities of its propagandists' imaginations.

At the peak of the anti-American campaign of 1952 when all previous limits of virulence were exceeded, a Soviet philosopher, G. F. Aleksandrov, charged that Americans considered themselves a 'master race' with the right to reduce the number of persons belonging to 'inferior' groups. Aleksandrov also claimed that the world could support from 8 billion to 11 billion persons, if capitalism were abolished. Because of the capitalist exploitation, he asserted, 50 per cent to 75 per cent of the soil in leading capitalist countries was becoming unsuitable for agriculture.[13]

Such propaganda has only too often sought to create the impression that the governments of Western nations, particularly the United States, were mass murderers. Soviet propaganda, like that of Communist China, is bitterly opposed to birth control, which is regarded as a 'capitalist' policy directed against life itself.

Soviet propaganda has charged that the United States 'dumps' vast amounts of surplus and obsolete goods abroad. It attacks American aid programs for allegedly exporting moldy flour in order to keep up food prices at home. It charges that the United States deliberately forces down the price of raw materials, such as tin and rubber, the export of which is important to the economies of many countries.

These alleged policies are presented as carefully planned by Wall Street. American 'imperialism' allegedly seeks to organize the economy of the non-Soviet world exclusively for military purposes.[14] To sow dissension among the Western powers, and to narrow the focus of propaganda against America, Soviet propaganda charges that American foreign economic policy is one of cutthroat competition in the 'spheres of influence' of other Western nations.

This pattern is applied in great detail to current developments, in every area of the globe. The Soviet reader, and non-Soviet audiences also, upon whom this propaganda exerts direct or indirect influence, receive a frightening impression of a world capitalist conspiracy operating everywhere and dedicated to the pursuit of profits derived from exploitation, corruption, and death. For example, the newspaper *Soviet Culture* for 31 May 1955 charged that the productions of 'bourgeois theaters' were weapons of ideological preparation for 'unjust' wars.

Distorted statistics are given on American military, particularly atomic, war preparations. The United States is accused of planning indirect attack on the 'socialist' camp and of subversive activities directed against the Soviet Union and the captive states. The outstanding example in recent years was the accusation against a number of Soviet doctors, members of the Kremlin medical staff, in January 1953, that they, as members of the spy network of the Jewish Joint Distribution Committee, served as agents of United States intelligence services.

We shall not deal in detail with the well-known communist 'germ warfare' propaganda. It may, however, be useful to point out that it furnished one of the best illustrations of the way in which communist governments manipulate irrational appeals to emotions calculated to stimulate mob passions and mobilize mass support against foreign governments. This aspect of communist propaganda tactics was most fully developed in the late Stalin period, but it has a long history. It may be traced at least as far back as the appeal to traditional Russian antipathy to the Poles during the Soviet-Polish War in 1920.

These tactics were perfected after Stalin's purges established Soviet totalitarianism as we know it today. The attempt to direct against external enemies, and their internal 'agents,' hostility generated by the frustration of expectations aroused by the revolution, became a major aspect of Soviet life with the inauguration of Stalin's drive for industrialization. It reached gigantic proportions during the great purges of 1936–8. In those days, and subsequently, technicians, scientists, veterinarians, and others were made to take the blame for mistakes of Soviet policy or for the inevitable consequences of an excessively rapid economic development of a backward society.

In March 1939, A. A. Andreev, then the Politburo member in over-all charge of Soviet agriculture, declared that losses of livestock on Soviet collective and state farms were due to the activities of agents of foreign powers who had injected farm animals with disease germs. A defendant at the Radek-Pyatakov trial in January 1937, one Ivan Knyazev, allegedly a spy for the Japanese, was accused of wrecking Soviet military trains and of having planned the infection of troop trains with deadly bacteria.[15]

Long before the 'germ warfare' charges, communists in Eastern European countries accused the United States of seeking to damage potato crops by introducing the Colorado Beetle. Soviet propaganda regarding the trial, at Khabarovsk in 1949, of Japanese military personnel accused of having conducted illegal experiments in the use of disease germs against Soviet war prisoners, linked the defendants with American intelligence agencies. The Korean War charges were not a new feature of Soviet tactics, although their sinister character cannot easily be overestimated. They had several purposes, both defensive and offensive; the point that perhaps needs most emphasis is that by establishing in advance an image of American 'barbarism,' the Soviet authorities would make it easier not only to rally their people for a defensive war, but to justify almost any action which they might choose to initiate against the United States.

The most violent anti-American propaganda began with the speech of Peter Pospelov, one of the leading Party specialists on ideological questions, on the twenty-seventh anniversary of the death of Lenin, 21 January 1951.[16] The American people were branded as the worst enemy of Soviet Russia throughout the period since the Bolshevik revolution. Pospelov quoted Lenin to the effect that American imperialism was the 'most savage beast,' and 'the active organizer and inspirer of military intervention against the young Soviet Russian republic in the first year of its existence.'

He charged that President Wilson, acting in his capacity as 'the leader of the American billionaires,' had been one of the chief organizers of armed intervention. A shocking feature of Pospelov's speech was his attempt to create the impression that any American who opposed intervention in Russia in 1919 was in imminent danger of death. The main significance of the speech, however, was that it inaugurated a campaign featured by accounts of alleged atrocities committed by Americans against Russians during the American participation in military intervention in the Russian North and in the Far East. The Party leadership cast itself as the protector of a Russia threatened by implacable, but not invincible, enemies.

A pamphlet by a distinguished Soviet jurist, who, prior to the beginning of the 'cold war' was friendly to the West, stated that 'in all countries indignant protests are mounting against the bestialities of the American monsters, trampling underfoot the elementary principles of international law, and violating basic rights of human morality and humanity.' [17] Denunciation of American 'crimes' in Korea and elsewhere was accompanied by publication of a spate of academic studies, historical novels, and other fictional works designed to show that Americans had always been the enemies of Russians.

Typical was a novel entitled *The Northern Aurora,* originally published, like most Soviet novels, in a literary magazine. *The Northern Aurora* in one passage had Winston Churchill telling one of his assistants that 'The United States already understands that Germany is at its last gasp and that the war will soon end. They are reaching out toward Russia. They are interested in timber, oil and copper. Thanks to the American Red Cross, the Russian-American Chamber of Commerce, and the Railway Commission, which was sent there under Kerenski, hundreds, if not thousands, of American agents are operating in Russia.' [18]

During the months before the death of Stalin, the Soviet Union was in the throes of a hysterical 'vigilance' campaign. The 'doctors' plot' was the high point of a campaign which may have been designed to pave the way for a vast purge of the type which shocked the world in 1936–8, and which attempted to create the impression that an army of American and British agents was operating in Russia. On 4 March 1953, the day on which *Pravda* first reported Stalin's last illness, items were published accusing the Americans of utilizing Japanese troops in the Korean War and of committing the most horrible crimes. The most inflammatory types of accusations against the United States have diminished in the Soviet press since the death of Stalin. An important exception to this statement is a series of arrests of Soviet persons allegedly acting as American agents. It is also important to keep in mind that since Stalin's death the Kremlin has intensified its psychological—and often more than psychological—offensive against Russian refugees abroad.

As James Reston reported in *The New York Times* for 20 November 1953, a Soviet color film entitled *Silvery Death,* shown in the summer of 1953, portrayed the United States as plotting to conquer the world by means of chemical warfare. A curious feature of the showing of this film was the fact that foreign correspondents were not permitted to send stories about it through the Soviet censorship. One type of anti-American propaganda, that which attempted to combine anti-Americanism and anti-Semitism, came to an abrupt end with the death of Stalin, although only the future will tell whether the policy of using anti-Semitism in Soviet domestic propaganda has been given up permanently. As late as 1 March 1953, *Pravda* published a despatch characterizing Israel as a 'semi-colony of American imperialism,' which furnished the United States with military bases and Zionist spies.[19]

During the summer of 1953 the newspaper of the Soviet Writers' Union, *The Literary Gazette,* continued to specialize in articles on alleged American brutality. The issue of this newspaper for 25 April 1953, for example, discussed murders allegedly committed by an American soldier and stated that 'he was raised without conscience and honor, with the morals of an animal.' The United States was accused of having instigated the East German uprising of 16 and 17 June 1953. The revolt of the German workers was treated as the work of 'fascist hirelings' of the American intelligence services.

The main theme of Soviet propaganda against Western 'reactionaries,' particularly in the United States, continued in the post-war period to be the alleged intention to destroy the 'camp of peace and democracy.' It is too early to predict what lasting effects the startling events of 1955 will have on this theme. The chief individual target of Soviet propaganda against America from the beginning of the Eisenhower administration until the spring of 1955 was Secretary of State John Foster Dulles. Soviet propagandists exploited the vulnerabilities associated with Dulles' previous reputation and with his actions and statements after he assumed office. *Kommunist* published in one of its May 1953 issues an article accusing Mr. Dulles of a policy of 'intervention in the internal affairs of the countries of Eastern Europe, and of restoration of the reactionary regimes hated by the peoples of these countries.' [20]

The new leadership in Moscow sought to create the impression that a new Soviet regime without the dread figure of Stalin was anxious for peace, trade, and cultural relations. The 'new look' was apparent from the beginning in appealing gestures and persuasive actions. A comparison of Malenkov's speech of 9 October 1952 and his major address of 8 August 1953, for example, reveals a sharp falling off of inflammatory symbols such as 'cannibal' or 'bloodsucker,' prominent in the vocabulary of the late Stalin period.

Another index of the new line is the 6 November and May Day slogans. In 1952, prominence was given to a slogan denouncing 'war mongers.' In 1953, 1954, and 1955, an appeal to 'proletarian internationalism' was substituted.[21] On the other hand, many of Stalin's slogans were retained, including the statement he made to a *Pravda* correspondent in February 1951 that peace would be preserved if the 'peoples' took the cause of peace 'into their own hands.'

We are aware that in a work of this kind the attempt to achieve up-to-dateness may result only in superficiality, but perhaps a few words about pertinent aspects of Soviet propaganda during the period of the 'Geneva atmosphere' in the summer of 1955 may be appropriate. Defeated in their attempts to prevent ratification of the Paris Agreements on West German rearmament, and worried about the Formosa crisis, the Soviet leaders carried out, with skill, a 'strategic retreat.' They did not cease to appeal to world public opinion, but they decided that much might be gained, at least for the time being, by convincing Western governments that they desired a *détente*. If successful, the policy of 'personal contact' among heads of state could 'relax tension' abroad and provide time for dealing with pressing problems at home. In their excellent power position, so different from that of the immediate post-war years, the Soviet leaders could afford to play the role of constructive statesmen.

This role required, among other things, diplomatic correctness and evidence of willingness to recognize the right of non-Soviet governments to exist. To create the right tone, the Soviet leaders and press proclaimed that a 'new stage' had begun in the relations among the four Geneva powers, and suggested that if further progress were achieved along the same line, the 'cold war' would end. Some credit for the results of Geneva was given to the Western leaders, but at the same time the Soviet leadership claimed the major share of the credit for itself. Soviet comment also emphasized that 'the enemies of peace have not laid down their arms,' thus putting the world and their own cadres on notice that the 'new stage' was not necessarily destined to be long lasting. As after earlier conferences, it was not difficult to see who would be blamed if Soviet objectives were not realized. On the other hand, perhaps, more spirit of 'give and take' was manifested than in comment on the results of Yalta or Potsdam.

It was clear that the attempt to revive something of the atmosphere of the 'coalition' of World War II would not involve surrender of any vital Soviet power positons. Bulganin also made it plain that discussion of the problem of international communism, which 'naïve people' had suggested, was not a matter of 'inter-state relations,' but concerned the 'activities of various political parties.' Soviet comment on Geneva also indicated clearly that Moscow did not intend to give up the struggle to extend its influence in the non-Soviet world. Its new goal would be 'neutrality' of the Austrian, not the Swiss, type. Almost immediately, pro-Soviet politicians like Nenni began to urge closer relations for their countries with Russia to 'balance' connections with America. A special twist of Soviet policy was assumed in Japan, where in August a conference, given wide publicity in the Soviet press, took place to denounce the American use of atomic bombs during World War II.

The struggle between 'two worlds' would go on, but by more complicated methods. The new tactics promised, at least to some degree, to 'disarm' the opponent. As usual, Moscow was in a better position to synchronize their implementation than was the disorganized non-Soviet world. This contrast had its positive implications for the non-Soviet 'camp,' however, as Soviet propaganda had earlier, and erroneously, called it. There remained a part of the world where smiles, like frowns, had not been 'nationalized.' In Russia a new purge of intellectuals seemed about to begin, this time of those who did not display the kind of appreciation of foreign culture appropriate to neo-Leninist 'internationalism.' Oddly enough, however, the attack on excessive chauvinism was being conducted in the name of Zhdanov and Stalin. The impasse at Geneva in October-November 1955 confirmed the suspicions of realists who even in the summer had emphasized the continuity of Soviet policy. But it still appeared that in a world in which all-out war had become obsolete, cultural penetration and promises of economic aid to underdeveloped countries would bulk larger and the cruder forms of subversion would play a smaller role in Soviet world strategy than under Stalin.

From the summer of 1946 until the death of Stalin, the Soviet Union was the scene of the most intensive campaign ever conducted against Western culture and against cultural exchange and cultural freedom. Apparently the most important motive of this campaign was the Kremlin's belief that all-out conflict between the Soviet Union and the West was ultimately inevitable. The campaign against 'bourgeois' culture was the ideological concomitant of the post-war Soviet political offensive.

The question under examination is, of course, only one aspect of the problem of relationships in the Soviet system between politics, culture, and basic doctrine. We are here concerned primarily with the injection into creative work of attitudes generated by strained post-war relations between the Soviet and the Western 'camp.' A few words must be said about the doctrine of *partiinost,* or 'partyness,' which governs the function of culture in Soviet society and determines the Soviet attitude toward "bourgeois' culture.[22]

According to the doctrine of *partiinost,* as set forth in Lenin's *Materialism and Empirio-criticism,* in 1908, and in other works by Lenin and other Soviet leaders, philosophy, history, literature, and the arts must reflect objective truths as revealed by and to the Communist Party in its interpretation of Marxism-Leninism.

Some elements of Lenin's cultural utilitarianism were derived from the populist aesthetics of nineteenth-century Russian radical writers such as Chernyshevski. This native Russian tradition, considerably distorted, was reflected in the concept of 'socialist realism,' authoritatively proclaimed for the first time at the first meeting of the Union of Soviet Writers in 1934.

A major element in a policy which views intellectual activity as a function of state interests is derived from Lenin's application of his doctrine of *partiinost* to national cultures. In 1913, Lenin wrote:

> In every modern nation there are two nations. In every national culture there are two national cultures. There is a great Russian culture of people like Purishkevich, Guchkov and Struve, but there is also a great Russian culture marked by the names of Chernyshevski and Plekhanov. The same manifold cultures exist among the Ukrainians,[23] in Germany, France, England, among the Jews, and so on.

The same idea in somewhat different words was set forth in Lenin's important works of 1914, on *The Right of Nations to Self-Determination,* and *The National Pride of the Great Russians.* Both of these works are among those included in the large editions of selected writings intended for mass circulation among the politically literate elements of the Soviet population.[24] The latter article, in particular, identifies patriotism and national pride with socialism.

These works furnished the doctrinal foundations for 'Soviet patriotism' and, indirectly, for the cultural chauvinism which has flourished in the post-war Soviet Union. On the other hand, it should be noted that even those works of Lenin, knowledge of which is part of the equipment of every educated Soviet citizen, contain much that conflicts with Stalinist chauvinism and xenophobia. For example, Lenin emphasized that a nation which oppressed other nations could not be free and he praised Marx for becoming 'half an Englishman.'[25] After Stalin's death it became possible for Soviet theoreticians to make a partial return to such views of Lenin.

During the 1920's, when Party doctrine was far more consistently Marxist than it subsequently became, Soviet cultural life was much less marred by xenophobic and chauvinistic attitudes than it has been since the beginning of the first Five Year Plan. Stalin's program of 'Socialism in one country' led, among other things, to the growth of cultural nationalism. Fear of war and the internal tension generated by rapid industrialization were also among the factors responsible. Particularly during and after the purges of 1936–8, everything foreign was suspect.[26] It was felt that not only were foreigners untrustworthy and likely to be agents of enemy powers, but that they took a snobbish attitude toward Russians and did not appreciate the sacrifices the Russians were making for the defense and development of the Soviet state.

Exigencies of international politics, however, forced the Soviet government during the period from 1938 to 1945 to seek the support of Western middle-class liberals, socialists, and other elements against the menace of Nazi Germany and an expansionist Japan. A measure of cosmopolitanism was tolerated in arts, science, and scholarship. Also, in the early stages of its industrialization, the Soviet Union desperately needed foreign machinery and the services of foreign experts. At the same time, the enemy states, particularly Germany, were vigorously attacked on the cultural as well as on the diplomatic and political fronts.

The regime attempted to arouse hatred against Germans by showing such powerful films as Sergei Eisenstein's *Alexander Nevski* and the indictment of Nazi anti-Semitism, *Dr. Mamlock*. On the other hand, 'American efficiency' was extolled as a model to be emulated by Soviet engineers and managers, even though the 'bourgeois' order which produced the American possessors of this virtue was reviled. Underlying the limited positive element in the official appraisal of Western civilization in the 1930's was the conviction expressed by Stalin in a speech, 'On the Tasks of Managers,' in 1931. Stalin said, 'We are fifty to a hundred years behind the advanced countries. We must make up the gap in ten years. Either we will do this or they will crush us.' He also pointed out that other countries had been contemptuous of Russia because of her backwardness. The 'wolfish law of capitalism' prescribed that he who is weak is in the wrong.[27]

An 'industrial' spirit began to invade all spheres of Soviet life. There developed a culture characterized by extremely centralized organization, mass training of scientific and technical cadres, and highly utilitarian scientific and scholarly output, with excellent work in the natural sciences and a high level of technical competence in many non-scientific fields not directly related to ideology and politics. For example, even in the field of history, Soviet scholars have done outstanding work in the assembly and publication of source materials.[28] Another non-natural science field in which Soviet work is first-rate is archaeological excavation. The combination, which prevailed in the 1930's, of pride in vast and increasingly visible achievements in all fields and the sense of urgency and of a race against time was probably certain to generate irrational attitudes of chauvinism and inflated national ego among those who achieved distinction.

A good example of the combination of national pride and incipient anti-Westernism which characterized much Soviet expression on cultural matters in the years before World War II is afforded by the article on Pushkin in *The Literary Encyclopedia* published in 1935.[29] On the one hand, the article admitted that the 'classics of world literature,' such as Byron and Shakespeare, had exerted much greater influence on Pushkin than had Russian writers such as Fonvizin and Radishchev. It quoted from a letter in which Pushkin had described himself as the 'Minister of Foreign Affairs of the Russian Parnassus.' This reasonable position, which in the post-war period was to be attacked as 'kowtowing to the West,' was accompanied by the statement that Pushkin had accomplished in twenty years an evolution from classicism to realism which had required a hundred years in the West.

By January 1937 statements such as the following were common: 'In the definition of the services of Pushkin to his motherland and to all mankind there is contained an acknowledgment of the very great importance of the Russian literary language and of Russian literature for the cultural development of the Russian people and at the same time of world culture.'[30] In a symposium on *The Style and Language of A. S. Pushkin,* the statement was made that Pushkin was 'the heir to everything progressive and advanced in European culture.'[31]

The attitude taken in the Soviet Union from about 1934 to late 1943 or early 1944, when a new phase began, was as follows. The Soviet Union, as the standard bearer of the Marxist cause, and the first 'socialist' country, had a culture superior to that of any other country. Soviet Russia could still learn from the West in technology, however. As for the pre-revolutionary period, there was an increasing tendency toward a positive evaluation of Russian achievements, even in technology. *Pravda*, for 15 January 1937, for example, referred to the Russian Popov, as the 'inventor' of the radio.

The next phase probably began shortly after the victory at Stalingrad; the regime, looking toward post-war opportunities as well as problems, was determined to exploit Russian prestige in all fields. A very important step was taken during the week of 5–12 June 1944 when a 'scientific conference' was held at Moscow University on 'the significance of Russian science in the history of world culture.' One of the main themes of this conference was indicated in a statement by the scientist A. N. Zelinski, who wrote: 'We know well that Russian science, like all Russian culture, has always been original and independent.' [32]

Emphasis upon the self-sufficiency of Russian culture was accompanied by criticism of 'harmful' and 'decadent' foreign influences. This rejection of 'bourgeois' culture was officially expressed in the well-known series of Central Committee decrees in 1946–8. These decrees and the speeches made by Andrei Zhdanov, on literature, music, and philosophy belong to the first of the three periods into which the development of Soviet post-war cultural policy may be divided. The second period began in January 1949 with a vicious attack directed against a group of 'anti-patriotic theatrical critics.'

The phase inaugurated by this attack was characterized, among other things, by an anti-Semitic tinge. This was indicated by denunciation of 'passportless cosmopolitans,' by the publication in parentheses of the originally 'Jewish' names of critics and others who had Russianized their names, and by numerous other features. It was also characterized by an increasing tendency to resort to administrative measures against its victims, a fact indicated by the disappearance of a number of Soviet writers and critics during the years from 1949 to 1953.

The third stage, in which we are living today, was, of course, ushered in by the death of Stalin. It has been marked, among other things, by a politically astute Soviet cultural exchange campaign. 'Zhdanovism,' however, did not die with Stalin. On the contrary, two of the most important Central Committee decrees usually associated with the name of Zhdanov, that of 14 August 1946, on the journals of *Zvezda* and *Leningrad,* and the 26 August decree of the same year on the repertoire of dramatic theaters and measures for its improvement, remain among the canons of Soviet doctrine. They were included in the seventh edition of the vitally important publication *The Communist Party of the Soviet Union in the Resolutions and Decisions of the Congresses, Conferences and Plenary Sessions of the Central Committee,* published in October 1953.[33]

The 14 August 1946 decree on literature attacked Mikhail Zoshchenko and Anna Akhmatova for 'specializing in the writing of empty, trivial works, without content and permeated with a rotten lack of ideas and political indifference, calculated to disorganize our youth and poison its consciousness.' These writers, and those who had allegedly fallen under their influence, were accused of presenting Soviet people as if they were primitive, stupid, and uncultured, with Philistine tastes and manners.

A serious charge against Zoshchenko and Akhmatova was that their influence had caused the magazines *Zvezda* and *Leningrad* to publish works 'which cultivated a spirit, alien to Soviet people, of kowtowing to the contemporary bourgeois culture of the West.' Works permeated with pessimism and disillusionment had appeared.[34] The decree of 26 August, regarding the repertoire of dramatic theaters, criticized Soviet dramatists for depreciating the Soviet people and sharply attacked the Committee on Art Affairs, the responsible government agency, for permitting certain foreign plays to be presented on Soviet stages.

Among those listed were Kaufman and Hart's *The Man Who Came to Dinner,* Somerset Maugham's *The Circle,* and *Penelope,* and other English and French plays. The decree stated threateningly that 'the presentation by our theaters of the plays of bourgeois' foreign authors amounted, in essence, to turning over the Soviet stage to the propaganda of reactionary bourgeois ideology and morality and to an attempt to poison the consciousness of Soviet people by a world outlook hostile to Soviet society, which brings back to life the survivals of capitalism in the consciousness and way of life' [of Soviet people].[35]

These decrees were backed up by a long speech given by

Zhdanov to the writers and Party activists of the city of Lenin-grad.[36] Toward the end of this self-righteous tirade, Zhdanov struck a xenophobic and messianic note which reveals much of the political motivation of the post-war cultural purges. He stated that 'the bourgeois world' was not pleased by the increased strength of the Soviet Union and of the 'positions of socialism' gained as a result of the Second World War. The imperialists were employing their writers, journalists, and diplomats to put the Soviet Union in a bad light. Under these circumstances, it was the task of Soviet literature not only to answer, blow for blow, slander directed against Soviet culture but also boldly to 'attack bourgeois culture, which is in a state of disintegration and decay.'

Zhdanov then made his well-known statement that 'of course our literature, reflecting a system many times superior to any bourgeois democratic order, a culture many times higher than bourgeois culture has the right to teach other people a new, universal human morality.' Finally, Zhdanov struck a blow to restore to the Party the psychological initiative over the Russian people by declaring that the Russian people owed their eminence to the Party's efforts. 'We,' he said, 'are not the Russians that we were before 1917 and our Rus is not the same, and our character is not the same.' The progress of the Russian people, he indi-cated, was based on the great transformations which had taken place since the establishment of Soviet power.

The Central Committee decree of 4 September regarding the film *A Great Life,* attacked those responsible for the production and showing of this film because it allegedly portrayed Soviet in-dustry and Soviet workers and engineers as backward and in-efficient. This criticism was doubtless, in part, intended to support the campaign inaugurated by Stalin in his 9 February 1946 pre-election speech in which the dictator called upon Soviet scientists to 'overtake and surpass' their Western competitors. The decree on the cinema struck another significant note. Eisenstein was lashed because he had portrayed Ivan the Terrible, 'A man with a strong will and character,' as 'weak-nerved and lacking in will, as if he were a Hamlet.' The Party attacked Eisenstein for al-legedly creating the impression that 'the progressive troops of

Ivan the Terrible's guards resembled a gang of degenerates, on the order of the American Ku Klux Klan.' [37]

An exceptionally xenophobic note was struck in the decree on music, dated 10 February 1948, and entitled 'Concerning the Opera "The Great Friendship" by V. Muradeli.' [38] Sharply criticizing compositions by Shostakovich, Prokofiev, Khachaturyan, Shebalin, at that time director of the Moscow State Conservatory, G. Popov, and N. Myaskovski, 'and others,' the decree stated that their music reflected the spirit of 'modernistic bourgeois music of Europe and America, reflecting the decadence of bourgeois culture, the complete denial of musical art, its blind alley.' [39] It added that 'all of this signifies that among a portion of the Soviet composers survivals of bourgeois ideology have not yet died out, survivals nourished by the influence of the contemporary decadent Western European and American music.' [40] Like writers, dramatists, and film workers, musicians were ordered to produce works which would foster Soviet patriotism.

The decree on music illustrates a major characteristic of Soviet cultural policy, namely, the use of selected elements of both 'Russian' and 'Western' cultural forms. The 'decadent'—more or less synonymous with post-Victorian—elements of Western art, music, and literature are rejected. But Western forms, styles, and influences upon which the Great Russian 'classical culture' of the nineteenth century was based, are not only approved, but are regarded as obligatory. To a considerable extent, mastery of approved Western forms, styles, musical instruments, and related features of 'classical' culture tends to be forced upon the non-Russian peoples of the Soviet Union, who are under pressure to give up such features of their own native and traditional artistic, musical, and literary culture as do not conform to the Kremlin-approved combination of Russian and Western patterns. The observations above apply with particular force to peoples that have incurred the displeasure of the Soviet rulers.

The music decree charged Muradeli with creating 'the false impression that such Caucasian peoples as the Georgians and the Osetins were at that time [1918–1920] hostile to the Russian people, which is historically false, since the obstacle to the establishment of the friendship of peoples at that time in the North

Caucasus was the Chechens and the Ingush.' [41] At the same time, the decree criticized the opera because it spurned the 'best traditions and experience of classical opera in general, and of Russian classical opera in particular,' which it unqualifiedly described as 'the best opera in the world.' It also criticized the composer because he had not made adequate use of folk motifs of the peoples of the North Caucasus, but it is clear from the above quotation that use of Chechen or Ingush forms was strictly forbidden. Thus the cutting edge of Soviet cultural policy is directed outward against 'bourgeois' culture while within the USSR it is often turned against non-Russian peoples of the Soviet Union. Selected features of Western culture are associated with Sovietization and Soviet totalitarian Russification.

An article in *Pravda* for 20 March 1938, entitled 'The Music of a Great People,' was devoted in the main to proving that Russian music was at least as 'self-sufficient' as that of Germany, Austria, or France. This article also, in effect, attributed to the Great Russians a kind of 'Westernizing mission,' however. It castigated non-Russian artists and musicians who had clung too zealously to their national traditions. It stated that 'The bourgeois nationalists opposed the introduction of European instruments into their national orchestras.' Viewed against this background, post-war Soviet cultural policy represents a continuation of the process, begun by Moscow in the 1930's, of imposing upon the entire population under its control a 'Soviet Russian culture' that rejects and proscribes the major trends and schools in the arts and literature which flourish in the contemporary West but demands conformity to those 'Western' norms considered respectable by Lenin.

Since Stalin's successors have not repudiated the 1946–8 cultural decrees, it seems safe to assume that the spirit which they express did not die with Stalin. This interpretation appears to be confirmed by the fact that on many occasions in 1954 and 1955 important organs of the Party press praised these decrees highly. *Kommunist,* No. 1, for January 1954 expressed the still dominant view that the Central Committee decrees were valuable because they were 'directed toward the unswerving struggle to overcome survivals of capitalism in the popular mind, and against manifestations of political and ideological indifference in literature and art, as well as against kowtowing to things foreign.' [42]

On the other hand, there have been encouraging signs during the last two or three years of restlessness and eagerness for greater freedom on the part of Soviet creative intellectuals. In the field of drama, for example, a report published in *Soviet Culture* for 26 May 1955 contained evidence of freedom of expression which would certainly not have been tolerated under Stalin. At a conference called on 'measures for improving the repertoire of drama theaters'—shades of Zhdanov!—leading dramatists and producers asked for more freedom in choice and presentation of plays. It was even suggested that there were merits in the pre-revolutionary situation in which the famous producer Stanislavski had enjoyed the right to 'create a theater at his own risk.'

Since such opinions were expressed after the renewed outburst of 'Zhdanovism' which followed the first period of relaxation of literary controls in 1953, they indicate considerable confusion, at least, in literary-artistic circles. Until such trends become far more powerful, however, it will be safe to assume that 'partisanship,' particularly in relation to Western culture, remains the basis of Soviet cultural policy.

The second, and most virulent phase of post-war anti-foreignism was conducted under the slogan of extirpation of 'cosmopolitanism.' This term is associated especially closely with the developments of 1949, but it has continued to remain a key symbol even in the somewhat more relaxed post-Stalin period. The Central Committee on literature had been foreshadowed by numerous premonitory symptoms. In fact, some alert Soviet readers probably began to become aware of the return to orthodoxy early in 1944. In its second issue for January of that year *Bolshevik,* in an article entitled 'Concerning a Certain Pernicious Story,' excoriated Zoshchenko, while praising Boris Gorbatov and other writers whose works constituted 'a burning call to life and struggle.' The trend became stronger with publication on 28 June 1946 of the first issue of a Central Committee newspaper, *Kultura i Zhizn,* which for more than three years was to exercise a powerful and baneful influence on matters ideological.

On 28 January 1949 *Pravda* published an article entitled 'Against the Anti-Patriotic Group of Theater Critics.' This was a sinister and furious attack. Among other things, it demanded 'the ideological annihilation of the anti-patriotic group of drama critics,' who were charged with despising the 'new Soviet man,' his patriotism, and his hatred of 'bourgeois' foreign ideas. Following *Pravda*'s blast, six leading drama critics were expelled from the Party and the Society of Theatrical Critics was reorganized. The 14 August 1946 decree had been followed by the expulsion of Zoshchenko and Akhmatova from the Union of Soviet Writers, and by the demotion of Nikolai Tikhonov from the post of head of the Union to mere membership on its board of directors. The attack on the 'cosmopolitan' critics was, however, the first incident in the post-war ideological reconversion involving expulsions of erring intellectuals from the Party, and open admission that such purges had occurred. The new campaign soon spread to music and other fields. On 20 February 1949 *Culture and Life,* for example, published an article entitled 'Bourgeois Cosmopolitans in Musical Criticism.'

The attack on the music critics accused them of having failed to take to heart the directives contained in the Central Committee's decrees of 1946–8. And, like Zhdanov's speech of August 1946, subsequent indictments searched the offenders' past for evidence of earlier failings. Half-forgotten moods, attitudes, and groupings of the 1920's were recalled. In literature, Zhdanov had attacked the 'Serapion brothers.' In music, the 'Association for Modern Music' which was dissolved about 1925, was now declared to be the model for the musical 'cosmopolitans' of 1949. The music critic L. Mazel was accused of echoing the reactionary influence of this long-defunct association. He was also accused of having, at a conference of music critics in 1945, argued that the criterion for judging a work of art was its 'universal human cosmopolitan significance.'

Many critics were castigated for having made favorable statements about American music. They had, it was said, attempted to divide American music into 'black' and 'white' sectors, and in their enthusiasm about the youth and energy of American Negro music they had forgotten that 'the American bosses are attempting to wipe Negro culture from the face of the earth.'

A major charge against music critics was that they had 'slandered the democratic ideals of Russian musical culture.' [43] *Culture and Life* enjoined the leadership of the Union of Soviet Composers to expose and 'smash completely the anti-patriotic moods in musical criticism.' Despite the fury of this campaign, during which a number of prominent literary and music critics disappeared, resistance survived in Soviet artistic and musical circles. Frank Rounds reports that even during the worst period of the Stalin era, in March 1952, excerpts from Richard Strauss's 'Salome' were included in a concert broadcast over the Leningrad radio; the applause was so enthusiastic that the orchestra replayed these selections.[44]

Culture and Life on 10 March 1949 published a front-page article entitled 'Expose the Propagation of Cosmopolitanism in Philosophy.' The attack on philosophers such as Boris Kedrov, M. Rozental, and others revolved largely around the theme of 'priority.' In June 1947 Andrei Zhdanov, in a long address, criticized a major work by the philosopher Georgi Aleksandrov entitled *A History of Western European Philosophy*, which had been awarded a Stalin Prize in 1947.[45] Following Zhdanov's 'report,' Aleksandrov was dismissed from his post as Chief of the Administration of Propaganda and Agitation of the Central Committee. The burden of Zhdanov's criticism was that Aleksandrov's study failed to stress the radical differences between the philosophy of Marx and that of Hegel, and to devote sufficient attention to the development of 'Russian classical philosophy,' a term employed with increasing frequency since 1943.

Zhdanov's contribution to Soviet philosophy represented a mixture of Soviet totalitarian and Russian traditional elements. He criticized Aleksandrov for concentrating 'not on that which is new and revolutionary in Marxism, but on its links with the development of pre-Marxist philosophy.' [46]

He complained that 'Philosophical schools are placed one after another, or one near the other, in the book, but are not shown in struggle against one another.' [47] Among reactionary systems to be attacked were, Zhdanov said, 'Neo-Kantianism, theology, old and new versions of agnosticism, the attempt to smuggle God into modern natural science, and every other cookery that has for its aim the freshening up of stale idealist merchandise for the market.' The 'philosopher lackeys of imperialism' were using this 'arsenal' to 'give support to their frightened masters.' [48]

Accusing Aleksandrov of neglecting the history of Russian philosophy, Zhdanov declared that 'whatever the author's motives' for this omission, it artificially divided the history of philosophy into Western European and Russian sections and belittled the latter.[49] Aleksandrov was reproached for using a quotation from Chernyshevski, in which the latter pleaded for tolerance in philosophic questions. He made it clear that although men like Chernyshevski and Lomonosov were to be regarded as 'great Russian scientists and philosophers,' only aspects of their heritage which conformed to the needs of the Politburo would be tolerated.[50]

Zhdanov demanded mobilization of the Soviet philosophical profession for militant performance of political functions. The Soviet 'philosophical front' resembled a 'bivouac far from the battlefield.' This was a deplorable situation, for the Party urgently needed 'an upswing of philosophical work.' [51] Soviet philosophers must arm themselves, he asserted, for a bitter struggle against the 'pimps and depraved criminals' who were serving as philosophers in the United States and Great Britain.[52] Zhdanov asked, 'Upon whom, if not upon us—the land of victorious Marxism and its philosophers—devolves the task of heading the struggle against corrupt and base bourgeois ideology? Who, if not we, should strike crushing blows against it?' [53] Zhdanov thus mapped out the work of Soviet philosophers in the post-war period. Anyone who reads the philosophical articles published in Soviet magazines and newspapers is likely to feel that in the period since 1947 Soviet philosophers have heeded the call to action sounded by Zhdanov in the name of Stalin.[54]

The philosopher Boris Kedrov was unlucky enough to have published, after Zhdanov's address, a book entitled *Engels and Natural Science,* in which he denied the importance of the principle of 'priority' in the study of the history of philosophy. Kedrov had, in addition, defended the 'pernicious' idea that there was a 'single world science' and had asserted that the study of philosophy by countries was a 'bourgeois' rather than a Marxist approach. For such views, Kedrov and other philosophers were attacked as champions of 'harmful cosmopolitan ideas.' On 22 March 1949, an abject confession of his 'mistaken positions,' together with a promise to 'struggle decisively' in the future against the 'ideology of bourgeois cosmopolitanism, hostile to our world outlook' was published by Kedrov in *Culture and Life*.

The treatment of Kedrov and other offending intellectuals should serve as a warning against misinterpreting the demand made by Stalin in 1950 for a 'struggle of opinions' in scholarship and science, a demand which was, after Stalin's death, echoed with much fanfare by Soviet plant scientists, for example, who criticized some of the theories of Trofim D. Lysenko. Of course Kedrov was lucky. Not all of those accused of cosmopolitanism were given the choice between 'recantation or Siberia.'

Among the intellectual fields engulfed in the campaign against cosmopolitanism, science and history were especially important. A vigorous campaign got under way in 1946 to eliminate from Soviet thinking the idea that Russia had ever been a technically backward country. This campaign was accompanied by the cutting off of personal contacts and correspondence between Soviet scientists and their foreign colleagues. The contrast between post-war xenophobia and the wartime official Soviet attitude was probably greater in the field of science than in any other. As late as May 1945, on the occasion of the celebration of the 220th anniversary of the Soviet Academy of Sciences, Soviet scientists had been gracious hosts to dozens of foreign colleagues.[55] From the fall of 1946 on, particularly from the summer of 1947, when it became obligatory for writers on the history of Russian science and on the role of Soviet and Russian science in the development of world science and culture to stress the 'priority' of Russian achievements in every conceivable field, efforts were made to inspire in Soviet scientists hatred and suspicion of foreign scientists.

The nature of the Soviet anti-foreignism disseminated among scientists may be suggested by a few examples. The influential Central Committee magazine *Party Life*,[56] for July 1947 [57] devoted its lead article to political work among the Soviet intelligentsia. It had been difficult, stated the article, for the Soviet state to establish its own intelligentsia. The ruling classes of pre-revolutionary Russia had put their own personal, selfish interests above the 'interests of the country and its national dignity.' The revolution saved the peoples of Russia from enslavement by foreign capital. But it was difficult to maintain this hard-won independence.

Consequently, in its work of forming and training the Soviet intelligentsia, the Party sought to inculcate among scientists and artists a 'feeling of Soviet dignity.' Russian science, the article continued, had always suffered from excessive respect for foreigners. Scientific discoveries made by Russians were often stolen by foreigners.

Despite Stalin's demand that Soviet science and technology surpass that of the West, there was still, warned *Party Life,* 'cases of kowtowing to things foreign.' Among other things, some Soviet scientists, 'inspired by a desire for petty glory' had published in foreign journals articles based on their work in the USSR. These scientists forgot that their work was the property of the state.

Konstantin Simonov, in his play *An Alien Shadow,* dealt with this problem in several statements, made by the character Makeev. Makeev stated:

There is, my dear fellow, another kind of exaggerated respect for things foreign which has serious consequences and from which you, too, are not free. It is caused by the opinion held by some of our people, that the world which is opposed to us consists of people who are much more admirable than they really are. Some of us consider the people from that world to be capable of much more noble motivations than those they actually entertain. They mistake the false freedoms that the Westerners have for real freedom, regard their conscience, which is sold to the capitalist system, as pure, and confuse their shameless advertisements of their achievements, talents, and abilities for a true reflection of life. And so, such Russians, upon receiving letters from those supermen are filled with pleasure. They are almost ready to hang the pages

of the foreign journal in which their work is printed on the
wall of their own room. And who does all these things? Scientists with a world reputation! [58]

It will be interesting to read a few excerpts from an article by
S. I. Vavilov, entitled 'On the Dignity and Honor of a Soviet
Savant,' contributed to a collection of essays on 'Soviet patriotism.' [59] Vavilov, who died shortly after this article was first published, in 1950, was at the time of his death the president of the
Academy of Sciences of the Soviet Union. It is interesting that
Vavilov's brother Nikolai, a world-famous geneticist, fell victim
to the purge which decimated Soviet geneticists in 1936–8. Sergei
Vavilov, in the article we are about to examine, may have been,
in a very real sense, warning his fellow scientists that holding
correct political attitudes was a matter of life and death.

Vavilov declared that 'An integral characteristic of the dignity
of a scientist of our country must be Soviet national pride, re-
fusal to tolerate manifestations of subservience to things foreign.' The greatest Russian scientists, men like Lomonosov,
Mendeleev, and Sechenov, had carried on a vigorous struggle
against the idealization of Western science. But many Russian
scientists, both in the nineteenth century and even during the
Soviet period, suffered from this shameful defect. Subservience
to the West was rewarded by the contempt displayed by foreigners toward Russian and Soviet science. Vavilov bitterly attacked the Nobel Prize Committee, which had awarded only
two prizes to Russian scientists, out of a total of 141 prizes thus
far conferred. In some cases, he charged, foreign scientists had
received Nobel prizes for discoveries which had actually been
made earlier by Russians.

Vavilov expressed bitter indignation because the Nobel Committee had not included the Russian language among the four
languages, namely, Swedish, French, German, and English, in
which it, in 1948, requested from Soviet scientists suggestions of
names of candidates for prizes. It is curious that in the course
of this denunciation Vavilov noted that 'many Soviet scientists'
had received such requests for information. Failure to include
Russian among the languages of the above correspondence, de-

clared Vavilov, must be considered 'an insult to our science and to culture in general,' especially in view of the fact that 'our army and people saved the whole world, including Sweden' from the threat of enslavement by Hitlerism. This insult was all the more infuriating because apparently the Swedes had a good knowledge of Russian, as was indicated by their having written Vavilov's name in perfectly good Russian in the text of a letter otherwise written in Swedish.[60]

In addition to its xenophobic aspects, Vavilov's article was interesting in many other ways. It stressed the debt owed by Soviet scientists and scholars to their government, which had given them the best conditions of work of any scientists in the world. Moreover, Soviet scientists enjoyed the inestimable advantage of Marxist-Leninist theory, upon which all intellectual activity in the Soviet Union was based. In return, Soviet scientists must display their love for their country not only by doing first-rate scientific work but also by carrying on propaganda among the public. In the first three months of 1950, the All-Union Society for the Dissemination of Political and Scientific Knowledge, organized in 1947, had given about 200,000 lectures. However, 'life demands more,' continued Vavilov; not merely hundreds of thousands, but millions, of lectures must be given by scientists.[61]

Anti-foreign pressure on Soviet scientists was further intensified after the anti-cosmopolitan drive got underway. The State Secrets Act of 1947, imposing draconian penalties for the disclosure, not merely of military or political but also of economic, technical, and other kinds of information to unauthorized persons with permission from the appropriate authorities, was only one of many measures intended to hermetically seal Soviet scientists off from contact and exchange of ideas with foreign scientists.[62] There can be no doubt, however, that Soviet scientists continued to receive, under official supervision, at least some of the books, periodicals, and other foreign materials needed in their work. As in so many other fields, the effort continued to be made to utilize foreign achievements against the foreign enemy. One phase of this operation was to give Russian and Soviet names to foreign discoveries, and to claim them for 'native' science so as to add to the prestige of Russian science abroad and to the self-confidence of Soviet scientists. Fortunately, there have been indications since the death of Stalin that some of these practices are being abandoned.

Let us now survey developments in Soviet post-war historiography.[63]

History is with the possible exception of Russian classical literature, the most potent of the Kremlin's ideological weapons. In all countries and at all times there is, of course, a large element of relativism in the study of history. It is a truism that 'history is past politics.' Perhaps it is more accurate to say that history is the past seen in the light of present interests. But in relatively free societies, this aspect of the relationship of men to their ancestors is balanced and corrected by respect for objective truth, and by the competition of views which permitted Carl Becker to coin the expression, 'Every man his own historian.'

By contrast, in the eyes of totalitarian rulers, history is a kind of synthetic mythology. The Soviet rulers have made an unusually systematic effort to tailor the consciousness of the living by doctoring the images of the dead. If during World War II Stalin wanted his subjects to gain courage by identifying themselves with a romanticized vision of Mother Russia, once the immediate military threat had been eliminated, he considered it necessary to reconvert his historical apparatus for the glorification of the Party. The symbol of Russia had been found to be too valuable and too powerful to dispense with, but henceforth historians were to serve the Party leadership by extolling the virtues and demonstrating the services to Russia and to 'progressive' mankind of that special breed of Russians, the Russian Bolsheviks. It was to be made clear that Soviet Russians were Russians to which something had been added.

A regrouping of forces on the historical front was begun by the reorganization and change of name of the major Soviet historical magazine in 1945, in connection with which a demand was made for a return from a largely traditional to a more 'Marxist' interpretation of history, especially of the history of 'capitalist' society, by preparation of a Five Year Plan for historical research, and by carefully staged public denunciations of historians whose works failed to conform to the post-war requirements of the Kremlin. The standard university textbook on the history of the USSR was revised, along with other basic works, but the first revised edition was not considered sufficiently militant. A leading Soviet historian, K. Bazilevich, attempted to defend the authors of the textbook against the charge that they had overemphasized the influence of Western revolution-aries' and socialists' movements on their counterparts in Russia, by pointing out that Stalin himself, a few years earlier, had criticized Soviet historians for underestimating this influence.

It is interesting to contrast the post-war attitude on the rela-tionship between Western and Russian revolutionary movements with the official view in force from 1934 until 1947. The 'observa-tions' of Stalin, Zhdanov, and Kirov, dated 9 September 1934, which inaugurated, on the administrative level, the modern So-viet system of rewriting Russian and world history to fit Party needs—the rewriting of Party history had begun still earlier—were severely critical of the draft of a text on the history of the USSR because it minimized the contributions of Western revolu-tionaries to the Russian movement.

Asserted the Politburo historians: 'The authors of the project apparently forgot that the Russian revolutionaries considered themselves pupils and followers of well-known coryphaei of bourgeois revolutionary and Marxist thought in the West.' [64] Obviously, if either political leaders or scholars in Soviet Russia permitted themselves the saving grace of humor the contrast between this position and that of 1947–9 would have evoked sheepish amusement. Since Stalin's death, the Party, anxious to make a good impression on Western European intellectuals, has begun again to demand that historians display proper respect for 'progressive' foreign traditions.

Under anything approaching normal conditions, an equally magnificent distance would have been noted between the inter-pretations contained in earlier 'observations' and decrees and those that Stalin and Zhdanov forced on Soviet scholars after World War II. Thus, in 1934, the triumvirate ruled that a text-book was needed in which the history of Great Russia would not be separated from that of the other peoples of the USSR, and, second, the history of the peoples of the USSR would not be separated from general European and world history.

But, of course, even in 1934, the rule that the right to think, at least in print, was reserved to Politburo members had already been established. If any doubts thereon remained alive in the minds of Soviet scholars they were eliminated, together with many of the scholars, by the purges of 1936–8. Even unauthorized quotation from or reference to previous official statements was, from the late 1920's, tacitly forbidden. The fact that some Soviet intellectuals felt free to resort, however cautiously, to this dangerous tactic in the post-war period indicated that the Stalin regime was no longer in a position to treat its valuable, probably on the whole patriotic, but perhaps diffusely discontented, cadres with the savagery to which it had resorted earlier.

It is not surprising that such courageous voices of consistency as that of Bazilevich were ignored. Probably Bazilevich, a strong Great Russian nationalist, escaped punishment because he was considered to be one of the 'cadres' too useful to be destroyed or damaged.[65] Perhaps the most prominent scapegoat in the historical profession was N. A. Rubinstein, author of a massive, excellent and scholarly study, published in 1941, entitled *Russian Historiography*.[66] Although, anticipating the future, he publicly criticized himself in writing in February 1948, his 'errors' were one of the main themes of the violent denunciations of late 1948 and early 1949 directed against 'cosmopolitan' historians.

We do not, of course, wish to give the impression that Rubinstein's work would satisfy critically-minded, conscientious Western scholars. To a disturbing degree, Rubinstein's work bore the marks of conformity to an abstract, Party-imposed scheme. For example, Rubinstein's judgment on Milyukov's work was that it 'regressed, like all bourgeois ideology.' [67]

In a mild form one finds in Rubinstein's work the justification of the policies of Ivan the Terrible which Stalinist historiography elevated to such a shocking level during and after World War II. Rubinstein criticized Plekhanov for sympathizing with Ivan's opponent, Kurbski. This indicated that Plekhanov failed to understand the social significance of Ivan's policies.[68]

Common to the 1936–8 period, and to the post-war era, was a

curious attempt to increase the moral authority of Soviet 'socialism' by associating it with reactionary, chauvinistic nationalism. It is instructive to compare contemporary Soviet history textbooks with the works of Dmitri Ilovaiski, whose name was a byword before 1914 for pedantic, fact-crammed super-patriotic historical writing. I looked up the reign of Ivan the Terrible in Volume III of Ilovaiski's *History of Russia* and was surprised to find that it was treated in what by Soviet standards would be considered an excessively objective, tolerant, and even 'cosmopolitan,' spirit.[69]

Distortion, demagogy, and anachronism in the presentation of the historical record were reinforced by limiting factual knowledge about the foreign world to a bare minimum. An examination of Soviet secondary-school syllabi used by teachers of history, and of the authoritative Soviet handbook on methods of teaching history by M. A. Zinovev indicate that this is a system of historical instruction intended to 'condition' the mind, almost in the behavioristic or Pavlovian sense, rather than to instruct, enlighten, or challenge. This effect is produced by heavy doses of rote learning about 'native' history, institutions, personalities, and so on, combined with a bare minimum of facts regarding, and an abundance of vilification of, the 'alien' world. To conclude this short excursion into the implementation of historical xenophobia and chauvinism, it may be noted that in 1950 foreign history and literature were included among the subjects no longer required for the secondary school [70] diploma.[71]

It seems probable that this trend toward cultural isolation, at least as far as the mass of the Soviet population is concerned, was still further intensified by the reduction, in the school year which began in September 1954, of time devoted to non-technical and non-utilitarian subjects.

Among the most basic documents, in reality directives, for the enforced re-injection of militant Stalinism into Soviet historiography, with which we are concerned here, were two major articles, published, respectively, in *Problems of History*,[72] No. 12, 1948 and No. 2, 1949. The first article was entitled 'Against Objectivity in Historical Science,' while the second bore the title 'Tasks of Soviet Historical Science.' Indicative of the crisis among

Soviet historians caused by the campaign against cosmopolitanism was the fact that the issue of *Problems of History* containing the second of these articles did not appear until July, although it should have come out in February. The state of terror which must have been produced among Soviet intellectuals by such developments of the late Stalin era helps us to understand why Stalin's successors considered it wise to make conciliatory gestures to Soviet intellectuals.

The documents under discussion sharply criticized the Institute of History of the Academy of Sciences, the top policy body in the field of history, for its alleged failure to 'fully reconstruct' its work in conformity with the decisions of the Party on ideological problems. Among other things, the Institute was taken to task for failure to participate in criticisms of the Rubinstein book. In this connection, *Problems of History* stated that 'The Institute, in practice, reacted but feebly to the Party's summons to organize a struggle against kowtowing to the West, and did nothing to expose the false theory of the lack of originality of Russian culture and science.'[73] While Soviet historians in general were attacked for failing to view the history of Russia and that of Western 'imperialist' countries from a Marxist point of view, non-Russian Soviet historians were criticized for 'bourgeois nationalistic theories' which allegedly led to distortions in their attitude toward relations between their own nations and the Great Russians in the pre-Soviet period. An indication of the completeness with which the field of history was covered by the Party authorities was offered by the fact that the highly specialized field of Byzantine history was dealt with at length in the December 1948 article. Soviet Byzantinists, the article alleged, had 'tried to establish a united front with foreign Byzantine scholarship.' [74] Another important feature of the December article was criticism of Soviet historians who made extensive use of foreign source materials in their research. Finally, this article reversed the tendency of Soviet historians of the 1930's to rehabilitate the great Russian non-Marxist historians such as Sergei Solovev and V. O. Klyuchevski, the latter one of the greatest historians produced by any country.[75]

The second of these two major articles struck a still sharper note. It asserted that the 'homeless cosmopolitans' had slandered the great Russian people, had disseminated the false view that it was 'eternally backward,' and had accepted the legend of the foreign origin of Russian culture. Their activities were calculated to undermine the spirit of patriotic pride of the Soviet people. The article connected the struggle against cosmopolitanism in historiography with major problems of international relations.

Cosmopolitanism, it declared, was an ideological weapon of American imperialism in preparation for war against the Soviet Union. This article also associated Zhdanov's speech at the founding of the Cominform in September 1947 with the campaign against cosmopolitanism. This point is of some interest, for, although the fury of this campaign and the daily publication of items using its key terms—'passportless tramps,' 'homeless cosmopolitanism,' et cetera—abated after 1949, it was, in the larger sense, a continuation of the campaign inaugurated by Stalin and Zhdanov in 1946.

Among other things, the 1949 document attacked *émigré* Russian historians, such as Michael Karpovich and George Vernadsky. These scholars were charged with seeking to present the Russian people as if it were 'located somewhere in the by-paths of history, incapable of independent development.' Cosmopolitanism, continued the article, was allied with bourgeois objectivity and bourgeois nationalism, with Cadet liberalism and social reformism. Both articles devoted attention to the problem of relations between the Great Russian and the non-Russian peoples of the Soviet Union.

The historian Razgon, who together with his colleague I. I. Mints, had been dismissed from his post, was criticized for giving a 'completely incorrect picture of relations between the Russian people and the peoples of the North Caucasus, and for "showing" the Chechens and Ingush as revolutionary and the Osetins as counter-revolutionaries.' In view of the fact that the Chechens had been deported during World War II, such references to them in official documents on music, history, and other subjects seem particularly vindictive.

It is perhaps to the credit of Mints—or possibly it indicated that there was some difference of opinion in high Party circles—

that he attempted to defend a 'Leninist' position against the nationalist line favored by the majority of Soviet historians under Party pressure. As A. Avtorkhanov has pointed out, the position of Mints and his friends was hopeless, among other things because they had earlier achieved eminence by helping the Party to silence and destroy the followers of Pokrovski in the 1930's.

The campaign against 'cosmopolitanism' in the historical field was, to a considerable extent, directed against historians whose method was most faithful to Marxism.[76] One wonders, in view of the generally anti-Semitic tone of the purge of 'cosmopolitans,' whether some of the purged historians did not suffer in part because of their Jewish origin. It should be noted again that the post-war purges, while they struck heavy blows at intellectuals, seldom involved exile or 'liquidation.' Certainly, however, they were intended to terrify intellectuals into smooth and ready compliance with Party policy. And, as Professor Kulski notes, forcing intellectuals to denounce their colleagues destroys normal solidarity among members of learned professions.[77]

Some Soviet historians, such as I. A. Zvavich, were accused of glossing over the evils of American and British imperialism. Zvavich was one of those unfortunate Soviet intellectuals who, undoubtedly with the approval and probably at the instigation of the Kremlin, had, during World War II, maintained rather cordial relations with the British Embassy. He had also studied in England. He had come to be considered dangerously objective in his attitude toward Britain. His situation was similar to that of the geneticist Zhebrak, one of the principal victims of the purge of anti-Lysenko geneticists in 1948. Zhebrak's chief error probably consisted in the fact that he had dared, at a time when this seemed a harmless and certainly not an anti-Soviet action, to publish an article in the American magazine *Science* criticizing the views of Lysenko.

Such men fell easy victims to a campaign in which any normal association with foreign colleagues in their fields of work became identified with lack of patriotism.

A fundamental theme of the criticism of 'cosmopolitanism' was the denunciation of the so-called thesis of 'a single current in the development of world historical science.' [78] Here, as in philosophy and other fields, this 'single current' theory was attacked because it seemed to deny the official Party doctrine of the uniqueness and superiority of Soviet Russian culture. It violated the official doctrine that 'bourgeois' and Soviet scholarship were in irreconcilable conflict. It was probably regarded as dangerous also because by implication it legitimized the desire of Soviet intellectuals to give expression to a tendency to regard fellow-workers in their respective fields in other countries as colleagues, rather than as spies.

We close this survey of Soviet xenophobia in the field of historical studies with a summary of the lead article in *Problems of History,* July 1954, entitled 'On the Study of Modern and Contemporary History of the Capitalist Countries.' [79] Commenting on a recent conference of leading Soviet scholars in the fields of modern and contemporary history, the article stated that 'Soviet science must demonstrate the boundless superiority of Soviet socialist democracy to bourgeois democracy.' It followed the line taken by Stalin in his farewell address at the Nineteenth Party Congress, in which he emphasized that the *bourgeoisie* 'has changed substantially, has become more reactionary, has lost its connection with the people and thus has weakened itself.'

In the light of this conception, according to the article, Soviet historians should attack the contemporary, reactionary, *bourgeoisie,* but at the same time might recognize the 'progressive role' of such men as Benjamin Franklin in an age when the *bourgeoisie* was a 'progressive' class. This seems like a very slight concession to the idea of a 'united front' of communist and other 'progressive' forces. It reflects a less accommodating attitude than was characteristic of the 'united front' of the 1930's.

Thus far we have not discussed the way in which the Party sought to inject xenophobia into economics. Correction of the 'mistakes' made by the venerable economist Eugene S. Varga, in his major work, *Changes in the Economy of Capitalism as a Result of the Second World War,* played a prominent part in the mobilization of economists for the 'cold war.' [80] Since Western readers know more about developments in this field than those in almost any other, and since we have already dealt extensively with post-war Soviet economic 'analysis' of the 'capitalist' world, we discuss the mobilization of economists very briefly.

The keynote was struck by K. V. Ostrovityanov, who replaced Varga in 1947 as the Party's overseer of economists, when he said that Varga's work suffered from 'separation from politics.' Just as Soviet musicians had shirked their political duty by failing to compose tunes which would cultivate a martial spirit so Varga and his economist colleagues had failed to produce propaganda tracts calculated to sustain the faith of a tired people and to inspire among foreign communists and fellow-travelers confidence in the inevitability of the doom of capitalism and in the Kremlin's omniscience.

Varga set to work on a new book to correct his 'errors.' The new work appeared in the fall of 1953, under the title *Fundamental Problems of the Economy and Politics of Imperialism*.[81] According to the author's preface, the book was written during the period 1948 to 1951, but in 1952–3 it was revised in the light of Stalin's article, 'Economic Problems of Socialism in the USSR,' and of the materials of the Nineteenth Party Congress. The preface, as well as the content of the work, make it clear that Varga made an earnest effort to take to heart the criticisms of his colleagues and of the Soviet press. The basic theme of the work is the 'struggle of two systems.'

This theme of struggle is presented, particularly in the concluding chapter, within the framework of the current official Soviet interpretation of 'co-existence.' Thus, for example, Varga quotes from a statement made by Malenkov in March 1953, a few days after Stalin's death, regarding the ardent desire of the Soviet Union for peace, and follows this with the statement that the Soviet peace policy does not indicate fear of the imperialists. In the final paragraph of this book Varga declared that if the Soviet Union had been able, 'one for one,' to smash Hitler's powerful military machine, there could be no doubt that in a new war, the Soviet Union, no longer alone, but in alliance with 'the countries of people's democracy, and the democratic republics of China and Germany, and also with the aid of the peoples of the colonies, fighting for their liberation,' would certainly be victorious.[82]

It is not necessary to comment on the scholarship of such a study. In this connection, however, it might be well to note that a deterioration in quality of scholarship similar to that represented by the contrast between the relative objectivity, and even a slight measure of orginality, of Varga's 1946 work and his recent book, seems to have occurred in most branches of social science and the humanities in the Soviet Union since the onset of 'Zhdanovism' in 1946. Thus far, there is no reason to believe that 'Malenkovism' or 'Khrushchevism' will prove to be more favorable to the development of sound and objective scholarship.

In Soviet psychology a standard work, which had been awarded a Stalin Prize in 1942, was harshly attacked in 1947, apparently because it had been decided that its author had 'deliberately ignored the psychology of the "new Soviet man"' and that he was moreover a 'servile fawner' on Western theories.[83] In the closely related field of physiology, it was officially decided, at a conference held during the summer of 1950, that there existed 'only two physiologies, Pavlovian and post-Pavlovian.' [84]

These developments in psychology and physiology are, in some ways, closely related to better-known events in the field of genetics, in which the Party Central Committee officially ruled, in August 1948, that Trofim D. Lysenko was correct in upholding the doctrine that acquired characteristics of living organisms are inherited. By implication at least, it could be deduced that the Soviet leadership, by its guidance of work in these three fields, wished to convey the impression that the new, and superior type of human being, 'Soviet man,' fit to decide the destinies of all mankind, had come into existence under the favorable conditions of Soviet 'socialist' society. In these and other fields, in fact in every conceivable field from statistics to archaeology, architecture, and atomic physics, Soviet intellectuals are mobilized for spiritual battle against the 'decadent' West.

The pattern we have described seems distorted and sinister to us, despite its ludicrous aspects, but to the Soviet leadership, and, to a considerable extent to members of the Soviet ruling class in general, it may seem the only logical response to the actions of the 'imperialist' enemy as they perceive them through the distorting prism of Russian xenophobia and Marxist historicism.

Moreover, the Soviet leadership might be expected to feel deep concern about the survival of the traditional Russian cultural inferiority complex, various aspects of which have been touched upon in this and the preceding chapter.

From the days in 1944 and 1945 when disturbing reports reached Moscow of the unsettling, even disintegrating, impact of foreign ways and wares on Soviet military personnel, the Kremlin was worried about the new climate of popular opinion, particularly among intellectuals and youth.

As the war ground to a weary and sanguinary end, hopes and desires for physical and spiritual rest and change waxed stronger. To a considerable extent the regime itself had encouraged such aspirations, mainly if not entirely by typically Soviet methods of indirection, suggestion, and implication which in fact left it uncommitted. The worse feature of the situation, from the Kremlin's point of view, was that, in part, these moods were stimulated by the glimpse many Soviet citizens had had of the, to them, fascinating West. As is often, and correctly, pointed out, the favorable popular reactions to this experience, and the alarmed and indignant official response recall Russian experience after the Napoleonic wars. Could a historically conscious Politburo forget that that earlier experience was followed by the Decembrist uprising of 1825?

As for Soviet soldiers and even, in many cases, officers of low or medium rank—about the colonels, generals, and marshals we know less—faith in Soviet ideology was shaken when even the supposedly backward Balkans seemed vastly richer than the Soviet homeland. And life abroad also seemed free and gay in comparison with the regimented existence at home. I remember many conversations with Soviet acquaintances in Moscow in 1945 and even, though contacts were fewer and fearful, in 1946, in which my Soviet friends complained bitterly of the scarcity of facilities for relaxation and leisure even in Moscow, the show window of the USSR.

To the Soviet leaders, self-appointed engineers of human souls, to use a well-known expression of Stalin such moods seemed wicked and dangerous. At the very time when communism abroad had attained new heights of influence, there was danger of a loss of vitality at home. When the violent propaganda blasts of 1946 and 1947 did not produce the full desired effect, and the West stiffened its resistance to Kremlin efforts to proceed with what Zhdanov said in 1946 was 'the order of the day,' the further spread of Soviet 'socialism,' the still stronger medicine of the anti-cosmopolitan drive was prescribed.

The nature of this remedy, and an indication that it, too, did not take immediate effect, was contained in a sharply worded public lecture on 'Proletarian Internationalism and Bourgeois Cosmopolitanism' delivered in Moscow in 1951, and published by the All-Union Society for the Dissemination of Political and Scientific Knowledge. This is the vast organization of Soviet intellectuals, engaged in lecturing and other activities by means of which, in terms of their various fields of interest, Soviet intellectuals assist the Party in bringing the 'line' to the better-educated strata of the population.

The lecturer, F. Chernov, attacked the 'homeless cosmopolitans' as continuators into the Soviet period of a 'vile, barbarous survival,' which owed its origin to the fact that the ruling classes of Tsarist Russia, cut off from the people and hostile to it, had been economically dependent upon foreign capital. The first source of cosmopolitan ideology in the Soviet Union was the 'vile tradition of servility to the capitalist West.' The second was the existence of the 'imperialist camp.' The 'world *bourgeoisie*' relied, in its struggle against the Soviet Union, on the 'survivals of capitalism in the minds of man,' which it sought to stimulate. One could not fail to see a direct connection between the manifestations of bourgeois cosmopolitanism among 'some backward intellectuals,' and such manifestations of bourgeois ideology as lack of interest in politics and bourgeois objectivity. The elimination of this 'national nihilism,' and the cultivation of 'Soviet national pride,' asserted Chernov, were among the major tasks of the struggle of socialism against capitalism. Soviet people must feel their immeasurable superiority to citizens living under capitalist slavery.[85]

Among the ludicrous irrationalities of the cultural purge might be mentioned such absurdities as a resolution by the Vladivostok City Council [86] prohibiting indulgence in that city in such decadent Western dances as the fox trot. 'Sport for sport's sake' followed 'art for art's sake' to the Soviet index of prohibitions. While learned journals and scholarly books rejoiced in the fact that Soviet Russia had enriched the languages of the world with such terms as 'Stakhanovite,' and the genuinely Russian word *prizyv* [87] had replaced the German word *lozung* [88] in May Day slogans, 'foreign' words, such as 'eclair,' and 'biscuit,' were, at least for a time, frowned upon. Such bathos resembled similar features of Nazi cultural policy, as well as counterparts in the Russia of the mad Tsar Paul I or the anti-foreign hysteria connected with the names of Admiral Shishkov or Rostopchin, whose pinning of the epithet 'cannibal' [89] on the French reminds us of Soviet invective against the American 'cannibals' in 1949–53.

Very crude emotional appeals were often employed, for example, in the book *The Truth about American Diplomats,* by the American Embassy clerk, Annabelle Bucar, published in serial and book form in 1949, after her desertion to the Soviets. A long string of anti-American plays, beginning with Konstantin Simonov's *The Russian Question* in 1946, also belong to this type of propaganda. So also does the republication, abstracted from their context, of threatening anti-Western statements by Pushkin and other Russian men of letters in earlier times of crisis.[90]

In the post-war period, the fact that writers such as Pushkin, Chernyshevski, or even the much more chauvinistic Dostoevski, were careful to balance their criticisms of the West by at least equally sharp criticisms of their own country, was allowed to fade from the Soviet mind, in so far as the efforts of the regime could achieve this result.[91]

Let us now attempt to place in perspective the post-Stalin leaders' re-establishment of a measure of formal cultural contact with the outside world. It has already been suggested that the regime has not repudiated the essential features of the Lenin-Stalin ideology, at least up to the time of writing, late in 1955. The 'new course' appeared under the quite different circumstances of the mid-1950's, to resemble somewhat the 'united front' policy directed against Nazi Germany from 1934 to 1945. This hypothesis would not necessarily preclude a simultaneous effort to expand cultural exchange with the United States.

It appeared that while seeking to gain all possible scientific, technological, and perhaps even commercial advantages by improving relations with the United States, Moscow had not given up its long-range objective of undermining the American security system. One way of facilitating attainment of this objective was by utilizing cultural exchange to win friends in the Western 'camp.' This hypothesis might help to explain the friendlier treatment according to Europeans as against Americans.[92] It should be remembered, however, that in terms of relative standards of living, as well as in terms of ideological susceptibility, most of the peoples of the world are far easier for Moscow to deal with than are Americans.

Hints regarding political purposes of the post-Stalin cultural exchange policy emerged from statements made in connection with its launching in the spring and summer of 1953. The *Pravda* editorial for 15 June 1953, which was devoted to cultural relations, stated that 'the Soviet Union hospitably opens its doors to all who, with honorable intentions, wish to see our country.' The editorial went on to say that 'simple people,' as well as cultural leaders and other visitors, belonging to various political parties and social strata, were now visiting the USSR on an increasing scale.

Such visits enabled people to learn the truth about Soviet Russia and to expose 'the falsity of imperialist propaganda.' Visitors to the Soviet Union were 'unanimous' in praising the struggle of the Soviet people for peace. For this reason, 'everything progressive and honorable' was attracted to the Soviet Union. The growth of cultural exchange would benefit the 'progressive elements of all humanity, and the strengthening of peace throughout the world.'[93]

Two days after publication of the above *Pravda* editorial, the prominent Polish Communist and cultural leader Wanda Wasilewska, who became a Soviet citizen during World War II, made a significant statement on the subject of cultural exchange at a conference of the World Peace Council in Budapest. Speaking as the head of the Soviet delegation to the conference, Wasilewska stressed the importance of the exchange of cultural and scientific knowledge. She said that during the several years preceding her speech hundreds of foreign 'delegations' had visited the Soviet Union. She urged that cultural exchange be vastly expanded. 'Millions' of people must learn the truth about Soviet culture, and must become acquainted with the Soviet people in order that 'ignorance, prejudice, slander and indifference may be overcome.' [94] The conference passed a resolution endorsing Wasilewska's appeal.

Malenkov in his important address to the Supreme Soviet on 8 August 1953 devoted two paragraphs to cultural relations. He took advantage of difficulties which had arisen in connection with the projected visit of Soviet chess players to the United States to attempt to create the impression that it was not the Soviet Union, but America, which was obstructing cultural exchange.

The Khrushchev-Bulganin regime added almost spectacular propaganda impetus to Malenkov's international cultural program. Khrushchev had already, in November 1953, contributed conspicuously to the anti-isolationist trend by receiving the American lawyer and former UNRRA administrator in the Ukraine, Marshall MacDuffie, within the sacred precincts of Party Central Committee headquarters.[95] This event symbolized a new policy devoting increased attention to non-communists and anti-communist elements. In broad terms, this policy was consistent with Stalin's rather wishful appeal, in 1952, to communists everywhere to exercise leadership within broad coalitions of 'patriots' and 'progressives,' but its tone and tempo were refreshingly and indeed seductively different from the Stalinist pattern.

Once in power, the Khrushchev-Bulganin leadership made it clear that they were committed, at least for a time, to a bold attempt to alter the negative image of Bolshevik behavior throughout the non-communist world. As we have indicated, we consider that in view of the historical record, it will be prudent for non-communists to hope for the best but be prepared for the worst in connection with this and other aspects of Moscow's 'new look.'

A number of at least superficially encouraging developments occurred in 1954 and 1955. Americans in particular were inclined to be optimistic when the Soviet leaders at Geneva in July 1955 subscribed to 'directive' number three, instructing the foreign ministers of the four participant powers to study measures capable of 'leading to the gradual elimination of barriers which hinder freedom of communication and peaceful trade among peoples and to the assurance of free contacts and relations mutually beneficial for the interested countries and peoples.' [96]

Probably, to the extent that these objectives are attained, the Western world will favorably revise its estimate of Soviet intentions. Certainly one useful operational index for measuring xenophobia is the willingness of a state to permit interaction between its citizens and those of other states. The present fluid situation may be so altered by the time this book is published as to make everything said here seem foolish. But this is a risk that all who have the temerity to write on Soviet affairs must take, and we shall permit ourselves the luxury of some cautious speculation on the significance and further development of Soviet cultural exchange policy.

Americans tend, perhaps somewhat naïvely, to assume that 'international' activity of any kind is conducive to world peace. Doubtless the Kremlin is shrewdly aware of this. Available data seem to indicate, however, that the national stereotypes held by peoples regarding other peoples 'may be attributed to relations between their governments,' and that they are not 'causative,' but 'symptomatic.' [97] If this is true, the future trends of propaganda and education, especially in Russia, will be more important than other factors both as indexes and as determinants of Soviet-non-Soviet relations. If the 'venom content' of post-Stalin propaganda continues to fall, this will be a favorable sign.[98]

Our reading of the Soviet press to date indicates that only the most objectionable features of its basic anti-foreignism have been modified and, perhaps temporarily, eliminated. The pattern in August 1955 was contradictory, with negative features still predominant. Yet some minor but encouraging symptoms were visible. A sense of humor, absent for years from Soviet comment on the United States, was manifested in some Soviet press comment on America in 1955. In fact, aesthetically conservative Americans might not have objected to Soviet derision of American modern art. At least this sort of material was a relief from grim Stalinist tenseness.[99]

There was also a new, if not very flattering, note of realism in some appraisals of features of the American scene. Quite interesting was the characterization in a review of the American film *Test Pilot* in *Soviet Culture* for 31 May 1955 of American males as 'sport-loving,' 'coarsely masculine,' 'practical and down to earth.' At the same time, however, the standard image of 'bourgeois,' particularly American, culture continued to be dominant. Thus for example, *Soviet Culture* for 9 July reprinted a long article from *Masses and Mainstream* by Charles White, an American Negro artist, full of communist clichés regarding the relationship of Negroes, and Negro culture, to American and Soviet Russian culture.

On the high policy level realism was manifested in a renewed determination to learn from the capitalist West. Khrushchev's 'corn-hog' agricultural measures, numerous statements regarding continued Western superiority in various branches of technology in Bulganin's speech of 17 July 1955, and the sending of scientific and technological delegations to Western nations were some of the many indications of this desire. Probably, together with the political factors already mentioned, this was the most significant motive force of Soviet cultural exchange policy in 1953–5, as far as the advanced Western nations were concerned.

It was of course easy to overestimate the extent of post-Stalin cultural exchange activity. The few thousand participants by 1955 constituted a minuscule total in comparison with nearly a million foreign visitors to the United Kingdom every year. The police and informer system still made normal personal contacts between Soviet citizens and foreigners difficult, or impossible. The continued, though diminished, tendency to favor 'progressive' foreigners, and cultural materials produced by 'progressives,' further distorted the 'exchange.'[100] It seemed safe to predict in August 1955, however, that cultural contact between Russia and the West would increase, that it would pay political dividends to the Kremlin, and that if it continued long enough and grew sufficiently in scope it might perhaps lead, despite the Soviet control system, to a mutually beneficial process of diffusion. But it was apparent that a great deal would have to be accomplished before Soviet-American cultural exchange could regain the levels attained in the 1930's, when thousands of Americans lived, worked, and studied in Russia. It is startling to be reminded that American engineers, alone, in the Soviet Union numbered more than 1000 around 1930, and that even in 1940 they 'were counted in tens.' [101] In the 1920's, of course, freedom to travel and to associate on normal and even intimate terms with Soviet people had been far greater. Thus looking back we see a steady growth of isolation and xenophobia as the Soviet totalitarian system was perfected.

To what degree this trend could be reversed, and to what extent its reversal could be paralleled by deeper trends toward a diminution, both on the Soviet and non-Soviet sides, of narrow, group-centered attitudes remained unanswerable questions. To hope for rapid progress was unrealistic. But it seemed reasonable to speculate that the worst excesses of Stalinist isolationism and xenophobia might gradually recede into history. It was perhaps not too naïve to hope that behavior changed for tactical reasons might, if it persisted long enough, react back on motivation and eventually even bring about a revision of doctrine.

Soviet Chauvinism and Messianism

This chapter deals with chauvinistic and messianic attitudes in Soviet ideology. Let us begin with a brief attempt at a definition of messianism in the Soviet setting.

Messianism, strictly defined, is a technical term associated with study of the Jewish and Christian religions. But it has been defined more broadly by Hans Kohn as 'a belief held with religious fervor by oppressed or unfortunate ethnic, social or religious groups or by men suffering either from the imperfection of their fellow human beings or the consciousness of their own inadequacy.' [1] Such groups profess to believe in the inevitability of a radical change which will end their suffering and fill the world with piety and justice. Usually, messianic movements insist upon an exclusive right to prescribe the nature of desired changes. The political messianism of modern times exalts the values of particular nations or social movements into universals.

Social psychologists have achieved a measure of agreement regarding factors which favor the development of extreme nationalism, chauvinism, and destructive messianism. Such attitudes seem to be 'compensatory,' 'substitutive,' and 'projective.' Individuals, and the groups of individuals who make policy in some states and nations, compensate for feelings of inferiority, individual insecurity, and real or fancied threats or insults by creating self-images which magnify their virtues, but depreciate and vilify enemies and outsiders. Feelings of guilt are 'projected' to socially approved foreign targets. Such tendencies are especially strong where social tensions are acute. Totalitarian governments are unusually well equipped to exploit such sentiments, and are perhaps forced to do so to protect themselves against popular discontent.[2]

'Compensation,' and related concepts help us to understand the virulence and persistence of Soviet chauvinism and messianism. This approach furnishes one of the best keys to understanding many aspects of Russian development. Much of the extremism of Russian thought has resulted from attempts to overcome handicaps imposed by geography and other factors. One tragic uniformity of Russian history is the vicious circle of extreme reactions against unfavorable situations which have led, after brief periods of apparent change, to a recurrence, often in intensified form, of the evils against which they were directed.

Chauvinism regarding Soviet achievements has been accompanied in Soviet thought by utopian-messianic pretensions with regard to the part of the world which has not yet experienced the blessings of 'socialism.' Moscow believes, or pretends to believe, that communism will inherit the earth. It holds out to mankind the vision of the harmonious society without coercion and inequality. But Soviet messianism justifies a plan for a Russian communist world organized and directed from Moscow.

For those who do not fully share it, including, I believe, the majority of persons living under communist rule, this is more a nightmare vision than a utopian dream. To many in the West it is so frightening that they prefer to ignore it. The pattern of sentiments and behavior with which it is associated is one of the most potent and menacing abroad today. Soviet Russian nationalism reflects defensive as well as offensive attitudes, however.

If the world can move toward stability, and the peoples of the Soviet Union toward more normal relations with one another and toward their government, Soviet chauvinism and messianism may gradually lose force. A partial offset to the dangers posed by these attitudes exists already, in the form of attitudes of discontent, escapism, and political apathy. One of the encouraging aspects of the Soviet scene is the continued existence of 'cosmopolitan' sentiments among Soviet intellectuals, and friendly curiosity about foreigners among ordinary people. Official xenophobia and chauvinism derive much of their virulence from the Kremlin's effort to overcome Russian xenomania.

The Party has considered it necessary to urge, from as far back as 1938, that propaganda work among the intelligentsia be conducted 'differentially,' with emphasis upon persons of high rank. The necessity of a major effort to arouse patriotic enthusiasm among 'commanders of production,' and the 'most cultured segment of the people,' has been stressed ever since.[3]

Such efforts would not have been necessary if the Kremlin had felt that it could count on the enthusiastic support of the intelligentsia, the section of the population most likely to entertain xenomanic, or at least 'cosmopolitan,' attitudes. The reluctance of members of this class to join the Party has been a source of suspicion and anxiety in the Kremlin. It is almost amazing that as recently as the end of 1953 apparently 'only 35 per cent of all teachers in higher educational establishments were members of the Communist Party.'[4]

Sentiments discussed in this chapter are expressed sometimes in Russian traditional terms and at other times in Soviet revolutionary symbols. Often both types of symbols are employed. A good example of this mixture of elements is furnished by an article published in *Kommunist* in July 1954, entitled 'The Great Russian Writer, A. P. Chekhov.' The author, V. Ermilov, one of the most influential Soviet critics, argues that Chekhov's service to Russian literature and the revolutionary movement consisted in his indictment of a dying order accompanied by expression of confidence that happiness for all Russians would soon be realized. Unlike Gorki, Chekhov did not understand that the true hero of Russian reality was the revolutionary worker, but he reflected many of the best traits of 'Russian national character.' Chekhov is 'one of the close and wise friends of our literature.'[5]

At times the relationship between 'Russian' and 'Soviet' elements is harmonious. But often it seems to be contradictory. Instead of a synthesis, there is a mere juxtaposition. This confusion reflects an insoluble contradiction of Soviet ideology derived from the fact that one national culture, interpreted by a single government, is arbitrarily combined with Marxist universalism.

A person who thinks of himself primarily as a 'Russian' and only secondarily as a 'communist' is in a better position to seek for himself an alternative to the present Soviet system than one who defines his world outlook in dogmatic Marxist terms. The former can oppose the regime and still consistently consider himself a patriot, identifying himself with millions of his fellow countrymen. For this reason, the regime, while often relying heavily upon traditional Russian sentiments, has always carefully refrained from committing itself to a wholehearted identification with these sentiments. Even when it has exploited them most intensively, it has been highly selective and it has always reminded Party members, in particular, and to a lesser degree the non-Party population, that only such Russian sentiments and traditions as are in accord with its interpretation of Soviet Marxism can be considered respectable.

For the most part, the healthy and positive elements in Soviet culture consist of carry-overs from pre-Soviet Russian culture or are borrowed from Western science and technology. The glaring contrast between the reality resulting from the impact of these factors, and the ideals of 'socialism' and of the 'communism' toward which Soviet society is officially declared to be moving, gives rise to a largely compensatory chauvinism and messianism. The regime cannot afford to admit to the non-Soviet world which it seeks to influence, or to the population under its control, or probably even to itself, that this glaring contrast exists. Hence the violent attacks on the 'decadent' non-Soviet world, and the sometimes ludicrously boastful assessment of Soviet achievements.

It seems to this writer that of the three sentiments discussed in this and the preceding chapter, chauvinism, or at least the normal national pride of which official Soviet chauvinism is often the distorted expression, is the most popular among the Soviet peoples. Messianism probably finds least support among the lower strata of the population. Fear and hatred of the 'capitalist' governments with whom they must contend have deep roots in the thinking of top echelons of the Soviet elite. Not entirely without justification, the Soviet leadership has always regarded foreign governments as malicious, if often inept, enemies. Messianism, which, as we have noted earlier, is difficult to distinguish from Soviet imperialism, also appeals to members of the elite, although it is probably not nearly as powerful a sentiment, even in the highest Soviet circles, as is xenophobia. Although in quite varied forms, national pride and chauvinism are common to elite and masses alike.

The Soviet chauvinism of the 1940's and 1950's resembles, but much surpasses in virulence, certain pre-Soviet attitudes. Chauvinistic tendencies were expressed by reactionary nationalists, such as Nicholas Danilevski, who in his *Russia and Europe* set forth an ambitious program for Russian territorial and cultural imperialism, together with a pseudo-biological justification for military expansion. Danilevski pioneered in adapting for political purposes a theory of 'social-cultural types,' somewhat similar to Oswald Spengler's concepts.[6]

The extreme reactionary nationalism of influential journalists like Michael Katkov, who, however, opposed Pan-Slavism, and the demagogic Pan-Slavism of Danilevski, were reflected in some of Dostoevski's novels and journalistic articles. Both in *The Possessed,* and in his well-known and mediocre anti-Western articles of the 1870's, there was a pre-Fascist note, balanced, however, by Christian faith and by rejection of any doctrine which completely sacrificed the individual to society. Reactionary Russian nationalists, somewhat like current Soviet propagandists, tended to lump together indiscriminately, and reject, ideas they regarded as liberal, skeptical, or insufficiently patriotic. Perhaps the most significant similarity between pre-Soviet thought, both radical and conservative, and contemporary official doctrine, consists in an excited, emotionally charged tone. All of the currents of thought which we are here comparing are characterized by dogmatism, arrogance, and angry and suspicious intolerance. All are worlds apart from the experimental and self-examinatory spirit of true liberalism or from the positive, constructive, but critical spirit of genuine conservatism.

Although there are significant resemblances, however, between the thought of men like Danilevski, and contemporary Soviet ideology, there is little continuity.[7] There are too many differences between pre-revolutionary Russian chauvinism and Soviet thought for us to speak meaningfully of continuity between these two patterns. Rather, we are confronted here by the type of resemblance which exists between modern communism and fascism. All of these forms of extremism represent, in all probability, more or less 'natural' but perhaps pathological reactions to peculiar and difficult situations.

On the whole, the Soviet 'line' has been consistent with respect to Danilevski and other reactionary nineteenth-century Russian thinkers.[8] Danilevski's thought cannot be reconciled with Soviet doctrine because of his opposition to Darwin. With regard to the Slavophiles, the position is somewhat more complex.[9] Dostoevski, with particular respect to his literary as distinct from his ideological heritage, was especially during World War II, sometimes praised in Soviet sources.[10] Such attitudes, however, were tolerated only in the wartime atmosphere characterized by a tendency to indiscriminate glorification of everything Russian. The subsequent revival of Stalinist dogmatism 'corrected' what was regarded as an unhealthy idealization of the Russian past.[11] But in 1956 the regime moved to claim the heritage of Dostoevski for Soviet culture.

Turgenev, who was hated by Dostoevski partly because he was too 'European' to sympathize with the latter's chauvinism, gave, in *Smoke*, an excellent description of the touchy nationalism, easily degenerating into chauvinism, which afflicted many Russian intellectuals. Potugin, in this novel, pokes fun at 'Russian inventiveness.' Grain, he remarks scornfully, is still placed in the kiln as it was in the days of Rurik. It is remarked that Russian intellectuals, or pseudo-intellectuals, often discuss 'the decadent West.' Yet, 'it beats us at every point, that West—but it's rotten!' One reason for Dostoevski's excoriation of Turgenev was that in *Smoke* the opinion was expressed that Russia had never created anything original in the course of its entire existence.[12]

In his famous work, *Fathers and Children*, Turgenev [13] had pilloried the emerging radical intelligentsia, the force that was eventually to transform Russia. In *Smoke*, he again attacked the radicals, but directed much of his fire also against extreme nationalism. The attitudes revealed in such novels as *Smoke*, and *The Possessed*, persisted down to the Bolshevik Revolution, and were allowed, during the nationalist revival which began in the early 1930's, to at least partially re-emerge.

In some of Lenin's writings there is a latent Great Russian chauvinistic and messianic potential. Although this sentiment was kept under strict discipline by Lenin, it occasionally surged to the surface.[14] This messianic note in Lenin, although its overt expression bulked small in his thought, can be usefully employed by Soviet propagandists in times of crisis.

Red Star for 1 July 1943 contained an interesting article, entitled, anachronistically, 'Lenin and Stalin on Soviet Patriotism,' which asserted, among other things, that Lenin in exile on Capri once reproached Gorki for having 'forgotten Russia.' Lenin is pictured as observing the native fishermen cautiously drawing in their nets, and saying 'ours work more boldly.'

Even a strictly orthodox interpretation of Lenin permits the Soviet leadership to make use of patriotism, though scarcely of chauvinism. The demands of ideological consistency and, more important, the necessity of maintaining doctrinal integrity as one means of assuring the organizational integrity of the Party, and its 'social distance' from the non-Party mass, seem to require that official Soviet use of the emotional appeal of chauvinistic sentiments not be permitted to go beyond rather strict limits. In general, despite zigzags, these limits remain those which were laid down by Lenin in such works as 'On the National Pride of the Great Russians.'[15] Lenin made it clear that the only patriotism which was legitimate for a Russian Marxist was 'socialist' patriotism.

Within this framework, we can understand why sentiments expressed in Soviet Russia during World War II, were sharply censured after the war, or simply ceased to be expressed. In still other cases, sentiments which during the war tended to acquire a certain autonomy and to bulk rather large in the total stream of communications, persisted after the war only as minor notes, and under guard, so to speak, of accompanying Stalinist concepts. The latter observation, perhaps, applies particularly to the cult of Russian military tradition which blossomed during the war, but which after the war was reduced to more modest proportions, within a framework of heightened Party surveillance.[16]

The fate of the writer Anna Akhmatova symbolizes the conflict between the 'two Russias.' The pure, idealistic but not at all chauvinistic Russian patriotism of Akhmatova was tolerated and even acclaimed during the darkest period of the war, when it could be useful, but it had no place on the post-war Soviet scene.[17]

The patriotic Russian nationalism of the wartime period differed both from pre-war and post-war 'Soviet patriotism' in one supremely important way. Although it certainly was not a free and spontaneous expression of 'public opinion,' it was a more accurate reflection of popular sentiment than either its pre-war or post-war counterparts. It is significant that the Russian patriotism of World War II was much less anti-Western than the official patriotism with which we are contrasting it. There are enough indications in Soviet published sources of the wartime period, and in the testimony of Soviet refugees, to warrant the conclusion that, at that time at least, Soviet people, Russians and non-Russians alike, who were most patriotic in the traditional sense of the term, were also friendliest to the Western allies.

This was very definitely the writer's impression during the war years in Moscow, based not only upon spontaneous expressions of friendliness on the part of hundreds of Russians, but also upon the fact that the overwhelming majority of the Russian writers, scholars, librarians, and other professionals with whom he had official or semi-official contact did their best, sometimes probably at some risk to themselves, to assist him in performing various functions connected with his duties as an embassy Press Attache.

By contrast, persons whose status and duties were more closely involved with the Party-State apparatus, were much less friendly and, by and large, far more inaccessible. Thus the impression was created that the least 'Russian,' or if you will, the least 'patriotic' of Soviet citizens were the most xenophobic and chauvinistic. I should like in this connection to mention a rare publication, of which a copy was given to me by an official of the State Lenin Library in Moscow, entitled *Eighty Years in the Service of the Science and Culture of Our Motherland*.[18]

This publication expressed the legitimate pride of Russian library workers in their own traditions and achievements, originating, in the case of the Lenin Library, in the famous Rumyantsev Library founded by a public-spirited Russian nobleman. But at the same time, the book contained many pages of obviously sincere expressions of admiration and gratitude for help rendered by British and American libraries and librarians to their Soviet colleagues.[19]

Nikolai Tikhonov, during the Soviet-German war one of the most popular Soviet poets, wrote in 1944 that 'National pride, hitherto buried in the hearts of the Soviet people, burst forth in a bright flame before the threat of enslavement and in the face of deadly danger.' [20]

However, a few months before publication of Tikhonov's statement, Alexander Fadeev, who in the shakeup of 1946 replaced him as head of the Union of Soviet Writers, made a significant statement reflecting the Kremlin's determination to retain the monopoly right to define the character of Soviet nationalism. In a lecture in Moscow on 'Soviet Patriotism and the National Pride of the Peoples of the USSR,' Fadeev said that the most important cause of the unprecedented patriotism of Soviet people consisted in the fact that 'the Soviet character of our patriotism' distinguishes it from any other kind of patriotism.[21]

Typical of wartime hatred of the enemy and love of country was a poem published in 1942 in the literary magazine *Znamya,* which referred to the Germans as the 'Pechenegs of the Rhine.' It hailed the 'mother of cities, Moscow, immortal Moscow, calm, glorious and confident.' [22] Another poem in the same issue said that Russia was so 'wealthy and generous that we gave Pushkin to the world,' and it added that 'magnanimous, wise, and young, inflamed by anger, having grown strong under the Kremlin star, Russia is invincible.' [23]

Hatred of the Germans was most effectively expressed by Ilya Ehrenburg in his newspaper articles, particularly those contributed to the army newspaper *Red Star.* Many other Soviet writers such as Sholokhov, in his series 'The Science of Hatred,' Simonov, in his famous play *Russian People,* and Nikolai Tikhonov in his vivid reportage articulated the hatred which developed when it became apparent that the Germans intended to wage a war of enslavement and extermination against the Russians. The savage passions aroused partly by this propaganda, but much more by the nature of the war itself, ultimately found expression in the behavior of Soviet troops in Germany.

Hatred of the enemy and love of the homeland were reflected particularly interestingly in the magazine *Leningrad,* the organ of the Leningrad section of the Union of Soviet Writers. Typical of the content of this magazine was a poem published in its second number, in October 1942. A dying Russian guerrilla fighter expresses his love for 'this land, and the forest and the grass,' and his satisfaction that with his last bullet he helped to avenge 'my Russia.' A table of contents of this magazine, published in March 1943, covering the first seven numbers for 1942, gives a good sample of the Russian wartime mood.

The illustrations contained in this and other Soviet publications, and the savagely effective 'Tass Window' war posters, conveyed the same message. The main theme in the seven issues of *Leningrad* referred to above, was the Red Army, closely followed by 'Leningrad during the Fatherland War,' 'the historic past of Leningrad,' and 'the Fatherland War.' Almost equal attention was devoted to 'the historical heritage of Russia.' By contrast, these issues contained only two items on Lenin and four on Stalin.

Although this magazine played down the Party, and 'ideological' themes in general, and for this reason, among others, was eventually suppressed, some of its articles were quite chauvinistic. Number three, 1943, praised the Tsarist general, Dragomirov, who, the article said, appreciated the special ability of the Russian soldier in bayonet and sword fighting. Number six, 1943, contained an article on a Cossack hero of the War of 1812 who had aroused curiosity and enthusiasm while on a visit to London. Interestingly and characteristically, this item drew much of its material from an extreme nationalist magazine of the nineteenth century, *The Son of the Fatherland.*

Like other Soviet publications, because of pressure from Party authorities, *Leningrad* struck an increasingly chauvinistic and messianic note after the Russian victory at Stalingrad. An article by the prominent writer Vsevolod Vishnevski in number seven, 1943, boasted that 'No one could resist the advance of Russia,' and stated that the history of Russia pivoted around Leningrad, 'the most beautiful city in the world.' Vishnevski hailed Russia's 'advance to the borders of Asia,' and also the extension after the accession to the throne of Peter the Great, of cultural, economic, and political relations with the West, as one result of which the Baltic became a 'Russian sea.'

An interesting article in Number 12–13, 1943, on the victory of the Russian Prince Dmitri Donskoi over the Mongols in 1380, included the following statement: 'The Russian Prince, gathering around Moscow almost the whole of the Russian state, and the Russian people, uniting around Moscow, threw off the Tatar yoke, and organized that tremendous Russian force, which now rules a sixth of the earth, and is the most advanced and democratic principle in the world, and the guiding principle of world history.'

The same issue quoted the Tsarist admiral Makarov to the effect that the Arctic Ocean would be mastered by Russian sailors for the glory of Russia.

Chauvinist sentiments were expressed in *Leningrad*. The magazine, however, was not openly anti-Western—it did not, for example, stress the 'second-front' problem—and its image of Russia differed substantially from that of Party propagandists such as Georgi Aleksandrov, Emilyan Yaroslavski, or P. F. Yudin, whose wartime articles, mainly by innuendo, continued to convey the Leninist thesis that the Soviet Union, on the one hand, and the entire non-Soviet world, on the other hand, represented two radically different social systems. The stubborn devotion of the Kremlin and its Party cadres to Bolshevik symbols even in the darkest days of the war, impresses anyone who takes the trouble to carefully read wartime issues of such Soviet political journals as *Bolshevik*.[24] Articles in such organs made frequent references to the struggle against Allied intervention in 1918–21, to the 'world' mission of the Soviet Union and its Communist Party, and to Soviet victories against the Germans resulting from the principles of Leninism.

Two Russias, or two very different images of what in the West was represented by the word 'Russia,' were depicted in Soviet wartime propaganda. One of these was the Russia of tradition, the Russia symbolized by icons in corners of peasant cottages, by folklore and folk memories with roots in pagan Slavic mythology, by Tatyana in Pushkin's *Eugene Onegin*, by Platon Karataev in

Tolstoy's *War and Peace,* or by the sometimes corrupt and cow-
ardly, in other instances brave, conscientious, and public-spirited
Russian officers, officials, and scholars whose memory was honored, though with qualifications and reservations, in Soviet literature and drama of the early war years.[25]

Features of this multi-faceted traditional Russia were at least
dimly discernible in much that Soviet censors allowed to be published at a time when the Party needed, as never before, the support of the Russian people. Not only was the traditional Russia
beginning to emerge, but the non-Russian peoples also were,
though to a lesser degree, permitted to express pride in their
national traditions. After the war, they, even more than the Great
Russians, were to pay a high price for this partial gift of cultural
freedom.

Even during the war, Soviet totalitarianism remained basically
intact. However, many potentially dangerous, pluralistic, and
anarchistic tendencies emerged. Some of the anti-totalitarian
trends discernible during the war served the Kremlin's purposes
by arousing false hopes in the West. Even some Russian *émigré*
intellectuals thought that a healthy Russian patriotism had developed, with which the world could live much more easily than
with doctrinaire Bolshevism.[26]

Hopeful observers of Soviet wartime trends were not entirely
wrong. The 'two Russias' were confusingly present even in Stalin's speeches and other major wartime documents. In Stalin's
speeches, to be sure, as well as in May Day and November sixth
slogans, and the like, Marxist themes were only tactfully muted,
leaving at the center of attention a 'patriotism' too easily accepted at its face value. Especially confusing was—and is—the
mixture, in the very core of Leninism-Stalinism, of 'Western'
technocracy and 'Russian' despotism and messianism. The military ordeal, and the imperialist expansion made possible by Soviet military power, welded together more firmly this amalgam
of elements symbolized by Peter the Great, Suvorov, and Kutuzov, and the already Russified Marxism of Lenin and Stalin.[27]

We are dealing with a broad spectrum. At one extreme were
the most unpolitical Russian nationalist sentiments, such as those
of Akhmatova, or the highly 'cosmopolitan' sentiments of other

Russian intellectuals. At the other extreme were the attitudes of Party fanatics. In between were those of most Russians, including writers such as Simonov or Tikhonov. Tikhonov, a member of the group that contributed to *Leningrad,* was sufficiently tinged with 'traditional' Russian sentiments to suffer demotion, but not disgrace, in the post-war literary purge. Certainly he went very far, even in newspaper pieces, toward forgetting that Russia had become Soviet. 'Russia,' he wrote in one such piece, 'is our soul and our heart!' 'Russia was, is and will be, eternal!' Russia, the home of our forefathers, Russia, joy and freedom—such was the hymn to Russia penned by Tikhonov in one article published in August 1942. In the eight pages of this article the words 'Russia,' 'Russian,' and cognates—occur 49 times.[28]

Even Konstantin Simonov, hailed by Tikhonov, then writing as head of the Union of Soviet writers, as 'the voice of the present day younger generation,' was to be forced, or at any rate considered it expedient, in 1946, to sharply criticize the literary themes which made his reputation during the war. In his self-castigation, in November 1946, Simonov wrote that in his 'Russian People' he had been unable to rise to the 'higher,' the 'Soviet' conception of Russian patriotism. He called upon Soviet writers to make it plain to the whole world that they considered communism to be the only correct path to the future for humanity.[29]

During the war, some Soviet writers, like other Soviet citizens, had perhaps forgotten what they should have known: that it was their duty to 'struggle for the triumph of socialism.' [30] It was this 'duty,' more than the patriotic emotions aroused by the bitterest of wars, that demanded of Soviet people the xenophobic, chauvinistic, and messianic attitudes with which we are concerned. After the war, not only were deviant notes eliminated, but the Party effected more than a mere return to pre-war 'normalcy.' New ground was broken on the path toward creating the 'new Soviet man,' arrogantly convinced of his superiority, full of hatred for the 'bourgeois' world.

Zhdanov's address to the Leningrad writers was representative of the official post-war attitude toward Russian nationalism and toward non-Soviet culture. Non-Russian Soviet emigrant scholars often assert that only non-Russians were accused after the war of 'bourgeois nationalism.' These assertions are partly correct, but they overlook the fact that a radical change occurred also in the Party's attitude toward the Great Russian cultural heritage.

Several months before Zhdanov's thunderous blast, *Culture and Life* published a sharp criticism of plays by N. Pogodin and other Soviet dramatists dealing with the 'unplumbed depths' of the 'Russian soul' and other ideas, now denounced by the Party as harmful nonsense.[31] Plays about 'Tsars, noblemen and Khans,' were also condemned.

At the same time, novels and dramatic works which allegedly played down the role of the Party or did not depict Party apparatus personnel in an appropriately positive fashion, were castigated.[32]

Alexander Fadeev was required to rewrite his highly successful novel *The Young Guard,* in 1948–51.[33] The case of Fadeev carried to its logical conclusion a process of demanding, in effect, that the Party, and the Soviet order in general, be depicted as perfect in essence and infallible in action.

Let us now survey the post-war expression of Russian chauvinism and messianism in Soviet thought. Claims of Soviet superiority increased in intensity as tension mounted between the Soviet and non-Soviet powers. Fundamentally, this relationship between the international situation and the reflections of anxiety and hostility in Soviet sources exists with regard to all of the sentiments we here discuss. Wrapping itself in the mantle of Russian patriotism, the Party leadership declared that those whose interpretation of Russian traditions differed from its own were in reality traitors to the Russian heritage. There was much that was contradictory and paradoxical in this effort of an 'internationalist' leadership, deeply enmeshed in a particular national culture, to reject parts of that culture while seeking to integrate other, arbitrarily selected parts of it, into its supranational ideology. Because this whole process is so inherently difficult, the post-war Soviet 'line' has seemed to be and to a large degree has been self-contradictory.

As we indicated in Chapter I, with reference to Stalin's linguistic pronouncements of 1950, realization of this fact may have been reflected in the effort to disassociate language and other features of Russian culture from the 'superstructure.' Regarded as in a sense outside the process of dialectical development, language, law, morality, and other cultural residues could be claimed by the Soviet regime as its own with less embarrassment. A number of ideological articles published after June 1950 suggested such an interpretation. For example, an important paper by G. F. Aleksandrov, read in November 1950, attacked the Marr school of philology on the ground that it 'artificially contrasted Soviet culture with its national form.' The Marrists, in effect, argued Aleksandrov, carried on a struggle against Soviet culture.

The Marr theory that language, as well as culture, was class-determined, was, if we may paraphrase Aleksandrov, a 'highbrow,' anti-popular and, above all, anti-Russian theory. Aleksandrov's and other glosses on Stalin's ruling argued, in effect, that socialism, and Russian culture and language, were integral parts of one complex. To be anti-socialist, or to oppose Soviet policy, was to be anti-Russian. Language, said Aleksandrov, was 'the means of communication of people in contemporary socialist society, the means of consolidating all the adherents of peace, democracy and socialism into a unified, all-powerful camp, inspired by the great Stalinist ideas.' In a word, the Russian-speaking, Kremlin-led 'camp' is identified with world socialism. This argument also furnishes, from the Stalinist point of view, justification for energetically supporting a program of Russian cultural expansionism.[34]

One way to rationalize Soviet use of the Russian historical legacy and to explain the failure of the new regime to develop an original culture of its own, as some Bolsheviks had once hoped it would, was to exempt from the dialectic certain categories formerly regarded as superstructural. This was, probably rightly, apparently regarded as too dangerous to be more than suggested for most categories other than language. Stalin, in Klaus Mehnert's expression, 'relativized' Marx by his statements on language and on the out-modedness of earlier concepts of Marx, Engels, Lenin, and himself. As long as the regime remains an absolute dictatorship, however, it will presumably reserve to itself alone the 'relativizing' function.

Yet there would be danger of stimulating undesirable speculation among intellectuals by removing fields such as law and morals from the category of the superstructure. What would remain of Marxism if this process were carried too far? And how could it be argued, if some basic superstructural features were considered independent of the economic basis, that Soviet culture owed its superiority to that of the non-Soviet world, to the 'socialist' economic system?

Perhaps a safer and more logical rationalization was presented by F. V. Konstantinov in 1951. Konstantinov argued that the 'classical Russian literature and art' of the nineteenth century could not be regarded as part of the superstructure of 'feudal-serf-owning society,' because it 'did not serve to consolidate the feudal-serf-owning basis, but, on the contrary, served to arm the enemies of that basis.' [35]

Matyushkin's illuminating manual of 'Soviet Patriotism,' to which we have already referred several times, contains many illustrations of the mixture, in Soviet texts, of Great Russian national chauvinism and Marxist internationalist messianism. For example, in his first chapter, the author presents some ten pages of material demonstrating the moral and cultural superiority of the Great Russian people, with particular emphasis upon their allegedly unsurpassed devotion to national freedom. In the course of this highly chauvinistic section, he refers to or quotes from numerous patriotic statements by Russian writers from Radishchev to Lenin. Among other things, he quotes Gogol's famous comparison of Russia with a 'troika-bird, which thunderously rushes forward.' [36]

Matyushkin follows this exercise in ancestor-worship, however, with other material expressing unlimited devotion to the concept of world revolution. At the end of the nineteenth century, he states, Russia 'occupied the most advanced position in the revolutionary struggle of the workers of the whole world.' And he adds that 'one of the historical services of Leninism to our Motherland and to the history of humanity consists in the fact that it discovered the dependence of the nationality problem on the socio-economic conditions of the development of society, and pointed to the only reliable method for the solution of this problem, the path of revolutionary struggle.' [37]

One major theme of post-war Soviet ideology might be characterized, either as the chauvinistic exaggeration of a partly correct thesis, or, as a kind of 'retroactive messianism.' This is the theme of 'Russia's military services to humanity.' A second basic theme is that of the 'internal mission' of the Russian people. Third, we are concerned with claims made for the superior achievements of the Soviet social order. Closely related claims are made for Russian and Soviet culture. Interesting in this connection is the Soviet Russian linguistic chauvinism, which has been touched upon earlier. We shall deal briefly in this section with some of its international aspects.

The retroactive Russian military messianism referred to above is closely related to the Soviet combination of militarization of all phases of life, with the propaganda of the 'struggle for peace.' The Kremlin asserts a strict self-censureship of overtly bellicose utterances. To foster the martial spirit of the population, and of the armed forces in particular, however, enormous effort is devoted to the celebration of past Soviet and Russian military achievements. Many Soviet historians, including V. Bazilevich and the better-known historian, Professor Eugene Tarle, made brilliant careers as historians of Russian expansionism, military prowess, and diplomatic sagacity. In fact, regiments of historians and journalists, military men and political figures, including of course Stalin himself, contributed to the development of this theme.

Tarle, in his well-known work *Napoleon's Invasion of Russia*, published in 1938, depicted his native country as the savior of Europe in the earlier 'Fatherland War,' that of 1812. Soviet historians have also assigned to Russia the major role in the defeat of Germany in the First World War, and, as we have noted in Chapter II, they have revived, in an especially chauvinistic form, the old Russian conviction that Russia saved Europe from enslavement by the Mongols. One wonders, incidentally, how this Soviet attitude toward the Mongols impresses the Chinese and other peoples of Eastern Asia.

Typical of Soviet Russian cultural chauvinism and messianism is the statement in Zhdanov's address to the Leningrad writers that 'Of course, our literature, which reflects an order higher than any bourgeois-democratic system and a culture many times more advanced than bourgeois culture, has the right to teach other people a new, universal, human morality.' [38] Speaking a few months later, Zhdanov struck a note of moral indignation with regard to the alleged failure of Western countries to appreciate the good qualities of the Russians. He said:

> Recently a great many 'researches' have been published on the character of Soviet people in general, and on the national character of Russians in particular. In connection with all this, many articles do not spare efforts to depict Soviet people in the most unpleasant light. Read, and you will be surprised how quickly Russian people have changed. When our blood was flowing on the battlefield, they were thrilled by our bravery, our high moral qualities and our unlimited patriotism. But now when we, in co-operation with other people, wish to realize our equal right to participate in international affairs, they begin to pour torrents of slander and abuse upon us.[39]

The note of wounded pride prominent in Zhdanov's claim of Soviet moral and cultural superiority was soon replaced by a more strident and intolerant attitude. David Zaslavski, a leading Soviet journalist, stated flatly in the *Pioneer* newspaper for 24 October 1947 that 'To us belongs the first place in humanity.' It was no accident, he continued, that Soviet chess players, artists, and athletes were the best in the world. An article in *Pravda* for 12 July 1948 stated that 'The Soviet people are proud that their country stands at the head of mankind.'

An unusually interesting combination of Soviet Marxist universalism and of traditional Russian messianism was reflected in *Pravda*'s editorial of 6 June 1949. On that day and for several days thereafter, the entire Soviet press was dominated by the celebration of the two-hundredth anniversary of the birth of Pushkin. The spirit of the 1949 celebration was far more bellicose and strident than its 1937 counterpart.

The editorial stated, oddly enough for a communist newspaper, that Pushkin understood the 'soul' of the Russian people, the people 'for whom history prepared the great mission of the liberation of mankind.' [40]

After the presentation in 1946 of Konstantin Simonov's violently anti-American play, *The Russian Question,* the arts were increasingly employed as vehicles for xenophobic and chauvinistic indoctrination. One of the most interesting examples of recent Soviet novels written for this purpose is Yuri Trifonov's *Students,* published in an English translation in 1953.

Vadim Belov, the smug hero of *Students,* is described as 'a true son of the Soviet era and a typical "positive" character of our times.' [41] He is contrasted with the 'negative' type, Palavin, a 'hang-over' from an earlier period. Such types are rare, according to Trifonov, but must be 'remade,' and taken 'into the bright future when communism will have been achieved.'

The positive characters in *Students* display such praiseworthy attitudes as a desire to work 'at the very end of the earth,' in Siberia or the Urals—an attitude obviously not as widespread as Trifonov would have us believe, if this writer's observations in Moscow were at all accurate. Negative characters shy away from such expressions of desire for enthusiastic participation. One character is criticized because he, 'a citizen of the largest industrial country in the world,' had never been inside a factory shop.

Students abounds in chauvinistic statements. Thus, in describing Vadim's war experiences, Trifonov writes:

'He had seen foreign countries, and found them quite unlike the descriptions in books. He had seen them as they really were, felt their quality, breathed their air. And he had found it stifling and impure, not like the air his lungs were accustomed to.' He had seen American soldiers near Pilsen beating up a Negro driver, while two officers stood by, laughing. 'Yes,' concludes the author, 'the people living beyond our frontiers would have to introduce great changes in their countries . . . they still had much to learn.' [42]

A peculiar impression is made by the injection of the same chauvinistic note into basic reference books. A few examples taken from the second edition of the *Large Soviet Encyclopedia* will serve as illustrations. It would be interesting to make a comparative qualitative and quantitative analysis of chauvinistic and messianic sentiments expressed in this work, with those in standard European or American encyclopedias, or to compare the degree of concentration in the Soviet encyclopedia on 'native' personalities, themes, and symbols with corresponding characteristics of an American or European counterpart.

Of the seventeen entries in the first 21 pages of Volume 23 of the *Encyclopedia,* twelve deal with Russian or Soviet Russian persons. An exceptionally high percentage of space in this encyclopedia is devoted to military material, particularly to the biographies of Tsarist generals and admirals. The article in Volume 17 of the *Great Soviet Encyclopedia* on the city of Izmail, in the Ukraine, is illustrated by four photographs, of which two are connected with the name of Suvorov, who was in command of the Russian troops that captured the city from the Turks in 1790, and more than half of this article is devoted to military exploits of Tsarist commanders associated with the history of the town.

The article on art in Volume 18, released by the censor in January 1953, states, among other things, that Soviet art is 'the most advanced art in the world,' because it is the product of a society free from exploitation and dedicated to the welfare of humanity. This article emphasizes that 'mastery of the "national heritage" is an essential prerequisite for the development of culture.' Russian art of the nineteenth and twentieth centuries, it asserts, represents 'one of the highest achievements of humanity.' Interesting in connection with Soviet efforts to win friends among the peoples of Asia is another statement of this article to the effect that 'despite the claims of bourgeois theorists' the peoples of Asia have contributed greatly to the development of art. China, India, Korea, and Japan are specifically mentioned.

Another 'Eastern' note is struck in the article on the Russian poet Alexander Blok in Volume 5, published in 1950. Although Blok is highly praised for his hatred of 'bourgeois culture' and for impressing upon the peoples of the world the 'world-historical significance of the Russian people, which in the Middle Ages saved Europe from the nomads,' he is also criticized because he allegedly contrasted the West, 'the creator of the machine civilization,' with the East, 'the bearer of an elementary culture.'

The article on military science in Volume 8 of this work, published in 1951, proclaims the superiority of Russian military science to the defeated German military science, which, the article states, is now continued by Americans such as Bradley, Eisenhower, and others. It traces Russian military science back to medieval Russian princes such as Igor, Vladimir Monomakh, and others. It is interesting also that pages 404 through 488 of this volume are devoted to military topics, including military geology, military science, and so on. Of a similar character was the statement contained in the *Pravda* editorial for 20 June 1954, that 'our country is the motherland of aviation.' This assertion was accompanied by praise of Russian inventors, such as Mozhaiski, who contributed to the development of aircraft or air engine design.[43]

In May and June 1955 added impetus was given to the inculcation in the Soviet Union of pride in the national military heritage. A conference was held, under the auspices of the Union of Soviet Writers, on 'the military theme in literature.' The keynote of the conference was sounded by the writer Polevoi, as reported in the *Literary Gazette* for 28 May, with a demand for poetry and prose, reportage and drama, which would give full expression to the 'grandeur of the feat performed by the Soviet people,' and would discharge the debt owed by writers to the Soviet armed forces. It is difficult to judge whether this new drive represented a concession to the military as an interest group or a contribution, scarcely in harmony with Khrushchev's effort to 'relax international tension,' to Soviet military chauvinism.

Although it is concerned with world revolutionary messianism, which we reserve for the final section of this chapter, we mention here the article on 'Bolshevism' in the *Large Soviet Encyclopedia*. It is, perhaps, not surprising in a Soviet reference book that this topic is treated without mentioning, either in the text or in the bibliography, a single non-Soviet source. The article on Bolshevism states, among other things, that the victory of the revolution in Russia was not merely the product of the peculiar character of the development of capitalism in the 'epoch of imperialism' but represents also 'the beginning, and the prerequisite for, the world revolution.' It also gives an indication of what seems to be a condescending attitude on the part of the Russians toward foreign Communists. It states that the communist parties of foreign countries began, after the October revolution, to reorganize their work on the basis of the 'world historical experience' of the Party of Bolsheviks.[44]

Soviet Russian linguistic messianism and chauvinism represent an unusually interesting and significant combination of defensive and offensive, rational and irrational elements. Like many other great peoples, including the English, whose upper classes spoke French for several centuries, the Russians passed through a stage in which the native tongue was regarded with condescension by the aristocracy, which included, until about the end of the first third of the nineteenth century, most of the educated and cultivated elements of the Russian population. In early nineteenth-century Russia, as in the Prussia of Frederick the Great, French was the language of culture. One of the greatest services of Pushkin to Russian culture was that he, more than any other single individual, helped to make Russian one of the great literary languages of the world.

The development of pride in the Russian language and of concern regarding linguistic and cultural xenomania extends back as far as the mid-eighteenth century and is associated with the name of the Russian 'Leonardo,' Lomonosov, who bitterly resented German influence in the imperial Russian Academy of Sciences. Lomonosov was one of the first Russian men of genius to voice with eloquence and passion the claim of Russian to be one of the great world tongues. Every Soviet work on the Russian language, and many books and articles in other fields, since 1936, has referred to or quoted Lomonosov's famous statement according to which Russian was superior to Latin, Greek, Italian, and German, even in respect to the strong points of these languages, and indeed was superior to all European languages.

In line with such sentiments, the *Pravda* editorial for 7 July 1938 declared that 'The Russian language is becoming the international language of socialist culture, just as Latin was of medieval society and French was in the eighteenth and nineteenth centuries.' A rich store of messianic utterances regarding the Russian language, culled from dozens of Russian writers, is

contained in the book *The Language of a Newspaper*. It is interesting that this book, published in 1941, quotes even the arch-
conservative N. M. Karamzin, who wrote, among other things,
that the Russian language in its 'tender simplicity' was richer
and more harmonious than the French.[45] Perhaps the most amazing statement in this book is the assertion, with respect to Karl
Marx, that 'Mastery of a language, superior to the classical languages of ancient Greece and ancient Rome, surpassing the German, the French and the Italian languages, gave Marx a new
and mighty weapon in the struggle for the cause of communism.' [46]

In the case of much of the literature of Russian linguistic
chauvinism, it is often sufficient to mention the titles of works
to suggest adequately their content and implications. In 1944, the
Central Committee of the Communist Party of the Soviet Union
published a substantial brochure by the noted Russian philologist, Vinogradov, entitled 'The Grandeur and Might of the
Russian Language.' In the following year, Vinogradov published
The Mighty Russian Language. In 1949, Soviet newspapers proclaimed again and again that, just as Latin had been the language
of feudalism, English was the language of world capitalism, and
Russian, the future world language, was the language of socialism. The operational significance of this attitude had already
been suggested by the linguistic policy of the Soviet bloc at
the Belgrade Conference on the Danube in 1948. Although two
of the four sponsoring powers were English-speaking, the Soviet
bloc voted to exclude English as an official language.[47]

Stalin's pronouncements on linguistics, as we have pointed
out, disengaged language from particular social systems. Thus
the Kremlin could with more consistency than before proclaim
that Russian was the 'language of socialism,' although Stalin,
probably to avoid offending the Chinese and other Asian peoples, was careful to emphasize that 'national' languages have a
long and bright future, and that the development of a world
language will not occur until long after the victory of socialism
on a world scale. The post-1950 line facilitates a three-pronged
linguistic strategy for countries such as India: Attacks on English
as the instrument of 'Anglo-Saxon racialism'; encouragement of

native linguistic pluralism; and, simultaneously, fostering of Russian as a cultural link to Moscow.

The linguistics 'discussion' over a period of several months preceding Stalin's intervention in the summer of 1950, offered many hints that Russian chauvinism, and messianism played a role in the repudiation of N. Y. Marr's philological theories. For one thing, both Marrists and anti-Marrists accused one another of 'cosmopolitanism,' and champions of both schools vied in acclaiming the superior virtues of Russian.[48] Marr's relegation of Russian to a 'stage' of development inferior to English, French, or German—Russian was in 'stage' 5, German in 6, and English and French in 7—must have been irritating to Stalin. Similarly, Marr had placed Chinese—but also his, and Stalin's—native Georgian in low 'stages' of development because of certain characteristics of their grammar. This classification of Chinese, combined with the Marrist doctrine that existing languages would give way to a world language with the transition to socialism, must have seemed tactless as well as impractical.

Subsequent Soviet statements, such as the quotation on the world leadership of Russian from *The Teacher's Newspaper* of 7 April 1954 cited in Chapter II, indicate that linguistic chauvinism, and domestic Russification policies, survived the 'liquidation' of Marrism. Numerous statements are contained in Soviet philosophical works regarding the Russian language, 'synonym of a new world and a new culture,' and regarding the unusually tender love of the Russian people for their language.[49] Perhaps particularly disturbing was Stalin's statement in 1950, echoed and emphasized subsequently, that in its encounters with other languages, the Russian language had always emerged victorious.

This leads to the conclusion that although Stalin foresaw the eventual emergence of a 'single world language' of socialist society, to which various present living languages would contribute, the 'world' language might well turn out, if Stalin was correct, to be Russian with some foreign borrowings. Also, Stalin's suggestion, in an article first published in 1949, and repeated in 1950, that 'between the initial stage marked by the proliferation of emancipated languages and the final stage in which all national differences fade away,' there would be an intermediate stage of 'zonal' economic centers, with 'a separate common language' for each such center, indicated determination to begin early to build a Russian 'zonal' center, which would eventually become the center of a socialist world.[50]

It is often suggested that Soviet Communism has some characteristics of a 'new medieval age.' [54] Soviet Russian linguistic chauvinism, though it is associated with 'socialism,' and with Soviet technocracy, is one of the features of Russian communism that supports such an interpretation. For there is a certain similarity between the 'apocalyptic visions' of Soviet Russian pronouncements regarding language, and the vision of the sixteenth-century monk Filofei, of Moscow as the 'Third Rome.' [52]

We conclude this chapter with a survey of Soviet world revolutionary messianism. Like most of the other aspects of Soviet nationalism with which we have dealt, this is a blend of Great Russian imperialism—remembering always that this imperialist threat is only partially identifiable with pre-revolutionary Russian foreign policy, and of Marxist determinism, monism, and universalism. The Russian component of Soviet messianism places particular emphasis upon the claim that a Russian, Lenin, rendered unique and incomparable service to humanity by his application of, and immeasurably superior understanding and development of, Marxism. Marxism, in effect, becomes a political religion. Russia is the chosen nation, not only entitled but duty bound to bring light and truth to the 'toilers' of those parts of the world who have not yet been saved from 'capitalist slavery.'

As we have indicated earlier, this claim rests upon the obvious fact that Russia did make the first 'socialist' revolution—tragic historical accident though we may consider it. In doctrinal terms it is based in large part upon a few important passages in some of the works of Lenin. Perhaps the most important of these is the passage in his *What Is To Be Done?* in which Lenin described the 'immediate tasks' of the Russian Social Democrats as the most revolutionary in the world, and prophesied that the Russian proletariat would take a place in the vanguard of world revolutionary struggle if it successfully resolved them.

The somewhat embarrassing fact that Marx and Engels were Germans and, on the whole, bitterly and suspiciously anti-Russian, is dealt with in various devious ways. In terms of quantitative or qualitative analysis, we may conclude that Marx and Engels, in comparison with Lenin, or even with Stalin, have become minor figures. The official Soviet attitude toward them is to a large extent honorific, ritualistic. To the extent that Marxism is an operational factor in Soviet behavior, it is so in terms of Leninist interpretation of Marxist strategy, and of Stalinist political tactics. Engels, in particular, has been 'corrected' on many points. Many important statements of Marx and Engels, particularly those incompatible with the fact that 'socialism' has proved most attractive to the societies least prepared for it in Marxist terms, have been deleted from the corpus of works of Marx and Engels to which Soviet citizens are permitted access.

In various ways, the attempt has been made, so to speak, to 'Russify' Marx. We have referred to the extraordinary dilation in Soviet sources upon the fact that Marx studied Russian. Every scrap of favorable evidence of interest in Russia on the part of Marx and Engels is exploited to the full in Soviet works. Facts such as the publication in Russian in 1872 of the first foreign language translation of the first volume of *Das Kapital* are stressed, naturally enough.[53]

The assertion and demonstration of Russian 'priority' in the appreciation and acceptance of Marxism is obviously a matter of primary importance to the Soviet regime. This has become even more true since the victory of the Chinese communists created the potentiality of rival claims of the governments of great 'socialist' powers to doctrinal supremacy. In this connection it is interesting to notice that from time to time the Soviet press prominently reports statements by Chinese communist officials acknowledging Russian doctrinal priority.[54]

One of the major arguments of post-war Soviet sociology is that the superiority of Russian thought was in large measure a reflection of the favorable—from the point of view of an anticapitalist revolution—situation of Russia in the late nineteenth and early twentieth centuries. Although Stalin laid the foundation for this concept by his assertion that the center of the world revolutionary movement had shifted to Russia at the turn of the century, it has undergone considerable development in recent years.[55] Celebration in January 1955 of the fiftieth anniversary of the 1905 revolution stressed this theme.

The principal change which has been made in this doctrine is the replacement of earlier admissions concerning the economic 'backwardness' of Russia, and the imitativeness of Russian economic and social thought, by claims of originality and superiority. The philosopher Shariya wrote in 1951 that one of the great merits of Chernyshevski and Dobrolyubov was that they were the first thinkers 'before Marxism, but of course not in the strictly chronological sense,' who combined ethics with social progress.[56] Shariya also emphasized that one must not 'deny the positive role of the national traits of the Soviet peoples, especially the Great Russian people, in the socialist revolution and in the socialist construction of our country.' [57]

Another Soviet scholar, Professor V. M. Shtein, observed in 1948 that Engels was correct in saying that the day of 'chosen peoples' had passed, but that his words 'do not in any way eliminate the problem as to which country is entitled to win the honored role of pioneer of socialism.' [58] Shtein devoted several pages to arguing that Marx and Engels 'belong to the whole world, not to Germany.' Russian economic thought of the mid-nineteenth century, when Marxism was taking shape, was far superior to that of Germany. Thanks to Marx, German economic thought attained an unprecedented level, but it proved incapable of remaining on this level. Shtein emphasized the interest in, and the 'revolutionary passion' experienced by Marx for Russia. In a sense, Shtein made of Marx and Engels 'honorary Russians.'

Despite Shtein's highly positive evaluation of eighteenth- and nineteenth-century Russian social thought, however, he was severely taken to task in 1949 in connection with the celebration of the two-hundredth anniversary of the birth of Alexander N. Radishchev, author of a well-known book, *A Journey from Saint Petersburg to Moscow,* in which, for the first time, a member of the Russian upper classes presented an indignant protest against serfdom. Even the minimization by Shtein of the German and French influences which played probably a decisive role in Radishchev's thought did not save him from the accusation of having 'depreciated' Radishchev and other Russian thinkers.

Some Soviet writers, in 1949, went so far as to claim that Radish-chev's thought 'anticipated' that of the nineteenth-century Western utopian socialists, while others asserted that it was far superior to that of Rousseau.[59]

The current Soviet attitude toward the primary role of Russia in disseminating Marxism reflects a deeply rooted aspect of Russian messianism. It is in some ways a continuation of the Russian tendency to claim that Russians understand the culture, ideas, and best traditions of other peoples better than those peoples themselves. One of the most famous manifestations of this tendency in the nineteenth century was Dostoevski's speech in 1880 in honor of Pushkin, which emphasized the 'Pan-human' qualities of the Russians.

This attitude has an historical basis in the cosmopolitan traits of the Russian intelligentsia, based on travel in Europe, knowledge of European languages, and eager interest in the trends of European and American thought. It certainly has positive implications, or had until the Soviet regime adopted its violently anti-cosmopolitan attitude. However, especially in our period of Soviet imperialism, this old Russian tendency can become a rationalization for the claim that Russians are the heirs to the best features of all cultures and, as a partial consequence, the natural teachers of the arts of civilization to lesser, more provincial peoples.[60]

The simplest and best-known form in which Soviet revolutionary messianism finds expression is the endlessly repeated assertion that the Soviet Union is destined to bring to all mankind the blessings of 'peace, democracy, and socialism' already enjoyed by the peoples of the USSR, the 'people's democracies' of Eastern Europe, and China, North Korea, and, most recently, Northern Vietnam. The desirability and inevitability of universal 'socialism,' and, eventually, of ascent to the 'starry heights of communism' are proclaimed in every Soviet sociological, economic, or political science treatise.[61] More important is the fact that major Soviet policy statements including speeches to the Supreme Soviet by Khrushchev, Molotov, and others, and the annual Lenin Anniversary and November sixth speeches are, in essence, applications to the current situation of the 'manichaean' vision of life referred to at the beginning of the last chapter.

It has been said again and again, as Molotov put it in his 6 November 1947 address, that 'We are living in an age in which all roads lead to Communism.' *The History of the Communist Party of the Soviet Union,* the bible of Soviet political education, usually known as the 'short course,' contains on the first page the statement that 'The study of the history of the C. P. S. U. (b) strengthens our certainty of the ultimate victory of the great cause of the Party of Lenin-Stalin, the victory of Communism through the world.' All Soviet newspapers still carry on their mast head the slogan 'Proletarians of all countries, unite!'

Experts have always differed regarding the relative weight in Soviet thought and behavior which should be assigned to normal political 'realism' and to world revolutionary messianism. Legitimate differences of opinion regarding this and related problems will continue to exist. No one, however, who takes the trouble to read Soviet 6 November speeches, May Day, and 6 November slogans or any of the other numerous and readily available indicators of basic Soviet attitudes can doubt that revolutionary messianism, expressed in action as Soviet imperialism, remains a part of official Soviet theory.

Despite the post-Stalin campaign for 'relaxation of international tensions,' 'proletarian internationalism' has been increasingly emphasized in Soviet propaganda in the past year and a half. In this, as in most major features, post-Stalin policy is to a considerable extent a continuation of the policy which Stalin and his associates announced at the Nineteenth Party Congress in October 1952.[62]

Stalin's statement, in his article 'Economic Problems of Socialism in the USSR,' that the concept of the 'temporary stabilization' of capitalism, developed by him in the 1920's, was now outmoded, reflects the confidence with which a recovered Soviet Union views current progress toward universal achievement of the Marxist mission. That this is the case, despite negative factors, such as the Soviet agrarian crisis and political problems connected with the succession to Stalin, is indicated by many features of post-Stalin policy, including, in all probability, the limited, strictly expediential revival of cultural exchange, which we have discussed in other contexts.

The mixture of traditional and revolutionary elements in Soviet ideology has been likened by Klaus Mehnert in his provocative and stimulating study, *Stalin versus Marx,* to an airplane flying on two motors, Marxism and Russian nationalism. Mehnert suspects that these two very different motors cannot operate indefinitely in synchronization. Perhaps a more realistic view is that which regards Soviet ideology as a synthesis of parts of the Russian tradition and parts of Marxism.[63]

There is in 'Soviet patriotism' 'ideological division of labor,' between Marxism and Russian nationalism. Marxism is a science of destruction of old societies rather than of construction of new ones. Its appeal, moreover, is largely to intellectuals, although this fact did not prevent Lenin, demagogic genius that he was, from associating Marxist goals with emotionally appealing and inflammatory slogans. Bolshevism needed Russian nationalism to fill the void left by the destruction of beliefs and customs capable of satisfying the Russian—and the universal human—need for emotionally satisfying social myths. The Kremlin also may have felt it necessary to buttress its claim to leadership of the forces of 'progress' in the whole world by the doctrine, highly dubious, from a Marxist point of view, of Russian 'priority' in revolution and hence in all spheres of life.

A great weakness inherent in the Kremlin's use of Russian nationalism—and of other elements of traditional culture, such as the Russian Orthodox religion—is that it cannot, if it is to retain its ideological and power monopoly, be 'sincere' in relation to those elements. Traditional nationalism, whatever its defects, and these are many, is not totalitarianism. As long as the Soviet system remains as totalitarian as it is today, there will be tension between government and people and an unexpressed, but possibly widespread feeling among the Soviet population that the government and the people do not really speak the same language, though they may use the same words.

The Party leadership, being totalitarian, will feel it necessary to stress its monopoly right to speak for 'the people,' and to enhance its legitimacy by bestowing on its policies all available 'familiar, vague and emotively moving' words. Likewise, it will continue to attempt to convince the Soviet and other Communist-ruled peoples that their enemies are its enemies.[64]

Those who have lived in Soviet Russia and have succeeded in establishing more than merely official relations with Soviet people, tend to agree that the old Russian characteristic of external conformity combined with a stubborn effort to maintain a measure of personal integrity, has not been eliminated by the pressures of life in a totalitarian state. Probably more significant than resistance to psychological pressure, which, even if it is not expressed in any overt manifestation, requires a strength of character rare in all countries, are the myriad forms of escapism rampant among Soviet citizens.

Soviet escapism manifests itself in such diverse ways as the tendency to 'go overboard' for foreign novelties, craving for 'decadent' forms of entertainment, tendencies toward alcoholism, about which the Soviet press has had a good deal to say since the death of Stalin, and, on a higher plane, an effort on the part of able young people to avoid political pitfalls by 'retreating into the past,' or by entering technical occupations as little connected as possible with ideological or political responsibility. We refer again near the end of this chapter to some of the psychological vulnerabilities of Soviet society because we feel that, since it is difficult to be aware of these factors without having either resided for a protracted period in the Soviet Union or without intensive interviews with former Soviet citizens, there is some danger that the material presented in this chapter might create an exaggerated impression of the ideological strength of the Soviet regime.

Unlike the Nazis, who enjoyed a far greater measure of enthusiastic popular support than the communists ever did in Russia, and unlike even their predecessors of the 1920's, the present Soviet leaders are still so afraid to trust their own people that when they make a slight move toward more normal cultural and personal relations with non-communist countries, they make headlines all over the world. The Soviet Union is probably the most frightened of the powerful nations of the world.

In this situation, a government is likely to seek to gain, if not the affection of its subjects, which is extremely difficult in a totalitarian regime, especially if living standards are kept unneccessarily low, at least their support in common hatred of the foreigner. Fear, envy, and indignation aroused by real or fancied offenses against the dignity of the community become instruments by which the political authorities seek to foster national solidarity. These are, of course, powerful weapons and they can achieve considerable effects, though I have always felt that, in the case of Russia at least, their effectiveness is more superficial than most of us believe. Men can be conditioned by propaganda, and that is very important, but it is impossible for the merely 'conditioned' to achieve the inner convictions upon which, in the long run, a stable political community must rest.

Human nature and totalitarian governments being what they are, the Kremlin is probably more successful in establishing in the minds of the populace identity between 'bad' images and the 'capitalist' enemy than in associating itself with 'good' images. It is apparently easier, especially for people under severe pressure, to hate foreigners than it is to love neighbors. Probably because of their shrewd knowledge of such matters the party leaders pillory as 'anti-patriotic' all whose conception of patriotism does not include hatred of the 'bourgeois' world which, after all, saved Russia by its aid during World War II. The official Soviet view reverted to a conception of patriotism which requires not only love of country but hatred for all groups and individuals considered by the Kremlin to be hostile, or not sufficiently loyal, to the communist cause.

Retrospect and Prospect

No single factor could have produced the pattern of sentiments discussed in this book. War and the expectation of war have bulked largest in shaping Soviet Russian nationalism. But these factors operated within a peculiar context. Communist doctrine impelled the Soviet authorities to give unusual weight to preparation for clashes which the Kremlin tended to regard as unavoidable. To some degree the international situation, to which Soviet preparation for war was a logical response, was itself a product of the Soviet attitude toward the 'capitalist' world.

This uneasy attitude, reflecting doctrine and experience, rendered plausible the 'self-fulfilling prophecy' of inevitable conflict. Other major elements in the Soviet situation are closely related to the military factor. Economic and technological backwardness, for example, constituted a danger which, in Moscow's eyes, could be balanced by vigilance, military preparedness, and rapid industrialization. The tendency of Russians to idealize Western civilization impelled the Soviet authorities to put special emphasis upon the development of a chauvinistic national pride. But this, in turn, was closely related to the official policy of mobilizing the population for all possible eventualities.

The military factor in Soviet policy stimulated the revival of Great Russian nationalism. This was made necessary by the regime's desire to obtain maximum support from the Great Russian population, which has always played a particularly important role in the Soviet armed forces. There is an intriguing element of paradox in the relationship between militarism and nationalism in Soviet Russia. War contributes to the development

263

of totalitarianism by stimulating centralism, chauvinism, and anti-foreignism.

But at the same time, the revival of Great Russian nationalism in the Soviet Union, must, to a certain extent at least, be regarded as an anti-totalitarian development. We should not, of course, exaggerate the contradiction between these elements in Soviet ideology. The Kremlin has, to a considerable degree, succeeded in synthesizing them. And yet, it is not impossible that the concessions made by the Kremlin to Great Russian nationalism may have introduced modifications in Soviet ideology which contain a promise of easier Soviet-Western relations in the long-term future.

During World War II, the connection in Soviet thought between fear of foreign enemies and patriotism became particularly close. This involved an identification of 'Russia' with the Soviet Union. It also involved preference for relatively concrete symbols for the Soviet state, such as 'motherland,' 'fatherland,' 'state,' and 'government,' to more abstract ideological concepts. Similarly, negative symbols of the current enemy, Nazi Germany, were almost entirely calculated to arouse hatred of Germans as a nation rather than as representatives of a social order.

Stalin clung to a 'Soviet' meaning for symbols, however, which, to the embattled Russian people or to Russia's allies in the 'Anglo-Soviet-American coalition,' held quite different meanings. Even in his first wartime address Stalin held up as the ideal of courage for the Soviet armed forces, the 'splendid virtues of the Bolshevik,' as defined by Lenin.

Many features of pre-war and wartime Soviet policy can be more easily understood if we keep in mind the Kremlin's attempt to exploit Russian nationalism as a shield against dangers emanating from the 'capitalist' world. A national conception of military service, and of Soviet citizenship, replaced the earlier, more strictly Marxist conceptions. Prior to 1939 the military oath, for example, began as follows, 'I, a son of the working people and a citizen of the USSR, am becoming a soldier of the Red Army of Workers and Peasants.' The oath enforced since January 1939 emphasizes devotion to 'my people, my Soviet motherland, and the Soviet government.'[1] A still more traditional Russian note was struck by the oath taken by Soviet guerrillas during World War II. The first sentence of this oath read as follows: 'I, a son of the great Soviet Union, and a true son of the heroic Russian people, swear that I will not lay down my arms until the last Fascist in our territory is destroyed.' [2]

Full treatment of the relationship between military pressure and Russian nationalism would require several chapters. Such themes as the restoration of traditional military forms, the revival of military historiography, or the elaborate system of military orders and medals which make the 'socialist' Soviet society far more rank conscious than that of royal Britain, would repay analysis. Bertram D. Wolfe has underlined the influence of the military factor on some aspects of Soviet nationalism in the statement that, 'step by step, a number of decisions of a "purely" or predominantly military character resolved matters of national structure—unintentionally, but, just for that reason, all the more decisively.' [3]

The 'political-administrative' factor operates in a somewhat different way than the military factor. Preparation for war has, doubtless against the will of the Kremlin, necessitated concessions to national sentiments and traditions. But essential features of the Soviet political system have exerted anti-traditional influences and have worked to strengthen the 'Soviet' at the expense of the 'Russian' element in official doctrine. Three characteristics of Soviet political power seem to be especially relevant. These are the relationship between the central political authority and the population which it controls, the monolithic structure of power, and the hypertrophy of the functions of government. These characteristics make for an exceptionally powerful influence of the state upon society.

The Soviet regime lacks legitimacy, representativeness, and popular control. A free and critical body of thought which could subject the basic principles of the regime to rational examination cannot exist. Soviet social thought consists largely of a tissue of calculated ambiguities, the authority of which is sustained, in the final analysis, by terror. Like other unrepresentative national leadership groups, the heads of the Soviet Party-state seem to find it necessary to strike an aggressively 'popular' attitude.

The pluralistic tendencies set in motion by industrialization, and by the development of a functional bureaucracy to perform the complex tasks of administration have, thus far at least, been held in check, although there seem to be increasing possibilities that this will not always be true. Central controls require doctrines of social harmony. They have given rise, among other things, to a struggle against the tendency of scientists and other members of the Soviet skill groups to identify in some degree with their foreign counterparts. One result of this struggle, as Huxley has pointed out, is that, 'as a result of recent events in the USSR, science as a whole has lost its unity.' [4]

The highly centralized state monopoly economy of the Soviet Union is an important force impelling the Party leadership to develop the nationalist ideology which we have discussed. Within its framework, individual work performance tends to be regarded, to an unusual degree, as a matter of public concern. A completely nationalized economy must find substitutes for 'capitalist' incentives of profit and bankruptcy. There is a strong temptation to substitute patriotic slogans for more tangible rewards. It must be remembered that labor cannot employ the weapon of the strike under Soviet 'socialism.'

Industrial life is relatively new to the Russian and other Soviet peoples, and stronger emotional incentives and harsher controls are required to impose labor discipline than is the case in countries with well-established habits of individual and group discipline, team work, and punctuality.

It is likely that the men in control of a state-directed economy think of foreign states as their competitors, somewhat in the way in which the executives of great corporations view competing firms. It seems logical that they should expect the Soviet labor force to share their concern regarding the international competitive position of 'their' national enterprise.

War and the exigencies of totalitarian administration in a scarcity economy bulk largest among the forces which have shaped Soviet nationalism. We should mention some other socio-cultural factors, however. The Russian inferiority complex resulting from consciousness of industrial and technical underdevelopment has been dealt with in various contexts. To the extent that the Soviet regime has been successful in overcoming Russian backwardness, it has undoubtedly stimulated nationalism in the ranks of the new Soviet ruling class, although satisfaction based upon material progress is partly offset by discontent engendered by the high cost of Soviet industrialization. Nevertheless, I am convinced that to the extent that the Soviet regime succeeds in persuading the population, and particularly its leadership strata, that its policies are in the national interest it can count on much willing support.

American Ambassador William H. Standley reported to Secretary Hull in 1943 that he believed that 'the continuing support given to Marshal Stalin and his Supreme War Council by the common people of Russia brought Stalin to the conclusion that his effort to make Mother Russia over into a Communist-Socialist state has been successful.' [5]

The testimony of Soviet defectors and the accounts of recent foreign visitors to the Soviet Union offer considerable evidence that in spite of the low Soviet standard of living, satisfaction and national pride are derived from Soviet industrial progress, as well as from certain features of the Soviet social system. Among these, the most important are probably wide access to education and, despite their serious deficiencies, the Soviet social security and public health systems.

And yet there are limitations to national pride based upon material progress. The Kremlin has failed to create a vital and emotionally satisfying new culture. The literary and artistic preferences of Soviet people indicate that their values, tastes, and ideas remain surprisingly unaffected by the efforts of the new regime to create the 'new Soviet man.' [6]

Occasionally, works of imaginative literature contain unusually revealing evidence of nostalgia for the past. In his play *For the Power of the Soviets*, V. Kataev wrote: 'The habit of surrendering themselves to recollections was very characteristic of all people of their generation [pre-revolutionary].' Even for a child brought up after the revolution the days of 'papa's childhood' were extremely attractive and romantic. [7]

Much of the old Russia, good and bad, has survived. Among other things, romantic love as depicted in Russian classics like

Tolstoy's *Anna Karenina* still moves Soviet women. Over the generations, some of the surviving elements of the pre-revolutionary culture of the Russian and other Soviet peoples are being slowly but gradually transformed under the influence of industrialization, administrative centralism, widespread technical and scientific education, and other powerful forces. The 'new Soviet man' is taking shape, and yet neither the Kremlin nor outside observers can predict or control his future development with any degree of certainty.

We can probably be sure that the stubbornly persistent culturally-determined differences between the peoples of the Soviet Union and those of the West strengthen Soviet nationalism. Even those who are convinced, as I am, that there are deep tensions between attitudes derived from the traditional culture patterns and the institutions and attitudes created by the Soviet regime must recognize that in a world of rival states governments can exploit nationalist sentiments for their own purposes. However, their ability to do so is, to some extent, limited by the degree to which other governments are sensitive to cultural values, to national peculiarities, and to the problems of international communication.

What is the future of Soviet nationalism? In what ways will the Kremlin continue to utilize national symbols to sustain its power and realize its political program? In our effort to push ahead a bit the veil of obscurity we face two sets of problems. One is concerned with the scope and content of the Soviet 'symbol sphere,' and the other with the tone and intensity of the sentiments contained in 'Soviet patriotism.'

Despite the apparent crudity of their thinking, the Soviet leaders have shown themselves to be extremely able practical sociologists. In fact, the capability of the communists in applied psychology and sociology may constitute their real 'secret weapon.' Marxism has given the Soviet leaders a framework of analysis which, with all its defects, at least makes them aware of some important factors of social action. Soviet Marxism, combined with the power monopoly and the administrative instruments and skills of the Kremlin, is a formidable tool.

This study will have served a useful purpose if it has succeeded in conveying some sense of the way in which the characteristics referred to above have been manifested in the Soviet treatment of problems of social sentiments. There is no reason to believe that the present rulers are lacking in the flexibility and adaptability by which, together with ruthlessness, the Soviet state was built. They seem to be operating with considerable success on several levels of national symbol manipulation.

On the one hand, they are continuing Stalin's policy of consolidation of the area under direct Soviet administrative control. Their ultimate goal on this level is the achievement of cultural homogeneity and administrative standardization, ends which may be summed up under the term 'Sovietization.' Barring all-out war with the West in the near or short-term future, it seems likely that the process of integration will continue and will enjoy substantial success. Increasing homogeneity with respect to nationality factors, however, by no means precludes the possibility of increasing heterogeneity with respect to other factors, such as a system of status based on social function.

We can probably expect continuation of the effort to Sovietize the captive countries of Eastern Europe, and, in a different fashion, of China. If and when it becomes expedient, some captive countries may be incorporated into the Soviet state. Some of the most powerful weapons of Soviet policy consist in the dissemination of translations of Soviet technical and political material, as well as of the classics of Russian culture, and a systematic program of instruction in the Russian language.

In Czechoslovakia, for example, children are required to have a speaking and writing knowledge of Russian by the time they finish elementary school. They must master the Cyrillic alphabet by age nine.[8] The Czechoslovak Communist Party decree prescribing the foregoing also stipulated that the Czech and Slovak languages must be taught according to the precepts of Stalin's essay on 'Marxism and Linguistics.' In Hungary, Joseph Revai, an outstanding communist theoretician, defined the cultural program of Hungarian communism as follows:

'We wish to acquaint the Hungarian people with the most advanced culture in the world, the culture of the Soviet Union.'[9]

In Bulgaria, according to *The Teacher's Newspaper* for 1 May

1954, 110,000 'toilers' were studying Russian in special study circles. This was of course in addition to those persons receiving regular instruction in the schools. Soviet Russian cultural influence includes inculcation of the idea of Russian superiority in the technical arts. *Pravda* for 1 February 1953 quoted a deputy to the Polish Parliament as saying, 'If it had not been for the brotherly help of the Soviet Union, we could never have built such a factory.' [10]

Since the Nineteenth Congress the claim that the Soviet Union and the Soviet working class are altruistically sharing their superior industrial techniques and knowledge with the workers of China, North Korea, Poland, East Germany, Bulgaria, and increasingly, with free Asian nations such as India, has become conspicuous. Sometimes the propaganda on this topic emphasizes the benefits derived by Bulgarians, Rumanians, and others from residence in the Soviet Union as students of Soviet industrial methods. One Soviet book stressed the building, by Soviet engineers and Soviet-trained Bulgarians, of the Bulgarian city of Dimitrovgrad. It should be stressed that Moscow assures Asian countries, in particular, that Russia offers not only technical assistance but also respect for the cherished patterns of folk culture.

Soviet cultural pressure on the captive countries is a much more powerful weapon than old-fashioned Russification. The new program is bilingual. No overt attempt is made to deprive the peoples of their native language, but they are expected to learn Russian. At the same time, the study of languages of the 'brother' countries is popularized in Russia.[11]

There is much evidence that Russian is becoming the second language of China. *Pravda* for 2 May 1953 stated that 'The study of the Russian language becomes more and more a mass movement: the knowledge of the Russian language aids in the study of advanced Soviet experience.' Soviet influence in China and Eastern Europe is intensified by the use of translations of Soviet secondary school and university textbooks, by visits of Soviet artists and scientists, by lectures by visiting Russian professors, and by the manifold activities of the Soviet-sponsored Friendship Societies, which have many millions of members. Probably because of Soviet experience with Tito, care is taken to avoid giving offense to the Chinese.[12]

In the case of China, and even, since the death of Stalin, in the Eastern European countries, there is some give and take in cultural relations. Frequent flattering references are made to the 'great Chinese people' in editorials and in the 6 November and May Day slogans. Soviet newspapers and magazines publish appreciative articles on Chinese literature. It seems probable that this calculated flattery of the Chinese has the double aim of overcoming Russian condescension toward Chinese 'backwardness,' and of convincing the Chinese that the Kremlin highly respects their ancient culture.

The large-scale domestic and foreign operations by which this program is supported constitute a well-planned exercise in information engineering. They include extensive scholarly publication, language and area studies, and the activities of the Soviet State Publishing House for Foreign and National Dictionaries. *Pravda* for 11 April 1954 stressed the connection between dictionaries and Soviet foreign policy, and reported that dictionaries were being prepared for 'a number of the languages of India' and, among others, for various African languages. A statement by a leading Indian scholar was quoted to the effect that a recently published Russian-Hindi dictionary had become an 'object of pride' to Indians. Dictionary production, manuscript translation, and related topics were stressed at a conference of Soviet philologists specializing on oriental languages held in March 1955 under the auspices of the Academy of Sciences of the USSR and attended by more than 500 scholars.[13] There have been many other impressive indications of the current Soviet attempt to demonstrate appreciation for foreign, particularly oriental cultures.

The use of cultural instruments to forge bonds between Moscow and the 'people's republics,' in Eastern Europe and China, has been accompanied by the development of doctrinal concepts designed to stimulate a consciousness of common destiny, among the populations controlled by the 'socialist camp.' As far back as 1949, official Soviet statements began to place renewed emphasis upon 'proletarian internationalism,' with special reference to the new 'fraternal' regimes established as a result of the 'falling away from capitalism' of a number of countries.

At the same time, the press began to publish articles by Chinese communist theoreticians on problems of nationalism and internationalism. For example, *Pravda* for 9 June 1949 devoted more than half a page to an article by the ranking theoretician of Chinese Communism, Liu Shao Chi, which criticized 'reactionary bourgeois nationalism' and proclaimed that 'the real patriotism of the masses of the peoples of all countries is not in contradiction to proletarian internationalism, but is closely linked with it.' True patriotism, said Liu Shao Chi, consists in love for 'the motherland, the people, the language and their literature and for the best traditions of one's own nation, developed over the centuries.' Soviet scholars in apparent response began to revert to earlier Leninist views concerning problems involved in the 'fusion' of nations, first into groups and finally into a world society.[14]

An article by Ts. Stepanyan revived a significant view presented before the war by Stalin on the problem of 'capitalist' versus 'socialist' internationalism. He asserted that,

> The true unification of the peoples is possible only in the struggle for communism. Communism teaches that the unification of peoples takes place . . . only under the slogan of the federation of the socialist republics of developed countries, and of colonies, which have broken away or are breaking away, from the imperialist system. This federation is opposed in its struggle for world socialism to the world capitalist system.[15]

Stalin subsequently developed further the current Soviet idea, discussed in Chapter I, that the world is divided into capitalist and socialist 'camps.'

Beginning in 1949, with Stalin's well-known telegram to Wilhelm Pieck beckoning Germany to partnership in 'great actions of world significance,' an attempt has been made to appeal to the national sentiments and interests of Germans.[16] In a speech delivered at the Fourth Congress of the Socialist Unity Party of Germany on 1 April 1954, A. I. Mikoyan offered what would, a few years earlier, have seemed like an amazing paeon of praise to the German people.[17]

Mikoyan's praise of the German people was within a Soviet Marxist framework. He observed, among other things, that 'the German people and the German labor movement gave to the world Karl Marx and Friedrich Engels, the founders of the theory of scientific socialism, and armed the workers with a program for social liberation.' He reminded his German communist audience that Lenin had once declared that the German working class had been for half a century the model of socialist organization for the whole world. Mikoyan also praised the Germans for having given the world the music of Bach and the poetry of Goethe.[18]

In spite of these and subsequent appeals to German national identity, Soviet doctrine has not elevated East Germany to the level of a 'people's democracy.' It seems pretty clear, however, that the reason for excluding East Germany from the happy family to which Poland and the other 'socialist' countries of Eastern Europe belong is that the Kremlin does not wish to alienate West Germans who might be antagonized by inclusion of any part of their country in the category of 'people's democracies.'

The Kremlin still hopes, apparently, that it can ultimately succeed where earlier empires have failed, in the universal diffusion of a national cultural pattern. Its experience inside the Soviet Union in presenting a universally applicable policy in terms of local patterns has indeed been formidable.[19] And, of course, despite the manifold internal tensions of the 'socialist camp,' the growth of communist power since 1917 has been such as to furnish grounds for optimism regarding the future.

The Kremlin is aware of the difficulties confronting the Western powers in their efforts to check the further extension of Soviet influence. The United States, in particular, faces most perplexing problems. For many reasons, most of which are mainly not of its own making, the United States has become the whipping boy of discontented people everywhere in the free world. One important, even obvious, reason for this situation is that Washington cannot operate according to a single plan to nearly as great an extent as Moscow can.

And yet it is easier for communists to document their thesis regarding 'Yankee imperialism' than it is for the forces of democracy to show how much more alien Soviet communism is to the patriarchal, traditional, and individualist cultures of many lands than is the less centralized Western system. American influence, whether in the form of business enterprises, missionary activities, military forces, or even tourists, is far more visible and hence vulnerable to criticism than is that of Soviet Russia, which works for the most part indirectly. Of course, many other factors militate against the Western nations in the world cultural competition.

Perhaps the best known of these is the resentment of the peoples of Asia, Africa, and Latin America against European and American 'imperialism,' with its accompanying attitudes of ethnocentrism, provincialism, and arrogance. It should also not be forgotten that although the end results of Soviet communism are profoundly alien to the spirit of the societies which it seeks to seduce, its criticism of the current evils of 'capitalist' and, especially, 'colonial and semi-colonial' societies is partly correct and is dangerously plausible. This criticism can certainly not be refuted by mere denunciations of communism and of Soviet imperialism, which, if they are not accompanied by sympathetic understanding, cultural sophistication, and above all by a positive program, only tend to confirm existing prejudices against those who make them.

We should not like to end this book on a note of pessimism. The prospects for further consolidation of the 'socialist camp' and for its continued expansion give pause indeed. Despite the integrative tendencies of modern technology, however, the odds are probably against the chances of the adherents of any ideology establishing a world empire. Central control creates as many problems as it solves. Will the dogmatic, albeit culturally experienced, Soviet Russian be able to dissolve the ancient civilizations of the East and the skeptical, proudly nationalistic cultures of the West into the monotonous conformity of a Russianized, 'Marxist' totalitarian industrialism?

Were it not for the existence of modern super-weapons which may have rendered attempts at conquest by purely military means obsolete because they are so nearly synonymous with suicide, the Kremlin might still have a chance of realizing its dream of a world communist society, dominated from Moscow, leaving for future settlement problems of the locus of sovereignty in a 'socialist' world society. Of course, the military stalemate does put a premium upon internal subversion, but too eager efforts in this direction tend to stimulate resistance. And the question arises whether in spite of the imperialist surge still contained in Soviet nationalism, the Kremlin's will to power is not balanced somewhat by counter forces operating within Soviet society.

We hope that, given a sober use of power on the part of the leadership of the non-Soviet world, together with sensitivity to the problems and aspirations of the peoples, the attitudes discussed in this study may gradually be modified in the direction of greater reasonableness and tolerance. The urge toward self-aggrandizement, domination of other peoples, and political expansion contained in Soviet Russian nationalism derives from an 'abnormal' pattern. If this pattern changes for the better with the passage of time, the attitudes to which it gave rise may become weaker. Such reasoning should not inspire facile optimism.

The development for which we hope requires on the part of Western leadership the balancing of Soviet power with wisdom, strength, and skill. It requires a diminution of the international and internal social tensions and instabilities which offer tempting targets for communist penetration. Moreover, although the relaxation of the internal tensions which have shaped Soviet Russian nationalism might make the Soviet Union a more 'normal' country, they would also make it a more powerful country because it would in fact enjoy more of the internal harmony of which Soviet propaganda now falsely boasts.

In the short run, Soviet aggressiveness is to at least some degree limited by the discontent and apathy engendered by the present political system. There has probably been some loss of self-confidence at the top because of the death of Stalin and the difficulties confronting a rather unstable oligarchy in operating Stalin's design for autocracy. The increased power of the military, even if it is unlikely in the foreseeable future to lead to major changes of institutions or policies, is probably, on the whole, a force for stability and peace. In the Soviet system, the super-militarists are the Party leaders, who think of 'peace' as the continuation of war by non-violent means, or at least with the employment of only a necessary minimum of violence. The Bolsheviks were, from the beginning, a political army. For this reason, among others, they are certain to resist with great skill and tenacity any tendencies toward the establishment of a military dictatorship in any way resembling the types of such dictatorships known to modern Western societies.

But they have been forced to grant a greater weight to the military in Soviet political councils than was the case under Stalin. Since the military professionals are more representative of Soviet society as a whole than are the Party leaders, and since they probably have a better understanding of the military capabilities and intentions of the West than their more doctrinally-oriented Party professional superiors, they can take a more realistic and less dogmatic attitude toward the West. Their influence is probably bolstered by that of some members of the Soviet administrative and professional classes, whose outlook is increasingly 'functional' and decreasingly 'ideological,' and who do not wish to risk the loss of the status, material advantages, and other privileges for which they have worked so hard.

The largely unreported discussion in Soviet official and intellectual circles in 1953–5 over the degree of priority to be given to capital goods over consumers' goods indicates that one current of Soviet thought is sensitive to values other than total concentration upon the maximization of national power. But we are in a realm of speculation. It is not clear to what degree 'vested interests' of the Soviet ruling class coincide with the desire of the sensible elements in Western society to work toward rational solutions of international problems.

It is by no means certain that the 'vested interests' of the Soviet ruling bureaucracy are developing in such a way as to coincide eventually with the desire of the sensible elements in Western society to work for rational solution of international problems. Moscow's goal remains a Soviet world. This is indicated by such statements as the one following: 'In its nationality policy, the Communist Party of the Soviet Union assumes that the development of socialist nations, and their culture, national in form, will continue for a long time after the world dictatorship of the proletariat has been realized,' and 'Human society is moving, thus, to a single, universal world culture.' [20]

What can 'co-existence' mean as long as such attitudes persist in Moscow? Although the Soviet press proclaimed that the 'summit' conference confirmed the possibility of peaceful co-existence, it is significant that it also, at the same time, stressed that Soviet-Yugoslav co-operation could be especially fruitful, on the basis of common acceptance of Marxism-Leninism, thus indicating no change in basic thinking.

Nevertheless, we are confident that by insisting on a non-Soviet definition of 'co-existence,' the democracies can gain sufficient 'survival time' to get safely through 'the world revolution of our time' and eventually to regain the initiative for constitutional government in the world. Democracy is, after all, much newer and more hopeful than any form of despotism, including the neo-feudalism perfected by Stalin.

NOTES

Chapter I

1. Hans Gerth and C. Wright Mills, *Character and Social Structure* (London, 1954), p. 198.
2. Alfred Cobban, *National Self-Determination* (first published in the United Kingdom, 1944, and reprinted by University of Chicago Press, 1951).
3. Carlton J. H. Hayes, *The Historical Evolution of Modern Nationalism* (New York, 1931), p. 12. Hayes, incidentally, displayed unusual insight when he referred, in this work, to the 'peculiarly integral nationalism' of the Russian Bolsheviks, 'worshipping at the shrines of their dictators that are now their national heroes.'
4. *Nationalism and Social Communication* (New York, Cambridge, Mass. and London, 1953), p. 81.
5. E. K. Francis, 'Sociological Concepts and the International Order,' *The Review of Politics* (October 1954), Vol. 16, No. 4, p. 481.
6. Article on 'Nationalism' by Max Hildebert Boehm in *Encyclopedia of the Social Sciences* (originally published 1933, reissued 1938), Vols. 11–12, p. 231.
7. *The Web of Government* (New York, 1947), p. 445. MacIver also emphasizes, more effectively than many other writers, the danger which faces a community in which the state asserts such great economic power that the implementation of its economic functions 'conveys with it the effective domination of the cultural life' (Ibid. p. 446).
8. The contributions of Sidney Hook and Calvin Bryce Hoover to the symposium on 'Ideology and Reality in the Soviet System,' sponsored in November 1954 by the American Philosophical Society, furnish part of the analytical basis for my characterization of Soviet society as 'state monopoly capitalism,' although neither of the authors uses this expression. See *Proceedings, American Philosophical Society*, Vol. 99, No. 1, 27 January 1955 (Philadelphia, 1955).

279

9. *Administrativnoe pravo* (Moscow, 1946), p. 3. This is the most valuable of the post-war Soviet textbooks on administrative law. Later editions are less revealing; this version was criticized for an alleged tendency to identify administration too closely with police controls, a tendency obviously descriptive of reality.

10. Ibid. p. 5.

11. *Sovetskoe administrativnoe pravo* (Moscow, 1950), p. 5.

12. Ibid. p. 5.

13. Florian Znaniecki, *Modern Nationalities* (University of Illinois Press in Urbana, 1952), p. 136.

14. *The New York Times,* 1 June 1954.

15. I. Stalin, *Marksizm i voprosy yazykoznaniya* (Moscow, 1950), p. 12. A Ciliga, in *La Yougoslavie sous la menace intérieure et extérieure,* says that Stalin was in the habit of telling his intimates that Alexander the Great did not succeed in creating a lasting empire because he did not know how to deal with nationality questions. See esp. p. 50. It is interesting that Stalin first emphasized the instability of empires which lacked the integrating cement of nationality in 1913. See I. Stalin, *Sochineniya* (Works), (Moscow, 1946), Vol. II, p. 293. Hereafter Stalin's *Works* will be referred to as *Soch.* The last volume published was No. XIII, 1951.

16. *Red Star.*

17. Quoted by Fedotoff White, op. cit. p. 413. It is not entirely clear from White's note whether this quotation refers to *Red Star* or to another military organ, but there is no reason to doubt the accuracy or representativeness of the quotation.

18. *Politicheskaya ekonomiya* (Moscow, 1954), pp. 609-19.

19. I. Gadourek, *The Political Control of Czechoslovakia* (Leiden, 1953), p. 205. The author's observations seem applicable to all Soviet-controlled areas.

20. Isaac Deutscher in *Manchester Guardian Weekly,* 18 November 1954; *Pravda,* 15 May 1955; Molotov's Supreme Soviet speech of 8 February 1955 in *Pravda* for 9 February. Deutscher's phrase, though it antedated the other events referred to, has been quoted as an excellent summation of one influential interpretation, with which on the whole I disagree. It is possible, however, that Moscow may eventually be constrained to move toward granting 'commonwealth' status to its satellites.

21. An excellent example of this effort is furnished by the article by the leading philosopher M. Yovchuk, entitled 'Leninizm vysshee dostizhenie russkoi i mirovoi kultury' ('Leninism, the Highest

Achievement of Russian and World Culture'), *Kommunist,* No. 1, January 1955, pp. 23-38.

22. N. I. Matyushkin, *Sovetski patriotizm-moguchaya dvizhushchaya sila sotsialisticheskogo obshchestva* (Moscow, 1952), p. 4.

23. *Slovar inostrannykh slov* (Moscow, 1949), p. 482.

24. Matyushkin, op. cit. p. 291.

25. Article by D. I. Chesnokov, entitled 'Marksizm-Leninizm ob ote-chestve i patriotizme,' in the symposium *O sovetskom patriotizme,* rev. ed. (Moscow, 1952), p. 14.

26. Matyushkin, op. cit. p. 6.

27. *Pravda,* 14 October 1952.

28. *Slovar,* op. cit. p. 435.

29. Ibid. p. 340.

30. G. E. Glezerman in *O sovetskom patriotizme* (Moscow, 1950), p. 164. This is an earlier version of the work of the same title cited above. Both symposia were published by the Institute of Philosophy of the Academy of Sciences of the USSR.

31. For this view regarding the 'covert' role of Russian symbols and attitudes I am indebted to Mr. Paul W. Friedrich.

32. *Making Bolsheviks* (New York, 1931), p. 18.

33. *tseleustremlennyi.*

34. On the crucial importance of 'consciousness' for modern Soviet concepts of personal responsibility and duty to the state, see Raymond A. Bauer, *The New Man in Soviet Psychology* (Cambridge, 1952), pp. 140, 141.

35. *Entsiklopediya gosudarstva i prava* (Moscow, 1925-7, 3 vols., Vol. III, pp. 252-4.

36. *otechestvo.*

37. Solomon S. Bloom, *The World of Nations* (New York, 1941), pp. 24, 26.

38. *otechestvennaya voina.*

39. V. I. Lenin, *Sochineniya* (Works), 2nd ed. (Moscow, 1929), XXXIII, p. 13.

40. *derzhava.*

41. It was not until later in the same year that the name of the Party was changed to All-Union Communist Party.

42. *strana.*

43. Stalin, *Soch.,* Vol. VII, pp. 109-19.

44. Stalin, ibid. p. 130.

45. 1902.

46. motherland.

47. All-Union Leninist-Communist Union of Youth.

48. *Dvenadtsaty sezd rossiiskoi kommunisticheskoi partii* (Moscow, *Krasnaya Nov,* November 1923), p. 169. Referred to in subsequent chapter as *Twelfth Congress.*

49. Stalin, *Marksizm i natsionalno-kolonialny vopros* (Moscow, 1938), p. 173. This letter was first published in 1938, according to a foot-note.

50. Stalin, *Soch.,* Vol. xiii, 1951, pp. 23-7.

51. Stalin, *Soch.,* Vol. ii, p. 296.

52. Ibid. p. 303.

53. Stalin, *Soch.,* Vol. xi, pp. 338-9, 353.

54. *Marksizm i natsionalno-kolonialny vopros* op. cit. p. 158.

55. Ibid. p. 159.

56. References in this section are to the English translation, Moscow, 1950.

57. Ibid. pp. 17, 18-22, 49-50.

58. Referred to in article 'On the Marxist-Leninist training of the cadres of the Soviet intelligentsia,' *Bolshevik,* No. 9, 1944, p. 5.

59. Ibid. p. 25.

60. Ibid. p. 23.

61. D. Fedotoff White, *The Growth of the Red Army* (Princeton, 1944), p. 361.

62. W. V. Pillsbury, *The Psychology of Nationality and International-ism* (London and New York, 1919), p. 221.

63. D. I. Chesnokov, *O sovetskom patriotizme,* 1952 ed., p. 54.

64. *Pedagogika,* 5th ed. (Moscow, 1950), p. 7. The importance of this statement is indicated by the fact that it is underlined in the text.

65. Page 239.

66. *Sovetski narod.*

67. *Malaya sovetskaya entsiklopediya,* Vol. viii, column 33.

68. Column 326.

69. *Malaya,* Vol. ix, col. 326.

70. F. V. Konstantinov, *Istoricheski materializm* (Moscow, 1951) p. 705.

71. Michael Karpovich, 'The Historical Background of Soviet Thought Control,' *The Soviet Union* (Notre Dame, 1951), p. 18.

72. *Nasha velikaya rodina* (State Publishing House for Political Liter-ature, Moscow, 1953).

73. Ibid. p. 435.

74. The term 'Soviet people' occurs hundreds of times in the text.

75. Ibid. p. 403.

76. Ibid. p. 430.

Chapter II

1. *Folkways* (Boston, 1907), pp. 13-15.

2. Michels, *Der Patriotismus* (Munich and Leipzig, 1929).

3. 'Human Nature in American Thought,' *Political Science Quarterly*, Vol. LXVIII, No. 4, December 1953, pp. 492-510. Quotation, p. 507.

4. The term 'Great Russians' is normally used in this study to refer to the most numerous of the Slavic peoples, and their culture and language, in distinction from other Slavic peoples, such as the Ukrainians.

5. The words 'nation' (*natsiya*) and 'people' (*narod*) are used interchangeably in Soviet sources. Professor Abram Bergson of Columbia has called my attention to the fact that the term 'national income' (*natsionalny dokhod*) has apparently recently tended to replace the older term 'popular income' (*narodny dokhad*).

6. *Vneshnyaya politika sovetskogo soyuza* (Moscow, 1947), III, 47.

7. The term 'national' seems to be taking on a slightly patronizing connotation. This is still more true of the term 'natsmen,' referring to a member of a non-Russian 'national minority.'

8. *Uchitelskaya gazeta*, Number 28 (3842) 7 April 1954.

9. V. I. Lenin, *Sochineniya*, 2nd ed. (Moscow, 1929), XXIII, p. 188.

10. Ibid. 33.

11. Stalin, *Soch.*, I (1946), *Kak ponimaet sotsial-demokratiya natsionalny vopros*, pp. 33-35. First published 1904.

12. This factor is stressed from various angles by such writers as Isaac Deutscher, in *Stalin: A Political Biography*, by Roman Smal-Stocki in *The Nationality Problem of the Soviet Union*, and Walter Kolarz in *Stalin and Eternal Russia*.

13. Walter Biehahn, 'Marxismus und Nationale Idee in Russland,' *Osteuropa*, Berlin, Vol. 9 (1933–1934), pp. 461-76. Quoted material on p. 463. Biehahn and to a lesser degree Kolarz argue that Marxism in Russia was essentially a form of Russian nationalism.

14. *Rossiiskaya kommunisticheskaya partiya, Desyaty s'ezd* (Tiflis, 1921). See pp. 29, 156-8, 165, 168, and 187; the last-mentioned contains Lenin's statement on the Ukraine and Russia.

15. *Twelfth Congress*, pp. 645-7.

16. Ibid. p. 529.

17. Ibid. p. 563.

18. Ibid. p. 547.

19. Ibid. pp. 471-5.
20. It is interesting to note, incidentally, in view of Stalin's claim to have originated the formula of 'socialism in one country' that Zinovev, still in 1923 the titular leader of the Party, stated that 'until the complete victory of Communism on an international scale, I think that the system of authority which now exists will be continued.' *Twelfth Congress*, p. 7.
21. Ibid. pp. 598, 604, 605.
22. Ibid. pp. 605-6.
23. J. Stalin, *On the Draft Constitution of the U.S.S.R.* (English translation, Moscow, 1950), p. 65.
24. *Twelfth Congress*, p. 524.
25. Change of landmarks.
26. On Ustryalov, see *Malaya sovetskaya entsiklopediya* (Moscow, 1930), Vol. VIII, cols. 45-6; (1931), IX, 209; second ed. of same, (1941), XI, cols. 797-8. The fate of Ustryalov was somewhat similar to that of the brilliant 'returnee' scholar, Prince Dmitri Mirski, who, however, was converted to communism. Nothing was heard of him after the purges.
27. *Shestnadtsaty sezd vsesoyuznoi kommunisticheskoi partii* (Moscow, 1931), pp. 54-6.
28. *Semnadtsaty sezd vsesoyuznoi kommunisticheskoi partii* (Moscow, 1934), pp. 31-2.
29. *Vosemnadtsaty sezd vsesoyuznoi kommunisticheskoi partii* (Moscow, 1939), pp. 26-7.
30. B. Volin, 'Veliki russki narod,' *Bolshevik*, No. 9, 1938, p. 36.
31. The best analysis of the developments of which the above is a part is Georg von Rauch, 'Grundlinien der sowjetischen Geschichtsforschung im Zeichen des Stalinismus,' *Europa Archiv*, Nos. 19, 20, and 21, 1950.
32. *Malaya sovetskaya entsiklopediya* (Moscow, 1941), Vol. IX, cols. 319-26.
33. I. Stalin, *O velikoi otechestvennoi voine sovetskogo soyuza* (Moscow, 1944), pp. 11, 28.
34. The words and music of the anthem were published on the front page of *Pravda* for 1 January 1944. Words by Sergei Mikhalkov and El Registan, and music by A. E. Aleksandrov.
35. *Izvestiya*, 4 November 1943.
36. *Uch. gaz.*, 30 June 1943.
37. Walter Kolarz, *Stalin and Eternal Russia* (London, 1944), pp. 115, 116.

38. *KPSS v rezolyutsiakh* (Moscow, 1953), Vol. II, p. 1018.

39. Walter Kolarz, *Russia and Her Colonies* (London, 1952), p. 19.

40. G. M. Malenkov, 'Comrade Stalin, leader of progressive mankind,' (Foreign Languages Publishing House, Moscow, 1950), p. 15.

41. For example, A. M. Pankratova, 'Veliki russki narod' (Moscow, 1947), and editorial of same title in *Literaturnaya gazeta*, 24 May 1950.

42. On the rewriting of Fadeev's *The Young Guard* see Boris Shub, 'Humanity Deleted,' *Problems of Communism*, No. 2, 1952, pp. 13-17.

43. Full translation in *Problems of Communism*, No. 6, 1953, p. 49; *Central Asian Review*, Vol. III, No. 2, 1955, p. 151.

44. Merle Fainsod, 'The Soviet Union since Stalin,' *Problems of Communism*, No. 2, 1954, pp. 4-6. See also Isaac Deutscher in *The Reporter*, 1 September 1953. Similar views were expressed in connection with the fall of Beria by Harry Schwartz in *The New York Times* and by the *Ukrainian Bulletin*, organ of the Ukrainian Congress Committee of America, which follows Soviet developments from a militant Ukrainian nationalist point of view.

45. Pryzyvy.

46. *Pravda*, 28 June 1953. Since Beria's arrest was not announced until 10 July, items appearing before that date may be considered to belong to the period discussed above.

47. The name of this authoritative Central Committe theoretical journal was *Bolshevik* until the Nineteenth Party Congress in October 1952, at which time the word 'bolshevik' was dropped from the Party's terminology. See P. Fedoseev, 'Sotsializm i patriotizm,' *Kommunist*, No. 9, 1953, pp. 12-28.

48. Ibid. p. 13.

49. Gosudarstvennost.

50. Ibid. pp. 25-6.

51. Ibid. p. 25.

52. *Kommunist*, No. 9, 1953, pp. 29-45.

53. Narodnosti.

54. Rodovoi stroi.

55. p. 29.

56. Natsiya, and narodnost.

57. Interesting statistical material on pp. 37, 39, 41, 43.

58. Yakubovskaya's reference to 'mutual enrichment' of cultures is interesting. Many books have been published in the Soviet Union since 1945 in which literary and other relations between the Great

Russians and other peoples of the USSR are discussed from the official point of view. Typical is *Russko-ukrainskie literaturnye svyazi,* edited by the noted literary scholar N. K. Gudzi (Moscow, 1951). Although Gudzi stresses the benefits conferred upon Ukrainian literature as a result of the sympathetic interest of Herzen, Chernyshevski, and other Russians, he also occasionally criticizes the 'unjust' attitude sometimes displayed by Belinski and other 'progressive' Russian men of letters toward Ukrainian writers. See for example, pp. 18-19.

59. Ibid. p. 44. The term 'oblast' corresponds roughly to 'state' in the American political system. Special 'national oblasts' exist where the population of a particular nationality is not great enough to establish a 'republic'; the next lowest level of nationality is the 'autonomous republic'; then come autonomous oblasts and finally 'national areas' *(natsionalnye okrugi).* Although the political significance of this system is very much less than is claimed by Soviet propaganda, it is one that takes into account linguistic and other national attributes.

60. *Pravda,* 9 October 1952, p. 2. Beria also included in his speech several strong paragraphs on the leading role of the Russian people, which included a paraphrase of Stalin's 1945 Toast.

61. The Presidium replaced the old Politburo at the Nineteenth Party Congress, 1952. A relatively large body of 25 members and 11 alternates from the congress until shortly after Stalin's death, this became in March 1953 a body of the same size as the old Politburo, and it has continued at this smaller size.

62. On one occasion a Soviet refugee of Great Russian extraction, whom I was interviewing in Germany, jumped from his chair and denounced Stalin as a 'stinking Georgian'; on the basis of conversations with Soviet refugee Georgians, I have the impression that Beria, much more than the more Russified and probably more convinced communist, Stalin, was to a considerable extent influenced by his Georgian national background.

63. Definitely Georgian were Dekanozov and Goglidze, the latter just before his downfall head of the M.G.B. in the Ukraine. Merkulov and Kobulov were, to my knowledge, Caucasians with Russianized names. It is interesting that the other henchmen of Beria, Meshik and Vlodzimirski, were apparently also non-Russians. It is also interesting that after the reorganization of the political police and the setting up of the Committee on State Security, Serov, who apparently is a Russian, was made the head of this Committee; the

successor of Beria as the head of the MVD, Kruglov, is also apparently a Russian.

64. *Kommunist,* No. 11, 1953, pp. 42-5, 54.

65. On Georgia see *The New York Times,* 21 and 24 February 1954. I am also indebted to Mr. N. M. Kay for valuable material on Georgia. A wealth of material based on a careful study of the Soviet sources on Central Asia and Kazakhstan is available in the quarterly *Central Asian Review* which the Central Asian Research Centre in London has been publishing since January 1953.

66. No. 16, pp. 22-36.

67. Ibid. p. 29.

68. *Nasha velikaya rodina,* op. cit. pp. 410-11.

69. *Pravda,* 21 June 1954. John S. Reshetar, Jr., 'National Deviation in the Soviet Union,' *The American Slavic and East European Review,* Vol. XII (April 1953), p. 173.

70. *Izvestiya,* 17 January 1954. The same issue included items from Kazakhstan reporting similar celebrations on collective farms in that Republic.

71. *Vossoedinenie ukrainy s rossiei* (Moscow, 1953, 3 vols.). These contain materials in Polish, Russian, Ukrainian, and Latin. The editorial committee, judging by the names, consisted of two Russian and four Ukrainian historians.

72. Karl Deutsch, *Nationalism and Social Communication* (New York, 1953), Ch. III, esp. p. 49.

73. Council.

74. Ukrainian spelling Bohdan Hmelnitskyi.

75. John S. Reshetar, *The Ukrainian Revolution* (Princeton, 1952), pp. 15, 16.

76. Ukrainian; in Russian, malorusski.

77. 'The Ukraine at the Turning Point,' *Annals of the Ukrainian Academy of Arts and Sciences in the United States,* Vol. III, Fall-Winter 1953, pp. 605-15. Quotation on p. 606.

78. Article on 'Ukraine' in *Malaya sovetskaya entsiklopediya,* IX, cols. 112-21.

79. Ibid. col. 115.

80. Col. 1013.

81. A. L. Patkin, *The Origins of the Russian-Jewish Labor Movement* (London and Melbourne, 1940), states that 300,000 Jews perished in these massacres. See p. 25.

82. *Istoriya srednikh vekov* (Moscow, 1946), p. 108.

83. E. A. Kosminski, *Istoriya srednikh vekov* (Moscow, 1950), p. 99.

84. Kolarz, *Russia and Her Colonies*, p. 123.

85. *Nasha velikaya rodina*, op. cit. p. 101.

86. *Izvestiya*, 10 March 1954.

87. *Bulletin of the Institute for the Study of the History and Culture of the USSR* (Munich), April 1954, pp. 30-33.

88. *The Young Communist*.

89. *Uch. gaz.*, 18 December 1954.

90. *Pravda*, 27 March and 1 April 1955.

91. *Vossoedinenie ukrainy s rossiei*, Vol. I, p. 5.

92. Ibid. p. 28.

93. Natsionalnost.

94. Rodina.

95. Strana.

96. An indication of unconscious, covert, and irrational Russian nationalism in the Soviet Union called to my attention by Paul W. Friedrich is that the images of workers, peasants, and intellectuals in cartoons in *Krokodil* and other Soviet illustrated magazines, as well as verbal descriptions of these types, seem to be almost invariably in terms of what are known by physical anthropologists as 'East Baltic' traits. It would appear that this type is a Russian nationalist symbol; the fact that nothing is ever said about this lends strength to the hypothesis. In this connection, it is interesting to note that at various times in the history of the Soviet regime, for example during the campaign against 'cosmopolitanism' in 1949, Semitic types were shown in cartoons and articles directed against 'negative' social elements.

97. See 'Public Statements of G. M. Malenkov,' issued by Department of State in May 1954, which contains no expression of Russian nationalism.

98. *Bolshevik*, No. 14, July 1945, pp. 17-18. See also article in Nos. 10–11, May-June 1944, correcting 'defects' in the work of the magazine, *Bolshevik of Kazakhstan*.

99. Potok.

100. M. I. Matyushkin, *Sovetski patriotizm* (Moscow, 1952), p. 281.

101. Solomon M. Schwarz, 'Revising the History of Russian Colonialism,' *Foreign Affairs*, April 1947, pp. 488-93. Dr. Schwarz incorrectly calls the treatment of Guseinov unprecedented. It was applied for example, in 1943 to G. F. Aleksandrov, and again to him in 1947, for works on the history of philosophy which after publication were condemned by the Kremlin as incorrect.

102. Bertram D. Wolfe, in *Foreign Affairs*, October 1952, p. 40.

103. On developments in Latvia see Jurgen von Hehn in *Ost Europa,* Vol. III, No. 3, June 1953, pp. 219-24.

104. Walter Kolarz, *The Peoples of the Soviet Far East* (New York, 1954), pp. 126-7; Roman Smal-Stocki, *The Nationality Problem of the Soviet Union* (Milwaukee, 1952), p. 294.

105. *Kommunist,* No. 6, 1954, pp. 45-59.

106. Stalin in his article 'The National Problem and Leninism,' first published in 1949, argued that to regard as a characteristic of a nation 'the possession of its own national state' would mean to remove oppressed nations deprived of their independent statehood, from the category of nations. *Soch.,* Vol. XI, p. 334. Quoted by V. Galkin, *Vozniknovenie i razvitie sotsialisticheskikh natsii v S.S.S.R.* (Moscow, 1952), p. 33.

107. Galkin, p. 23; Matyushkin, *Sovetski patriotizm,* pp. 285-6.

108. *Pravda,* 12 March 1954.

109. *Kommunist,* No. 3, 1955, p. 49.

110. The preferred status of the Russians over other Soviet peoples, however, was clearly indicated in a speech given by A. M. Puzanov, Chairman of the Council of Ministers of the RSFSR. Puzanov concluded his speech with salutations first to the 'mighty Soviet people, builder of a new human society,' second to 'the great Russian people and to all of the peoples of the Russian federation,' and third to 'the brother Ukrainian people.' Finally, he hailed the Party as 'the organizer of our victories.' *Pravda,* 27 March 1955.

Chapter III

1. Philip E. Mosely, 'Aspects of Russian Expansion,' *The American Slavic and East European Review,* Vol. VII, No. 3, October 1948 pp. 197-213. Quotation on p. 213.

2. Some anthropologists regard language as separable from the other elements of culture. For his own purposes, Stalin drew such a distinction in his pronouncements on linguistics in 1950. In this study language is regarded sometimes as a separate element but in the main we follow the usage according to which language is a part of culture.

3. Clyde Kluckhohn, *Mirror for Man* (New York, 1949), p. 17.

4. 'Kultura.'

5. However, *Voprosy yazykoznaniya,* No. 3, March 1954, p. 147, reported an academic conference at which Professor Blagoi argued

that the famous writers Karamzin and Radishchev belonged to opposing 'camps' of one 'culture.'

6. I am indebted for this term to the excellent study of John S. Armstrong, *Ukrainian nationalism, 1939–1945* (New York, 1955), p. 8.

7. Quoted by Kolarz, *Russia and her Colonies,* p. 7.

8. Warren B. Walsh in *Great Issues* (New York, 1951), p. 226.

9. *Terror and Progress* (Cambridge, 1954), p. 199.

10. Unfortunately, it is necessary here to use the term 'culture' sometimes in the ordinary rather than the 'anthropological' sense.

11. 'Has Soviet Anti-Semitism Faltered?' *Commentary,* July 1954, pp. 1-9. Quotation on p. 9.

12. Traditional Great Russian historiography, the centralist bias of which has been intensified by Soviet scholars, regarded the Russian Empire as the continuation of 'Kievan Rus,' originating in the Dnepr valley. The Ukrainian nationalist view is that the Ukrainian people of modern times is the heir of Kiev, while the Russian Empire and the Soviet state continue the tradition of 'Muscovy.' According to the Ukrainian view, the 'Muscovite' culture which developed under strong Tatar influence in the northeastern forest regions in the middle ages is different from, and does not include, Ukrainian culture.

13. Frank Lorimer, *The Population of the Soviet Union* (The League of Nations, Geneva, 1946), Ch. VI, pp. 137-40, 198-9. See also Kolarz, op. cit. and Eugene Kulischer, *Europe on the Move* (New York, 1948).

14. 1928–32.

15. Ivan Kurganov in his article 'Natsionalnaya Problema v Rossii, *Novy Zhurnal,* xxv, 1951, pp. 263-89, argues that denationalization of all nationalities, including even the Russians, is the Kremlin's ultimate purpose. English translation available under the title of 'The Problem of Nationalities in Soviet Russia,' *Russian Review,* October 1951, pp. 253-67.

16. Michael Prawdin in *The Mongol Empire* (London, 1941), Ch. XXXIII, points to significant Russian affinities with and borrowings from the 'Tatar heritage.' He argues that by the 'conscious and deliberate acceptance' of this heritage Moscow became great and powerful. Quotation on p. 514.

17. 21.3 per cent as against 10.5 per cent but far behind the Jews, 82.4 per cent of whom lived in cities. (Lorimer, op. cit. pp. 50, 52.)

18. *Bolshaya sovetskaya entsiklopediya* (Moscow, 1948), col. 60.

19. Not counting natural increase within the old borders during 1939–40.

20. *The New York Times,* for 17 January 1954, gave a figure of 215,-000,000 for the total Soviet population of which 107,000,000 were Russian and 42,000,000 Ukrainians. On this basis just under 50 per cent of the population would be Great Russians. The periodical publications of the Ukrainian Congress Committee of America consistently maintain that the Great Russians are in the minority in the USSR. At the other extreme Barrington Moore, Jr., *Terror and Progress,* op. cit. p. 198, estimates the non-Russians as about 40 per cent of the population. One recent estimate of the Soviet population by a reliable source was the figure of 210,000,000 in *Ost-Europa,* April 1954, p. 120.

21. *Malaya sovetskaya entsiklopediya,* 2nd ed., x, col. 1,046, gave a figure of 'about 38 million Ukrainians' within the USSR. This was before the Soviets took Bessarabia from Rumania.

22. Lorimer, op. cit. p. 140.

23. Basilius Martschenko, *Soviet Population Trends* (in Russian with English title; Research Program on the USSR, New York, 1953), pp. 33-4. Martschenko estimates that in the Soviet Union as a whole about 11 million persons died, or were not born, as a result of the famine, p. 23. He is critical of Lorimer for paying almost no attention to the famine.

24. Ukrainian scholars whom I have interviewed believe that because of this 'passing,' the number of Ukrainians is underestimated by Soviet censuses. They also believe that under favorable conditions these 'Russians' would reveal their true identity. Smal-Stocki, op. cit. p. 368, even compares non-Russians in the USSR to Jews forced to become 'Christians' in medieval Spain.

25. W. H. Chamberlin, *Russia's Iron Age* (Boston, 1934), pp. 88-9.

26. *Bolshaya,* special edition, op. cit. cols. 61, 62.

27. *Malaya,* x, col. 1046.

28. *Russia and Her Colonies,* op. cit. p. 123.

29. It is interesting, in connection with this discussion of the roles of the three Slavic peoples, that Stalin asserted, in March 1939, that the Russian republic had replaced the Ukraine as the Soviet 'breadbasket.' Present Soviet policy envisages a larger grain production in Kazakhstan than in the Ukraine.

30. G. A. von Stackelberg, 'The Tashkent Conference on the History of the Peoples of Central Asia and Kazakhstan—1954,' *Bulletin of*

the Institute for the Study of the History and the Culture of the USSR, Munich, May 1954, p. 12.

31. See *Pravda vostoka*, 4 May 1954.

32. 'Soviet Affairs Notes,' U.S. State Department, No. 144, 20 April 1953.

33. *Bolshaya*, special edition, col. 60. I have listed above only those of a population close to a million; other smaller groups such as the Kara-Kalpaks with almost 200,000 and the Abkahazians with about 60,000 would have to be included in a complete list.

34. Lorimer, op. cit. p. 58.

35. No historical study had appeared on water reform in Soviet Central Asia until publication of an article on the reform in the Uzbek Republic by A. A. Gurevich in *Voprosy Istorii*, No. 11, 1948, pp. 50-59. I am indebted to Dr. Albert Burke for calling this article to my attention.

36. Olaf Caroe, *Soviet Empire* (London and New York, 1953), p. 156.

37. Vyborg.

38. Population figures from Lorimer, op. cit. pp. 55, 56.

39. *Bolshaya*, op. cit. col. 60.

40. *Ost-Europa*, April 1954, p. 123.

41. The two books by Walter Kolarz referred to earlier contain a wealth of detailed descriptive material regarding even the smallest peoples of the Soviet Union.

42. Caroe, op. cit. p. 170. *Pravda*, 11 August 1955; *The New York Times* 11 and 15 August 1955.

43. *Bolshaya*, op. cit. cols. 61, 62.

44. The 1939 census gave a figure of 1,423,534.

45. Lorimer, op. cit. p. 56; *Bolshaya*, op. cit. col. 60; Bertram D. Wolfe, 'Operation Rewrite,' *Foreign Affairs*, Vol. 31, No. 1, October 1952, p. 39; Anatole Goldstein, 'The Soviet Attitude towards Territorial Minorities and the Jews,' published by Institute of Jewish Affairs (New York, 1953), p. 11; Kolarz, op. cit. Ch. III.

46. Goldstein, p. 12; Kolarz, *Russia and Her Colonies*, pp. 84-6.

47. A. Avtorkhanov, *Narodoubiistvo v SSSR* (Munich, 1952), p. 69.

48. Goldstein, op. cit. pp. 12-13; *Malaya sovetskaya entsiklopediya* (Moscow, 1937), v, col. 1012. Theodore Shabad in *The New York Times*, 30 June 1955; *Kazakhstanskaya Pravda*, 17 May 1955.

49. Based on figure of 832,300 persons in the region in 1934, of which 25 per cent were Tatar. At that time 48 per cent of the population were Russians, and 10 per cent Ukrainians. There were also con-

siderable numbers of Germans, Jews, Greeks, Bulgarians, etc., *Malaya,* loc. cit. col. 1012.

50. Jurgen von Hehn in *Ost-Europa,* April 1953, pp. 219-24.

51. *Europe on the Move,* op. cit. pp. 294, 297.

52. Ibid. p. 306.

53. G. P. Fedotov, *Novy grad* (New York, Chekhov Publishing House, 1952), p. 196.

54. Esp. in Ch. II 'The policy of the White Soviet Far East.' He asserts that the Soviet government wants only European colonization in its Far Eastern territories, and states that with regard to the Japanese problem 'the nationalist Russian trend has prevailed in practice' while the internationalist-communist approach has remained largely theoretical. See esp. pp. 32 and 50.

55. *Soviet Strength and Strategy in Asia* (Seattle, 1950), pp. 9, 11.

56. *K.P.S.S. v rezolyutsiyakh,* 7th ed. (Moscow, 1953), I, p. 516.

57. The foregoing attempt to relate Soviet doctrine on the nationality problem to the main body of Soviet thought is based for the most part on my article 'Nationality Doctrine in Soviet Political Strategy,' *The Review of Politics,* (July 1954), Vol. 16, No. 3, pp. 283-304. Subsequent to writing the article, I discovered Stanley W. Page's, 'Lenin, the National Question and the Baltic States, 1917–1919' in *The American Slavic and East European Review* (February 1948), VII, pp. 15-30, which takes a similar view of Soviet nationality policy. The excellent study by Richard E. Pipes, *The Formation of the Soviet Union* (Cambridge, 1954), written from a similar point of view, is a brilliant history of the application of Leninist-Stalinist doctrine to the creation of the Soviet 'federation.' See also Bertram D. Wolfe, *Three Who Made a Revolution* (New York, 1948), Ch. XXXIII, and, for an interpretation much more favorable to the Bolsheviks, E. H. Carr, *The Bolshevik Revolution* (New York, 1951), Vol. I, Part III, 'Dispersal and Reunion,' and Note B.

58. Russian for 'men of the majority.'

59. V. I. Lenin, *Izbrannye proizvedeniya* (Moscow, 1943, 2 vols.), I, p. 280; hereafter referred to as *Iz. proiz.* This collection of some of Lenin's most important works is useful as a guide to current Soviet interpretation of the heritage of Lenin. All or most of the works republished in these two volumes have subsequently been published in individual brochures or small books, and are frequently quoted in Soviet political journals.

60. Ibid. pp. 272-3.
61. *Three Who Made a Revolution,* op. cit. pp. 233-4.
62. Stalin, *Soch.,* pp. 49, 50.
63. Ibid. p. 55.
64. Avram Yarmolinsky, *The Jews and Other Minor Nationalities under the Soviets* (New York, 1928), p. 50.
65. Ibid. pp. 11, 112.
66. 1914.
67. Lenin, *Iz. proiz.,* I, pp. 657-9.
68. Ibid. p. 679.
69. Lenin, *Iz. proiz.,* I, p. 227.
70. *Current Soviet Policies* (New York, 1953), p. 29.
71. *Voprosy organizatsionnogo stroitelstva bolshevistskoi partii* (Moscow, 1945), p. 30.
72. Merle Fainsod, *How Russia Is Ruled* (Cambridge, 1953), p. 218.
73. Fainsod, op. cit. p. 219.
74. Fainsod, op. cit. pp. 230, 236-9.
75. *The Nationality Problem of the Soviet Union,* op. cit. p. 60.
76. An excellent and carefully qualified brief statement is 'The Concept of Basic Personality Structure as an Operational Tool in the Social Sciences,' by Abram Kardiner in Ralph Linton, ed., *The Science of Man in the World Crisis* (New York, 1945), pp. 107-22. In the work of Nathan Leites, *A Study of Bolshevism* (Glencoe, 1953), and in writings of Henry V. Dicks, Margaret Mead, and Geoffrey Gorer attempts are made from various angles to explain aspects of Soviet politics on the basis of 'national character' or other 'psycho-cultural' formulations similar to the concept of 'basic personality.' In my opinion the most successful and useful is Henry V. Dicks, 'Observations on Contemporary Russian Behavior,' *Human Relations* (1952), Vol. v, No. 2, pp. 111-74.
77. Lenin, *Iz. proiz.,* I, p. 147.
78. Smal-Stocki, op. cit. p. 95.
79. *Nationalism and Social Communication* (New York, Cambridge and London, 1953).
80. See esp. Chs. 6 and 7.
81. Fedor Mansvetov in *Novoe Russkoe Slovo* (New York), for 2 and 5 August 1948, argued rather convincingly that if pre-revolutionary trends had continued, the Ukrainians and Belorussians would have been assimilated in the general East Slavic population by that year.

Chapter IV

1. *Bolshevik*, No. 11, June 1951, p. 21; V. I. Lenin, 'Critical Remarks on the National Question' (Moscow, Foreign Languages Publishing House, 1951). Originally published in 1913.

2. Mr. Paul W. Friedrich suggested the use of this term and gave other assistance in dealing with the problems of 'acculturation' involved in this and the following chapter.

3. See Kolarz, *Russia and Her Colonies*, pp. 191-3, on the 'good' (from the Soviet point of view) Osetins.

4. By no means complete, judging by charges by *émigré* Osetins in the United States that the Soviet authorities have distorted beyond recognition, for political purposes, the history of the Great Osetin poet Kosta Khetagurov.

5. M. E. Rasul-Zade, *O panturanizme* (Paris, 1930), p. 21. Richard Pipes, 'Muslims of Soviet Central Asia: Trends and Prospects,' *Middle East Journal*, Vol. 9, No. 2, Spring 1955, pp. 147-62; No. 3, Summer 1955, pp. 295-308.

6. According to Albert Kalme, *Total Terror* (New York, 1951), the aim of the anti-communist resistance movement is 'to survive the present regime if at all possible.' Pp. 271-2.

7. S. A. Zenkovski, 'Ideological Deviations in Soviet Central Asia,' *The Slavonic and East European Review*, Vol. XXXII No. 79, June 1954, pp. 424-37. Quotation on p. 436. This article offers an excellent treatment of the Kremlin's struggle against cultural nationalism in central Asia subsequent to World War II, particularly with respect to the purge of central Asian, and also Russian, historians who had written on central Asia, in 1951–2.

8. Section on Soviet education in Nicholas Hans, *Comparative Education* (New York, 1949); popular work on Soviet education in N. Medinsky, *Public Education in the USSR* (Moscow, 1950); *Komsomolskaya pravda*, 8 May 1946; *Pravda*, 20 August 1952, and 15 October 1953.

9. A survey by Benjamin Fine in the *New York Times* for 21 January 1948 reported that the Soviet school system had 'seriously deteriorated,' and that between a third and a half of Soviet children did not go beyond the fourth grade. Apparently a very rapid recovery was made from this situation to that of 1955.

10. Harold R. Weinstein, 'Language and Education in the Soviet Ukraine,' *The Slavic Year-Book*, American Series, Vol. I, 1941, pp.

124-48. Material referred to on p. 144; *Pravda,* 26 March 1938, 'Russki yazyk v shkolakh ukrainy.'

11. Secondary.

12. Weinstein, pp. 146-7.

13. *Bolshaya sovetskaya entsiklopediya,* USSR volume, op. cit. col. 1821.

14. *Pravda,* 26 March 1938.

15. *Pravda,* 16 June 1938.

16. For example, *Pravda* for 25 April 1938 reported that the intelligentsia of the Crimean Tatar Republic had 'requested' introduction of the Russian alphabet, a request which was of course granted.

17. *Politicheskoe obespechenie velikoi pobedy pod leningradom* (Leningrad, 1945), pp. 145-50.

18. Zaki Ali, *Islam in the World* (Lahore, 1947), p. 351. I have been told by Ukrainian Soviet refugees that a similar policy was applied in 'liberated' Soviet Ukrainian territory. The motive in both cases seems to have been to get rid of 'unreliable' elements. On the other hand, Great Russians, inside the USSR and in exile, often told me what poor soldiers the Moslems were. They asserted that they were easily frightened.

19. *Sbornik rukovodyashchikh materialov o shkole,* Narkompros RSFSR. (Moscow, 1944), p. 16.

20. *Pedagogika,* 5th ed. (Moscow, 1950). This publication is one of the most important of all Soviet educational and propaganda sources.

21. Ibid. pp. 119, 121.

22. Russian title *Uchitelskaya gazeta,* hereafter referred to as *Uch. gaz.*

23. Numerous articles regarding technical problems of teaching Russian to non-Russians appear in the journal *Russki yazyk v shkole.*

24. Georgia includes also the Southern Osetin and the Adjarian autonomous republics.

25. *Zarya vostoka,* 5 February 1954.

26. Translation of this material, published in the Georgian language, furnished to me by Mr. M. N. Kay.

27. *Kultura i zhizn,* No. 13, (105), 11 May 1949.

28. *Uch. gaz.,* 10 July 1954.

29. *Uch. gaz.,* 26 June 1954.

30. I obtained in Moscow several issues of this rare publication of the Central Committee of the Communist Party in Latvia.

31. No. 7/8.

32. P. 32.

33. No. 7/8, 1945, p. 40.

34. Mr. Ulo Sinberg, in a review of the Soviet Estonian newspaper *Rahna Haal* for September 1952, noted propaganda on the value of Russian to Estonians, and a tendency to replace Estonian terms with counterparts derived from international stems which also exist in Russian.

35. The most comprehensive treatment of Soviet language policies, giving considerable attention to Russification, is the unpublished doctoral dissertation of Jindrich Kucera, entitled *Language Policy in the Soviet Union,* on deposit in the Harvard University Library. The forthcoming publication of this study will be a valuable addition to the literature on Soviet cultural policies. Uriel Weinreich gives a good brief summary of Soviet linguistic Russification policy, especially with respect to introduction of Russian elements into non-Russian languages, in 'The Russification of Soviet Minority Languages,' *Problems of Communism,* Vol. 2, No. 6, 1953, pp. 46-56. Kolarz and Smal-Stocki, particularly the latter, have dealt extensively with this problem. On Stalin's views on linguistics see 'The Stalin-Marr philological controversy in the USSR,' *The World Today,* Vol. 6 (1950), pp. 335-64, and J. Ellis and R. W. Davies, 'The Crisis in Soviet Linguistics,' *Soviet Studies* (January 1951), Vol. 2, No. 3, pp. 209-64.

36. The state Publishing House for Pedagogical Literature, in 1953, published an effective pedagogical tool entitled *A Picture Dictionary of the Russian Language (Kartinny slovar russkogo yazyka),* for use in non-Russian schools and for adults studying Russian.

37. *Russia and Her Colonies,* op. cit. p. 241.

38. In Russian, with English title, published by Research Program on the USSR (New York, 1953), introduction.

39. *Pravda,* 4, 5, 6 March 1926.

40. See Weinreich, op. cit. As late as 1949, T. P. Lomtev, in an article in *Voprosy filosofii,* attacked 'bourgeois nationalists' who had allegedly attempted to introduce Polish words into the Belorussian and Ukrainian languages. See No. 2, p. 135.

41. *Selected Writings of Edward Sapir* (Berkeley and Los Angeles, 1951), p. 565.

42. On the restoration, in 1934, of entrance examinations in Russian language and literature see Nicholas Hans, 'Recent Trends in Soviet Education,' *The Annals of the American Academy of Political and Social Science,* Vol. 263, May 1949, p. 116.

43. *Spravochniki.*

44. *Spravochnik dlya postupayushchikh v vysshie uchebnya zavedeniya soyuza s.s.r. v 1947 g.* (Moscow, 1947), pp. 5, 6, 7; 1954 ed., pp. 4, 5. On the abolition of the oral Russian requirement in 1955, see *Izvestiya,* 20 May 1955.

45. See for example *Tekhnikumy chernoi metallurgii. Spravochnik* (Moscow, 1941), p. 9, stipulating Russian language and one foreign language as part of the general educational 'cycle' for technical schools of the Peoples Commissariat of Ferrous Metallurgy. But *Spravochnik dlya postupayushchikh v srednie spetsialnye uchebnye zavedeniya,* 1954, refers to some institutions in which 'the language of instruction is not Russian.' See p. 12. However, required study of Stalin's works on language, and stress on Russian as 'one of the most important world languages,' is significant. See p. 23. The 1955 entrance requirements for higher educational institutions dropped foreign languages in non-Russian institutions, probably to leave more time for Russian.

46. *Kultura i zhizn* No. 6, 20 August 1946, and subsequent annual announcements.

47. M. Morozov, 'Natsionalnye traditsii i vospitanie sovetskogo patriotizma' (Moscow, 1950.

48. *Bolshaya sovetskaya entsiklopediya,* special number (Moscow, 1948), cols. 1233-5.

49. Hans, *Comparative Education,* p. 323.

50. Alex Inkeles, *Public Opinion in Soviet Russia* (Cambridge, 1951), p. 146.

51. Ibid. p. 147.

52. Data taken from articles on Union republics in *Bolshaya,* special USSR volume, op. cit. See esp. cols. 1821, 1831, 1842, 1852, 1862, 1870, 1903, 1930. It is interesting that the republics are listed, not alphabetically but in order of population, with the Russian republic first.

53. Inkeles, op. cit. p. 238.

54. *Pravda,* 9 August 1953.

55. Alexander Vucinich, *Soviet Economic Institutions* (Stanford, 1952), p. 92; A. Poplyuiko, 'The Change in the Social Aspect of the Peasantry in the USSR,' *Bulletin of the Institute for the Study of the History and Culture of the USSR* (Munich), April 1954, pp. 3-12.

56. A. Poplyuiko, in *Vestnik instituta po izucheniyu istorii i kultury S.S.S.R.,* March 1954, p. 14.

57. *Central Asian Review,* No. 3, 1953, pp. 85-95. This journal is hereafter referred to as *C.A.R.*

58. Village.

59. *C.A.R.,* Vol. II, No. 1, 1954, pp. 67-73.

60. On Sultan Galiev's 'case' see *KPSS v resolyutsiyakh* (Moscow, 1953), I, pp. 759-61. This item refers to 1923, when Sultan Galiev was expelled from the Party for allegedly attempting to organize a conspiracy against the Party's nationality policy in the Eastern regions, especially in Tataria and Bashkiria.

61. Among many authors of highly optimistic works on this area were Egon Erwin Kisch, William Mandel, Anna Louise Strong, and Owen Lattimore.

62. *C.A.R.,* No. 3, 1953, p. 52.

63. A. Grigolia, *Custom and Justice in the Caucasus* (Philadelphia, 1939), p. 176.

64. *Khaty.*

65. A wealth of factual material on the Ukraine is contained in *Entsiklopediya ukrainoznavstva* (Munich, 1949).

66. *The New York Times,* 1 August 1954.

67. Ivan Kurganov, 'Natsionalnaya problema v Rossii,' *Novy zhurnal,* Vol. 25, 286.

68. Based on conversations with members of Harvard Russian Research Center Refugee Interview Project.

69. See F. C. Barghoorn, 'Stalinism and the Russian Cultural Heritage,' *The Review of Politics,* Vol. XIV, No. 4, April 1952, pp. 178-203.

70. Alexander Werth, *The Year of Stalingrad* (London, 1946), p. 153.

71. Theodore Shabad, *Geography of the USSR* (New York, 1951), pp. 425-6. I am indebted to Mr. Ronald Joel for calling this to my attention.

72. *Pravda,* 10 December 1954; *The Ukrainian Bulletin,* 1-15 October 1954.

73. Based on material of Harvard Russian Research Center Refugee Interview Project.

74. *Soviet Opposition to Stalin* (Cambridge, 1952), pp. 137-8.

75. Committee for Liberation.

76. Ibid. p. 90.

77. Caroe, *Soviet Empire,* Ch. xv.

78. Armstrong, pp. 282, 286-7.

79. New York, 1954. See also Boris Shub, *The Choice* (New York, 1950).

80. A very useful recent contribution to the literature on this subject is K. Karov, *Partizanskoe dvizhenie v S.S.S.R. v 1941–45 gg* (Munich, 1954).

In addition to the books by Lyons and Shub, a considerable number of newspaper and magazine items on defection or armed resistance to the Bolsheviks have been published. Among the most valuable sources for this material are the bulletins of Ukrainian, Baltic, and other refugee organizations and such American publications as *Plain Talk* and *The New Leader*. Particularly noteworthy was an article by Paul L. Martin, entitled 'Wartime Runaways from Stalin's Army,' in *The New Leader* for 16 August 1947. An outstanding argument for a 'liberation' policy with regard to the Soviet peoples was Wallace Carroll's article 'It Takes a Russian to Beat a Russian' in *Life,* 19 December 1949. A useful contribution to the literature on discontent and resistance, including that of national minorities, is 'Tensions within the Soviet Union' (83rd Congress, 1st Session, Document No. 69, Washington, 1953), prepared by Sergius Yakobson.

81. The two articles by Richard Pipes, cited earlier, go further than any other scholarly studies known to me in their optimism regarding not merely the continued survival but the probable future growth of national consciousness among non-Russian peoples in the Soviet Union. Pipes even considers it possible that the entire area of Central Asia, Russian and Chinese, 'will tend to move with time in the direction of independent statehood.' Although I have the highest respect for Pipes' scholarship, I am inclined to interpret the available evidence differently, particularly in view of statements made to me by people who have traveled in Soviet-non-Russian republics, including those of Central Asia, since the death of Stalin, to the effect that Russian seems to be becoming the language of everyday speech among the children of the Turkic peoples, at least in and near large cities.

Chapter V

1. Avtorkhanov, *Narodoubiistvo v S.S.S.R.,* op. cit. p. 68. It is ironic that *Pravda* for 4 February 1939 highly praised the Chechen-Ingush for their patriotism, and that *Bolshevik* No. 15, August 1942 reported participation of Chechens and other North Caucasian peoples in a patriotic conference.

2. Avtorkhanov, op. cit. p. 68.

3. *Uch. gaz.*, No. 54, 1946.

4. For an excellent account of the application of these tactics against the peoples of Central Asia, see Uluktuk, 'Sovetizatsiya Turkestana i ee resultaty,' *Turkeli*, Munich, ⅔, 1951, pp. 8-20. The interpretive notes in Jurij Lawrynenko, *Ukrainian Communism, a Bibliography* (Research Program on the USSR, New York, 1953), present a very illuminating account of the application of this method in the Ukraine. See also *Investigation of Communist Take-Over of the Non-Russian Nations of the U.S.S.R.*, 83rd Congress, second session (Washington, D.C., 1954).

5. Molotov used this term in justifying the 'liberation' of Belorussians and Ukrainians by the Red Army in 1939.

6. F. Krushinski, *Byelorussian Communism and Nationalism* (Research Program on the USSR, New York, 1953); in Russian, with English titles.

7. Areas.

8. *Entsiklopediya gosudarstva i prava* (Moscow, 1927), iii, pp. 47-50.

9. V. K. Vlasov, *Sovetski gosudarstvenny apparat* (Moscow, 1951), pp. 93, 97, 107.

10. For brief observations, see F. C. Barghoorn. "The Ideological Weapon in Soviet Strategy,' in *The Threat of Soviet Imperialism* (Baltimore, 1954), note 14, p. 96.

11. On this point see Julian Towster, 'Soviet Policy on Nationalities,' *The Antioch Review*, Vol. xi, December 1951, pp. 437-48.

12. M. Shalamov, *Sudebnoe ustroistvo kazakhstana* (Moscow, 1941), p. 45. The shariat and adat are bodies of Moslem law.

13. The preceding paragraphs are inspired in part by the concepts of Otto Bauer in his *Die Nationalitaetenfrage*, and by observations in John S. Reshetar, Jr., 'The Nationality Problem in the Soviet Union,' a report prepared for the Russian Research Center, Harvard University, Project on the Soviet Social System.

14. Caroe, in the final section of his *Soviet Empire* says of the Soviet Turks that 'The tide will turn and bring with it either liberation or disappearance from the pages of history,' p. 268. For a contrary opinion, see the two articles by Pipes referred to in Ch. iv.

15. New York, 1951.

16. Alfred Skerpan, in 'Aspects of Soviet Anti-Semitism,' *The Antioch Review* (Fall 1952), takes a considerably more somber view than Schwarz. An interesting indication of 'covert' anti-Semitism is dele-

tion from the standard *Khrestomatiya po istorii SSSR*, 2nd ed., Vol. III, of the material in the 1st ed. denouncing Alexander III's anti-Jewish policy. I am indebted to Professor Marc Szeftel for bringing this to my attention.

17. *The New York Times*, 22 June 1954. Salisbury's figure of 100,000 Jews in Birobidzhan far exceeds earlier estimates. If correct, it may indicate mass deportations of Jews from other parts of the country to Birobidzhan. *N. Y. T.* 25 May and 15 August 1955; *Pravda vostoka*, 19 February 1955.

18. The preceding paragraphs are based on personal observations in the Soviet Union and on Goldstein, op. cit. pp. 27-39.

19. 'Jews in Soviet Literature,' in *Through the Glass of Soviet Literaature*, ed. by E. J. Simmons (Columbia University Press, 1953), p. 156.

20. Choseed, p. 111, quoting Harry Schwarz in *Commentary*, February 1948, p. 129. According to a reliable Ukrainian refugee, journalism and 'office work' in the Ukraine before World War II were dominated by Jews.

21. There are indications that since 1948 the participation of Jews has been drastically reduced by a 'quota' system more strict than that of the Tsars. Intelligence Report, U.S. State Department, 'The Position of the Jews in the USSR' (Washington, D.C., 26 January 1953), p. 32.

22. One get this impression from earlier works on Soviet nationality policy, such as those of Avram Yarmolinsky and Hans Kohn.

23. The political framework within which Russification takes place is exhaustively treated in Merle Fainsod, *How Russia Is Ruled* (Cambridge, 1953). Much essential factual information is contained in Julian Towster, *Political Power in the USSR* (New York, 1948). The standard work on Soviet propaganda is Inkeles, *Public Opinion in Soviet Russia*, op. cit.

24. For an excellent discussion of assimilation and national minorities, in terms of alternative policies of 'coercion,' 'discrimination,' 'toleration,' and 'equality,' see *Nationalism*, a report by a study group of members of the Royal Institute of International Affairs (London, New York, Toronto, 1939), pp. 285-7.

25. Robert H. Lowie, *Social Organization* (New York, 1948), p. 283.

26. *Ustav garnizonnoi sluzhby krasnoi armii* (Moscow, 1946).

27. *Nachalnik i podchinennye* (Moscow, 1945).

28. G. K. Schueller, *The Politburo* (Stanford, 1951), pp. 11, 12, 42.

29. Julian Towster, 'The Soviet Union after Stalin,' *The American Slavic and East European Review*, Vol. XIII, No. 4, December 1954, pp. 471-99. See esp. p. 484, footnote.

30. See Reshetar, 'National Deviation in the Soviet Union,' op. cit. pp. 170-71.

31. Some valuable material on the growth of the Ukrainian ethnic element in the Ukrainian Party organization and also on the effects of the purge of 1937–8, are contained in an article by D. Feliks in *Vpered*, Munich Ukrainian Labour Magazine, No. 6, (43), 1954. Feliks, in his article entitled 'Ukrainska byurokratiya-novii politichnii faktor,' states that the percentage of Ukrainians in the Central Committee of the Ukrainian Communist Party increased from 61.7 per cent in 1952 to 72 per cent since the fall of Melnikov.

32. Testimony of Mikola Abramtschik, in 'Investigation,' op. cit. p. 59.

33. For above data, I am indebted to Mr. M. N. Kay, in letter of 22 April 1955, based on Georgian-language Soviet press and on monitoring of Radio Tbilisi. On the turnover of personnel after Stalin's death, see Boris Meissner, *Die Kommunistische Partei der Sowjetunion vor und nach dem Tode Stalin's* (Frankfurt, 1954), pp. 22, 26, 28.

34. Jan Dubicki, *Elements of Disloyalty in Turkmenistan* (New York, 1954) in Russian (English title), Research Program on the USSR.

35. *Izvestiya*, 29 April 1940, cited in *The American Quarterly on the Soviet Union*, Vol. III, No. 2-3, November 1943, appendix, pp. 97-100.

36. *Partiinaya zhizn*, No. 14, 1947, pp. 77-8.

37. *Uch. gaz.*, 34 (3,163), 1946, published an unusually interesting article on 'Certain Causes of the Backwardness of the Kazakh School' stressing poor training of teachers, the low percentage of Kazakhs in the upper grades of the secondary schools, and the vital necessity of improving instruction in Russian if qualified cadres were to be trained in the national republics.

38. United States Department of State, *Soviet Affairs Notes*, No. 168, 11 April 1955, p. 7.

39. 'Die Kaukasischen und Zentralasiatichen Gebiete,' *Ost-Europa* Heft 6/2 Jahrgang, pp. 464-8. Muratov's speech in *Pravda*, 8 October 1952.

40. The most recent material, assembled by William H. E. Johnson, indicates 'a rather equitable apportionment on the basis of total population.' See George B. De Huszar, ed., *Soviet Power and*

Progress (New York, 1955), pp. 214-15, giving data on distribution of higher educational institutions by republics, etc. According to *Pravda,* for 1 June 1955, the number of secondary schools in Moldavia grew from 37 in 1945 to 319 in 1955 and four times as many pupils in Turkmenia finished secondary school in 1950–55, or earlier.

41. Eugene Staley, *The Future of Underdeveloped Areas* (New York, 1954), Part II, esp. Ch. 8.

42. *Ukrainian Nationalism,* op. cit. p. 17.

43. For a penetrating discussion of the contemptuous attitude of the Party elite toward the 'masses' see F. Beck and W. Godin, *Russian Purge and the Extraction of Confession* (New York, 1951), pp. 216-18. The same attitude is taken by the main characters in Igor Gouzenko's insightful novel, *The Fall of a Titan* (New York, 1954).

44. Fainsod, op. cit. p. 495. For a significant indication of post-Stalin concern about the strength of 'survivals of nationalism' see M. Yovchuk, 'Rol sotsialisticheskoi ideologii v borbe s perezhitkami kapitalizma,' *Voprosy filosofii,* No. 1, 1955, pp. 3-16. See esp. pp. 8-9 and 12-13. Among other things, Yovchuk attacks attempts, allegedly exposed in literature, art, and scholarship, to 'alienate the culture of the peoples of the USSR' from the 'advanced Russian culture.'

45. K. C. Wheare, *Federal Government,* 3rd ed. (New York, London, 1953), pp. 26-8.

46. M. Holdsworth, quoted in Staley, op. cit. p. 157, footnote. For penetrating observations on this problem, see 'Ukraine and the Budget of the USSR,' by T. S., *Ukrainian Quarterly,* Vol. IV, No. 1, 1948, pp. 19-27.

47. See for example, *Sobranie postanovlenii i rasporyazhenii pravitelstva s.s.s.r.,* No. 28, June 29, 1938, decree number 182, on the livestock plan for 1938.

48. *Pravda vostoka* (Tashkent) 10 September 1949, and 31 January 1951.

49. Kolarz, *The Peoples of the Soviet Far East,* p. 120, footnote.

50. County.

51. On folklore, for example, see Yuri Sokolov, *Russian Folklore* (English translation, New York, 1950), esp. pp. 531-2, 653, 658, 681-90.

52. *Sbornik rukovodyashchikh materialov po bibliotechnoi rabote* (Moscow, 1947), p. 23.

53. Ibid. p. 23.

54. *Programma doprizyvnoi podgotovki* (Moscow, 1942), pp. 77-8.

55. *Bibliografiya sovetskoi bibliografii, 1939* (Moscow, 1941), pp. 15-18, 20.

56. The studies of Kolarz and others have made a good start. Works in progress at various university research centers will fill many of the remaining gaps.

57. One of the points made to the author by Soviet refugees interviewed in Germany was that German propaganda to Soviet people during World War II failed partly because it was 'primitive.' Its archaic terminology betrayed failure to understand the technical and cultural developments which have taken place in Russia under the Soviet regime. Another point, often made by Great Russian refugees, is that the Rosenberg school of thought in Germany aroused resentment among Russians precisely because it envisaged the 'dismemberment' of Russia.

Chapter VI

1. Waldemar, Gurian, *Bolshevism* (Notre Dame, 1952), p. 101; Thomas G. Masaryk, *The Spirit of Russia* (London, 1919, 2 vols.), *passim.*

2. G. P. Fedotov, *The Russian Religious Mind* (New York, 1946), pp. 351-3.

3. K. Waliszewski, *A History of Russian Literature* (New York, London, 1927), p. 22.

4. Edward Crankshaw, *Cracks in the Kremlin Wall* (New York, 1951), p. 268.

5. Some of these works are in many ways, especially in technical matters, of a high order of scholarship. One might cite, for example, in very different fields, *Russkoe derevyannoe zodchestvo* (*Russian Wooden Architecture*) (1942), or *Russkie biologi-evolyutsionnisti do darvina* (*Russian Evolutionary Biologists before Darwin*) (1951-2).

6. A. S. Popov, *Izobretatel radio* (Moscow, 1945), flyleaf.

7. I have emphasized this 'synthetic' aspect of Soviet patriotism in my article 'Stalinism and the Russian Cultural Heritage,' in *The Review of Politics*, April 1952, and in my contribution to the Arden House Conference on Change and Continuity in Russian and Soviet Thought.

8. See, for example, the London *Economist* for 14 August 1954.

9. Boston, 1953.

10. 'Religion must be eliminated, sooner or later, and above all it must not gain the younger generation' p. 325.

11. See, for example, photograph of club in village of Borisovo in *Arkhitektura i stroitelstvo,* Moscow, 1954, No. 4. This shows a very ornate building with eight columns in front. In the same issue there is a photograph of the foyer of the House of Culture of the Moscow Energetics Institute, with pilasters, a huge crystal chandelier, and a gleaming parquet floor.

12. Items in *The New York Times* for 16 and 21 August 1954. On the other hand, adoption of uniforms for school children in 1954–5 was a 'democratic' development.

13. F. C. Barghoorn 'D. I. Pisarev: A Representative of Russian Nihilism,' *The Review of Politics,* Vol. 10, No. 2, pp. 190-211; April 1948; F. C. Barghoorn, 'The Russian Radicals of the Eighteen Sixties and the Problem of the Industrial Proletariat,' *The Slavonic and East European Review* (American series), Vol. II, 1942–3, Part I, pp. 57-69.

14. For a penetrating criticism of such 'situation-bound' thinking, see Karl Popper, *The Open Society and Its Enemies,* 2nd ed. (Princeton, 1952). Popper does not, however, discuss Sumner.

15. Sumner, *Folkways,* op. cit. p. 14.

16. 1689–1725.

17. I agree with Professor Michael Karpovich of Harvard that the translation of Ivan Grozny as John the Dread is preferable to the one used above, but I employ the translation familiar to most American readers.

18. *Voprosy istorii,* No. 2, February 1954, recorded a meeting of the historical faculty of Leningrad University at which the above problem was discussed. See pages 182-4.

19. *Voprosy yazykoznaniya,* No. 3, March 1954, p. 133; *Voprosy istorii,* No. 6, June 1955, pp. 168-72.

20. A sensitive and at times brilliant attempt at a geographic interpretation of Russia, which continues the great pre-revolutionary traditions of Leroy-Beaulieu and Mackenzie Wallace, is Edward Crankshaw's *Russia and the Russians* (New York, 1948). Among works on Soviet Russia by professional geographers, which have much to offer to the student of politics, the best known is George Cressey's *The Basis of Soviet Strength,* 2nd ed. (New York, 1954). Dinko Tomasic in *The Impact of Russian Culture on Soviet*

Communism (Glencoe, 1953) interestingly combines a geographical with a 'psycho-cultural' approach.

21. Henry Thomas Buckle, *Civilization in England,* new ed. (London, 1871), Vol. I, p. 196.

22. Aleksandr Ivanovich Gertsen, *Polnoe sobranie sochinenii i pisem* (Petrograd, 1917), Vol. VI, pp. 311, 377.

23. Ibid. p. 377.

24. *Nationalism,* a report by a study group of members of the Royal Institute of International Affairs (London, 1939), p. 57. Very interesting material on the early stages of development of the Russian national consciousness is contained in George Fedotov, *The Russian Religious Mind* (New York, 1946). For an excellent brief survey of the development of Russian national consciousness from the earliest times see also Roman Jakobson, 'Comparative Slavic Studies,' *The Review of Politics,* Vol. 16, No. 1, January 1954, pp. 67-90.

25. G. Samarin, *Patrioticheskaya tema v pessennem tvorchestve russkogo naroda* (Frunze, 1946).

26. *Der Patriotismus,* op. cit. Pp. 181-248 are devoted to the 'sociology of national songs.'

27. For the First World War, there is much impressive evidence on this point in Bernard Pares, *The Fall of the Russian Monarchy* (New York, 1939).

28. *Rodina* (Moscow, 1942), p. 88. Hereafter cited as *Rod.* This is a very interesting anthology of patriotic statements by Russian writers.

29. *Rod.,* p. 88. For Chernyshevski's statement on Hungary, see *Dnevnik Chernyshevskogo* (Moscow, 1931), Part I, pp. 305, 315.

30. A wealth of material on the Muscovite-Tatar struggle in its later phases is contained in the book by A. A. Novoselski, *Borba moskovskogo gosudarstva s tatarami v XVII veke* (Moscow, 1948).

31. Quoted by Lewis Galantiere in *Foreign Affairs,* Vol. 28, No. I, p. 120. Galantiere's article, entitled 'Through the Russian Looking-Glass,' contains numerous striking quotations.

32. See, for example, Jan Kucharzewski, *The Origins of Modern Russia* (New York, 1948).

33. Parliament.

34. Gosudarstvennaya Duma, fourth convocation, stenographic report (Moscow, 1913), III, pp. 902-7.

35. See George Denicke, 'Links with the Past in Soviet Society,' Department of State External Research Paper, 21 March 1952, p. 7.

36. V. O. Klyuchevski, *Skazaniya inostrantsev o moskovskom gosu-darstve* (Petrograd, 1918). Although based upon reports by foreigners, this work is brilliantly original in design and execution.

37. Ibid. pp. 5-23.

38. Ibid. p. 48.

39. *Elf Jahre in Sowjetischen Gefaengnissen und Lagern* (Zurich, 1950), pp. 234-6.

40. Among these the best recent account is *Russian Assignment* (Boston, 1953), by retired Vice Admiral Leslie C. Stevens.

41. Closed by Soviet order in 1948.

42. Nobility.

43. Ibid. p. 65.

44. See *The Russian Menace to Europe*, ed. by Bert Blackstock and Paul Hoselitz (Glencoe, 1952).

45. *Bolshevik*, No. 20, 1937, pp. 35-45.

46. See, for example, Salisbury in *The New York Times*, 29 September 1954.

47. Local self-government organs, performing educational, health, and other services, set up in 1864.

48. G. P. Fedotov, 'Russia and Freedom,' *The Review of Politics*, Vol. VIII, No. 1, January 1946, p. 34.

49. Leon Trotski, *Stalin* (New York, 1946), p. 385.

50. Ibid. pp. 404-5.

51. Loc. cit.

52. Isaac Deutscher, in *Russia: What Next?* (New York, 1953) and in other works seems to argue that Stalinism was reactionary in form but progressive in essence because Stalin's industrialization of Russia paved the way for a 'democratic regeneration' which set in, at least in its incipient stages, after the death of the dictator. This view rests upon the Marxist assumption that economics determines politics. It is certainly partly correct, but it underestimates the importance of political traditions and institutions.

53. Jacob Walkin, 'The Attitude of the Tsarist Government toward the Labor Problem,' *The American Slavic and East European Review*, Vol. XIII, No. 2, May 1954, pp. 163-4.

54. Even Lenin, until 1905 and to a certain extent until his 'April theses' of 1917, held to the view that Russia must first experience a 'bourgeois' revolution; then, after accumulating further experience of capitalist development, it could eventually make the 'proletarian' revolution which would usher in socialism. We cannot here discuss such very complicated problems as whether or not

it would have been possible for Russia to have followed the pattern of first establishing a parliamentary government, which was clearly the path of development envisaged in classical Marxism, and then have proceeded to convert the bourgeois parliamentary republic into a socialist parliamentary republic according to the pattern set forth by Engels in his Preface of 1891 to Marx's *Civil War in France.* E. H. Carr seems to take the position, in his *Bolshevik Revolution,* that Russia had arrived at a situation in which it could no longer continue under capitalism without suffering catastrophe, but at the same time was not ready for socialism.

55. Quoted by Peter Gay, *The Dilemma of Democratic Socialism* (Columbia University Press, 1952), p. 294.

56. Robert A. Feldmesser, 'The Persistence of Status Advantages in Soviet Russia,' *The American Journal of Sociology,* Vol. LIX, No. 1, January 1953, pp. 19-27. Quotation on pp. 26-7.

57. Denicke, op. cit. maintains that a majority of the old intelligentsia survived physically and that its literary and other values play a very important role in Soviet culture.

58. Dicks, 'Observations on Contemporary Russian Behavior,' and Tomasic, *Impact of Russian Culture on Soviet Communism* op. cit. esp. Part III, 'Personality Development.'

59. Nathan Leites, in *The Operational Code of the Politburo* (New York, 1949) and *A Study of Bolshevism* (Glencoe, 1953), has attempted to codify these rules of political action and to connect them, though more implicitly than explicitly, with psychological drives, using a Freudian interpretation. To these factors as studied by Leites must be added the more general ones explored by Dicks and Tomasic.

60. Among scholars who tend to emphasize the rational factors in Soviet policy, E. H. Carr and Barrington Moore, Jr., are outstanding.

61. Suvorov fought against Napoleon in the famous Alpine campaign of 1798. Earlier he had distinguished himself, by, among other things, crushing the Polish Republic set up in 1791.

62. The term 'cultural' is here used in the sense of 'value culture,' referring to systems of religious, ethical, and other ideas.

63. Nicholas Berdyaev, *The Origin of Russian Communism* (London, 1937).

64. Milyukov's learned and brilliant historical analysis of the development of Russian culture is available in English in *Outlines of*

Russian Culture, 3 vols. (Philadelphia, 1942), edited by Michael Karpovich. Part I is entitled *Religion and the Church.*

65. Masaryk's book was published originally in German in 1913. The English translation was published in London in 1919.

66. Bertrand Russell, *Bolshevism: Practice and Theory* (New York, 1920).

67. The 'defensists,' who supported the Tsarist government in the war against Germany, were reviled by Lenin.

68. *Vekhi* (Moscow, 1909, 4th ed.); *Intelligentsiya v rossii* (St. Petersburg, 1910). I am indebted to Professor Sergei Pushkarev for calling my attention to these works. The places of publication are interesting. They recall the earlier polemic between St. Petersburg 'Westernizers' and Moscow 'Slavophiles.'

69. *Vekhi*, pp. 6, 11, 17.

70. An excellent recent treatment of Slavophile thought is contained in Nicholas A. Riasanovsky, *Russia and the West in the Teaching of the Slavophiles* (Cambridge, Mass., 1952).

71. *Intelligentsiya*, op. cit. pp. 89-191.

72. This was the approach I took in my article 'Stalinism and the Russian Cultural Heritage.' A similar conception furnishes one of the main themes of Igor Gouzenko's *The Fall of a Titan.*

73. This point of view is argued most brilliantly in Walter Biehahn's article 'Marxismus und Nationale Idee in Russland,' cited earlier.

74. Stolypin's assassination in 1911 was a severe blow to this policy and deprived Russia of perhaps its ablest conservative statesman.

75. On these points, see Biehahn, op. cit., and Walter Kolarz, *Stalin and Eternal Russia* (London, 1944).

76. Alexander von Schelting, *Russland und Europa* (Bern, 1948), p. 14.

77. Biehahn, op. cit. p. 464.

78. For my views on the attitude of Soviet people toward Americans, based upon personal experience, see Ch. XI of my book *The Soviet Image of the United States* (New York, 1950).

79. For additional details see my article 'Russian Radicals and the West European Revolutions of 1848' in *The Review of Politics*, Vol. XI, No. 3, July 1949, esp. pp. 340-42.

80. I went several times to the special Library for Foreign Literature and found a few English language magazines about a year old, none of which were popular mass circulation journals.

81. J. H. Adam Watson, in *The Threat of Soviet Imperialism* (Baltimore, 1954), p. 39.

82. A great deal of fascinating material on this and related subjects is contained in G. V. Plekhanov, *Istoriya russkoi obshchestvennoi mysli* (3 vols. Vol. I, St. Petersburg, 1915, Vols. II and III, Moscow, 1917).

83. On various phases of this subject see: Eugene Lyons, *Our Secret Allies: the Peoples of Russia*, Boris Shub, *The Choice*, and George Fischer, *Soviet Opposition to Stalin*.

84. *Znamya*, No. 1, 1947, pp. 130-42. I am indebted to Mr. Robert Hankin for calling this article to my attention.

85. Ibid. p. 137.

86. *Pravda*, 9 December 1947, p. 3.

87. The books by Frank Rounds, Jr., *A Window on Red Square* (Boston, 1952), Vice Admiral Leslie C. C. Steven's *Russian Assignment*, and Marshall MacDuffie's *The Red Carpet* present many interesting observations on this and other aspects of the outlook of the Soviet people.

88. Karl W. Deutsch, *Nationalism and Social Communication,* furnishes valuable suggestions as to how such a project might be set up.

89. Gosudarstvennost.

90. *Intelligentsiya v rossii,* op. cit. p. 152.

91. Shirokaya natura.

92. The Slavophiles and also Herzen and many other nationally conscious and in various ways anti-Western writers attacked Western 'narrowness' and philistinism.

93. N. Bukharin, 'A Great Marxian Party,' *Communist Review* (London), Vol. IV, No. 1, p. 16.

94. Ivan the Terrible.

95. Ibid. p. 129.

96. Ibid. pp. 155-6.

97. Ibid. p. 157.

98. Ibid. p. 166.

99. Obviously implicit and to a small degree explicit in Milyukov's discussion was the idea that the views of the *Landmarks* group represented, among other things, a Great Russian chauvinism which would arouse bitter resentment among the non-Russian peoples of the Empire.

100. Leaders and Duma deputies whose names are associated with 'black hundred' bands responsible for pogroms against Jews. Lenin in his 1914 article, 'On the National Pride of the Great Russians,' castigated Purishkevich and contrasted chauvinism with what he

considered to be the genuine Russian patriotism of Chernyshevski and other revolutionaries. Little did Lenin imagine that his successor as leader of the Soviet state would bring to perfection a nationalism exceeding in its intolerance even that of Purishkevich.

101. Some of the contributors to *Landmarks* criticized the 'cosmopolitanism' of the Russian intelligentsia. Ironically enough, they directed this criticism with particular force against the radical Marxists, including the Bolsheviks. Of course, it was not the *Landmarks* group, but the 'cosmopolitan' Bolsheviks, who gained power in Russia.

102. The work of Otto Bauer, *Die Nationalitaetenfrage und die sozialdemokratie,* 2nd ed. (Wien, 1924), and the recent work of Karl Deutsch present valuable sociological explanations of the relationship between industrialization and nationalism.

103. For an excellent discussion of the contrast between the mainly negative 'official nationality' policy of nineteenth-century Russia and that of the Soviet regime, see Michael Karpovich 'Historical Background of Soviet Thought Control,' in *The Soviet Union,* Waldemar Gurian, ed. (Notre Dame, 1951), pp. 16-30.

104. *O kommunisticheskom vospitanii* (Moscow, 1952), p. 8.

105. On this point, see for example, Peter Yershov, 'Soviet Literature in the New Encyclopedia,' *The American Slavic and East European Review,* Vol. XIII, No. 1, 1954, pp. 89-99.

106. Ibid. p. 19.

107. Dicks, op. cit. pp. 150-58.

108. *Bolshevik,* 1951, No. 2, p. 16.

109. *Pravda,* 15 March 1953.

110. *Doklad t. Zhdanova o zhurnalakh 'zvezda' i 'Leningrad'* (Moscow, 1946), pp. 35-6.

Chapter VII

1. Raymond Aron, 'La Russie après Staline,' *Preuves,* 32 (October 1953), pp. 5-13.

2. V. Berestnev, 'Kniga o sovetskoi kulture,' *Kommunist,* No. 17, 1954, pp. 123-8. The book reviewed was written by G. G. Karpov and entitled *O sovetskoi kulture i kulturnoi revolyutsii v SSSR.* Karpov presents the Stalinist view that culture is a function of politics. He asserts on the first page of this work that the Soviet Union is the 'citadel' of the most advanced, scientific thought and

culture, while 'bourgeois' culture is the main obstacle to the 'progressive' advancement of mankind, and successfully maintains this tone throughout. The reviewer does not criticize this messianic, intolerant view. Judging by his initials, this is the Karpov who heads the Soviet agency for liaison with the Russian Orthodox Church. While I was in Russia I was told by several Soviet acquaintances that G. G. Karpov was a former high official of the security police, whose experience had been principally in anti-religious activity.

3. Ibid. p. 123.
4. Ibid. p. 124.
5. Ibid. p. 127.
6. *Bolshaya sovetskaya entsiklopediya*, 2nd ed. (December 1953), Vol. 24, p. 31.
7. I believe that this 'post-Stalin' line was foreshadowed in Stalin's article 'Economic Problems of Socialism in the USSR,' and in his farewell speech to foreign Communists at the Nineteenth Party Congress, delivered on 15 October 1952. Stalin's successors, however, displayed more intelligence in applying the tactics adopted by the Party high command to exploit Western 'contradictions' and frustrate Western unity, than the perhaps senile Stalin. The difference between the 'Stalin,' and 'post-Stalin,' lines is less than is widely supposed in the West.
8. *Voprosy istorii*, No. 7, July 1954, p. 9.
9. Front page of *Pravda*, 15 October 1952.
10. See my article 'The Soviet Image of the United States: A Deliberately Distorted Image,' *The Annals of the American Academy of Political and Social Science*, Vol. 295, September 1954, pp. 42-51.
11. See, for example, excerpts from the poem by the Soviet author Dolmatovski on the 'Next Nuremberg Trial,' quoted by Sergius Yakobson in *Proceedings of the American Society of International Law*, 1950, p. 21.
12. For the period up to 1950, with special reference to the United States, see Barghoorn, *The Soviet Image of the United States* (New York, 1950).
13. Harry Schwartz, *The New York Times*, 20 June 1952.
14. Such charges were made in the Soviet press in connection with the formation of S.E.A.T.O., for example, in the summer of 1954.
15. *Report of the Court Proceedings in the Case of the Anti-Soviet Trotskiite Center* (Moscow, 1937), pp. 366-8.
16. *Bolshevik*, No. 2, 1951, pp. 9-16.

17. E. A. Korovin, 'Chudovishchnye zlodeyaniya amerikanskikh agressorov v Koree,' (Moscow, 1952), p. 3.

18. *Znamya,* No. 10, 1950, p. 15.

19. The books by Admiral Leslie C. Stevens and Frank Rounds, Jr., already referred to, furnish much additional factual material as well as vivid on-the-spot impressions of the effect on the Soviet public of anti-American propaganda.

20. *Kommunist,* No. 7, 1953, p. 30.

21. For additional details see my article in the *Annals* referred to earlier. The value of studying May Day slogans has been demonstrated by Sergius Yakobson and Harold D. Lasswell in their article 'May Day Slogans in Soviet Russia, 1918–1943' in *Language of Politics* (New York, 1949), pp. 233-97.

22. The word 'culture' is here used in the sense of arts, literature, etc.

23. Quoted by Sergius Yakobson in *Nationalism,* op. cit. p. 73. This concept of 'two nations' is found earlier in Disraeli's novel, *Sybil.*

24. See, for example, V. I. Lenin, *Iz. proiz,* op. cit.

25. Ibid. pp. 678, 679.

26. Alexander Weissberg in *The Accused* (New York, 1951), and Anton Ciliga, in *The Russian Enigma* (London, 1940), give much evidence concerning the pathological suspicion displayed toward foreigners in Russia during the early and mid-1930's.

27. Stalin, *Soch.,* Vol. xiii, pp. 38-9.

28. See, for example, V. Gitermann, 'The Study of History in the Soviet Union,' *Bulletin of the Atomic Scientists,* Vol. x, No. 6, June 1954, pp. 206, 240.

29. *Literaturnaya entsiklopediya* (Moscow, 1935), ix.

30. *Pravda,* editorial, 5 January 1937. *Pravda* was commenting on the decision taken on 16 December 1935 to set up a committee to plan for the celebration of the anniversary of Pushkin's death in 1937.

31. *Stil i yazyk A. S. Pushkina* (Moscow, 1937), p. 14.

32. *Pravda,* 5 June 1944.

33. *K. P. S. S. v rezolyutsiyakh i resheniyakh sezdov, konferentsii i plenumov ts. k.,* 2 vols. (Moscow 1953), ii, pp. 1028-31, and 1032-7.

34. *K. P. S. S. v rezolyutsiyakh,* ii, pp. 1028, 1029.

35. Ibid. p. 1033.

36. *Pravda,* 30 September 1946.

37. Cited from brochure in Russian containing the Central Committee's decrees on literature, the theater, the cinema, and music. Russian title: *O zhurnalakh zvezda i leningrad: o repertuare drama-*

ticheskikh teatrov; o kinofilme bolshaya zhizn; ob opere velikaya druzhba (Moscow, 1951). Hereafter cited as 'brochure of decrees.' Above quotation, p. 21.

38. Libretto by G. Mdivani.

39. Brochure of decrees, pp. 26-7.

40. Ibid. p. 29.

41. Brochure of decrees, p. 25.

42. *Kommunist*, No. 1, January 1954, p. 48.

43. *Kultura i zhizn*, 20 February 1949.

44. Rounds, op. cit. p. 163.

45. As noted earlier, the award of the Stalin Prize for this work was revoked.

46. A. A. Zhdanov, *On Literature, Music and Philosophy* (London, 1947), p. 80.

47. Ibid. p. 90.

48. Ibid. p. 91.

49. Ibid. p. 85.

50. Ibid. pp. 86-7.

51. Ibid. p. 103.

52. Ibid. pp. 108-9.

53. Ibid. p. 110.

54. In the case of philosophy, as in all other fields, speakers and writers made it clear that the ideological re-conversion was conducted at the initiative of Stalin. Zhdanov attributed leadership in the field of philosophy to Stalin and the Central Committee of the Party. Ibid. p. 100.

55. Very interesting material on the attitude of Soviet scientists toward their Western colleagues and toward international scientific co-operation is contained in Eric Ashby, *Scientist in Russia* (Penguin, London, 1946).

56. *Partiinaya zhizn*.

57. Issue No. 14.

58. I am indebted to Mr. Leo Bromwich for bringing this passage to my attention. See K. S. Simonov, *Pesy* (Moscow, 1950), pp. 464-5.

59. *O sovetskom patriotizme*, 2nd ed., op. cit. pp. 460-84.

60. Ibid. pp. 464-7.

61. Ibid. p. 482.

62. English translation of State Secrets decree in *The American Review on the Soviet Union*, Vol. VIII, No. 3-4, October 1947, p. 86.

63. For more general treatments of post-war Soviet historiography, including additional material on some of the aspects treated in this

chapter, see Klaus Mehnert, *Stalin versus Marx* (London, 1952. German original, 1951); Sergius Yakobson, 'Postwar Historical Research in the Soviet Union,' *The Annals of the American Academy of Political and Social Science,* Vol. 263, May 1949 pp. 123-33; Georg von Rauch, 'Grundlinien der Sowjetischen Geschichtsforschung im Zeichen des Stalinismus,' *Europa Archiv,* v, pp. 3383-8, 3423-30, 3489-94. One of the best treatments of the plight of historians and other intellectuals during the period of the great purges, is Philip E. Mosley, 'Freedom of Artistic Expression and Scientific Inquiry in Russia,' *The Annals,* Vol. 200, November 1938, pp. 254-74.

64. *Krasny arkhiv,* 1936, Vol. 2, p. 5. This volume contains, on pp. 3-9, the major documents embodying the Stalinist historical revolution.

65. On this point see Yakobson, op. cit. pp. 128-9.

66. *Russkaya istoriografiya.*

67. *Russkaya istoriografiya* (Moscow, 1941), p. 534.

68. Ibid. p. 552.

69. D. Ilovaiski *Istoriya rossii,* Vol. III (Moscow, 1890), pp. 151-287. Even the highly patriotic preface pales by comparison with Soviet boasting. It is not even notably anti-foreign.

70. Ten year school.

71. *Communist Offenses against the Integrity of Education, Science, and Culture* (U. S. State Department, 1951), p. 14.

72. *Voprosy istorii.*

73. *Voprosy istorii,* No. 12, 1948, p. 5.

74. *Vop. ist.,* No. 12, 1948, pp. 6-7.

75. For additional material on several of these points, particularly criticism of Eugene Tarle for writing in a 'spirit of subservience to foreign historians,' see my article, 'Stalinism and the Russian Cultural Heritage,' esp. pp. 188-91.

76. A. Avtorkhanov, 'Polozhenie istoricheskoi nauki v SSSR' (Munich, Institut po izucheniyu istorii i kultury SSSR, 1951), pp. 15-35.

77. W. W. Kulski, *The Soviet Regime* (Syracuse, 1954), p. 116.

78. *Vop. ist.,* No. 2, 4 February 1949, p. 7.

79. *Vop. ist.,* No. 7, July 1954, pp. 2-12.

80. For a full discussion, see E. Domar, 'The Varga Controversy,' *American Economic Review* Vol. XL, No. 1, pp. 132-51, and Frederick C. Barghoorn, 'The Varga Discussion and Its Significance,' *The American Slavic and East European Review,* Vol. VII, No. 3, October 1948, pp. 214-36.

81. *Osnovnye voprosy ekonomiki i politiki imperializma* (Moscow, 1953).

82. Ibid. p. 572.

83. Ivan D. London, 'Soviet Psychology and Psychiatry,' *Bulletin of the Atomic Scientist*, Vol. VIII, March 1952.

84. Ivan D. London, 'Contemporary Psychology in the Soviet Union,' *Science*, 31 August 1951, p. 1. For a well-rounded account of the development of psychology in the Soviet Union see Bauer, *The New Man in Soviet Psychology* op. cit.

85. F. Chernov, 'Proletarski internatsionalizm i burzhuazny kosmopolitizm' (Moscow, 1951), esp. pp. 22-30.

86. Soviet.

87. Appeal.

88. Slogan.

89. Lyudoed.

90. See for example long quotation from Pushkin's well-known poem 'To the Slanderers of Russia' in Matyushkin's *Sovetski patriotizm*, op. cit. p. 15. This poem was published in full, together with other inflammatory material, in *Pravda* for 6 June 1949.

91. Even during the war, *Rodina*, the collection of patriotic statements referred to earlier, omitted from a celebrated passage from Chernyshevski's diary, the writer's gloomy dictum that although Russians could 'conquer Europe if we want to, like the Huns, like the Mongols,' Russia had contributed 'nothing' to the sum of human knowledge. *Rod.*, op. cit. p. 85. Compare with the whole passage, quoted by Richard Hare, *Pioneers of Russian Social Thought*, op. cit. pp. 179-80. The well-known Soviet philosopher M. Yovchuk, asserted that Hare 'hated' Chernyshevski. See *Kommunist*, No. 11, July 1953, p. 91.

92. Among many comments on this tendency, those of Harrison Salisbury in a series of articles in *The New York Times* in September 1954, and in *American in Russia*, are especially interesting.

93. Similar statements, including the phrase 'with good intentions' were made by the leading Soviet political commentator, David Zaslavski, over the Moscow radio on 29 November 1953.

94. *Pravda*, 18 June 1953.

95. Khrushchev received MacDuffie in his capacity as First Secretary of the Party Central Committee.

96. *Pravda*, front page, 24 July 1955.

97. William Buchanan and Hadley Cantril, *How Nations See Each Other* (University of Illinois Press, Urbana, 1953), p. 57.

98. Harrison Salisbury, *The New York Times,* 13 August 1955.

99. See, for example, a satirical item, ironically sympathetic to the decision of the city fathers of Bristol, Virginia, to return to Italy a piece of modernistic, and completely incomprehensible, sculpture which they had ordered. *Sovetskaya kultura,* 5 May 1955.

100. For example, the agenda for a second All-Union Congress of Soviet Composers, scheduled for April 1956, includes a report on 'progressive foreign music.' *Sovetskaya kultura,* 22 March 1955.

101. Andrew J. Steiger, *American Engineers in the Soviet Union* (New York, 1944), p. 7.

Chapter VIII

1. *Encyclopedia of the Social Sciences* (New York, 1933, reissued 1938), Vols. 9–10, pp. 356-63.

2. See, for example, Hadley Cantril, *The Psychology of Social Movements* (New York, 5th printing, 1947) which applies the above concepts to several messianically-tinged social movements. Stimulating comment on the tendency of nationals of relatively poor, technologically underdeveloped, or in other ways 'low-status' countries to develop chauvinistic or messianic attitudes is contained in several articles in the September 1954 issue of *The Annals of the American Academy of Political and Social Science.*

3. See, for example, *O postanovke partiinoi propagandy v svyazi s vypuskom 'kratkogo kursa' istorii VKP (b)* (Moscow, 1944), and M. Protsko, *Sovetskaya intelligentsiya v borbe za kommunizm* (Moscow, 1950).

4. Nicholas De Witt, 'Professional and Scientific Personnel in the U.S.S.R.,' *Science,* 2 July 1954, p. 3.

5. *Kommunist,* No. 10, 1954, pp. 56-71. Quotation on p. 56.

6. *Russia and Europe* was first published in book form in 1869. It is available in a German translation, but not in English. On Danilevski's thought, see Robert E. MacMaster, 'The Question of Heinrich Rückert's Influence on Danilevski,' *The American Slavic and East European Review,* Vol. xiv, No. 1, February 1955, pp. 59-66.

7. On the resemblance referred to above, see B. I. Nikolaevski, *O kornyakh sovetskogo imperializma, Sotsialisticheski Vestnik,* February 1954, pp. 29-32.

8. See, for example, articles in the 1st and 2nd eds., respectively, of the *Large Soviet Encyclopedia,* the latter in Vol. 13, published in 1952.

9. V. N. Shtein, in his *Ocherki razvitiya russkoi obshchestvenno-ekonomicheskoi mysli XIX-XX Vekov* (Leningrad, 1948), Ch. IV, takes a quite favorable view of Slavophile thought; in particular he argues that in its sociological aspects it was superior to contemporary Western thought. Haxthausen, argues Shtein, did not, as is commonly believed, give to the Slavophiles and similar Russian thinkers their ideas regarding the Russian peasant commune, but on the contrary, Haxthausen, Custine, and other Europeans in effect stole their ideas on this subject from the Slavophiles.

10. For example, *Kratkaya sovetskaya entsiklopediya*, 1943, p. 452, referred to him as 'a writer of genius.'

11. This 'correction' applied to Dostoevski, has been excellently documented by John Fiske in his article 'Dostoevski and the Soviet Critics,' *The American Slavic and East European Review*, Vol. ix, No. 1, February 1950, pp. 42-56.

12. *Smoke*, Hapgood translation (London, 1904), pp. 43, 148-60. Originally published in Russian in 1867-9.

13. 1862.

14. For example, see Lenin's long and emotional tribute to 'the predecessors of Russian social democracy' in *What Is To Be Done?* Particularly significant is the concluding portion of this tribute, in which Lenin, addressing his reader, says, 'Let him think about the world significance which Russian literature is acquiring today; let him—but enough of that!' It is as if Lenin here allowed feelings to erupt which, for a disciplined revolutionary, were taboo. He had, momentarily, spoken the 'unspeakable.' Cited here from Lenin, *Iz. proiz.*, I, pp. 145-6. I am indebted for this interpretation to Mr. Paul W. Friedrich.

15. 1914.

16. On the 'cutting down to size' of military symbology in 1945, see my article 'The Soviet Union between War and Cold War' in *The Annals of the American Academy of Social and Political Science*, Vol. 263, May 1949.

17. The works of Akhmatova published in the Soviet Union during World War II have been gathered in the volume, *Anna Akhmatova: Izbrannye stikhotvoreniya* (Chekhov Publishing House, New York, 1952).

18. *80 let na sluzhbe nauki i kultury nashei rodiny.*

19. Alexander Werth, in *The Year of Stalingrad* (London, 1946), takes the position that although the mass of the Soviet population desired 'a long-term policy of co-operation with the West,' not only

Party members, but 'everybody,' shared a distrust for England and America, because of the existence of anti-Soviet forces in those countries. See esp. pp. 103, 139-261. I do not think Werth's view necessarily is incompatible with mine, although I disagree strongly with his assumption that the Party 'line' expressed the sentiments of the population as a whole. However, Werth is probably correct in emphasizing that even pro-Allied Russians were mistrustful of the intentions of their allies. The fact seems to be that many, perhaps most, Soviet Russians, but probably in particular members of the very insecure Soviet elite, trust neither their own authorities, nor those of other countries.

20. *Bolshevik*, No. 3–4, February 1944, p. 27.
21. *Izvestiya*, 4 November 1943.
22. *The Banner*.
23. *Znamya*, No. 12, 1942, p. 112.
24. Cf. for example, articles in *Bolshevik*, No. 19–20, 1942, by M. Mitin, G. F. Aleksandrov, and others, in honor of the 25th anniversary of the Bolshevik revolution.
25. For an excellent discussion of some of this literature, see 'Soviet Historical Novel,' by Michael Karpovich, *The Russian Review*, Vol. 5, No. 2, Spring 1946, pp. 55-63.
26. See for example Helen Iswolsky, 'Soviet Culture Today,' *Commonweal*, 28 May 1943, pp. 138-41, and *Soul of Russia* (New York, 1943). With many wise qualifications, Nicholas Timasheff presented a similar thesis in *The Great Retreat* (New York, 1946). Solomon Schwarz, Raphael Abramovich, and the other leaders of the Menshevik group who wrote for the *Sotsialisticheski Vestnik* were, with the exceptions of Fedor Dan and Aaron Yugov, completely free of illusions about the post-war shape of Soviet things to come. So was G. P. Fedotov, who in a discussion reported in *Novoe Russkoe Slovo* for 23 February 1942 noted a return in Russia to 'irrationalist nationalism,' but never deceived himself as to the power of totalitarian elements in Bolshevik nationalism.
27. During the war it again became quite common for Soviet historians, even when writing for Party publications, to use the term 'Peter the Great.' Cf. K. Bazilevich in *Bolshevik*, No. 11–12, June 1945, p. 35. Post-war practice, as for example in Anna Pankratova's standard secondary school text, has continued this usage.
28. N. Tikhonov, *Leningrad prinimaet boi* (Leningrad, 1943), pp. 3-11.
29. *Bolshevik*, No. 3–4, February 1944, p. 27; *Pravda*, 22 November 1946.

30. Quoted by Robert Ramsey, in Master's Essay submitted to Russian Institute, Columbia University, 1952, on Political Instruction in the Red Army, 1941–5, p. 7, on deposit at Russian Institute. As Ramsey correctly notes, this formulation 'embraced the concept of revolutionary expansion as well as that of national defense.'

31. A. Egolin and P. Lebedev, 'On the Repertoire of Dramatic Theaters,' *Kultura i zhizn*, 10 July 1946.

32. See for example criticism of play by A. Surov, in *Kultura i zhizn*, 10 October 1946, for giving 'an incorrect, distorted presentation of the work of Party organizations.'

33. For an account of this episode, see Boris Shub, 'Humanity Deleted,' in *Problems of Communism*, No. 2, 1952, pp. 13-17.

34. *Materialy obedinennoi nauchnoi sessii posvyashchennoi trudam I. V. Stalina po yazykoznaniyu* (Moscow, 1951), pp. 20-23, 35-7.

35. Quoted from p. 20 of article 'Vydayushchiisya vklad v razvitie istoricheskogo materializma,' *Bolshevik*, June 1951, No. 11, pp. 9-23.

36. *Matyushkin*, op. cit. p. 14. The reference is to the apostrophe to 'Rus,' in Gogol's *Dead Souls*. In this celebrated passage, coming at the end of the first part of the work, Gogol pictures Russia, 'inspired by God,' as flying past the 'other peoples and states,' who look askance, but make way.

37. Ibid. 18-19.

38. *Doklad t. Zhdanova o zhurnalakh 'Zvezda' i 'Leningrad'* (Moscow, 1946), pp. 35-6.

39. *Bolshevik*, No. 21, November 1946, p. 11.

40. It is interesting that in connection with the 1949 celebration, a careful search was made of Pushkin's works with a view to uncovering every possible expression by Pushkin of anti-foreign, as well as Russian nationalist, feeling. Among other things the Soviet propagandists discovered and published in *Pravda* a review by Pushkin of a book by one John Jenner expressing Pushkin's indignation at American treatment of the North American Indians.

41. The author resorts to the rather unusual device of describing the significance and general traits of his characters in an introduction. It is interesting to note, incidentally, that the English translation of this novel is by Ivy Litvinova, apparently Maxim Litvinov's widow. I am indebted to Mr. Francis De Tarr for calling this novel to my attention.

42. Ibid. pp. 35-6. Interestingly, the author's biography, given in the preface, indicates that he had not been outside his own country before the writing of *Students*.

43. *Pravda* for 20 and 21 March 1955, published several long articles on Mozhaiski, 'creator of the first airplane in the world.'

44. (Moscow 1950), Vol. 5, p. 513.

45. *Yazyk gazety,* op. cit. p. 39.

46. Ibid. p. 43; this book contains, among other things, a long section entitled 'Declare War on the Unnecessary Use of Foreign Words.' It is a veritable treasure house of linguistic messianism.

47. *Department of State Bulletin,* Vol. 19, August 1949, p. 200. I am indebted to Dr. Stephen Gorove for calling this fact to my attention.

48. For an English translation of this material, see *The Soviet Linguistic Controversy,* Columbia University Slavic Studies, E. J. Simmons, ed. (New York, 1951), esp. pp. 40, 48-57, 78.

49. *O sovetskom patriotizme* (Moscow, 1950, 1st ed.), pp. 51-2. Same material on pp. 52-3 in 2nd ed., 1952.

50. George Morgan, in *The Threat of Soviet Imperialism* (Baltimore, 1954), pp. 33-4.

51. Nicholas Berdyaev, in *The Origin of Russian Communism,* eloquently presents this thesis.

52. Suggested by Radovan Lalic, 'The Russian Language and Great Russian Chauvinism' (New York, Yugoslav Information Center, 1950), p. 5. Lalic also points out that Soviet writers on the subject of the 'series' of 'world languages' have remained silent on German, probably because they could scarcely attack the language in which Marx wrote, as 'the language of Fascism.' I am indebted to Mr. George Carnett for calling this pamphlet to my attention.

53. See for example B. Chagin, *Proniknovenie idei Marksizma v rossiyu* (Moscow, 1948).

54. See for example, article by N. Fedorenko, occupying two-thirds of a page in *Pravda,* 19 October 1953, stressing statements by Mao Tze Tung indicating China's debt to Lenin and Stalin.

55. Stalin developed this concept, together with the claim that Russia was both the most revolutionary country and the 'weakest link of imperialism,' in his article 'On the Foundations of Leninism,' 1924; contained in all editions of *Problems of Leninism.*

56. P. A. Shariya, *O nekotorykh voprosakh kommunisticheskoi morali* (Moscow, 1951), p. 24.

57. Ibid. p. 143. Shariya, incidentally, is a Georgian.

58. Shtein, op. cit. p. 352.

59. For an interesting discussion of these points, see Avtorkhanov, op. cit. 30-31.

60. An example of the assumption of such an instructor's role is the article by Aleksei Surkov in *Pravda* for 1 May 1953. Surkov asserted, *inter alia,* that a steady stream of foreigners visited Moscow to learn 'from the experience of the people who have built socialism.' He also stated that it was the 'wise and strong' machines, built by Soviet engineers, that were reconstructing the economy and technology of Eastern Germany and of Eastern Europe in general. A great volume of similar material is published with respect to China.

61. Sociology and political science are treated in Soviet scholarship within the framework of 'dialectical and historical materialism.'

62. Slogans such as 'the international solidarity of toilers of all countries,' and 'raise higher the banner of proletarian internationalism,' have, since October 1953, become the most prominently featured of the November 6 and May Day 'calls.' The 'calls' (*prizyvy*) are published about two weeks in advance.

63. This view is taken by George A. Morgan, in *The Threat of Soviet Imperialism,* op. cit. p. 35. As noted earlier, still greater emphasis was put on continuity with Russian tradition by Kolarz and Biehahn.

64. For interesting observations on the use of the technique of the 'persuasive definition' in this type of deception, see 'Is Man an Animal,' by Russell Kirk, in *ETC* (Chicago), Vol. xi, No. 3, pp. 204-16.

Chapter IX

1. Fritz Lieb, *Russland unterwegs* (Bern, 1945), p. 276; Raymond L. Garthoff, *Soviet Military Doctrine* (Glencoe, 1953), pp. 228-9.

2. Maurice Hindus, *Hitler Cannot Conquer Russia* (New York, 1941), p. 299.

3. Bertram D. Wolfe, 'The Influence of Early Military Decisions upon the National Structure of the Soviet Union,' *The American Slavic and East European Review,* Vol. ix, pp. 169-79. Quotation on p. 170.

4. Julian Huxley, *Soviet Genetics and World Science* (London, 1949), p. 193.

5. William H. Standley and Arthur Ageton, *Admiral Ambassador to Russia* (Chicago, 1955), p. 495.

6. In addition to material in earlier chapters on this point, see *Pravda* for 7 December 1952, and *Moscow Pravda* for 11 December

1952, complaining about the failure of Soviet theaters to perform plays devoted to contemporary Soviet themes.

7. *Zvezda,* No. 6, June 1952, p. 172. Subsequently, the Party forced Katayev to revise this work. I am indebted to Mr. Stanley Wilcox for calling my attention to this passage.

8. Dana Adams Schmidt, *Anatomy of a Satellite* (Boston, 1952), pp. 267-8.

9. 'Russian Cultural Penetration in Hungary,' National Committee for a Free Europe (Washington, D.C., 1950).

10. The factory referred to was an automobile factory.

11. *Slavnyi put rabochego klassa nashei rodiny* (Moscow, 1953), pp. 316-19. The last chapter of this work is devoted mostly to Soviet 'aid' to the 'Peoples' democracies.' At the Geneva conference on peaceful use of atomic energy in August 1955 a Soviet program of aid to these countries in this field was promised. On Soviet study of Chinese, etc., see *Sovetskaya kultura,* 30 June 1955.

12. On the strength and weaknesses of Chinese-Soviet cultural ties see Richard L. Walker, 'Pattern of Sino-Soviet Relations,' *Problems of Communism,* Vol. 3, No. 3, May-June 1954, pp. 5-13.

13. *Pravda,* 29 March 1955.

14. See, for example, Ts. A. Stepanyan, in the symposium *Velikaya sila idei Leninizma* (Moscow, 1950), pp. 266-331. Stepanyan's article was entitled 'In Our Era All Roads Lead to Communism,' a title taken from a statement in Molotov's speech of 6 November 1948.

15. Stepanyan, op. cit. p. 324.

16. Some brief but interesting comment on the significance of the Stalin-Pieck exchange is contained in the article by George A. Morgan, in *The Threat of Soviet Imperialism,* op. cit. p. 34.

17. Compare a somewhat similar statement by Mikoyan at the Leipzig Fair in 1955. *Pravda,* 1 March 1955.

18. *Pravda,* 2 April 1954.

19. On the problems of 'diffusion' of a world revolutionary pattern see H. D. Lasswell, *World Politics and Personal Insecurity* (New York, 1935), pp. 6-7.

20. Karpov, op. cit. pp. 76-7.

INDEX